Luther's Legacy

Luther's Legacy

Salvation and English Reformers,
1525–1556

CARL R. TRUEMAN

CLARENDON PRESS • OXFORD
1994

Oxford University Press, Walton Street, Oxford OX2 6DP
Oxford New York Toronto
Delhi Bombay Calcutta Madras Karachi
Kuala Lumpur Singapore Hong Kong Tokyo
Nairobi Dar es Salaam Cape Town
Melbourne Auckland Madrid
and associated companies in
Berlin Ibadan

Oxford is a trade mark of Oxford University Press

Published in the United States
by Oxford University Press Inc., New York

British Library Cataloguing in Publication Data
Data available

Library of Congress Cataloging in Publication Data
Luther's legacy : salvation and English reformers, 1525–1556
Carl R. Trueman.
Revision of thesis (doctoral)—University of Aberdeen, 1991.
Includes bibliographical references and index.
1. Reformation—England. 2. Luther, Martin, 1483–1546—Influence.
3. Salvation—History of doctrines—16th century. I. Title.
BR375.T784 1994 274.2'06—dc20 93–35766
ISBN 0–19826352–X

1 3 5 7 9 10 8 6 4 2

Typeset by Seton Music Graphics Ltd., Bantry, Co. Cork, Ireland
Printed in Great Britain
on acid-free paper by
Bookcraft (Bath) Ltd., Midsomer Norton, Avon

TO MY PARENTS

PREFACE

THIS book is based upon my doctoral dissertation, 'The Soteriology of the Early English Reformers, 1525–1556', which was researched and written at the University of Aberdeen between 1988 and 1991 and financed by the generous award of a scholarship by that same institution. During that time, my friend and supervisor, Professor Peter Stephens, patiently encouraged and guided my work. I will always be grateful to him for all that he has done for me.

As well as having such a supervisor, I was singularly fortunate to have as my examiners Revd Benjamin Drewery and Professor James Atkinson. Their comments on my thesis were most helpful and encouraging, and their efforts on my behalf since that time have been above and beyond the call of duty. I am most thankful for all of their help.

Others to whom thanks are due include Professor Malcolm Lambert, Mr Arthur Johnson, and my friend from Cambridge days, Mr Andrew Ball who suggested the title Luther's Legacy. As undergraduates together, Andrew and I shared a mutual love of the theology of the sixteenth and seventeenth centuries, and it was thanks to his encouragement that I first considered postgraduate study on the Reformation. It is perhaps fitting that my path to writing this book started with conversations over coffee in St Catharine's College, Cambridge. Part of this college is, I am told, built on the site of the White Horse Inn, the very place where, 450 years previously, men such as Robert Barnes also met to discuss the works of Martin Luther and his fellow Reformers.

While the bulk of the research was done at Aberdeen, the book was completed at the University of Nottingham during my first months as lecturer. I am grateful to my colleagues here for making those months so pleasant. Thanks are especially due to Dr Richard Bell who brought my attention to a number of relevant items of scholarship and who also kindly read through the section on Luther for me. I, of course, take full responsibility for any remaining errors. I am also grateful to Dr Mary Charles Murray for suggesting Holbein's Bible as a source for the jacket illustration.

This book would quickly have become a long-forgotten doctoral thesis if it had not been for Oxford University Press. I will always consider it a great privilege to have had my work published by OUP, and am most grateful for the help and advice I have received from my editor, Hilary O'Shea, and my two anonymous readers.

Final thanks must go to my wife, Catriona. The bulk of the revision work was carried out during a long and difficult period of unemployment. Without the love and support of Catriona, it would never have been completed. Only she knows how much it cost her.

CARL R. TRUEMAN
Department of Theology
University of Nottingham
Pentecost, 1993

CONTENTS

NOTE ON TEXTS

THERE is, sadly, no modern critical edition of the works of the five men examined in this study. As a result, I have used the nineteenth-century Parker Society editions of Tyndale, Hooper, and Bradford. These texts are reliable and certainly the best available. Tyndale's earliest work, the so-called *Cologne Fragment*, was reproduced in facsimile last century, and I have used this edition, following the pagination in that edition rather than that of the original folios.

For Frith, I have used the edition of his works which was edited by Thomas Russell and published in 1831. The text of this edition has been published in the Courtenay Reformation Classics series in a volume edited by N. T. Wright. Wright's book also includes an excellent introduction and some material not included by Russell. As such, it is the best edition of Frith available.

No modern edition of Robert Barnes exists and so I have used the original sixteenth-century editions of 1531 and 1534. A microfilm copy of each is held at Cambridge University Library and I am grateful to the Librarian for allowing me to take copies of these. The Day edition of Barnes's work, published in 1572, should not be used by any serious student of Barnes as it is a conflation of the two original editions and is thus not suitable for tracing his development during the crucial years between 1531 and 1534.

In some quotations, I have taken the liberty of modernizing some of the spelling and some of the punctuation. This is for the sake of fluency and consistency, and it does not violate the original meaning. Translations from other sources are my own, unless otherwise acknowledged in the notes.

ABBREVIATIONS

AM	*Acts and Monuments*
ARG	*Archiv für Reformationsgeschichte*
CD	Barth's *Church Dogmatics*
CH	*Church History*
EQ	*Evangelical Quarterly*
EW	*Early Writings of John Hooper, D.D.*
JEH	*Journal of Ecclesiastical History*
JR	*Journal of Religion*
JTS	*Journal of Theological Studies*
LW	*Later Writings of John Hooper, D.D.*
NDT	*New Dictionary of Theology*
NT 25	Tyndale's New Testament (1525)
OC	*Opera Calvini*
OL	*Original Letters*
OM	*Opera Melanthonis*
PG	*Patrologia Graeca*
PL	*Patrologia Latina*
Russell	*The Works of Frith* (Russell edition)
SCJ	*Sixteenth Century Journal*
SJT	*Scottish Journal of Theology*
Summa	*Summa Theologiae*
WA	*D. Martin Luthers Werke: Kritische Gesamtausgabe*
WA (DB)	*D. Martin Luthers Werke: Kritische Gesamtausgabe: Deutsche Bibel*
Work	*The Work of John Frith* (Wright edition)
Works 1	Tyndale: *Doctrinal Treatises*
Works 2	Tyndale: *Expositions and Notes*
Works 3	Tyndale: *Answer to More*
Writings 1	*The Writings of John Bradford*, 1
Writings 2	*The Writings of John Bradford*, 2
Z	Zwingli's *Sämtliche Werke*
1531	Barnes's *A Supplicatyon* (1531)
1534	Barnes's *A Supplicatyon* (1534)

INTRODUCTION

IT is only in the last fifty years that serious interest has been shown in the theology of the English Reformation. Before that time, the English Reformers had loomed larger as symbols of the ferocity of the religious conflict of the sixteenth century than as theologians. With the exception of the attempts made by the members of the Oxford Movement and their opponents to claim them as precursors, the English Reformers were largely ignored in terms of their theology and were generally regarded as poor copies of their continental counterparts.

However, in recent decades an increasing interest has been shown in the works of these men in terms of their theological content, and many previous presuppositions have been called into question.

As a result of this renewed interest, the theology of the English Reformers is now the subject of a growing number of secondary studies. Many of these studies are concerned with Eucharistic theology. This reflects the fact that the Eucharist was a central issue of the English Reformation. However, the doctrine of salvation was also important. After all, salvation lies at the very heart of Reformation theology and determines, to a large extent, the nature of Eucharistic doctrine. Various scholars have dealt with aspects of soteriology to varying degrees, but no single study has taken this as its theme and examined the thinking of the English Reformers in this area.

This study is divided into three parts. Part One deals with the historical and intellectual context of the five English Reformers: Chapter 1 contains brief biographies of the five men, highlighting the political forces which shaped their careers; Chapter 2 examines the influence of various non-Reformation traditions upon their thought; and Chapter 3 is a brief outline of those aspects of continental Reformation theology which are particularly relevant for a correct understanding of the

nature of English Reformation thought.[1] Part Two then examines in detail the doctrine of salvation as taught by three
Reformers during the reign of Henry VIII: William Tyndale;
John Frith; and Robert Barnes. Part Three does the same
for the Reformation under Edward VI and Catholic reaction under Mary, taking John Hooper and John Bradford as
its subjects.

While any selection of Reformers is doomed to be in some
way unrepresentative, the three men covered in Part Two of
this study are as near to 'obvious choices' as possible. In
general, there were few English theologians of any significance
who were truly Protestant during the reign of Henry VIII.
Men such as Cranmer and Ridley came to Reformation
convictions relatively late in life. Indeed, Cranmer sat on the
committee which condemned John Frith to death. Amongst
those who did advocate true Reformation doctrine, the leading
figures were undoubtedly Tyndale, Frith, and Barnes. Their
writings constitute the first significant English expressions of
Reformation theology and thus form the focal point of any
study of English soteriology during this time.

The choice of William Tyndale as a subject needs no justification. As the translator of a Bible that was used extensively in
the sixteenth century and later incorporated, to a large extent,
into the Authorized Version, he exerted a profound influence
on the religious language of the English people. For this reason
alone, his other writings merit examination. Furthermore, he is
now the subject of a growing body of secondary literature
concerned with his merits not just as a translator but also as a
theologian. While his soteriology has been examined in some
detail, the subject has not been exhausted. In particular, little
attempt has been made to set his theology within the wider
context of English Reformation theology. This study seeks to
rectify this deficiency.

John Frith is widely lamented as the great loss of the English
Reformation. By the time of his death, aged 30 he had already
converted John Rastell, a Catholic polemicist, to the Reformation

---

[1] Chapters 1 and 3 are intended as aids to those unfamiliar with either the history
or the theology of the period. As such, they provide a basic introduction to their
respective fields. Those wishing to know more about these areas should consult the
books referred to in the footnotes.

cause and beaten Thomas More in controversy. His writings show a clarity and conciseness never obtained by Tyndale and give tantalizing hints of what might have been had he lived. His works, particularly on purgatory, represent some of the earliest English expressions of Reformation soteriology and must therefore be included in any study of this aspect of the English Reformation.

Robert Barnes has been largely ignored in studies of English Reformation theology, yet he wrote a treatise which deals with various commonplaces of theology and which forms the nearest thing to a work of systematic theology that the Henrician Reformers produced. He composed essays on justification and on the will, and these constitute important statements of soteriology. That the work was reprinted after his death is a sign of the continuing appeal of his thought.

The choice of Hooper and Bradford for Part Three of this study is perhaps less obvious than that in Part Two. The most famous Reformers of the period 1547 to 1556 were Cranmer, Latimer, and Ridley. Nevertheless, they are of little significance for a study of the soteriology of the early English Reformation. Latimer was a great preacher, but he contributed little to the theology of the period. In contrast, Cranmer and Ridley were probably the major theological influences in England at that time. However, their most important contributions were in the matters of Eucharistic theology and Anglican ecclesiology. Neither Cranmer nor Ridley wrote a major work upon salvation.[2] Cranmer was, of course, the guiding influence behind the formulation of both the Homilies and, more importantly, the Anglican Articles. These defined the doctrinal framework of the Anglican Church, and thus also defined the Church's views on soteriology. However, there are major drawbacks involved in basing a study of English Reformation soteriology upon the Articles. Their confessional purpose meant that they were both brief, in order to present a concise summary of the Church's doctrine, and broad-based, in order to provide a doctrinal framework which would not place undue doctrinal constraints upon the Church's membership. Therefore, any secondary study

---

[2] Ridley did reluctantly write a treatise on election at the request of John Bradford. However, it has not survived. Ridley himself confessed that the work was scarcely more than a catena of relevant verses from the Bible: see Ch. 8.

of the Articles would reflect the broad and undetailed nature of
their content. More importantly, such a study would also fail to
show either the variety of opinion that existed within the Church
concerning the details of salvation or the issues which provided
the focal points of controversy. For these reasons, the writings
of individual Reformers provide a much better source for
studying English Reformation soteriology than the Articles.

While the soteriological views of Cranmer, Latimer, and
Ridley could be extracted to a certain extent from their writings
on other topics, there are two English theologians of the same
period who did write soteriological works: John Hooper and
John Bradford. Because they directly addressed the issue of
salvation, they are more suitable for a study of soteriology than
the three more famous Reformers. Both men were also involved
in separate disputes concerning the nature of salvation. The
first of these arose during the reign of Edward VI because of a
clash between the views of Hooper and Bartholomew Traheron,
a Calvinist. The second occurred during the reign of Mary
when certain 'free willers' objected to the predestinarian doctrine of John Bradford. The disputes led to major statements of
belief by both Hooper and Bradford, and these comprise the
most significant extant works on soteriology from the period.
However, despite the fact that they both wrote important
works on salvation, no attempt has previously been made to
examine in detail this aspect of their thought.

Their significance becomes even more apparent when one
realizes that they were in fundamental disagreement on a number of central issues. As such, their writings reveal the tensions
concerning the doctrine of salvation which existed within
English Reformation theology at this time. It also indicates the
diverse continental influences which were at work upon English
theologians. Thus, the works of Hooper and Bradford offer a
unique glimpse into the soteriology of the English Reformation
under Edward VI and Mary.

Before commencing the study proper, a number of methodological points need to be made. First, in presenting the thought
of these five men, my primary concern has been to expound
what they themselves say, and only secondarily to indicate possible sources for their ideas and similarities or contrasts with
other Reformers.

Secondly, while these men did cover many of the same topics, they had different methods and approached the various issues from different backgrounds and in different contexts. Such considerations prevent a point-by-point comparison of the thought of each.

Thirdly, the literary output of each of the subjects was not great and consisted mainly of brief works. If a purely chronological approach was to be adopted and every work was to be examined separately, the result would be fragmentary and repetitive. It would therefore run the risk of missing the essential unity of the Reformer's thought. However, a purely thematic approach could miss areas of development or impose an alien structure upon the writings which might distort results.

Therefore, in Part Two, the method employed is basically a mixture of both chronological and thematic approaches. The careers of the three men are divided into chronological divisions, and then those themes which appear to be the central concerns in each period are individually examined. Such an approach allows for the possibility of development over time and does not undermine any fundamental theological unity that there may be. However, in Part Three, the nature of the writings of Hooper and Bradford makes it necessary to modify this approach. This is discussed at the relevant points in Chapters 7 and 8.

The picture of the English Reformers that emerges from Part Two is of theologians who demonstrated a variety of different emphases and concerns, but who were united in their belief in two basic principles: that justification is by faith alone, and that works are a vital part of salvation. However, Part Three reveals that by 1556, serious tensions and divergences of opinion on central soteriological themes had emerged within the ranks of the English Reformers. While the Anglican Church now accepted justification by faith alone as its official doctrinal position, the focal point of soteriological debate had shifted to the doctrine of election, and disagreements over this were a dark omen of future controversies.

At the end of the book, the reader may wonder why I chose to call this work *Luther's Legacy*, when my basic argument is that Luther's thought is considerably modified by the theologians of the English Reformation. My intention in using such a title was to underline the fact that, while Tyndale and his fellow Reformers were not Luther and had differing concerns and emphases from him, it was nevertheless contact with Luther's work which radicalized their thinking and changed them from Catholic Humanists to Protestant Reformers. Thus, the earliest English Reformation theology is, in the broadest sense, Luther's legacy. As for Hooper and Bradford, the influence of Luther is much harder to substantiate, but, at the risk of appearing to indulge in special pleading, one must not forget that the intellectual world of the Edwardian Reformation was made possible only through the efforts of men such as Tyndale and his pioneering Bible translation. Thus, this too is, in a certain sense, Luther's legacy.

PART ONE

The Historical and Intellectual Context

1

Five Roads to Martyrdom

ALL five of the English Reformers in this study died at the stake because of their theological stance. While martyrdom in itself does not validate the beliefs which bring it about, it does indicate the passion with which those beliefs were held or rejected. To the twentieth-century Western mind, schooled in the philosophy of liberal democracy, sentencing a man to die because he disagrees with the Church's teaching on the Eucharist appears as nothing more than murder and, indeed, the willing acceptance of death for such a belief an act of total insanity. All this does, however, is to remind us of the massive difference between the intellectual and social values of our century and that of the Reformers. Because of this difference, it is of the utmost importance that something of the biographical and historical background of these men is known before a valid assessment of their theology can be made. These Reformers were no ivory-tower academics, playing a kind of theological 'glass-bead game'. They were men intimately involved in the events of their day. For them, theology was something of profound social, as well as personal, importance, something for which they were willing to pay the ultimate price.

WILLIAM TYNDALE

William Tyndale, the greatest and most influential Bible translator in the English language, was born around the year 1494 in Gloucestershire, near to the Welsh border.[1] Because

[1] The best biography of Tyndale is J. F. Mozley's *William Tyndale* (London, 1937). The most recent scholarly study of Tyndale's life is C. H. Williams's *William Tyndale* (London, 1969). However, Williams's general agreement with the interpretation of Tyndale proposed by W. A. Clebsch renders his work unreliable in terms of its theological analysis. For Foxe's account, see *AM* 5. 114–30.

of his silence concerning his background, little is known of his early life. In the one reference which he does make to his childhood he recalls reading in the English Chronicle about an early vernacular translation of the Bible.[2] Whether this childhood event exerted a formative influence on his mind is a matter for speculation.

In 1512 he proceeded BA at Oxford, followed by MA in 1515. After Oxford, sometime between 1516 and 1519, he transferred to Cambridge.[3] Cambridge, which had recently enjoyed the presence of Erasmus, would certainly have provided Tyndale with a more liberal intellectual environment and exposed him to the New Learning.[4] While he does not appear to have been a member of the group who met at the White Horse Inn to discuss recent intellectual developments and study Humanist and Reformation writings, Foxe tells us that he left 'further ripened in the knowledge of God'.[5]

After Cambridge, Tyndale returned to Gloucestershire to become tutor to the children of a Master Walsh who lived in Little Sodbury.[6] Here, he soon became known as one who baited local clergy about the corruption of the Church during dinner-parties held by the Walsh's. Indeed, Mistress Walsh became so confused by the dinner-time debates that she asked Tyndale for a brief guide to the Christian faith. This he duly gave her by translating Erasmus's *Enchiridion Militis Christiani*, a choice not without considerable significance for a correct under-standing of Tyndale's intellectual development.[7]

---

[2] See *Works* 1. 149, where Tyndale mistakenly ascribes the translation to the reign of Athelstan, not Alfred.

[3] For a full discussion of the intellectual impact of Cambridge upon Tyndale at this time, see Ch. 2. Clebsch dismisses Tyndale's life prior to 1524 as 'of little impor-tance for a theological estimate of Tyndale': *England's Earliest Protestants* (Yale, 1964), 139. This utterly a *historical* approach to intellectual development sets the scene for Clebsch's later misunderstanding of Tyndale. In fact, Tyndale's later theological concerns are profoundly shaped by these early years.

[4] Preserved Smith makes the claim that Tyndale studied under Erasmus while at Cambridge. As Tyndale was certainly not at Cambridge before 1516, and prob-ably not until 1519, this cannot be true. See P. Smith, *Erasmus: a Study of his Life, Ideals and Place in History* (New York, 1962), 66. Cf. Mozley, *William Tyndale* 17; Clebsch, p. 139.

[5] See *AM* 5. 115.

[6] Local tradition has it that the pulpit which stands in Little Sodbury Parish Church is the one from which Tyndale himself preached.

[7] See Ch. 2.

When his attacks on the clergy made his continued residence in Gloucestershire impossible, Tyndale went to London where, with the help of a wealthy merchant, Humphrey Monmouth, Tyndale sought the sponsorship of Cuthbert Tunstal for a vernacular translation of the scriptures. Tunstal was not only Bishop of London but also a leading Humanist scholar. In his own account of his decision to approach Tunstal, Tyndale claimed that Erasmus praised the bishop in his *Annotations*, but no such praise occurs in editions prior to 1527, years after Tyndale's visit to London.[8] However, Tunstal was famous as a brilliant Humanist scholar by 1517, particularly as regards his competence in the Greek language.[9] It was almost certainly his reputation for linguistic excellence which made him the obvious choice as sponsor for a vernacular Bible.[10]

Despite his reputation for learning and his Humanist sympathies, Tunstal wanted nothing to do with Tyndale's project. The impact of this rejection upon Tyndale must have been immense. Years later, in referring to the incident, he wrote that Erasmus had praised a little gnat as if he were a huge elephant.[11] Indeed, it is quite probable that it was this incident which marked Tyndale's thorough disillusionment with Catholic Humanism as it was at this point that he turned towards Wittenberg and Luther for inspiration.

It is worth noting at this point that Tyndale's desire for a vernacular Bible was not, in itself, something which would necessarily have involved him in a break with the Catholic

[8] *Works* 1. 395.

[9] In a letter to Erasmus in 1516, Thomas More praised Tunstal for his scholarship. In 1517 Erasmus wrote to William Latimer that he considered Tunstal's learning in Greek to be equal to that of the Italians. Even allowing for the Humanist habit of hyperbole, Tunstal's ability must be beyond doubt. For the full text of these two letters, see *The Collected Works of Erasmus*, trans. R. A. B. Mynors *et al.*, (Toronto, 1974 ff.) vol. 3, p. 135 (Letter 388), and vol. 4, p. 259 (Letter 540).

[10] Tyndale's choice of Tunstal is of immense significance in the understanding of his intellectual development at this point: see Ch. 2.

[11] *Works* 1. 395. Tunstal himself played an important role in opposing the Reformation in England. He helped introduce the Six Articles in 1539 which enforced belief in the Real Presence and made deviation on this point a capital offence. During the reign of Edward VI, he was Bishop of Durham and, in 1550, had John Knox, then active as a Reformer in England, brought before the Council of the North for denying the Real Presence. However, Tunstal misjudged the political climate and, in the autumn of 1550, he was framed by the Earl of Warwick for conspiring against the king. He ended his days in the Tower of London, writing on the subject he loved best: the Real Presence. See J. Ridley, *John Knox* (Oxford, 1968) 90, 94–8.

Church. On the Continent, Bible translation was not that uncommon. For example, the first complete German translation, the Mentel Bible, was printed in 1466, fifty years before the Reformation started.[12] However, England was not the Continent. Unlike Germany, England stood in the shadow of Wyclif and the Lollards. Lollardy was synonymous with vernacular Bibles, heresy, and social revolution. Thus, any move towards a translation of the scriptures also carried connotations of heterodox belief and radical politics. As a result, the obscurantist suspicion with which Bible translation was viewed by otherwise forward-thinking men such as More and Tunstal is, perhaps, understandable. Furthermore, the advent of Lutheranism, with its perceived schismatic results, served only to reinforce English Catholic prejudices against placing the Bible in the hands of the laity.

Tyndale matriculated at the University of Wittenberg on 27 May 1524 under the name Guilelmus Daltin.[13] While here, he met his future assistant, William Roy. Together they made an abortive attempt to publish a New Testament at the press of Peter Quentel in Cologne. All that remains of this so-called *Cologne Fragment* is the preface and the first few pages of Matthew's Gospel. These, however, are quite enough to reveal the profound influence which contact with Luther had had on Tyndale.

It was in March 1526 that Tyndale and Roy produced the first English New Testament at Worms. Shortly afterwards, the relationship broke up. Tyndale, however, stayed in Worms to print a short, Luther-based introduction to Romans and to study Hebrew, the language required for a translation of the Old Testament.

At some time in the next few years, Tyndale established contact with John Frith, possibly at Marburg in 1528. In that same year, two of his major treatises, *The Parable of the Wicked*

---

[12] *The Cambridge History of the Bible 2: From the Fathers to the Reformation*, ed. G. W. H. Lampe (Cambridge, 1969) 433.

[13] The entry in the matriculation register lists one 'Guilelmus Daltici Ex Anglia. This was amended to 'Daltin', an anagram of 'Tindal', by Preserved Smith, an amendment which was confirmed by Professor F. A. Weissenborn, an expert on manuscripts. Mozley, unaware of Smith's research, made the same discovery independently some years later: see P. Smith, 'Englishmen at Wittenberg in the Sixteenth Century', *English Historical Review* 36 (1921), 422; Mozley, *William Tyndale*, 53.

Mammon and *The Obedience of a Christian Man* were printed at Antwerp. Tyndale was not merely a Bible translator: he was also a theologian who aimed to make the teaching of the Bible both comprehensible and practical.

In 1529, he went from Antwerp to Hamburg, and there recruited Miles Coverdale to help with the translation of the Pentateuch. He then returned to Antwerp in early 1530 and made this his publishing base and thus an important centre for English Protestantism in exile. He was to remain here until his execution in 1536.

Between the autumn of 1531 and 1534, Tyndale published nothing. According to a letter sent in early 1531 from royal agent Stephen Vaughan to Thomas Cromwell, Tyndale was delaying publication of his *Answer to More* in order to establish how the king would receive the work. Vaughan claimed that Tyndale was at that time writing a letter to the king and might well be persuaded to return to England under a safe-conduct. In December 1530 Hugh Latimer had circulated an open letter, asking the king to authorize an English translation of the Bible. This must have been good news for Tyndale and he would have been the natural choice to head such a project.[14]

Vaughan met Tyndale in May 1531 and recorded Tyndale's words in a letter to Henry VIII:

I assure you . . . if it would stand with the king's most gracious pleasure to grant only a bare text of the scripture to be put forth among his people . . . I shall immediately make faithful promise never to write more, nor abide two days in these parts after the same; but immediately to repair into his realm, and there most humbly submit myself at the feet of his royal majesty, offering my body to suffer what pain or torture, yea, what death his grace will, so this be obtained.[15]

If this report is to be trusted, it marks the high point of Tyndale's career in terms of potential importance to the political establishment.[16] However, his hopes of official support for a vernacular

---

[14] Henry knew of Tyndale and thoroughly enjoyed his *Obedience of a Christian Man* which argued for the Lutheran notion of obedience to the prince. However, Henry would certainly not have enjoyed *The Practice of Prelates* which declared that it was not legitimate for Henry to divorce Catherine of Aragon, despite the fact that she was his brother Arthur's widow.

[15] Quoted in Mozley, *William Tyndale*, 198.

[16] Mozley is sceptical of Vaughan's report, but Clebsch is prepared to accept it as a fair account: see Clebsch, p. 178.

scripture were not to be fulfilled so soon. The experiences of Robert Barnes, who returned to England in 1531 only to have to flee back to the Continent, and John Frith, who returned in 1532 and was executed in the following year, showed clearly that adherents of the Reformation were still not really welcome in England. Therefore, Tyndale remained on the Continent and continued to work on his translation of the Bible.

The remaining years of his life are shrouded in mystery. Because secrecy was necessary for survival, we know little of his movements during these years. Then, betrayed to the authorities at Antwerp by a government agent, Henry Philips, who had pretended to be a friend, Tyndale was imprisoned in the Castle of Vilvorde and tried in 1536. That same year he was executed by strangulation and burning at Antwerp. Ironically, it was only one year later, in 1537, that Henry VIII authorized a vernacular Bible which was heavily dependent upon the ground-breaking translation work of Tyndale himself.

JOHN FRITH

John Frith was born in 1503 in Westerham, Kent, a county renowned for Lollards.[17] He was educated first at Eton and then, from 1523 to 1524, at Queens' College, Cambridge. In 1525 he gained his BA from King's College. While at Cambridge, his tutor had been Stephen Gardiner, later to become a bishop and a notorious architect of the English counter-Reformation. At this time, however, Gardiner was a frequenter of 'Little Germany', the discussion group which met at the White Horse Inn in order to debate the latest trends in theology. Thus, it is possible that Gardiner himself may well have opened Frith's eyes to the exciting intellectual possibilities opened up by Humanism.[18] That Frith readily absorbed Cambridge's liberal intellectual atmosphere is evident from the fact that, in December 1525 he was selected by Cardinal Wolsey as a junior canon of his new

[17] The best modern biography of Frith, which also includes excellent analysis of his theology, is by N. T. Wright in *The Work of John Frith* (Appleford, 1978). For Foxe's account, see *AM* 5. 2–18.

[18] The White Horse group has the popular image of having been thoroughly committed to the Reformation. While this is probably true of many of its members, it was really an informal gathering of intellectuals and not a clandestine theological cell: see E. G. Rupp, *The Making of the English Protestant Tradition* (Cambridge, 1947), 18–19.

foundation at Oxford, Cardinal College.[19] This college was to be staffed by the brightest of the country's youth and was intended to form a lasting monument to the liberality of its founder. While it was never to be the latter, at the time it did shine as a beacon of Humanist learning and culture amidst the rigidly orthodox spires of early sixteenth-century Oxford.

The interests of Frith and his colleagues extended well beyond Catholic Humanism and, in February 1528, John Longland, bishop of Lincoln, was informed that fellows of the college were reading all manner of heretical books by such authors as Hus, Wyclif, Bucer, Oecolampadius, Zwingli, and, of course, Martin Luther.[20] Wolsey was understandably upset and had the offenders charged with heresy and thrown into the college fish cellar. Some died, some recanted, but Frith somehow managed to escape and flee to the Continent in late 1528.

On the Continent, he made contact with Tyndale whom it is possible that he knew prior to his exile. He was to help Tyndale translate Jonah and the pentateuch, and he probably completed his friends *Answer to More* before seeing it through the press.[21] Exact details of Frith's movements during this period are impossible to establish. It is unlikely that he visited Wittenberg, and he certainly never matriculated at the university there as did Tyndale and Barnes. Possibly he visited Marburg as his first literary work was *Patrick's Places*, an edited translation of the doctoral disputation of the young Scotsman Patrick Hamilton. Hamilton studied at Marburg under Francis Lambert and his disputation theses clearly demonstrate the Lutheran cast of his mind.[22]

---

[19] Now Christ Church.

[20] The complete list of books is to be found in two letters from Dr London, Warden of New College, Oxford, to Longland, dated 24 and 16 February 1528. These are printed as Appendix 6 in *AM* 5.

[21] See Clebsch, p. 81. Clebsch's claim that Frith completed Tyndale's *Answer to More* is based on persuasive historical and textual analysis. Clebsch then uses this fact to strengthen his case for a fundamental shift in Tyndale's theology by ascribing to Frith those parts of the *Answer* which do not fit his own interpretation of Tyndale: see Clebsch, pp. 94–8, 168–9. While his claims for Frith's authorship of parts of the text are probably correct, a careful analysis of the treatise's theology lays bare Clebsch's mistake in using his conclusions about the texts composition to support his interpretation of Tyndale's theological development: see Ch. 5.

[22] On Hamilton, see the collection of essays *Patrick Hamilton: First Scottish Martyr of the Reformation*, ed. A. Cameron (Edinburgh, 1929). The theology of *Patrick's Places* is discussed in detail in Ch. 5.

That Frith's own sympathies lay with Luther at this time is evident from other early works, such as his translation of Luther's *On the Antichrist* and his *Disputation of Purgatory*. The latter work rejected the orthodox position on purgatory and advocated instead a theology of Christian justification and sanctification built around the cross of Christ. The similarity with Luther is obvious. In later works, however, Frith was to demonstrate greater affinity with the Reformed tradition stemming from Switzerland, but this need not imply that he ever spent any great period of time or study there.

In 1531, Frith returned to England. This was the period of time when Thomas Cromwell, via his agent Stephen Vaughan, was attempting to persuade exiled Protestants to return. Cromwell now thought that Protestantism might well prove useful in facilitating northern European alliances against Habsburg power and in undermining his own opponents at home. In this context, Robert Barnes did return under safe conduct late in the year as mediator between Henry and Luther on the matter of the king's divorce.

Frith himself probably returned in order to deal with George Constantine, a defector from the Protestant cause who was then working as an informer for Thomas More.[23] However, More found out about his visit and had him arrested at Reading, a fact which indicates that Frith was not travelling under a safe-conduct. Foxe tells us that Frith was cast into the stocks and, having been starved for some time, asked to see the local schoolmaster, Leonard Cox, They talked, first in Latin and then in Greek. Finally, Frith recited the opening of the *Iliad*. At this, Cox was so moved that he secured Frith's release. Frith used his new-found freedom to return to the Continent.[24]

Frith was to remain on the Continent until July 1532. As Clebsch points out, the years 1531–2 were a period of uncharacteristic silence for Tyndale, Frith, and Barnes. We can only assume that the constant vacillations of Henry's foreign and domestic policies left the Continental exiles confused, and perhaps hopeful, about the prospects for their cause.

Hopes must indeed have been raised in 1532 when Thomas More, up to that point a powerful and zealous persecutor of

---

[23] See Clebsch, p. 100.   [24] *AM* 5. 5–6.

Protestants, resigned as chancellor over the issue of the king's headship of the Church. It was probably this event, potentially pointing towards the official acceptance of Protestantism in England, that led Frith to sail home in July 1532. If that is so, he badly misjudged the situation: he was arrested near Southend in October of the same year, intending to make good his escape to Antwerp.

While awaiting trial, Frith was kept in the Tower of London where he continued to write in defence of Protestantism. According to Foxe, his continued attacks on the Catholic doctrine of the Eucharist led to him being examined by Cromwell and Cranmer before his trial in an effort to obtain a recantation. The examination itself appears to have gone Frith's way and to have had some impact on his hearers. Cranmer himself was later to subscribe to Frith's view of the sacrament, although a causal connection between Frith's examination and Cranmer's later doctrine is pure speculation.[25]

At his actual trial, Frith was condemned on two counts: first, he denied the reality of purgatory as taught by the Catholic Church; and secondly, he denied that Christ was physically present in the Eucharist. On both issues, he did not insist on his own interpretation of the doctrines but stressed that belief on these matters was not vital for salvation, that legitimate disagreements could exist as long as the central idea of salvation through faith in Christ was grasped. This ecumenical spirit was of no avail: he died at the stake on 4 July 1533.

ROBERT BARNES

Robert Barnes, the most significant Lutheran theologian of the English Reformation, was born near Lynn, in Norfolk, in

---

[25] In a letter of 17 June 1533, Cranmer refers to his examination of Frith who, he states, argued for the 'erroneous' view that it was 'not necessary to be believed as an article of our faith, that there is the very corporal presence of Christ within the host and sacrament of the altar, and holdeth of this point most after the position of Oecolampadius': *The Work of Thomas Cranmer* (Appleford, 1964), 250. P. N. Brooks sees the similarity between Cranmer and Frith as the result of both men drawing on the work of Oecolampadius, although to call Frith 'a blind disciple' of the Basle Reformer is something of an overstatement, especially as Brooks does not cite one jot of evidence in support of so sweeping a claim: see *Thomas Cranmer's Doctrine of the Eucharist* (London, 1965), p. 91.

1495.[26] In 1511 or 1512, he became a novice at the Augustinian priory in Cambridge. In 1514 he went to study at the University of Louvain where he remained until 1521. It is possible that it was during this period of time that he first became acquainted with the troubles which were erupting within the Church and which focused on a member of his own Order, Martin Luther. It has been suggested that Barnes may indeed have been present at the Heidelberg Disputation of 1518, where Luther boldly asserted his theology of the cross and attacked what he regarded as the rank Pelagianism of his medieval mentors.[27] There is no positive evidence of this, although it remains a possibility. Even if he had been present, however, the strictly theological impact must have been limited: Barnes shows no signs of true Lutheran theology until much later, and then he never uses the language or content of the theology of the Cross, although this need not mean that he was not present at the Disputation or that he was unimpressed by what he heard.[28]

Barnes returned to Cambridge in 1522 or 1523 where he instituted a number of cultural reforms in the Augustinian House which clearly indicate that the New Learning of Louvain had influenced him. However, his reforms appear to have involved the introduction of Latin authors only, and there is no evidence to suggest that he knew any Greek even though he had been at Cambridge at the same time as Erasmus and was probably at Louvain at the same time as the Dutch Humanist was establishing the Collegium Trilingue for the study of Latin, Greek, and Hebrew. Thus, while Barnes became known as a leading advocate of the New Learning in Cambridge, it is important not to exaggerate how radical he was at this stage.[29]

It was on Christmas Eve 1525 that Barnes career as a religious reformer, as opposed to a cultural reformer, really

[26] The best modern biography of Barnes is by J. P. Lusardi in *The Complete Works of St. Thomas More* vol. 8 (Yale, 1973), 1365–415. For Foxe's account, see *AM* 5. 414–38.

[27] See Clebsch, p. 43. On Luther's theology of the cross, see Ch. 3.

[28] Another young man, Martin Bucer, was also present at the Heidelberg Disputation and was overwhelmed by the impact of Luther. Indeed, W. P. Stephens describes this as 'the decisive encounter of his life': *The Holy Spirit in the Theology of Martin Bucer* (Cambridge, 1970), 5. However, like Barnes, he too never developed a Lutheran theology of the cross, a concept which formed the heart of the radical theology articulated at Heidelberg.

[29] See Clebsch, p. 43. For a fuller discussion of Barnes's intellectual development at this time, see Ch. 2.

started. Sometime previously, he had been converted through the ministry of Thomas Bilney and, as a result, had developed a concern about the corruption of the Church hierarchy.[30] This concern bore fruit in his Christmas Eve sermon, which was delivered in St Edward's Church, Cambridge. The sermon soon led to trouble for Barnes who was arrested, transported to London, and then examined for heresy by Wolsey on 8 February 1526.[31] Barnes eventually recanted and did public penance at St Paul's. After this, he was thrown into the Fleet. It was here that his famous meeting with John Tyball took place. Tyball, a Lollard, visited Barnes and purchased a copy of Tyndale's New Testament from him for three shillings and six pence.[32]

Having been transferred from London to Northampton, Barnes discovered that he was to be burned. Therefore, he planned to escape. Leaving a suicide note for Wolsey, he pretended to have drowned himself. In reality, he fled in disguise to London, from where he sailed to Antwerp. From Antwerp, he went to Wittenberg.

The chronology of the years 1529–30 is unclear, but we do know that Barnes was resident in Wittenberg by the summer of 1530, where he was staying with Luther's friend, Bugenhagen.[33] It was here, and at about this time, that Barnes wrote his first book: *Sentences gathered from the Fathers which present-day Papists vigorously condemn* (*Sentenciae ex doctoribus collectae quas Papistae valde hodie damnant*). The work was a series of nineteen theological assertions with supporting proof-texts drawn from the works of the Fathers.[34] Its purpose was to prove the true catholicity of Lutheran theology and demonstrate the deviant nature of medieval theology. Barnes followed this work in November 1531 with a treatise in English, *A Supplication unto King Henry VIII*. This was ostensibly an

[30] Thomas Bilney (?1495–1531) was responsible for the conversion of a number of significant Reformers, including Hugh Latimer. However, his own theological position was thoroughly ambiguous: see Ch. 2.

[31] There is considerable debate about whether it was the theology of the sermon or simply its attacks on clerical abuses which landed Barnes in trouble: see Ch. 2.

[32] See Ch. 2.

[33] See Clebsch, pp. 48–9.

[34] The nineteen assertions are listed in Latin in Clebsch, p. 50, and in English in Rupp, *English Protestant Tradition*, 39–40.

expansion by Barnes of his earlier work addressed to Henry VIII in an attempt to vindicate his position.[35]

Earlier in this same year, Barnes had become involved in 'the King's matter', that is, Henry's desire to have his marriage to Catherine of Aragon declared void so that he could marry Anne Boleyn. Henry hoped to have the marriage declared void on the grounds that Catherine was his brother Arthur's widow and that their union was therefore contrary to biblical teaching. In order to strengthen his position, or perhaps salve his own conscience, Henry had consulted numerous distinguished theologians, including Luther, in search of the answer he desired.[36] Luther's pronouncement on the matter was given to Barnes early in September, 1531. Barnes, under safe conduct, travelled to England and met Henry in December.[37]

The letter Barnes brought did not perhaps contain the sentiments for which Henry had hoped. Rather than permitting divorce, Luther advised the king simply to have more than one wife as the Old Testament patriarchs had done.[38] Nevertheless, the letter was significant because it brought Barnes into the king's service and back to England. However, the situation was still highly precarious and Barnes was a relapsed heretic. Indeed, the ever-vigilant Thomas More pushed for Barnes's arrest, claiming that he had outstayed his safe-conduct. This led to Barnes returning to the Continent in January 1532. He was also relieved of his responsibility to negotiate with Wittenberg on Henry's behalf as one William Paget had been appointed as the king's negotiator with the Protestant princes.[39]

[35] For a thorough discussion of this work, see Ch. 6.

[36] Various unsolicited theologians also gave their opinions on 'the King's matter': e.g. Tyndale, in *The Practice of Prelates*, and, quite possibly, John Calvin. While I have been unable to find any specific reference to this in the secondary literature, an undated letter written by Calvin has recently appeared in English translation which is addressed to 'an illustrious prince' who desires to marry his brother's widow. As such, the letter fits the situation of Henry VIII exactly. Calvin considers such a marriage inadmissible: see *Calvin's Ecclesiastical Advice*, trans. M. Beaty and B. W. Farley (Edinburgh, 1991), p 125–9.

[37] Barnes was also invited to England at this time by Cromwell who had been advised by Stephen Vaughan, a Royal agent, that Barnes would be a useful leader of the Protestant cause.

[38] P. Smith. 'Luther and Henry VIII', *English Historical Review* 25 (1910), 665–6.

[39] E. Doernberg, *Henry VIII and Luther: An Account of Their Personal Relations* (Stanford, 1961), 91.

For the next few years, Barnes devoted himself to theology. On 20 June 1533, he matriculated at the University of Wittenberg under the pseudonym Antonius Anglus.[40] It was at Wittenberg that he prepared a revision of *A Supplication* which was published in November 1534.[41] However, from August 1534 to January 1535, Barnes was back in London to negotiate with Henry on behalf of Hamburg and Lubeck. Henry was at this point seeking alliances with anyone who would help him cause trouble for the Habsburgs. An alliance with these two cities would have given the king a powerful influence in Denmark and the Baltic cities, thus consolidating anti-Habsburg power in northern Europe. While the negotiations did not go well, they helped bring Barnes once again to the attention of his king.[42]

Barnes's loyalty to the king seems to have been absolute and to have verged on sycophancy. Indeed, having been appointed Royal Chaplain in July 1535, in September of the same year he dedicated his next work, *History of the Popes* to his royal master. His relationship with the king was apparently so warm at this time that Melanchthon jested about him becoming a bishop.[43]

For the next few years Barnes acted on behalf of the king in a number of matters, such as baiting John Lambert for his sacramentarian convictions in 1538, the same year that Cranmer unsuccessfully attempted to obtain for him the Deanery of Tamworth College. However, in 1539 came Barnes's greatest opportunity for influence when the Danes called on Bugenhagen to reform their Church. Barnes, an old friend of Bugenhagen, was the natural choice as English representative. Thus, with full diplomatic status and pay, Barnes travelled to Denmark.

It was at this time that the Six Articles were passed. In 1536 the so-called Ten Articles had been passed which were a broad affirmation of Erasmian and Melanchthonian principles. However, the Six Articles of June 1539 contained a vigorous assertion of the Catholic view of the sacraments, backed up with threats of the severest penalties for those who did not agree. England in 1539 was thus somewhat less disposed towards

---

[40] Smith, 'Englishmen at Wittenberg', 423.
[41] The revisions are discussed in detail in Ch. 6. Many reflect shifts in the political climate while others have significance for Barnes's theology.
[42] Rupp, *English Protestant Tradition*, 41–2.
[43] The incident is recounted in ibid. 43, although no primary reference is supplied.

reform than it had been in 1536. In the context of negotiations between Henry and the Lutheran princes during 1537 and 1538, the passing of the Six Articles can only be interpreted as representing Henry's decision to terminate his somewhat flirtatious attempts to establish an alliance with north European Protestants.

For Barnes, the Articles effectively neutralized his importance as negotiations with Protestants no longer formed a significant part of Henry's policy. Unfortunately, Barnes had also helped arrange the disastrous marriage of Henry to Ann of Cleves, an act hardly likely to endear him to the king. Nevertheless, it was theology which was to prove his ultimate downfall. When he returned to England, he, along with Thomas Garrard and William Jerome, were appointed by Cranmer to deliver the Lent sermons at St Paul's Cross. However, Stephen Gardiner had his own name placed at the top of the list of preachers and used his sermon to attack Barnes directly. Barnes, perhaps over-confident of the king's personal affection for him, gave a suitably vitriolic reply which led to him being arrested. Unable to convince the authorities of his doctrinal soundness, and with Cromwell now fallen from grace, Barnes perished at the stake on 30 July 1540, along with Garrard, Jerome, and three Catholics.

JOHN HOOPER

Hooper was born *c.*1495 in Somerset.[44] He graduated BA from Merton College, Oxford in 1519. The next period of his life is shrouded in mystery, and it seems likely that he spent this time in the Cistercian monastery at Cleeve. In 1536, in search of revenue and a way of curtailing Church power, Henry VIII authorized Cromwell to proceed with the dissolution of the monasteries. Hooper was thus pushed back into the world and, in 1536, he appeared in Oxford where he clashed with with Richard Smith, Regius Professor of Divinity and a

---

[44] The secondary literature on Hooper is small. The best account of his life is W. M. S. West, 'John Hooper and the Origins of Puritanism', *Baptist Quarterly* 15 (1954), 347–68 and 16 (1955), 22–6, 67–88. This is basically an abridgment of his doctoral thesis 'A Study of John Hooper: With Special Reference to his Contact with Henry Bullinger' (University of Zurich, 1953). For Foxe's account of Hooper's life, see *AM* 6. 636–62.

strong Catholic. The implication of this encounter is that Hooper had already begun to develop sympathies with the theology of the Reformation which was already established in many places on the Continent.[45]

After this incident, Hooper became a steward in the house of Sir Thomas Arundel. It was here that he came across the works of Zwingli and a number of Bullinger's *Commentaries on the Epistles of Paul*, an event which marked the turning point in his career and later encouraged him to consider Zurich as a place to study.[46] This change in Hooper did not meet with his master's approval, and Arundel sent him to Stephen Gardiner with a view to bringing him back to the Catholic fold. Gardiner failed in this task and sent Hooper back to Arundel.

The encounter with Gardiner probably took place in the early 1540s.[47] With the passing of the Six Articles in 1539 transubstantiation was official Church doctrine, a status underlined by the death penalty for anyone who denied it. Thus, Hooper was probably pursuing the only realistic option when he left for the Continent, probably first to Strasbourg, where he married Anne de Tserclas, the nurse who helped him through a serious illness. Then, after corresponding with Bullinger, Hooper made his way to Zurich.

Hooper was welcomed to Zurich by Bullinger, Zwingli's successor, in whose house he became a lodger.[48] During this

---

[45] It is easy to forget just how far behind the Continent English theology was in the early decades of the sixteenth century. For example, in 1536, Zwingli had been dead five years, Luther had long since produced his greatest works, Bucer was already established as a leading theologian, and Calvin was engaged in publishing the first edition of his *Institutes*. English theologians, however, were writing only short treatises, much of the content of which was heavily dependent upon Continental models. Indeed, England really produced no Protestant theologian (in the strict sense of the word) of international standing until the advent of men such as Perkins during the reign of Elizabeth. Until that time, theological initiative and originality lay on the Continent.

[46] Hooper refers to these works as crucial early influences in a letter to Bullinger: see *OL* 33–4.

[47] See West, 'Origins', 348.

[48] Writing in 1954, West declared that 'Bullinger . . . deserves to be better known than he is.' Certainly, he was a highly important influence on the English Reformation as his *Decades* formed the basic theological textbook for students during the reign of Elizabeth I. Sadly, the amount of scholarship available on him in English is still not great. The best work is J. W. Baker, *Heinrich Bullinger and the Covenant: The Other Reformed Tradition* (Ohio, 1980). Useful, if brief, discussions of aspects of his theology can also be found in R. W. A. Letham, 'Saving Faith and Assurance in Reformed Theology from Zwingli to the Synod of Dordt', unpubl. Ph.D. thesis (University of

time, Hooper was to develop many of the fundamental concerns which guided his later ministry. For him, the most impressive aspect of the Zurich reformation was the absolute simplicity of the Reformed way of worship: Churches devoid of the ornate trappings associated with Catholic and Lutheran worship; ministers who did not wear ceremonial garb; and a primary emphasis on the preaching of the word, with the sacrament, understood in a symbolic sense, being given a secondary, although still important, role. Hooper's conviction that such Church order was the only truly biblical one was to lead him into violent conflict with the Church authorities under Edward VI.

Late in 1548, now that Edward was on the English throne, Hooper began to contemplate a return to his homeland. Thus, in early 1549, he set out with his wife and baby daughter for England. On arrival, the situation was not all he could have wished: Peter Martyr Vermigli and Martin Bucer, neither of whom were committed to the Zurich theology, were both gaining in influence and the Polish Zwinglian, John Laski (or à Lasco) had left. Nevertheless, Hooper set about propagating the Zurich theology by giving a series of lectures in the London diocese, an act which led to the inevitable clash with Catholic bishop, Edmund Bonner. However, it appears that the Protestant leaders saw in Hooper an opportunity for a decisive confrontation with the bishop and Bonner's failure to stress in his sermon against Hooper that the king was to be obeyed, even though he was but a boy, cost him dearly. The end result of the conflict was that Bonner was imprisoned in late 1549, and Hooper, whose preaching had provided the pretext for undermining the bishop's power, was looked upon with some favour by Thomas Cranmer.[49]

In 1549, the Duke of Somerset fell from power. Somerset had been the leading political light behind the Edwardian

Aberdeen, 1979); R. A. Muller, *Christ and the Decree: Christology and Predestination in Reformed Theology from Calvin to Perkins* (Grand Rapids, 1988); S. Strehle, *Calvinism, Federalism, and Scholasticism: A Study of the Reformed Doctrine of Covenant* (Bern, 1988); J. R. Beeke, *Assurance of Faith: Calvin, English Puritanism, and the Dutch Second Reformation* (Bern, 1991). Several scholars are currently engaged in major studies of Bullinger's theology and hopefully these will help to rectify such a glaring gap in Reformation scholarship.

[49] For a detailed account of the conflict between Hooper and Bonner, see West, 'Origins', 24.

Reformation and the patron and protector of Hooper. However, his successor, the Earl of Warwick (later the Duke of Northumberland) was committed to continuing the process of reform and thus Hooper's activities were not prematurely curtailed. Indeed, in February 1550 he was invited by Cranmer to preach a series of sermons before the king, a sign of how his influence had grown since his arrival in May the previous year. He accepted the offer, and preached a series on Jonah.[50] In one of these, he made a critical remark about the requirement to swear an oath by the saints in the ordination of officers in the Church.[51] For this he was summoned before the Council and severely reprimanded by Cranmer. Hooper, however, was not persuaded: as far as he was concerned, Church practice was determined by what God's word prescribed and not simply limited by what it prohibited. This basic principle lay behind the most famous incident of Hooper's career: the vestment controversy.

At Easter 1550 Hooper was offered the bishopric of Gloucester. Hooper refused the offer, partly because of the oath to which he had already objected in his sermons on Jonah, and partly because of the requirement that he wear clerical clothing. According to Anglican statutes, various kinds of dress were to be worn when officiating at religious ceremonies. These outfits varied from a simple surplice of the deacon to the red and white uniform of the bishop. Both the oath and the clothing were anathema to one used to the simple Church order of Zurich.

As a result of his refusal, Hooper was summoned before the Council on 15 May 1550. Here, with the support of the recently released Duke of Somerset, Hooper persuaded the Council that whether to wear vestments or not was a matter for the individual conscience. With this point conceded by the Council, Hooper could now accept the bishopric with a clear conscience. Thus, on 20 July, Hooper came before the king and Council to have the bishopric confirmed. Here, he even persuaded the king that the oath referring to the saints was unchristian, and Edward crossed out the offending passage with his own pen.

Hooper, however, had yet to deal with the bishops who had

---

[50] These sermons are reprinted in *EW* 431–560.

[51] For this comment, see *EW* 479. It is possible that this oath was that to which Bradford too objected in the ordination ceremony: see below.

been far from pleased at the Council's decision concerning vestments. Cranmer, while accepting the matter of the oath, referred Hooper to Ridley on the issue of vestments. Ridley, despite various appeals from the Council, refused to compromise on the need for Hooper to wear the prescribed clerical vestments at his consecration. The resulting confrontation served to polarize the situation, with Ridley insisting that matters of Church order should be decided by Church authorities and then simply enforced by the secular power. Hooper, however, now rejected the idea that vestments were a matter indifferent and insisted that they were positively sinful.

On 3 October Hooper submitted a paper outlining his position to the Council. Ridley had little difficulty in refuting his arguments.[52] Hooper then attempted to find support for his cause elsewhere but, while Laski was supportive, Bucer and Vermigli refused to take his side. At the beginning of December, he was placed under house arrest and forbidden to indulge in any public theological endeavour. He ignored this, issuing *A Godly Confession and Protestation of the Christian Faith* later that same month. Finally, at the end of January 1551, the patience of the authorities came to an end and Hooper was cast into the Fleet. Thus, a hardline Reformer joined the ranks of leading Catholics, such as Bonner and Gardiner—a graphic testimony to the intolerance of Reformation Anglicanism's 'middle way'.[53]

It was a mere fortnight before Hooper's resolve was broken and he submitted. Lack of support from the Continent was probably an important factor in this, but so too was threat of death. W. M. S. West has pointed out that in the 1559 Latin edition of *Acts and Monuments*, Foxe refers to a plan to have Hooper executed if he did not submit.[54] Hooper must have

---

[52] Hooper's arguments, and Ridley's replies, are summarized by West: 'Origins', 33–9. Ridley's reply is printed in full in Bradford's *Writings* 2. 375–95

[53] It is difficult to see that the controversy can really have escalated to the level it did unless there was at its root some violent personality clash between Hooper and Ridley. After all, John Bradford also objected to certain parts of the ordination ceremony and was ordained without the offending parts and without any major ecclesiastical dispute. He was, however, a close personal friend of Ridley. It seems likely that Hooper was such an outspoken and, to his opponents, arrogant individual that the Church authorities were deliberately awkward with him in order to put him in his place. Had they not done so, he might have become a dangerously destabilizing influence within the Church hierarchy.

[54] See 'Origins', 41–2.

decided that vestments were not worth dying for and so proceeded to the bishopric of Gloucester.

With his ordination as bishop, Hooper's life settled down to the mundane routine of ecclesiastical business. During his time in office, he focused his attention on the quality of ministry within his diocese, conducting surveys into the level of theological knowledge of the clergy and establishing basic standards in terms of Church practice and teaching. However, his time as bishop was short lived. Edward VI died in July 1553 and Mary took his place. Perhaps surprisingly, Hooper rallied support for Mary as the legal heir, opposing Warwick's scheme to place Lady Jane Grey on the throne. His loyalty, however, was not enough to save him. Refusing to flee abroad, he was arrested in September 1553, deprived of his bishopric in 1554, and tried for heresy in January 1555. Found guilty of denying the physical presence of Christ in the Eucharist, he was sentenced to death. He was burned at the stake in Gloucester on 9 February 1555.

JOHN BRADFORD

Like that of John Frith, the premature death at the stake of John Bradford most assuredly deprived the English Reformation of one of its potentially great theologians. The small collection of his work that we have points to a mind with a powerful grasp of Reformed theology and indicates that, had he lived, he would have made a significant contribution to the development of English Reformation thought.

Bradford was born *c.*1510 in the north of England, probably near Manchester.[55] We know very little of his early life, but, in *A Meditation upon the Ten Commandments*, he does give thanks to God for his 'parents, schoolmasters, and others' who had guided him from infancy onwards.[56] Perhaps this indicates that he had a genuinely happy childhood, or perhaps it is the nostalgic memory of a man facing death. Either way, it constitutes the only reference we have to Bradford's childhood.

As a young man he was employed as servant to Sir John Harrington of Exton in Rutlandshire. This man was treasurer

[55] John Bradford has attracted virtually no scholarly interest. The basic source for his life is John Foxe's account in *AM* 7 143–96.
[56] *Writings* 1, 162.

of the English forces at Boulogne in 1544, where Bradford acted as his paymaster. Three years later, just after the accession of Edward VI, Bradford entered the Inner Temple as a law student. It appears that, at about this time, he underwent the evangelical experience which was to transform his whole life. According to Foxe, Bradford's conversion led him not only to abandon many of his material possessions but also to abandon his legal studies and transfer to Cambridge in order to pursue a course in theology.

Before he left London, however, Bradford heard Hugh Latimer preach before Edward VI on the subject of the need to return stolen property. Bradford had himself known about a fraud committed against the king by Sir John Harrington and was so convicted by Latimer's sentiments that, having consulted the bishop, he immediately made a restitution.[57] The incident clearly indicates the scrupulous personal piety that undergirded Bradford's theology.

In the summer of 1548, Bradford matriculated at Catharine's Hall, Cambridge.[58] That he was an exemplary scholar is clearly indicated by the fact that twelve months later he was invited by Nicholas Ridley, bishop of Rochester, to become a Fellow of Pembroke, where Ridley was Master. Bradford accepted the offer, which apparently upset the Master of Catharine's Hall who hoped to retain him.[59] At about this time, Bradford also gained his MA, a remarkable achievement after only one year's study at the university.[60]

While at Cambridge, Bradford met the man who was to be the most important theological influence upon his thought: Martin Bucer. Invited to England by Cranmer, Bucer became Regius Professor of Divinity at Cambridge in 1549 where he was to remain until his death in 1551. Bradford was a regular attender at Bucer's lectures, and also a close personal friend.

---

[57] Several letters refer to this matter: see *Writings* 2, Letters 1, 4, 6, 9, 14.

[58] Catharine's Hall, now St Catharine's College, was home to a number of significant theologians: in the seventeenth century, Richard Sibbes, 'the heavenly doctor' who exerted a profound influence on English Puritan piety, was Master of the College, and Thomas Goodwin, another leading Puritan and Independent representative at the Westminster Assembly, was for a time a Fellow.

[59] See *Writings* 2. 27.

[60] The MA was a reward for Bradford's diligent study and opened the way for him to become a Fellow: see the Grace Book entry reprinted in *Writings* 2. xviii.

Indeed, Bucer's will stipulated that his widow was to take the advice of Bradford and another friend, Sampson, concerning the details of his burial.[61] Later, when facing death himself, Bradford warned the people of Cambridge to 'remember the readings and preachings of God's prophet and true preacher, Martin Bucer'.[62]

In 1550 Bradford accompanied Bucer on a trip to Oxford to meet Peter Martyr Vermigli, another Reformation exile who was then Regius Professor of Divinity at Oxford. Three weeks later, he was ordained deacon. Apparently, Bradford objected to something in the ordination service and so Ridley allowed his ordination to proceed with the offending part having been removed. What it was that caused Bradford's objection is a matter for conjecture. It may have been the clause 'by the saints' in the oath of supremacy or it may have been the need to wear a clerical surplice.[63] Whatever the problem, we can infer from his ordination that Bradford was one who wanted to see a more thorough reformation of Church practice.

After ordination, Bradford was immediately appointed as one of Ridley's chaplains and licensed to preach. In the following year, 1551, after the death of Bucer, Bradford was made a prebend of St Paul's and then one of the six itinerant chaplains of Edward VI. These six, who included Edmund Grindal, a future Archbishop of Canterbury, and John Knox, the Scottish Reformer, were officially appointed to preach the gospel to the remoter parts of the country where the new theology had not yet taken hold. The reception of Reformation theology and the success of the politics of the day were so intimately connected that the appointment of such preachers was as much an act of political expediency as of evangelistic fervour. Bradford performed his task with evangelical zeal, preaching all over Lancashire and Cheshire. According to Foxe, 'sharply he opened and reproved sin; sweetly he preached Christ crucified; pithily he impugned heresies and errors; earnestly he persuaded to godly life'.[64]

Bradford's reputation as a Christian leader was such that, late in 1552, Ridley suggested him for a new bishopric which

---

[61] See *Writings* 2. xxiii.   [62] Ibid. 1. 445.
[63] The editor of Bradford's writings favours the former interpretation: see ibid 2. xxii.
[64] *AM* 7. 144.

was to be created by dividing Durham into two sees. This was passed into law in March 1553, but by that time Edward VI was dying and Ridley's suggestion was never to be acted upon.

Edward died on 6 July 1553 and, on 19 July, Mary was proclaimed queen. She arrived in London on 3 August. Immediately, the tide of Reformation was turned back. At St Paul's Cross, the bishop of Bath preached a sermon attacking the Reformation. A riot ensued which was only calmed down by the intervention of Bradford, who apparently saved the bishop's life. This act of charity did not go unrewarded: soon after, Bradford was arrested and imprisoned in the Tower.

While imprisonment severely curtailed Bradford's preaching activities, he was able to continue his ministry through writing. The large number of extant pastoral letters and devotional tracts dating from this period are clear evidence of his continuing zeal for the Protestant cause and of his deep concern for those facing persecution from the Catholic authorities.

Bradford was not alone during this time. To begin with, he was held with Edmund Sandys and then with Cranmer, Latimer and Ridley. According to Latimer, they spent their time in Bible study, examining what the scriptures taught about Christ's sacrifice and Eucharistic presence, the key issue for which they were facing death.[65]

It was also while in prison that Bradford engaged in an important debate with members of a Pelagian sect known as 'the free will men'. The issue at stake was the perennial question of salvation by grace or by works. Bradford's vigorous defence of the former led him to adopt a strong predestinarian position, reminiscent of that of his mentor, Bucer, which was not altogether welcomed by the leaders of English Protestantism.[66]

With the revival of the Six Articles in January 1555, the way was open for the authorities to prosecute and then execute the Protestant leaders. Bradford was examined by Stephen Gardiner concerning his doctrine of the Eucharist and, having been found wanting, he was sentenced to death on 31 January 1555.[67] He was executed on 30 June 1555.

[65] See the quotation from Latimer in *Writings* 2. xxxiii–xxxiv.

[66] The writings relevant to this controversy and the attitude of other English Protestant leaders are examined in Ch. 8.

[67] The text of the three examinations Bradford underwent are printed in full in *Writings* 1. 465–92. The text is traditionally ascribed to Bradford himself, although it is written in the third person.

2

The Intellectual Context   1

THE greatest influences on the English Reformers were, of course, the exciting theological developments taking place on the Continent. However, while the theological endeavours of Luther and his fellow Reformers were the crucial intellectual force behind their thought, the English Reformers worked out their theology in the context of a number of other important influences. The precise impact of these influences can only be determined through a detailed examination of the English Reformers' written works, but certain general observations can and should be made as a prelude to such a task. With the exception of John Bradford, all of the men in this study were educated under a system which had yet to absorb the insights of Reformation theology, and it was from this pre-Reformation education that they were to emerge as Reformers.

PATRISTIC THEOLOGY

The English Reformers regarded the patristic writers as being of fundamental importance because of the need to establish that they were not theological innovators but restorers of the pure doctrine of the early Church. This does not mean that they regarded the Fathers as having an authority equal to that of scripture but that they considered them to be more reliable guides to Christian truth than the medieval scholastic theologians.

William Tyndale does not quote patristic sources as often as some of his contemporaries. As a result, some scholars have tended to minimize or ignore the role which patristic thought played in his theology.[1] In fact, Tyndale does demonstrate

---

[1] Clebsch devotes no attention to the role of the Fathers in Tyndale's theology. Examples of those who minimize their significance for Tyndale include C. W. Dugmore, *The Mass and the English Reformers* (London, 1958), 104; and S. L. Greenslade, *The*

knowledge of the Fathers, especially Augustine and Jerome, although he also refers to Cyprian, Chrysostom, Origen, and others. His attitude is one of critical respect: he regards the Fathers, especially Augustine, as great theologians, but stresses that their work must be subject to the test of scripture.[2]

There is evidence Tyndale was exposed to the teachings of Augustine before he travelled to Wittenberg. In his commentary on William Tracy's will, Tyndale makes the following comment concerning the author: he was 'a learned man, and better seen in the works of St Austin twenty years before he died, than ever I knew doctor in England'.[3] Tracy's patristic learning clearly impressed Tyndale, and it is possible that Tyndale's interest in Augustine dates from as early as 1510–11, twenty years before Tracy died. This means that his earliest theological impulses may well have come from first-hand encounters with patristic sources.[4]

John Frith quotes from and refers to the Fathers far more frequently than Tyndale. In part, this is due to his method of

---

English Reformers and the Fathers of the Church (Oxford, 1960), 4. The problem with such an approach is that influence is equated with explicit use. Such an equation is arbitrary and untenable. J. K. Yost ('Tyndale's Use of the Fathers: a Note on His Connection to Northern Humanism', *Moreana*, 6 (1969), 5–13) presents a more positive assessment of Tyndale's attitude to the Fathers, even going as far as to speculate (p. 11) that, had Tyndale lived longer, he would have produced a translation of his favourite patristic authors.

[2] *Works* 1. 330; 3. 136.

[3] Ibid. 279. Tracy was a native of Gloucestershire who, in 1530, made a will that was unashamedly Protestant in content. In it he advocated justification by faith and repudiated prayers for the dead. In 1531 the Prerogative Court of Canterbury found the will to be heretical, and Dr Parker, chancellor of Worcester Cathedral, was ordered to exhume Tracy's body. This he did, but went further and burned the body, an act that could only be sanctioned by the king's officers. As a result, Parker was himself fined £300. The will itself became something of a popular Protestant tract because of its content, brevity, and, no doubt, the scandalous light in which the whole incident portrayed the ecclesiastical authorities. Both William Tyndale and John Frith produced brief commentaries upon the work. See A. G. Dickens, *The English Reformation* (London, 1967), 139–40. For Frith's commentary, see Ch. 5.

[4] It is impossible to know how Tracy interpreted Augustine, but he appears to have been acquainted with his works at first hand and not simply through medieval collections. In his will, he demonstrates knowledge of a minor work by Augustine, *Of Care to be Taken for the Dead*, which he uses to support his assertions on burial: see *Works* 3. 272. This tract of Augustine was written for Paulinus, bishop of Nola. It dealt with the question of whether it was spiritually advantageous for the body to be buried after death near the tomb of some great saint. Tracy's knowledge of such a minor work possibly implies extensive first-hand knowledge of Augustine.

meeting his opponents on their own ground; thus, when John Fisher bases his case for purgatory on patristic sources, Frith refutes him by using the same.

Frith uses Augustine more than any other Father, although he also quotes from Jerome, Ambrose, Chrysostom, and Athanasius. Thus, he has knowledge of both Eastern and Western sources. While the majority of these references are concerned with the Eucharist, Frith also uses patristic sources in his discussions of salvation, particularly in the area of predestination. In this latter context, his thought is tied so closely to that of Augustine that he supports every step in his argument with a quotation from his writings. He never expands upon the content of these quotations.[5]

The influence of patristic writers upon the work of Robert Barnes can scarcely be overestimated. His earliest work consists of a collection of quotations from early Christian writers in support of a series of Reformation propositions, not unlike the collections of medieval *Sentences* in form. His purpose in this is to establish the antiquity of his views and highlight the un-Catholic position of his opponents.[6] His later work, *A Supplication*, is essentially an expansion of this collection with additional comments by Barnes himself and focused against the specific claims of his opponents.

In *A Supplication* Barnes stresses that the Church Fathers are to be his major authority. This position is to some extent influenced by the nature of the accusation against him, that he teaches doctrine that 'be condemned by the church, and by holy fathers, and by all long customs and by all manner of laws'.[7] Thus, in choosing the Fathers as a major source of his argument, he is meeting his opponents on common ground. However, Barnes himself clearly regarded the Fathers as fundamentally sound in doctrine or he would not have chosen them as the starting point for debate. His Humanist training

---

[5] For a discussion of Frith's predestinarianism, see Ch. 5.

[6] C. Anderson argues that Barnes probably used collections of patristic quotations, and not the original texts, as the source for his quotations. This is plausible, although impossible to prove. However, it does not undermine the claim that patristic theology did influence Barnes: see 'The Person and Position of Dr Robert Barnes, 1495–1540: a Study in the Relationship between the English and German Reformations', unpubl. Th.D. dissertation (Union Theological Seminary, 1962), 144.

[7] *1531* xxxvii. a.

would undoubtedly have exposed him to patristic writings and, in the light of his high regard for them, it seems reasonable to assume that patristic thought exerted a profound influence upon the formulation of his theology. This will become clear when his theology is examined in detail.[8]

However, Barnes's high view of patristic authority is qualified by his assertion that the Fathers are themselves fallible and that their teaching must therefore be tested by its conformity to the teaching of Christ. The contemporary theologian is no more bound to the doctrine of the Fathers than they were to their Fathers, but he is bound to the teaching of the master, that is Christ.[9] Thus Barnes regards the Fathers as important, but scripture alone as possessing ultimate authority.

Barnes's selection from the Fathers includes quotations from Origen, Athanasius, Ambrose, Jerome, Bernard, and, above all, Augustine. While Barnes's membership of the Augustinian Order does not necessarily imply that he would have been familiar with Augustine's writings from an early stage, he may well have desired to acquaint himself with the writings of the Order's namesake.[10] The Lutheran controversies on the Continent would undoubtedly have brought the writings of Augustine to the attention of Barnes by the early 1520s. It is certain that by the time Barnes engages in writing Reformation treatises, he regards the patristic authors in such high regard that he is prepared to use them in order to establish his doctrinal position.

John Hooper had a great respect for patristic theology, although he was careful to state that his doctrine rested upon the authority of the scriptures and not on that of any man 'be he Augustine, Tertullian, or other cherubim or cherabim'.[11]

---

[8] See Ch. 6. In later Lutheran dogmatics, it became standard practice to have a preliminary section dealing with the authority of the Fathers: see R. D. Preus, *The Theology of Post-Reformation Lutheranism: A Study of Theological Prolegomena* (St Louis, 1970), 35–6.

[9] 'But what right were it to bind us more to our fathers than our fathers were bound to theirs? Why did they not all believe the first father? Yea, why did they not all believe Christ, the master of all fathers?', *1531* xxxvii. a–b.

[10] The works of Augustine were not compulsory reading for Augustinians. Indeed, Luther did not study his writings until 1509, and declared that 'before I began reading his works he meant nothing to me': see H. A. Oberman, *Luther: Man Between God and the Devil*, trans. E. Walliser-Schwarzbart (Yale, 1989), 161.

[11] *EW* 29.

Hooper refers to Augustine more than any other patristic author, and the majority of these references occur in discussions of the Eucharist. For example, Hooper quotes Augustine on the nature of the sacramental signs, and also regards the latter's arguments concerning the presence of Christ's body in heaven as refuting any notion of corporal presence in the bread and wine.[12] However, his use of Augustine is not restricted to sacramental theology, and Hooper refers to his views on matters as diverse as the worship of images, the meaning of the Latin word *Papa*, and the nature of martyrdom.[13]

Hooper is critical of Augustine, along with other patristic authors such as Basil, Ambrose, Epiphanius, Bernard, and others, for having too high a regard for the authority of tradition. He gives no specific example of their error in this matter.[14] Such criticism of Augustine is an isolated occurrence and does not obscure Hooper's immense respect for him. However, it is perhaps significant that Hooper never refers to Augustine's views on predestination. His formulation of the doctrine without reference to an eternal decree of election reveals that his views on this subject were fundamentally different from those of Augustine.[15]

Other patristic authors quoted by Hooper include Ambrose, Athanasius, Cyprian, Epiphanius, and Jerome. In the majority of cases, the references are to teaching on sacraments or idols. Hooper does not appear to have drawn directly on patristic theology in order to formulate his doctrine of salvation.

Apart from a translation from Chrysostom, John Bradford's use of the Fathers is restricted almost entirely to his discussions either of the Eucharist or of the nature of the Church. In these matters, Augustine is cited most frequently, although Jerome, Irenaeus, Chrysostom and a host of lesser figures are also used. Bradford adopts such a method in order to demonstrate that the medieval teaching on the Eucharist, in terms of both Christ's presence and his sacrifice, is a departure from the view of the early Church. Underlying this is the idea that the

---

[12] Ibid. 233, 235, 529; *LW*, pp. 427–8, 488–91, 528–9.
[13] *EW* 319; *LW* 236, 504.
[14] *EW* 28.
[15] The eternal decree was fundamental to Augustine's doctrine of predestination: see J. B. Mozley, *A Treatise on the Augustinian Doctrine of Predestination* (London, 1855), 139.

Reformers are not theological innovators but rather restorers of doctrinal purity.

The other area in which Bradford emphasizes early Church teaching is that of the creeds. At various points, Bradford points to these as the basic framework for Christian dogma. Indeed, in *A Farewell to the City of London*, he declares his faith in terms of the Apostles' Creed.[16] While he is swift to emphasize that he sees the Creed as authoritative only because it reflects the teaching of scripture, Bradford is clearly concerned to set himself within the catholic tradition of the Church. This is undoubtedly the reason why he emphasizes the creeds of the early Church as the content of faith both in his interrogation before the bishops and in a statement to which he was one of a group of signatories in 1554.[17] However, Bradford's use of the creeds should not be interpreted as an attempt to find common ground with his opponents; rather, he is once again attempting to demonstrate their deviation from the early church.

SCHOLASTIC THEOLOGY

While both Oxford and Cambridge had been subject to varying degrees of Humanist influence during the first decades of the sixteenth century, it must not be forgotten that medieval thinking still formed a substantial part of university education. College libraries were the major source of reading material for the students, and these inevitably contained a heavy concentration of scholastic texts. At Cambridge, in many ways the more progressive university, Scotus continued to be taught as part of the basic syllabus, and it was not until 1535 that the medieval foundations of the divinity faculty were removed. Even then, individual academics continued to own sets of Aquinas and Scotus and quoted from them in lectures.[18] Thus,

---

[16] *Writings* 1. 435.

[17] Ibid. 371, 524. This zeal for establishing orthodoxy through a commitment to the creeds is in marked contrast to the approach of Calvin, who refused to subscribe to the Apostles', Nicene, and Athanasian Creeds in order to establish his orthodoxy against the attacks of Pierre Caroli: see F. Wendel, *Calvin: the Origins and Development of his Religious Thought*, trans. P. Mairet (London, 1965), 53–5; R. S. Wallace, *Calvin, Geneva and the Reformation* (Edinburgh, 1988), 294–5.

[18] D. R. Leader, *A History of the University of Cambridge 1: The University to 1546* (Cambridge, 1988), 314.

each of the five Reformers would have been exposed in some degree to scholastic theology.

Tyndale's attitude towards scholastic theologians was uniformly hostile. His criticisms of them focused on three main areas: the dogma of transubstantiation;[19] the subordination of the State to the Church in the political sphere;[20] and, above all, the obscuring of plain scriptural truth through the use of Aristotelian philosophy and the fourfold method of interpretation.[21] Tyndale does show some knowledge of specific differences in doctrine among the scholastics,[22] as well as their philosophical divisions,[23] but elsewhere he groups them all together and dismisses them as excessively verbose and contradictory.

Frith makes few detailed references to scholastic theologians, although on two occasions he does refer to the views of Thomas Aquinas where he sees the latter as contradicting statements made by Rastell in defence of the Catholic doctrine of purgatory. However, this is only done in order to demonstrate that Rastell's teaching is not representative of all of the Catholic Church's theologians, and not because Frith supports Aquinas' position. Elsewhere, he shows his contempt for scholastic theologians as theological innovators by describing them as 'certain new fellows' who have made the Pope into a God,[24] and as 'draffe' [rubbish].[25]

While Frith is dismissive of scholastic theologians, he is quite willing to use their terminology in order to engage in positive debate with his opponents. The most obvious example of this is his use of the term 'formed faith'.[26] This term was used by scholastic theologians in their discussions of what constituted true, saving faith.[27] He also preferred to use the

---

[19] *Works* 3. 241.

[20] Ibid. 2. 291.

[21] Ibid. 1. 154–5, 303–31.

[22] For example he refers to the difference between Aquinas and Scotus concerning the Immaculate Conception: see *Works* 3. 31.

[23] Ibid. 1. 157, where he refers to realists and nominalists and their division over universals.

[24] *Russell*, 360–1; cf. the identical criticism of Aquinas by Tyndale, *Works* 2. 291.

[25] *Russell* 412.

[26] Ibid. 251. Frith's use of this term is discussed in Ch. 5.

[27] A. Vos, *Aquinas, Calvin, and Contemporary Protestant Thought: a Critique of Protestant Views on the Thought of Thomas Aquinas* (Washington, 1985), 29.

word 'charity' instead of 'love'.[28] The significance of Frith's use of the term is that it represents a concession to his Catholic opponents and is indicative of his desire to engage constructively with those he considered to be in error.

Unlike Tyndale and Frith, Barnes was a member of a religious order, that of the Augustinians. This fact alone might be expected to locate him fairly accurately within a particular scholastic tradition. However, a recent study has demonstrated that the Augustinian Order contained within it a broad range of theological opinion.[29] In very general terms, two broad streams of thought can be discerned within the Order, one essentially Thomist, the other Scotist, although even these two categories in no way exhaust the variety of theological opinions which existed amongst Augustinians in the early sixteenth century.[30] If the Cambridge Priory is to be placed within one of these two groups it would seem most likely to be that of the Scotists. Barnes's familiarity with the thought of Scotus is shown in his work on free will which is formulated in opposition to the Scotist position.[31] Indeed, all his explicit references to Scotus are uniformly hostile, and this hostility is further demonstrated by his action upon returning to Cambridge from Louvain. Foxe tells us that Barnes was immediately made Prior and replaced the works of Scotus and his follower, De Orbellis, with Paul's Epistles as required reading.[32] Scotus is thus important to Barnes's thought as a target for his polemics.

Hooper's attitude to scholastic theologians is almost exclusively hostile. The reason for this hostility is that he regards scholastic theology as responsible for developing the doctrine of transubstantiation and thus eclipsing true eucharistic

---

[28] Tyndale, on the other hand, never used the term *formed* with reference to faith. He also refused to use the term *charity* in his scripture translations, although on linguistic, not theological grounds: see *Works* 3. 20–2. More criticized Tyndale for his rejection of the term charity: see *The Complete Works of St. Thomas More* 8. 288.

[29] A. E. McGrath '"Augustinianism?" A Critical Assessment of the So-called "Medieval Augustinian Tradition" on Justification', *Augustiniana* 31 (1981), 247–67.

[30] e.g. Luther's mentor, Staupitz: see McGrath, '"Augustinianism?"', 266.

[31] See Ch. 6. It is interesting that Luther's theological reading before his discovery of Augustine in 1509, had also consisted to a large extent of Scotus: see Oberman, *Luther*, 161.

[32] *AM* 5. 415. Another member of the Priory in Cambridge at the time was Foxe's friend, Miles Coverdale, and so it is more than likely that Foxe is here basing his account on the testimony of an eye-witness.

theology.[33] All of his explicit references to medieval theologians occur during discussions of the Eucharist.

Hooper refers to Peter Lombard more than any other scholastic theologian. While he generally does this in order to demonstrate Lombard's errors, he does quote with approval the statement in the *Sentences* that the Eucharist is a memorial of the sacrifice of Calvary.[34] In controversy with Stephen Gardiner, he points out that communion in both kinds was allowed in the time of both Lombard and Aquinas.[35] However, this hardly amounts to approval of their theology; rather, Hooper is saying that the practices of the Catholic Church have degenerated even since the dark ages of Lombard and Aquinas.

Elsewhere, Hooper criticizes Lombard, Aquinas and others for distorting the teaching of Augustine on Christ's presence in heaven. He regards them as corrupters of pure doctrine.[36] He attacks Duns Scotus for his subtlety and for his ignorance of scripture.[37] He also criticizes scholasticism in general for introducing Aristotelian sophistry into theology.[38] While Hooper himself is not above using Aristotle and other pagan philosophers to support his own arguments, his own leanings towards Aristotelianism do not prevent him from regarding scholasticism as essentially a distortion of true Christian theology.[39]

By the time Bradford matriculated at Cambridge, the medieval foundations of the Divinity Faculty had been removed and the presence of Martin Bucer as professor symbolized the triumph of Reformation learning. Bradford would thus have found himself in an atmosphere hostile to medieval scholasticism.

However, this does not mean that we can simply preclude any influence of scholasticism upon Bradford. College libraries would undoubtedly have contained a considerable number of medieval tomes which might have been read by students. Furthermore, a knowledge of scholastic theology would have been vital if Catholic opponents were to be engaged in debate or refuted in a satisfactory manner. As Bradford spent considerable time in demonstrating the apostate nature of the

---

[33] In his *Answer to the Bishop of Winchester's Book*, Hooper lists a number of theologians, from Lanfranc to Innocent, who he considers are to be blamed for the development of transubstantiation: see *EW* 117–18.

[34] Ibid. 530.   [35] Ibid. 229.   [36] Ibid. 192–3.   [37] Ibid. 325, 518.

[38] Ibid. 325.   [39] For Hooper's use of Aristotle, see Ch. 7.

Catholic Church's theology, it is reasonable to assume that he would have spent some time in studying the various positions of his opponents.

Bradford makes few explicit references to scholastic theologians. He does mention Scotus and Biel by name, but demonstrates no first-hand acquaintance with any particular work.[40] One exception to this is Thomas Aquinas, whose views on the restoration of all things are referred to in detail by Bradford.[41] However, this occurs in *The Restoration of All Things*, which is a translation from Bucer's commentary on Romans, and cannot therefore be interpreted as demonstrating first-hand knowledge of Aquinas.[42]

Nevertheless, it would be wrong to assume from the paucity of direct references that Bradford's knowledge of medieval theology was poor. Francis Clark, a Roman Catholic scholar, cites Bradford's statements on the medieval doctrine of Eucharistic sacrifice as not only reflecting a firm grasp of the Catholic position, but also 'reproducing the actual terms in which it was expressed in contemporary Catholic theology'.[43] Thus, Bradford was not ignorant of scholastic theology and had a good understanding of his opponents' position, even if his knowledge was possibly derived through a secondary source, such as Bucer. Nevertheless, his attitude to such thought was uniformly hostile, and he makes reference to it only in order to draw a contrast with that which he regards as the truth.

LOLLARDY

Some 150 years before the voice of Luther was heard in Europe, England had produced its own scourge of the Church in the shape of John Wyclif (c.1329–84). Wyclif's writings attacked the manifest abuses in the medieval Church, particularly its usurpation of secular power and its doctrine of transubstantiation. While his own works are in the main complex philosophical treatises, he provided the inspiration for a

---

[40] *Writings* 2. 275.
[41] Ibid. 1. 358–62.
[42] Ibid. 350, 355–6.
[43] F. Clark, *Eucharistic Sacrifice and the Reformation* (Oxford, 1967) 151–2. The passages which Clark cites can be found in *Writings* 2. 270, 277, 287, 289.

movement of popular reform, and his followers translated the Vulgate Bible into English. The extent to which this movement was a unified entity with common goals and doctrines has been hotly debated. However, in general the movement was associated with violent anti-clericalism, hatred of the doctrine of the mass, and, at least in the eyes of its opponents, with political radicalism.

Scholars are divided over the extent to which Lollardy survived into the sixteenth century and provided a fertile soil for the Reformation. While our concern here is not with the popular extent of the Reformation but with the shaping of the English theological perspective, it is nevertheless important that account is taken of the possible Lollard influence upon the five Reformers.

In *The Obedience of a Christian Man*, Tyndale recalls reading as a child that Athelstan commissioned a vernacular translation of the scriptures.[44] The reference is interesting as it raises the possibility that Tyndale's mind had been considering the matter of Bible translation from his early years. This in turn might imply that he grew up subject to Lollard influences. It is certainly true that two major practical concerns of his later years, scripture translation and preaching, were also two Lollard distinctives.[45] There is also evidence that he may have translated Lollard tracts.[46] However, even if this is so, it may indicate no more than that he felt these works were of value. In other areas, similarity does not necessarily prove influence. Had Tyndale been influenced at all by Lollardy, it is surprising that he does not acknowledge this even in a symbolic sense. Instead, at one point where such acknowledgement might have been expected, he is careful to reject any notion that he was influenced in his Bible translation by any predecessors.[47] Furthermore, he makes

---

[44] 'except my memory fail me, and that I have forgotten what I read when I was a child, thou shalt find in the English chronicle, how that king Adelstone caused the holy scripture to be translated into the tongue that then was in England, and how the prelates exhorted him thereto', *Works* 1. 149. It seems Tyndale's memory did fail him to a certain extent as it was Alfred the Great, not Athelstan, who ordered a vernacular edition of the scriptures.

[45] Dickens, *The English Reformation*, 144.

[46] See the argument of D. D. Smeeton, *Lollard Themes in the Reformation Theology of William Tyndale* (Missouri, 1987), 256–5.

[47] *Works* 1. 390.

no reference to Wyclif or to the Lollards at any point in his work. Such silence makes it impossible to assert specific links between Tyndale and earlier Lollardy with any degree of certainty.[48]

The fact that Frith was born in Kent raises the possibility of close contacts with Lollards from an early point in his life. It is generally agreed that Kent was an area of much Lollard activity, and that the Reformation made rapid progress there.[49] Frith's return to England on two occasions to help those working for reform indicates that he had links with popular Protestant groups, and it is probable that these groups originated in Lollardy.

However, the influence of Lollardy upon Frith is extremely difficult to assess with any degree of certainty. Indeed, Lollardy itself was a theologically diverse phenomenon, and we have no precise details of any groups with which Frith was in contact nor any statement of his own acknowledging an intellectual debt to them. He does refer to Wyclif once in his answer to More's sacramental writings. More has accused Frith of having derived his eucharistic doctrine from 'Wickliffe, Oecolampadius, Tyndale, and Zuinglius'.[50] Frith replies that he does not believe as he does because these men taught such a doctrine but because the scripture so teaches. He then proceeds to a brief outline of Wyclif's character that reveals his admiration for him. Thus, the reference to Wyclif here does not prove that Frith had read any of the Eucharistic works of Wyclif or his followers, but does show that he had a high regard for him as a man.

There are superficial similarities in doctrine between Frith and Lollardy, especially in regard to the Eucharist. His first treatise on this subject, *A Christian Sentence* (1532), was written in response to a request from a 'Christian brother' in England who wished to know Frith's thinking on the subject. It seems

[48] Even D. D. Smeeton, a keen advocate of Tyndale as a product of Lollardy, admits that his thesis is based upon demonstrating points of similarity and not upon documented connections: see *Lollard Themes*, 251.

[49] This is the view not only of A. G. Dickens and those who follow him in arguing for the rapid growth of Protestantism in England during the Reformation, but also of those who oppose this thesis: see Dickens, *The English Reformation*, 50–1, 356–7; 'The Early Expansion of Protestantism in England 1520–58', *ARG* 78 (1987), 199–200; J. F. Davis 'Lollardy and the Reformation in England', *ARG* 73 (1982), 222; C. Haigh, review of M. Bowker, *The Henrician Reformation. The Diocese of Lincoln under John Longland 1521–1547* (Cambridge, 1981) in *English Historical Review* 98 (1983), 371.

[50] *Russell*, 342.

highly likely that this was a Lollard contact.[51] Sacramentarianism was something both Lollardy and Frith held in
common, but there are important methodological differences
between them. On the one hand, Wyclif's doctrine, like much
of his theology, was built upon sophisticated philosophical presuppositions. Popular Lollard doctrine, on the other hand, was
crudely formulated and lacked sophistication. Frith's Eucharistic
writings, however, are marked by careful exegesis and detailed
patristic study. Thus, in approach he is less philosophical than
Wyclif and more sophisticated than the typical Lollard.[52] From
this it appears that the influence of either upon Frith in terms
of theological substance rather than in terms of mere symbolic
value is highly unlikely.

There is only one specific event which links Barnes to the
Lollard movement. According to the confession of John Tyball,
a Lollard, he visited Barnes while the latter was in the cus-
tody of the London Augustinians. Tyball purchased a copy of
Tyndale's translation of the New Testament from him for 3*s*. 6*d*.[53]
This indicates that Barnes was known to the Lollards, and also
that he himself was acquainted with the work of Tyndale from
an early point in the latter's career as a Reformer. However, it
is impossible to argue that the incident tells us any more than
this. It is perhaps significant that one of the distinctives of
Lollardy was crude sacramentarianism. While Barnes's position
on the Eucharist is itself complex, it appears that he held to the
position of Luther and was opposed to the sacramentarianism
of popular Lollardy.[54] For this reason, it seems unlikely that
Lollardy influenced Barnes in specific matters of doctrine.
Besides this obvious difference on the Eucharist, Barnes's

[51] The terms 'Christian Brethren' and 'Christian Brother' were commonly used
by Lollards to refer to each other: see Dickens, *The English Reformation*, 106.

[52] Wyclif did use biblical and patristic references to support his position on the
Eucharist, but his analytical framework was primarily philosophical: see S. H. Thomson,
'The Philosophical Basis of Wyclif's Theology', *JR* 11 (1931), 86–116; A. Kenny,
Wyclif (Oxford, 1985), 80–90.

[53] The confession is recorded in J. Strype, *Ecclesiastical Memorials* (Oxford, 1822),
1. 2, pp. 54–5.

[54] The evidence for Barnes's Lutheran view of the sacrament is the implication of
the following comment of Tyndale to Frith: 'Of the presence of Christ in the
sacrament, meddle as little as you can, that there appear no division among us. Barnes
will be hot against you. The Saxons be sore on the affirmative; whether constant or
obstinate, I remit to God', *Work*, 493.

education would have given him a theological sophistication far superior to that of Lollards in general.[55]

When we come to the Edwardian Reformers, it appears that Lollard influence can be virtually discounted: Hooper makes no reference to Wyclif or Lollardy, and there is no other evidence to connect Hooper with the movement. The same is true for Bradford. He makes no references to Wyclif in Bradford's works, and only one to Lollardy where the term 'Loller' (i.e. Lollard) forms a term of abuse hurled by a Catholic at a Protestant in an imaginary dialogue.[56] There seems to be no evidence that Bradford was knowledgeable about Lollard writings or influenced by the movement in any way.

It is clear from the above that the intellectual influence of Lollardy upon the English Reformers is impossible to establish with any certainty. Those themes they held in common with the Lollards were common currency in the continental Reformation. Furthermore, the tools of critical scholarship and biblical exegesis developed by Humanists such as Erasmus would have rendered obsolete the Bible translations of the Lollards. If Lollardy was an initial influence upon the shape of English Reformation theology, this influence was rendered invisible by the overwhelming impact of more recent and more sophisticated theological developments.

HUMANISM

Both Oxford and Cambridge had been subject to Humanist influence in the early years of the sixteenth century. Dean John Colet, a friend of Erasmus, had lectured at Oxford on Paul's Epistles between 1495 and 1504 using the grammatical-historical method.[57] It seems, however, that his influence was fairly localized, as in 1517 Bishop Fox found it necessary to write to his Reader in Theology instructing him to to lecture on the

---

[55] In fact, Barnes's distribution of Tyndale's New Testament is more significant for our understanding of the relationship between English Reformers than that between Barnes and Lollardy. It shows that they were not working in isolation from each other but that there was a level of co-operation at a practical level, and also an exposure to each others views. Tyndale's warning to Frith regarding Barnes's sacramental views is clear evidence of this last assertion.

[56] *Writings* 1. 11.

[57] N. P. Feldmeth's article, 'Humanism', in *NDT* 322.

Old and New Testaments in alternate years and to interpret them in line with the early Church Fathers. Had Humanist reform really taken hold at Oxford, such instructions would scarcely have been necessary.[58]

Cambridge, on the other hand, had proved more receptive to Humanist influence. The presence of a Humanist chancellor, John Fisher, along with Erasmus himself, had served to transform the university. Erasmus had taught Greek there between the years 1511 and 1514 and was the first man ever to receive a stipend for doing so. Furthermore, his lectures on Greek and theology had been free and open to all. His influence continued after he himself had returned to the continent. For example, in 1518 one John Bryan, an old Etonian who graduated BA in 1515, lectured on Aristotle from a Humanist perspective. That he was officially approved of is indicated by his being subsequently salaried for the year 1519–20. Also in 1518, the university appointed its first professor of Greek, one Richard Croke, who graduated BA in 1517. Thus, by 1520, Cambridge can accurately be described was an important centre of Humanist reform.[59]

The impact of Humanism upon William Tyndale in the years prior to his matriculation at Wittenberg in 1524 has been variously assessed.[60] Our source for this period, John Foxe, tells us that, during his time at Oxford, Tyndale was accustomed to reading 'some parcel of divinity' to fellow students, although we do not know of what exactly this consisted. Then, some time between 1516 and 1519 Tyndale went up to Cambridge. Foxe informs us that this was as a result of his 'spying his time', perhaps a hint that Tyndale was attracted by the university's Humanist atmosphere. Foxe tells us nothing of Tyndale's own stay in Cambridge beyond the fact that he left 'further ripened in the knowledge of God's word'.[61] It is also probable that it was at Cambridge that Tyndale learned Greek.

[58] S. L. Greenslade, 'The Faculty of Theology' in *The History of the University of Oxford*, ed. J. McConica (Oxford, 1986), 313.

[59] See Leader, pp. 295–8.

[60] J. K. Yost argues that Tyndale is never anything more than a Humanist and that his thought demonstrates little substantial continuity with Reformation theology: see 'The Christian Humanism of the English Reformers: a Study in English Renaissance Humanism', Ph.D. thesis (Duke University, 1965). W. A. Clebsch, however, dismisses Tyndale's life prior to 1524 as irrelevant to an understanding of his later theology: see Clebsch, p. 139.

[61] For Foxe's account, see *AMS*, 115.

That Tyndale left university with strong Humanist sympathies is clear from his subsequent career. While in Gloucestershire, he became well known as one who would advocate the beliefs of Erasmus and Luther.[62] As Erasmus had taught at Cambridge, and Lutheran books were in circulation in the university before 1521, Tyndale could quite easily have become knowledgeable concerning the teachings of both men before removing to Gloucestershire.[63] The reference to Luther is interesting as it raises the question of whether Tyndale was already moving beyond Humanism to a more Lutheran position.

At first glance, the question seems impossible to answer with any certainty. However, when Master Walsh and his wife asked for an explanation of the Christian faith, Tyndale gave them a copy of Erasmus' *Enchiridion Militis Christiani*, which he had been translating into English. The choice of this work is highly significant. Its influence can be discerned in Tyndale's later theology in the areas of Christology, justification, and covenant.[64] However, its importance here lies in the fact that it is to Erasmus and not to Luther that Tyndale turns for a summary of the Christian faith. It is inconceivable that he would have done this had he already grasped the radical nature of Luther's Reformation theology. Therefore, the only conclusion we can draw is that his basic position at this time is that of an Erasmian Humanist and not a Lutheran. This suggests that Tyndale's defence of Luther at this time arose from him interpreting Luther along Humanist lines. Other Reformers too first interpreted Luther in the light of Humanist convictions.[65] Thus, it is not legitimate to regard Fox's reference to Tyndale's familiarity with Luther as any sign that he was thinking in truly Lutheran terms at this time.

Confirmation of Tyndale's Humanist sympathies is found in his subsequent choice of Tunstal as the potential patron for his translation of the scriptures. First, the choice of a high ranking figure in the Church establishment is a clear indication that the reformation which he envisaged at this point was one which

[62] Ibid.

[63] The first burning of Lutheran books confiscated in Cambridge took place in late 1520 or early 1521, meaning that such works were being circulated at the university before that time: see Dickens, *The English Reformation*, 103.

[64] See Ch. 4.

[65] W. P. Stephens, *The Theology of Huldrych Zwingli* (Oxford, 1986) 21–2.

could be performed within the existing ecclesiastical framework, even though his experience of the Church had been so negative. Key to such reform was a vernacular edition of the scriptures. This suggests that Tyndale's interest lay primarily in combating the practical abuses that existed within the Church and not in reforming its dogmatic foundations.

Secondly, the choice of Tunstal in particular is important. By 1516 he had earned a reputation among Humanists for his learning and proficiency in the liberal arts.[66] Tyndale was no doubt aware of this and his choice of Tunstal as a potential sponsor is a clear indication that he expected Catholic Humanism to be sympathetic to his cause.

One final indicator of Tyndale's basic Humanist sympathies at this stage is his choice of a translation of Isocrates as a demonstration of his linguistic ability.[67] At its simplest level, this reveals that Tyndale was by this time proficient in Greek, but Isocrates was also a favourite classical author among Humanists, which may have influenced his choice.[68]

John Frith was also influenced by Humanism while at university. However, we have little information with which to build up a detailed picture of its impact upon his thinking beyond the fact that he was clearly sympathetic to its cause. While at Cambridge, he studied under Stephen Gardiner, the future bishop and champion of Catholic orthodoxy. Gardiner was at that time a frequenter of the meetings at the White Horse Inn, where the works of Erasmus and Luther were discussed. That Frith readily absorbed much of this Humanist influence while at Cambridge, as indicated by his excellent Greek and by Wolsey's choice of him for Cardinal's College,

---

[66] See Ch. 1.

[67] Isocrates (436–338 BC), was an Athenian orator, educationalist and rhetorician. His written work is noted for its stylishly polished prose.

[68] L. W. Spitz, *The Religious Renaissance of the German Humanists* (Harvard, 1963), 32–3. Here, he quotes from a letter sent by Agricola to his brother Johann along with Agricola's translation of Isocrates' *Parenesis*: 'There is nothing . . . that I could more fittingly offer you . . . than the furthering of your erudition and a better moral life. . . . I will surely not be doing something unworthy, if I gather ethical precepts for you related to the proper orientation of life. . . . May it then become not only an aid to your speech but truly also improve your soul.' J. K. Yost ('Christian Humanism', p. 24 n. 1) claims that Tyndale undoubtedly chose Isocrates because his ethical emphasis and precepts were in basic accord with Christianity. This may be the case, but it is speculating beyond the evidence to assert that it was certainly so.

activity had been conducted within the priory and was therefore not subject to the jurisdiction of the bishop.[75]

It is also possible that Barnes's conversion under Bilney may
not have been as significant as it appears. Bilney (*c.*1495–1531)
was educated at Trinity Hall and ordained as priest in 1519.
He came to exert a profound influence upon a generation of
Reformers at Cambridge, with men such as Hugh Latimer
converted under his ministry. Theologically, however, he only
just qualified for the Catholics as a heretic. It seems that he
embraced justification by faith, but his theology was generally
Catholic. He rejected idolatry, invocation of saints, image
worship, and trust in man's merits, but he agreed with the
mass, the primacy of the Roman See, and the Roman doctrine
of the keys.[76] Thus, when individuals were described as converted by Bilney, A. G. Dickens is probably correct when he
says that 'this may mean little more than the fact that he first
brought home to them the full meaning of a personal religion'.[77]
Therefore, if Bilney did influence Barnes, it was probably only
in terms of the earnestness with which reforms had to be
pressed, and not in terms of their doctrinal content.

Finally, the major piece of evidence against the view that
sees Barnes as a Lutheran Reformer in 1525 is the Christmas
Eve sermon itself. There are two problems in studying the
sermon of 1525, both pointed out by Charles Anderson in his
thesis.[78] The first is that we do not have the text of the sermon
itself but the articles gathered from it by opponents as the basis
for Barnes's prosecution. The second problem is that *A
Supplication* of 1531, written six years after the sermon, is our
sole source. However, Barnes's complaints with regard to the
articles concern the interpretation put upon them by opponents,
not the substance of the articles themselves. Thus he appears
to have regarded the articles as a fair representation of his
position. Furthermore, even allowing that Barnes may have
desired to make himself look more Lutheran in 1525 than he
really was, the articles can hardly be described as doctrinally

[75] N. S. Tjernagel, *Henry VIII and the Lutherans* (St Louis, 1965), 42; J. P. Lusardi,
'The Career of Robert Barnes' 1372.

[76] *AM* 4. 649–50, where Foxe acknowledges, with some regret, that Bilney held
many traditional doctrines.

[77] *The English Reformation*, 118.

[78] Anderson, 'The Person and Position of Dr Robert Barnes' 171.

radical. Indeed, Barnes appears to have made no retrospective attempt to impose Lutheran doctrine upon them. Therefore it is reasonable to grant the articles a degree of credibility.

While the text for the sermon was Phil. 4: 4–7 and based upon Luther's *Postil*,[79] the articles themselves are concerned mainly with clerical abuses, such as indulgences and pluralities, and the abuse of ecclesiastical power by Wolsey. There are a few that touch on doctrinal issues, but these latter are not distinctively Lutheran.[80] For example, saints' days are rejected on the ground that every day is holy.[81] Most significant is the absence of the axiom of justification by faith which is enough to disprove claims that Barnes was Lutheran at this point. It seems that it was the fact that he was publicly applying his Humanist reform programme to Wolsey, and not any conversion to Lutheranism, which led to his arrest.

The evidence which we have suggests that Barnes returned from Louvain to Cambridge as a man of broadly Humanist sympathies, and that this was his basic standpoint on Christmas Eve 1525. There is no solid evidence to ascribe Lutheran doctrine to him during this period of time.

Hooper received his university education at Oxford where Humanism had made less impact than at Cambridge. Upon leaving Oxford, he joined a Cistercian monastery which clearly indicates that his beliefs at this time did not prevent him from embracing the monastic life. This implies that he probably held traditional views concerning the Church and theology. Thus, it is unlikely that Humanism made a significant impact upon him at university.

In his writings, the only Catholic Humanist to whom Hooper refers is Erasmus. His high regard for the latter's biblical scholarship is indicated in his *Visitation Book*, which contains directives on Church doctrine and practice for ministers in his diocese. Hooper gives specific instructions that an English translation of Erasmus' *Paraphrases* is to be kept in every church as well as a copy of the Bible.[82] Elsewhere in his writings, he also mentions

[79] *AM* 5. 415.
[80] See Rupp's comment that Barnes was here prosecuted 'over a series of articles no single one of which was within a thousand miles of any central issue of the Christian truth': *Protestant Tradition*, 36.
[81] *1531* xxiii. b–xxv. b.   [82] *LW* 139, 143.

Erasmus' *Adages*,[83] his rejection of images,[84] his critique of pilgrimages,[85] and his scepticism concerning the antiquity of papal claims.[86]

There are also elements of Hooper's theology which resemble that of Erasmus, such as the emphasis upon Christ as teacher and example, and respect for classical sources. However, Hooper may well have imbibed these influences not directly from Erasmus himself but from those Reformers who had themselves been adherents of Erasmian Humanism.

By the time of Bradford's matriculation, Reformation thought had displaced the older Erasmian Humanism as the dominant ideology at Cambridge. Because of the similarities in emphases between the two movements, for example in terms of textual scholarship and respect for the Fathers, it is difficult to distinguish elements in Bradford's thinking which derive directly from Humanism rather than from the Reformed approach of men such as Bucer. Bradford makes only one explicit reference to Erasmus when, in a letter written in March 1548, he apologizes to his friend Traves for not having sent him the price of a copy of Erasmus' *Paraphrases*.[87] It appears that Traves had sent him a copy of this work. Thus, early in his Christian life, Bradford was exposed to the biblical scholarship of Erasmus. However, as there is no subsequent reference to him, it is impossible to prove any closer link between the thought of the two men. It is far more likely that, if Bradford was influenced by Erasmus, this would have been through the intermediate influence of Reformers such as Bucer whose background lay in Erasmian Humanism.

While it is true that the agenda of Humanism was soon overwhelmed in Oxford and Cambridge by the more radical theology of the Reformation, it remains an important fact that three of the five Reformers in this study were initially supporters of the Humanist cause and only later emerged from this background to become advocates of Reformation theology. When we come to examine their writings in detail, it will become clear that, while contact with continental thought took them well beyond the boundaries of Catholic Humanism, its concerns left a lasting impression on the shape of their theology.

---

[83] *EW* 484.   [84] Ibid. 46.   [85] Ibid. 40–1.
[86] *LW* 237.   [87] *Writings* 2. 6.

SUMMARY

From the above survey, it is clear that the five Reformers were more than mere empty receptacles for continental theology. Each of them had a good grasp of, and high regard for, patristic theology. For them, the medieval era was a period where theology was corrupted by pagan philosophy and it was their task to return to the purer doctrine of an earlier age. They were aware, however, that even the Fathers erred, and thus patristic authors were used as guides to the truth contained in scripture and not as authorities in their own right or merely on account of their antiquity.

The positive influence of England's own proto-reform movement, initiated by the life and work of John Wyclif and carried on at a popular level by the Lollards does not appear to have had a particularly powerful intellectual influence on the English Reformers. Far more important was the development of Humanism, particularly through the influence of Erasmus at Cambridge. Tyndale, Frith, and Barnes each came to Reformation convictions through Humanism, while Hooper and Bradford were both influenced by continental Reformers who had been greatly influenced in their thinking by Erasmus and his fellow-workers. It is this Humanism which provides the immediate intellectual context in which the English Reformers interpreted and developed the theology of the continental Reformation.

3

The Intellectual Context 2

LUTHER'S LEGACY

WHILE England never produced an organized Lutheran movement of any significance, it is simply impossible to understand
the nature of English Reformation thought without reference
to the theology of Martin Luther. Indeed, as the English
Reformers moved beyond Humanism, it was to Wittenberg
that they turned for inspiration. Both Tyndale and Barnes
studied at Wittenberg University and, along with Frith, used
Luther's writings as the textual basis for significant portions of
their own literary output. All three also adopted justification
by faith as a central motif of their theology, thus underlining
their sympathy with Luther's position. There can be no doubt
that they considered themselves to be allies of Luther in the
fight against a false Christianity. Indeed, this was the view of
their most talented opponent, Thomas More, who regarded
them as nothing more than Lutheran heretics.

Until fairly recently, this view was also that of scholars of
the English Reformation. Despite the fact that Barnes was the
only one to hold a Lutheran view of the Eucharist, it was
generally accepted that Tyndale, Frith and Barnes all advocated
a view of salvation which was substantially identical to that of
Luther. However, this position has been seriously challenged
in the last forty years, and scholarly opinion concerning
Luther's relationship to English Reformation thought is now
firmly divided.

The two most important revisionist scholars are W. A. Clebsch
and L. J. Trinterud.[1] In a historical and theological study of early

---

[1] W. A. Clebsch, *England's Earliest Protestants*; L. J. Trinterud, 'A Reappraisal of
William Tyndale's Debt to Martin Luther', *CH* 31 (1962), 24–45; 'The Origins of
Puritanism', *CH* 20 (1951), 37–57. J. G. Møller also regards Tyndale's theology as

English Protestantism, Clebsch claims that Tyndale and Barnes started their reforming careers as thoroughgoing Lutherans but later undermined the notion of justification by faith alone through developing a doctrine of 'double justification', which allows works a decisive role in salvation. Only Frith remained faithful to Luther's evangelical emphasis; the theology of Tyndale and Barnes becomes so legalistic that it is fundamentally the same as that of Thomas More.

Trinterud offers an even more radical assessment of Tyndale's theological development, arguing that he was never truly a Lutheran at all. Through a careful analysis of Tyndale's use of Luther's writings, Trinterud demonstrates that he did not simply translate passages from Luther but also edited and expanded them. Trinterud claims that these revisions subvert Luther's original intention and express a strong works-orientated view of salvation. In other words, Tyndale used Luther to establish his own legalistic view of salvation. In this, Trinterud argues, Tyndale's thought foreshadows the legalism of later Puritan thought.

The older view has found some notable defenders, such as E. G. Rupp and J. E. McGoldrick, who have been eager to stress the substantial identity of Luther and the Henrician Reformers.[2] However, the revisionist interpretation, particularly in the form advocated by Clebsch, has exerted considerable influence, and Clebsch's book remains a standard text on the theology of the early English Reformers.

One undisputed fact that emerges from all the secondary literature upon this subject is the crucial importance of Luther's thought to a correct understanding of English Reformation theology. As all three of the Henrician Reformers borrowed heavily from Lutheran works, the reality of his influence upon them is beyond question. Indeed, there is no evidence to suggest that they ever regarded themselves as deviating from Luther's

contractual: see 'The Beginnings of Puritan Covenant Theology', *JEH* 14 (1963), 50–4.

[2] E. G. Rupp, 'Patterns of Salvation in the First Age of the Reformation', *ARG* 57 (1966), 52–67; J. E. McGoldrick *Luther's English Connection* (Milwaukee, 1979). Others who regard Tyndale as fundamentally Lutheran include: J. F. Mozley *William Tyndale*; A. G. Dickens, *The English Reformation*, 105–12; E. Flesseman-van Leer, 'The Controversy about Scripture and Tradition between Thomas More and William Tyndale's, *Nederlands Archief voor Kerkgeschiedenis* 43 (1959), 143–65; 'The Controversy about Ecclesiology between Thomas More and William Tyndale', Nederlands Archief voor Kerkgeschiedenis 44 (1960), 65–86; W. D. J. Cargill Thompson, 'The Two Regiments: the continental setting of William Tyndale's political thought', in *Reform and Reformation: England and the Continent c.1500–c.1750*, ed. D. Baker (Oxford, 1979), 17–33.

position in arguing for justification by faith against the perceived justification by works of the Roman Church. What is at issue, then, is not the fact of Luther's influence, but the nature of that influence. When we ask the question, 'What view of salvation did the Henrician Reformers hold?', we are effectively asking how they interpreted Luther. Did they faithfully reproduce his thought in terms of emphasis and substance? Or, do their works reveal different emphases, even a totally different theology, to that of their German mentor? In studying their writings, Luther's theology must form one of the major criteria for evaluating their thought.

Of course, in outlining the immediate intellectual background of the English Reformation, we cannot confine ourselves to Luther alone. While his thought was the single most important theological influence on English Protestantism during the reign of Henry VIII, it was not the only source of theology. From the start, English Reformation thought was an eclectic phenomenon, drawing life from the teachings of a number of continental Reformers. This is hardly surprising when one considers that significant works of Reformation theology only start being written by Englishmen in the mid-1520s: by this time, the Reformation had already developed two distinct intellectual wings, Lutheran and Reformed. English theologians, not being territorially committed to either, were free to draw inspiration from wherever they found it. Later, with the accession of Edward VI, Luther really ceased to be a significant intellectual force in England. Then, it was the turn of the moderate Melanchthon and of Reformed theology to become the most significant sources of theological reflection. Thus, any consideration of the intellectual background of the English Reformers must not simply use Luther as the sole criterion for understanding how their theology took shape; it must also give due consideration to the fact that continental Reformation theology contained within it a variety of doctrinal positions and emphases. Only when this is done can we gain a correct understanding of English Reformation thought.

LUTHER AND THE RIGHTEOUSNESS OF GOD[3]

For Luther, the doctrine of justification is the article by

---

[3] Because this study is not an examination of Luther's theology for its own sake,

which the Church stands or falls, the acid test of what is truly Christian. His distinctive development of the doctrine is inextricably linked with the troubles of his own soul and his desperate search for a gracious God. The medieval system within which he was nurtured taught that justification involved a process of being made righteous and that the believer only had to do his best and God would save him.[4] The problem of how to decide whether one had done one's best was, of course, lethal for assurance: the subjectivity of the process left conscientious individuals in constant fear that they had not quite done as much as they could and were thus liable to be damned.

According to Luther's own account, his problems focused on the text of Rom. 1: 17, which declares that the righteousness of God is revealed in the gospel. The understanding of righteousness which Luther's teachers in the *via moderna* had taught him was the classic Ciceronian definition: righteousness was giving to each person what he deserved. Such a definition became problematic when applied to God. After all, how could such justice be gospel, that is, good news: for someone as conscious of his sin as Luther, being rewarded with what he deserved could only lead to despair. If God's righteousness was truly good news, it could not be understood in the way accepted by the *via moderna*.

The insight came when Luther realized that the righteousness of God was not some objective standard by which God assessed the individual's worthiness of entering heaven, but that by which God made the sinner righteous and saved him. Writing many years later, Luther himself describes his insight thus:

only those areas of relevance to Parts Two and Three will be dealt with. Furthermore, while the chronology of Luther's theological development is an area of much scholarly debate, by the time the English Reformers engaged with his thought (i.e. the mid-1520s onwards), his Reformation theology had already reached maturity. It is thus not my intention to deal in any detail with this matter, only to present a summary of the salient doctrinal points. An excellent introduction to Luther's thought, which includes surveys of recent scholarship and Luther's significance for modern dogmatics, along with a bibliography of works in English is B. Lohse, *Martin Luther: An Introduction to His Life and Work*, trans. R. C. Schultz (Edinburgh, 1987).

[4] The classic summary of this position is 'facientibus quod in se est, Deus non denegat gratiam', which translates as 'To those who do what is in them [i.e. who do their best], God will not deny grace.' This is the position of theologians of the *via moderna*, such as Gabriel Biel: see H. A. Oberman, *The Harvest of Medieval Theology: Gabriel Biel and Late Medieval Nominalism* (Grand Rapids, 1967). Further articles on the connection between Luther and late medieval theology can be found in Oberman's *The Dawn of the Reformation* (Edinburgh, 1986).

I hated this word 'the justice of God' which by the use and usage of the doctors I was taught to understand philosophically in terms of the so-called formal or active justice with which God is just and punishes sinners and the unrighteous. For, however irreproachably I lived as a monk, I felt myself before God to be a sinner with a most unquiet conscience, nor could I be confident that I had pleased him with my satisfaction. . . . At last, God being merciful . . . I noticed the context of the words, namely, 'The justice of God is revealed in it; as it is written, the just shall live by faith.' Then and there, I began to understand the justice of God as that by which the righteous man lives by the gift of God, namely, by faith, and this sentence 'The justice of God is revealed in the gospel' to be that passive justice with which the merciful; God justifies us by faith as it is written: 'The just lives by faith.'[5]

In making this 'breakthrough', Luther was in fact doing   no more than returning to the classic Catholic concept of God's righteousness that had been held by theologians such as Augustine and Aquinas. They too held that God's righteousness was that by which he justified the ungodly. However, Luther went well beyond Catholic tradition in the way in which he developed this idea in the context of his doctrine of justification.

Implicit in this understanding of God's righteousness is that it is God, not man, who takes the initiative in individual salvation.[6] Thus it is not surprising to find that Luther's theology of salvation has no need, and indeed no place, for the idea that man in any way earns or merits justification by his own unaided efforts. This, of course, is a standard Augustinian position. Where Luther departs from Catholic tradition is in his teaching on the revelation of God's righteousness and in his view of the relationship between this righteousness and the believer.

Luther's Theology of the Cross

In dealing with the knowledge of God, medieval theology had been faced with the problematic relationship between man's reason and God's revelation: to what extent could man gain

---

[5] I am using the translation in M. Luther, *Lectures on Romans*, trans. W. Pauck (London, 1961), pp. xxxvi–xxxvii. The original text is found in *WA* 54. 179–87.

[6] It is true that, according to Biel's system, God takes the initiative in salvation by setting up the *pactum*, with its requirement that man 'does what is in him'. However, by doing this God only makes salvation *possible*: it is the human response to the arrangement which is decisive for individual salvation. Thus, Biel's doctrine is inherently semi-Pelagian.

true knowledge of God without the aid of revelation. Two basic models were developed. The first model, exemplified by the theological method of Thomas Aquinas, adopted the Aristotelian notion that effects must resemble their causes. This allowed the creature to infer certain things about God simply from the fact that both creator and creature shared in existence and were related as cause to effect. This knowledge was limited in scope and negative in substance, i.e. it told man what God was not. It was, nevertheless, true knowledge of God. Revelation was necessary in order to supply positive knowledge of God, but the two sources complemented rather than contradicted each other.

The second model, which was developed by William of Occam and the *via moderna*, emphasized the freedom of God to act in any way he wished, subject to the law of non-contradiction. As a result, man could no longer have reliable knowledge of God based simply on the analogy between his being and that of the creator as this relationship was determined solely by God's will, not by Aristotelian notions of cause and effect. As a result, man needed to look first at God's revelation in order to see how God had decided to act.

Both of these models take as their starting point the relationship between creator and creature considered purely in terms of being. Aquinas sees this relationship as positive, allowing for knowledge of God based on rational reflection on the nature of existence; Occam sees it as negative, stressing that the difference between the existence enjoyed by God and that of his creatures is so great that rational reflection alone cannot be a basis for any reliable knowledge of God.

Luther, while nurtured in the tradition of Occam, adopts neither of these models. For him, knowledge of God is not simply a matter of being, in and of itself; it is a moral problem. Man is a fallen sinner. As such, his mind is clouded by sin and cannot build an accurate picture of God on its own. Thus, like Occam, Luther regards true knowledge of God as unattainable to reason without revelation; unlike Occam, however, he regards this impossibility as caused not just by man's finite creatureliness, but by his finite, *sinful* creatureliness. Thus, when God comes to reveal himself, he does it in a manner which contradicts all of man's rationally based, sinful expectations. This dramatic event takes place upon the cross at Calvary.

For Luther, the righteousness of God is revealed solely in the cross of Christ. This idea culminates in his famous 'theology of the cross' which formed a central part of the Heidelberg Disputation in 1518, with its radical contrast between the theologian of glory who approaches God through his own preconceptions and thus builds God in the image of sinful man; and the theologian of the cross who approaches God through his revelation of himself on the cross at Calvary. In the cross, God is revealed to man but in a manner which contradicts human expectations: for example, the glory of God is revealed through the humiliation of the Incarnate God, Christ; the strength of God in conquering sin is revealed through the apparent triumph of evil in effecting the death of Christ; the mercy of God towards sinners is revealed in his wrath poured out on Christ. Thus, on the cross, God paradoxically reveals himself in his hiddenness. In making the cross the methodological starting point for theological reflection, Luther develops a theology which teems with such exciting paradoxes. The theologian of glory builds a picture of God as powerful and glorious; while the theologian of the cross approaches God through his revelation on the cross, where he is seen as weak and humiliated. Here, God is revealed through his hiddenness, a revelation invisible to reason but visible to faith.

Luther and Justification

Luther's theology of the cross is more than just an abstract principle. Indeed, it is intimately related to the Christian's experience of justification and salvation. Throughout the Christian's life, God deals with him in a manner which contradicts sense and expectation. For example, in order to bring the believer to spiritual life, God must first kill him. He accomplishes this through the law: the law commands that man earn salvation by his works and obedience, but man can never achieve the level of perfection demanded. Thus, man is brought to despair of his own attempts to reach God through works. It is only at this point that the gospel offers him mercy through Christ and not through works of his own. There is no need for man to work for this salvation: all he needs to do is believe the gospel. Luther expresses this dichotomy between the law and the gospel in the most graphic terms in his *Lectures on Galatians*:

How great and horrible is this presumption of righteousness [the self-righteousness of the unbeliever]. To break and destroy it, God needs a huge, strong hammer, i.e. the law, which is the hammer of death, the thunder of hell, and the lightning of divine anger. Why? To fight the presumption of righteousness, which is a rebellious, tenacious, stiff-necked beast. So, when the law accuses and terrifies the conscience, saying 'You ought to have done this and this! You have not! Therefore you are condemned to the wrath of God and eternal damnation!, then that is the proper use and purpose of the law. Then the heart is crushed to the point of despair. Consciences which feel this use and function of the law are terrified and desperate: they long for death, or even wish to kill themselves because of the anguish of their conscience.[7]

However, in terrifying the conscience in this way, God is only preparing the ground for salvation. The law, in accusing the individual of sin and in revealing his imminent damnation, points him away from himself to the gospel of Christ:

When the law urges you, despairing of your own works, to seek help and solace in Christ, then that is indeed its proper use: thus, through the gospel, it serves justification. This is the best and most perfect use of the law.[8]

So, in using the law to bring the individual to the point of despair, God has in mind the ultimate purpose of drawing him to the gospel and thus to salvation. As on the cross, God achieves his proper work through his alien work.

Having been terrified by the law and having consequently fled to Christ and believed the gospel, the believer is justified. However, it is important to understand precisely what this justification involves. Faith in the gospel is not meritorious in and of itself: it is only effective in justification because of its relationship to Christ. Through faith, the believer is united to Christ, and it is this union which is the basis of justification. Luther describes this in the following terms:

It must be noted here that these three things, faith, Christ, and acceptance or imputation, are linked. Faith grasps Christ and holds him present, as a ring encloses a gem. Whoever is found with such faith, having grasped Christ within their heart, him will God declare righteous. This is the means and basis by which we obtain remission of sins and righteousness. 'Because you believe in me' says God 'and

---

[7] For Latin, see *WA* 40. 482. 22–483, 11.   [8] Ibid. 490. 22–24.

by faith have grasped Christ whom I have given to you to be your Justifier and Saviour, therefore you are righteous.' Thus, God accepts or accounts righteous only on account of Christ in whom you believe.[9]

It is clear from this passage that it is not faith which is the cause of justification: faith is the instrument through which the believer grasps Christ, and it is on account of Christ, grasped by faith, that God declares the believer to be righteous.

In *The Freedom of a Christian Man*, Luther describes this union by comparing Christ and the believer to a bride and groom:

Faith joins the soul with Christ as a bride is joined to her bridegroom. . . . Thus the soul which believes can boast of and glory in whatever Christ possesses as though it were its own. . . . and whatever the soul possesses, Christ claims as his own. . . . Christ is full of grace, life, salvation. The soul is full of sins, death, damnation. Let faith come between them and Christ will have the sins death and damnation, while the soul will have grace, life, and salvation.[10]

Thus, faith does not save in and of itself but because of the union it effects between the believer and Christ, a union which leads to the 'joyful exchange' of sins for righteousness. It is on account of this exchange that God is able to account the believer as righteous and thus to save him. This is the heart of Luther's doctrine of justification by faith.

There are a number of important aspects to note concerning Luther's doctrine. The first is that the faith which justifies is not simply an intellectual assent to dogma but a rich concept which has a strong personal reference: faith is not, for example, believing that Christ died and rose again; rather, it is believing that Christ died and rose again *for me*. Thus, faith involves the believer's personal relationship to the truth. As such, it is not simply belief in God as he has revealed himself but *trust* in God as he has revealed himself. Furthermore, Luther does not allow a distinction between faith as adherence to dogma and faith as a personal relationship: faith and its object go hand in hand and are not to be set over against each other. To have faith in Christ is also to believe his teaching.[11]

The second point of importance concerns the fact that the righteousness of the believer is an extrinsic, imputed

[9] *WA* 40, 233. 16–24.
[10] For Latin text of whole passage, see Ibid. 7. 54. 31–55, 36.
[11] E. G. Rupp, *The Righteousness of God* (London, 1953), 169.

righteousness. This separates Luther's doctrine from the medieval teaching which, stemming from Augustine, regarded Christ's righteousness as imparted, not imputed, to the believer. This imparted righteousness made the believer actually righteous, and it was this actual righteousness which was the formal cause of justification.[12] This is not to deny that there is a proleptic dimension to Luther's doctrine, whereby the believer is accounted righteous now through faith on the basis that he will be righteous in the after-life, but the stress in Luther is always on the extrinsic righteousness of Christ as opposed to the eschatological righteousness of the believer.[13]

The third point about Luther's doctrine of justification is that it leads to his so-called 'whole man anthropology'. Luther regards everyone, believer and unbeliever, as both fully righteous and completely sinful. He expresses this idea in the famous phrase 'simul iustus et peccator'— 'at the same time righteous and a sinner'. On the one hand, the unbeliever, who seeks to justify himself by works, regards himself as righteous, as do his fellow men. Before God, however, his righteousness is but filthy rags. Thus, while he is outwardly righteous before men, he is inwardly unrighteous, a sinner, before God. On the other hand, the believer, knowing he is sinful, does not strive to be justified by works but simply believes in Christ. Before the world, therefore, he is outwardly a sinner. He also knows himself that he is sinful and unrighteous. Before God, however, he is clothed with the righteousness of Christ and is regarded on this basis as fully righteous. This anthropology serves to underline that justification is, above all, an external event, primarily a change of status rather than being, a matter of imputation rather than impartation.

Luther and Good Works

While the overwhelming concern of Luther's theology is to emphasize that justification is by faith alone through imputation,

---

[12] For a discussion of the medieval development of justification, see A. E. McGrath, *Iustitia Dei: A history of the Christian doctrine of Justification 1: The Beginnings to the Reformation* (Cambridge, 1986).

[13] The German scholar, Karl Holl, emphasized the proleptic dimension of justification, but his views have been shown to be an overstatement of the case by, among others, P. Althaus and E. G. Rupp: see P. Althaus, *The Theology of Martin Luther*, trans. R. C. Schultz (Philadelphia, 1966) 241–2; Rupp, *The Righteousness of God*, 30–1.

and not by works, this should not be understood as implying that Luther sees no role for good works within the believer's life. By excluding works from justification, he is not excluding them from salvation as a whole.

For Luther, it is fundamental that good works do not precede justification but follow after as a consequence. One of his favourite images in this regard is that of the tree and the fruit, as in the following passage from his *Lectures on Galatians*:

So, we conclude with Paul that we are justified by faith alone in Christ, without the law and works. However, after a man has been justified by faith and now possesses Christ by faith and knows that he [Christ] is his righteousness and his life, he will certainly not be idle but, like a good tree, he will produce good fruits. You see, the believer has the Holy Spirit and where he is, he does not allow a man to be idle but drives him to all the exercises of devotion, to the love of God, to patience in times of trial, to prayer, to thanksgiving, and to showing love to all men.[14]

Thus, when a man is justified, he possesses the Spirit, and this Spirit drives him to do good works. Like a good tree producing good fruit, the works flow as a natural consequence of the believer's justification.[15] However, if he were not justified, his works would be evil in the same way that the fruit of a sick tree would inevitably be bad.

The motive and goal of these works is twofold: love to God and love to neighbour. Because man realizes that God loves him enough to save him, he loves God in return; and, because he realizes his own status as a wretched sinner saved only by grace, he loves his neighbour in order to show him the love of God in Christ. It is this love towards his neighbour which leads the Christian to manifest his justification before God in works before men

As I have said, therefore, in this passage [Gal. 5:6] Paul is dealing with the whole Christian life: inwardly it is faith before God; outwardly it is love and works toward one's neighbour. Thus a man is a Christian in an absolute sense, inwardly through faith before God,

---

[14] For Latin, see *WA* 40. 265. 29–36.

[15] 'fides habet ipsum facientem et facit arborem, qua facta fiunt fructus. Oportet enim prius esse arborem, deinde fructus. Poma enim non faciunt arborem, sed arbor poma facit. Sic fides primum personam facit quae postea facit opera', *WA* 40. 402. 14–17.

who does not need our works, and outwardly before men who gain benefit, not from our faith, but from our love and works.[16]

The thoughts contained in this passage are extremely important for a correct understanding of Luther's teaching on faith and works because they utterly undermine any notion that he is solely concerned with righteousness of faith before God and not with the righteousness of love and works before men. This point is underlined elsewhere in his *Lectures on Galatians* where he refers to the twin dangers of overemphasizing either faith or works to the detriment of the other:

It is difficult and dangerous to teach that we are justified by faith without works, and at the same time to require works. Here, unless the ministers of Christ are faithful and careful 'stewards of the mysteries of God' who correctly divide the word of truth, they will immediately confuse faith and works. Each topic, both faith and works, must be carefully taught and emphasised but in such a way that each remains within its proper boundaries. Otherwise, if works alone are taught, as happens in the papacy, faith is lost, and, if faith alone is taught, carnal men will immediately start dreaming that works are not necessary.[17]

From this, it is clear that Luther regards teaching on both faith and works as absolutely necessary. While he acknowledges that it is difficult to argue for justification by faith and, at the same time, to emphasize that works are vital, he is not prepared to allow an unscriptural resolution of the problem which stresses one to the expense of the other. Faith and works are two aspects of the one Christian life.

However, it is worth noting at this point that, in Luther's theology, works are definitely subordinated to faith. First, faith has both logical and chronological priority over works. As we have seen, faith is the cause of works, not vice versa. Secondly, it is faith which grasps Christ and clothes the believer in perfect righteousness before God. This is the righteousness which saves, not the weak, imperfect variety of the believer's works. Thirdly, the 'whole man' anthropology, with its emphasis on the believer remaining, in himself, always sinful, serves to underline the continuing centrality of the righteousness of

---

[16] For Latin, see *WA* 40². 37. 26–30.
[17] For Latin, see *WA* 40². 78. 17–23.

faith. Thus, while works are necessary in Luther's soteriology, they are not the primary concern: that is indisputably the righteousness of faith *coram Deo*, before God.

There is one last area of importance for a correct understanding of Luther's teaching on good works: the function of the law. Later Lutheran and Reformed thinking allowed the law a positive function as moral guide for the Christian life. This raises the question of how far this 'third use' of the law is present in the thinking of Luther.[18]

The attractions of such an application of the law are obvious: it is one thing to emphasize, as Luther does, that the law is fulfilled in the two commandments 'Love the Lord your God' and 'Love your neighbour as yourself'; but, human nature being corrupted by sin, it would be easy to misinterpret this principle in accordance with sinful ideas of behaviour. The need, then, is for some objective guide to the application of this twofold love in terms of the service of God and of neighbour. This need is met by pointing to the decalogue as normative for Christian behaviour.

If Luther does teach a third use of the law, it is in a very mild and very inconsistent manner. While he does speak of the decalogue as no longer having relevance to the believer in terms of his justification, he can also describe it as the highest expression of natural law, that is, of love to God and to neighbour.[19] However, such positive affirmations of the decalogue's value also highlight what is to be the fundamental principle of its interpretation and application: love. It is only to be used in a way which is fully consistent with love to God and to neighbour.[20] It is because the decalogue agrees with this universal natural law that it retains validity as an ethical code for Christians, and not because it was given by Moses to the Israelites.[21] For Luther,

[18] For a helpful discussion of the third use of the law in both Lutheran and Reformed theology, see 'Usus Legis' in R. A. Muller, *Dictionary of Latin and Greek Theological Terms* (Grand Rapids, 1985), 320.

[19] *WA* 16. 380–90.

[20] P. Althaus, *The Ethics of Martin Luther*, trans. R. C. Schultz (Philadelphia, 1972). While basically agreeing with Althaus, D. F. Wright points out the ambivalence of Luther's position: see 'The Ethical Use of the Old Testament in Luther and Calvin: a Comparison', *SJT* 36 (1983), 470–1.

[21] For a discussion of the relationship between the decalogue and natural law, see H. Bornkamm, *Luther and the Old Testament*, trans. E. W. and R. C. Gritsch (Philadelphia, 1969) 124–35.

Moses' continuing authority is thus 'accidental'.[22] Legalism, in the sense of being rigidly bound to the letter of the decalogue, is an alien concept to Luther's way of thinking. Justification is by faith alone; works naturally flow from such justification; but these are to be subject to the criterion of love, not Moses.

Luther on Predestination

Having discussed Luther's doctrine of justification in terms of its content and its relationship to good works, it is now necessary to look at his doctrine of predestination. The doctrine does not, in itself, hold a particular fascination for him. He deals in detail with the subject on only two occasions, in the *Lectures on Romans* (1515–16), and in *The Bondage of the Will* (1525). On neither occasion is he motivated by love of theological speculation for its own sake. In the former, he discusses predestination in the context of the exposition of Rom. 9; in the latter, predestination forms a central plank of his polemic against Erasmus' view of free will. It is his development of the doctrine in this latter context which is of great importance to a correct understanding of the relationship between his thought and that of English Reformers, particularly that of Robert Barnes.

Luther's exposition of predestination in the *Lectures on Romans*, is marked by caution. The basic components of his argument (original sin, God's will, and the unknowability of election) are all elements common in Western theology from Augustine onwards. Aquinas' discussion in the *Summa Theologiae* is far more detailed and far less hesitant. However, in *The Bondage of the Will*, written ten years later in the heat of Reformation controversy, Luther expresses his doctrine in far less cautious terms and introduces elements which take him well beyond Augustine's predestinarianism.

The most significant aspect of the formulation of predestination in *The Bondage of the Will* is the role played by the immutability of God. Luther argues that God is sovereign and that whatever he foreknows, he also wills. Because God is changeless, so is his will. Therefore, everything happens ultimately as a result of God willing it to happen.[23] Clearly, such a

---

[22] See Bornkamm, p. 125.
[23] 'Ex quo sequitur irrefragabiliter, omnia quae facimus, omnia quae fiunt, (et) si nobis videntur mutabiliter (et) contingenter fieri, revera tamen, fiunt necessario (et)

bold declaration points towards a doctrine of absolute determinism which allows man no freedom of will whatsoever. Unlike the position of Augustine, which regarded the Fall as the cause of man's loss of free will, *The Bondage of the Will* portrays man as in bondage because of his status as creature: he is subject to the sovereign will of God, the creator, and thus all his actions are caused by divine predestination, not the motion of his own will. The bondage of the will is part of creaturely ontology.[24]

Luther does try to soften the implications of the axiom of God's immutability by introducing a distinction between earthly matters, 'things below', and spiritual matters, 'things above', echoing his doctrine of the two kingdoms. Man has free will concerning the former, but none concerning the latter. However, the distinction is highly problematic, and it is difficult to see how Luther can maintain this position without radically altering his view of the relationship between God's immutability, foreknowledge, and will. As he does not do this, he remains open to the charge of inconsistency.[25]

Luther's use of God's immutability as an axiom has a number of radical implications for his theology. First, it effectively precludes him from giving a satisfactory account for the origin of evil. He merely assumes sin and the Fall as realities and does

immutabiliter, si Dei voluntatem spectes. Voluntas enim Dei efficax est, quae impediri non potest, cum sit naturalis ipsa potentia Dei, Deinde sapiens, ut falli non possit, Non autem impedita voluntate, opus ipsum impediri non potest, quin fiat loco, tempore, modo, mensura, quibus ipse (et) praevidet (et) vult', M. Luther, *Studienausgabe* 3 (Berlin, 1983), 191.

[24] It is hardly surprising that Luther himself dislikes the very term 'free will' and would rather that it was abolished: see *Studienausgabe* 3. 210.

[25] H. J. McSorley argues that Luther refused to draw the necessitarian conclusion logically demanded by his axiom and remained within the Catholic tradition. However, he proceeds to criticize Luther for failing to affirm free will, using absolute expressions regarding God's will, failing to distinguish carefully between different kinds of freedom, over-reacting to semi-Pelagianism, and failing to account for the origin of evil. In the light of these criticisms, McSorley's position seems to verge on self-contradiction. Furthermore, it is also arguable that Luther's statement of the necessitarian argument is, in its very essence, a statement of absolute determinism: see H. J. McSorley, *Luther: Right or Wrong? An Ecumenical–Theological Study of Luther's Major Work, 'The Bondage of the Will'* (Minneapolis, 1969), 313–29. In a carefully argued essay, L. Urban argues that Luther was a determinist and deals convincingly with the arguments of McSorley: see 'Was Luther a Thoroughgoing Determinist?', *JTS*, NS, 22 (1971), 113–39. Surprisingly, some scholars seem unaware of the problem, which makes their own treatments of *The Bondage of the Will* somewhat deficient, e.g. R. D. Shofner, 'Luther on "The Bondage of the Will": an Analytical-Critical Essay', *SJT* 26 (1973), 24–39, esp. 28.

not attempt to explain their existence in any way.[26] This is hardly surprising as his presuppositions demand that God is the one who is ultimately responsible for evil. No doubt it was Luther's desire to avoid imputing sin to God that led him to avoid this area despite the fact that it is directly relevant to the whole question of man's moral will.

In terms of sins committed after the Fall, Luther is on surer ground. He argues that God moves people to act in a way which is consistent with their own nature. They have to do what they do because God has willed it; but he only makes them act in a way which accords with their basic orientation. Thus, he moves people by necessity but not by compulsion.[27] That sin is the result is thus not the fault of God but of the evil in human nature. Luther illustrates this idea by comparing God to a good workman using a bad tool or a skilled horseman riding a lame horse: no matter what the skill of the workman or rider, the result is still disastrous.[28]

Secondly, Luther's argument demands a doctrine of double predestination. Augustine had regarded God as choosing for himself a certain number of individuals for salvation out of a fallen mankind. The rest were left to perish, not because God had predestined them to hell, but because he had not chosen them out of the mass of sinners. Augustine's argument rested on the idea that the Fall was the result of man's free will and not God's predestination. Thus, while salvation was the result of God's election, damnation was the result of man's sin and God's non-election. For Luther, every man is subject to the absolute predestination implied by God's immutability simply because of the nature of the Creator–creature relationship: as a result, the ultimate destiny of each man, whether heaven or hell, is also determined on the basis of this relationship. Because the Fall is itself predestined, Luther cannot opt for Augustine's view of predestination: reprobation must be regarded as the result of a positive act of God's will. Thus, Luther's formulation of the doctrine of predestination takes him well beyond the position of Augustine.

[26] See Althaus, *The Theology of Martin Luther*, 158; McSorley, p. 342; P. S. Watson, 'The Lutheran Riposte' in *Luther and Erasmus: Free Will and Salvation*, ed. E. G. Rupp *et al.* (London, 1969), 16.

[27] For the distinction between necessity and compulsion, see *Studienausgabe* 3. 207.

[28] See *Studienausgabe* 3. 277–8.

Thirdly, Luther's vigorous predestinarianism leads him to adopt an important theological distinction in order to overcome the exegetical problems raised by the conflict between biblical passages implying God's universal love and the fact that not all are given faith and thus saved: the distinction between God's hidden will and his revealed will.[29] The key passage occurs when Luther is responding to Erasmus's claim that the idea of God deploring the death of a sinner is ridiculous if God himself is directly responsible for willing that death. Luther replies as follows:

When the *Diatribe* argues 'Does the holy God deplore the death of his people which he himself works in them? This seems too absurd', then we reply, as I have already said, that we must discuss God, or the will of God, preached to us, revealed, offered and worshipped, not God as he is not preached, not revealed, not offered, not worshipped. Wherever God hides himself and does not wish to be known by us, there we have no business. . . . God as he is in his majesty and in his own nature is to be left alone. In this context, we have nothing to do with him, nor does he wish us to have dealings with him. We deal with him as he is clothed and displayed in his word by which he offers himself to us. . . . God does many things which he does not show us in his word, and he wills many things which he does not show us in his word that he wills. Thus, he does not will the death of a sinner according to his word, but he does will it according to his hidden will.[30]

These sentences must rank amongst the most important ever written by Luther. They contain the fundamental Lutheran stress on the need for the believer to approach God through his revelation and yet to be aware that God is much greater than this revelation. The believer is to restrict his meditations on God to that which God has chosen to reveal and not to probe into those aspects which God has chosen to keep secret.

However, is Luther himself not contradicting his own stated method in this very passage? By allowing that there exists a

---

[29] The distinction is not original and was used by Augustine: 'Ad occulta ergo Dei judicia revocate, quando videtis in una causa, quam certe habent omnes parvuli . . . huic subveniri ut baptizetur, illi non subveniri ut in ipsa obligatione moriatur; illum baptizetur in hac vita relinqui, quem praescivit Deus impium futurum, istum vero baptizatum rapi ex hac vita, ne malitia mutet intellectum ejus (*Sap.* iv. 11): et nolite in istis dare injustitiam vel insipientiam Deo, apud quem justitiae fons est et sapientiae.' *De Gratia Et Libero Arbitrio, PL* 44. 910.

[30] For Latin, see *Studienausgabe*, 3. 253–4.

hidden will which can, apparently at least, contradict God's revelation, it is arguable that he is both speculating beyond, and actually undermining the reliability of, that same revelation. Nevertheless, it is difficult to see how else he can deal with those exegetical difficulties which are always going to beset those operating within an Augustinian soteriological framework.[31] What is beyond dispute is that this distinction underlines Luther's framework of double-predestination: God reveals himself as not wanting the death of a sinner; but, according to his hidden will, he has predestined some for heaven and others for hell.

One last point of relevance is the relationship some scholars have perceived between references to God's hiddenness in *The Bondage of the Will* and Luther's theology of the cross. While allowing that there is significant theological development between the Heidelberg Disputation and the composition of *The Bondage of the Will*, these scholars see faith as the element which resolves the two notions of hiddenness.[32] However, even after allowing for legitimate development over time, the case for a positive connection between the two remains somewhat tenuous and fails to take into account the fundamental opposition between God's hiddenness on the cross and his hiddenness in predestination: on the cross, God's hiddenness and revelation are one and the same event seen in turn through the eyes of unbelief and faith. In predestination, God's hiddenness *is his hiddenness* and not connected in any direct way to his revelation. Election is only revealed in the fact that some have faith in Christ, reprobation only in the fact that some do not. Beyond that, they are utterly hidden. Thus, it would seem that any

[31] Luther does attempt to ease his difficulties by arguing that the contradiction between revelation and hiddenness is only apparent and not real, caused by mankind's finite minds. This scarcely solves the problem: if revelation is noetically unreliable, even if not ontically so, how can man have a trustworthy knowledge of God? This is just the objection raised by Karl Barth and G. C. Berkouwer to the classic Lutheran and Calvinist formulations of election. While one may not agree with their resolutions of the problem, it is hard not to acknowledge the importance and force of their criticism: see Barth, *CD* 2. 2, 188–94; Berkouwer, *Divine Election*, trans. H. Bekker (Grand Rapids, 1960), 102–31; see also Berkouwer's perceptive criticism of Barth, *The Triumph of Grace in the Theology of Karl Barth*, trans. H. R. Boer (Grand Rapids, 1956), esp. ch. 10, 'The Universality of the Triumph'.

[32] See B. A. Gerrish, '"To the Unknown God": Luther and Calvin on the Hiddenness of God', *JR* 53 (1973), 263–92; W. von Loewenich, *Luther's Theology of the Cross*, trans. H. J. A. Bouman (Belfast, 1976).

attempt to connect the two has to be based on the misconception that identity of terminology must imply degree of identity in terms of dogmatic content.

Philip Melanchthon

While Luther's theology, with its burning passion and earthy language, provided the major emotional backcloth to Lutheran theology, it was Philip Melanchthon, the gentle Humanist scholar, who set about organizing the thought of his friend into a coherent whole. Indeed, his *Loci Communes* were the first significant attempts at theological systematization made by a Reformation thinker. However, Melanchthon was more than a mere organizer of Luther's theology: his work contains a number of modifications of his mentor's thought, modifications which are highly significant for an understanding of the English Reformation.

One such development is that of the doctrine of forensic justification. Luther regarded justification as through the righteousness of Christ, a righteousness which is extrinsic to the individual and which is imputed to him through faith. Melanchthon's position is very similar, particularly in its emphasis upon the extrinsic nature of the believer's righteousness. However, unlike Luther, he sets this within a legal framework whereby the believer is declared righteous on account of Christ in a manner analogous to a judicial pardon.

Justification signifies remission of sins and reconciliation or acceptance of the person to eternal life. For the Hebrews 'to justify' is a legal term. . . . So Paul has taken the meaning of justification from the Hebraic usage to mean remission of sins and reconciliation or acceptance.[33]

The difference with Luther is arguably slight, but this is still none the less a key development in the understanding of the nature of justification, marking a shift away from Luther's dynamic emphasis upon union with Christ, as expressed in the marriage metaphor.

A second significant development introduced into the Lutheran tradition by Melanchthon concerns the use of the law. As a Humanist, he had a characteristically greater concern

[33] For the Latin, see *OM* 21. 742.

for good works than Luther.[34] In the first edition of the *Loci* in 1521, he is careful to stress that justification is causally related to sanctification and has an eschatological dimension: its beginning is not its end.[35] This concern is not weakened in later editions where he adopts the idea of forensic justification. Indeed, this is reflected by his increasingly positive approach to the law, to which he ultimately ascribes three functions: the good government of society; the condemnation of sin and self-righteousness; and the basis for Christian conduct.[36] The first two uses reflect Luther's own view of the law's functions, but the third is a new development in the Lutheran tradition. Here, the law acts as a normative principle for good works for those individuals who believe in Christ. As such, it is not the basis for a self-justifying works-righteousness but a guide for an obedient life subsequent to justification on account of Christ. While this idea is possibly implicit in Luther's thinking, he keeps interpretation and application of the decalogue strictly subordinate to love for God and one's neighbour and certainly never makes it into the formal principle which it is for Melanchthon. Indeed, such a positive view of the law contrasts sharply with Luther's radical dialectic of law and gospel and his overwhelming antipathy to anything which smacks of works-righteousness.

Perhaps the most significant difference between Luther and Melanchthon lies in their different understandings of the role of man's will in salvation. Luther rejected the idea that the will played an ultimately decisive role in this context. Salvation is all of God, and man is merely the passive recipient of God's gift. Such was the position of the young Melanchthon: in the

[34] For a thorough discussion of good works in Melanchthon, see C. E. Maxcey, *Bona Opera: a Study in the Development of the Doctrine in Philip Melanchthon* (Chicago, 1980).

[35] 'Qua vero opere iustificationem consequuntur, ea tametsi a spiritu dei occupavit corda iustificatorum proficiscuntur, tamen quia fiunt in carne adhuc impura sunt et ipsa immunda. Coepta enim iustificatio est non consummata. Primitias spiritus accepimus, nondum decimas', *OM* 21. 78.

[36] 'Quae sunt igitur legis officia in hac corrupta natura? Supra recensui tria. Primum est civile, videlicet, ut coherceat omnes homines disciplina quadam. . . . Secundum officium ac proprium legis divinae et praecipuum est, ostendere peccata, accusare, perterrefacere et damnare conscientias. . . . tertium officium legis in his, qui sunt fide iusti, est, ut et doceat eos de bonis operibus quaenam opera Deo placeant, et praecipiat certa opera, in quibus obedientiam erga Deum exerceant. Etsi enim liberi sumus a lege, quod ad iustificationem attinet, tamen, quod ad obedientiam attinet, manet Lex', *OM* 21. 405–6.

early editions of the *Loci*, he was careful to exclude man's will as a cause of individual salvation. For example, in the first edition of the *Loci*, he followed Luther in rejecting free will on the basis of God's predestination.[37] However, by 1543 he had changed his mind, arguing that the application of salvation needed the compliance of man's will as God gives the Spirit to those who seek him.[38] This teaching marks a clear departure from the teaching of Luther in *The Bondage of the Will*, with its overarching emphasis on the absolute sovereignty of God. It also leads Melanchthon to an inevitable softening of the doctrine of predestination whereby election is based on God's mercy but reprobation rests on man's sin. He does not allow that there is any predestinating decree behind either God's mercy in Christ or man's sin. This, coupled with his synergism, brings Melanchthon much closer to Erasmus than to Luther.[39] That Melanchthon did not suffer the same treatment from Luther as Erasmus had done says more about their friendship than about their theological convictions. When one remembers that Luther regarded the bondage of man's will as of more doctrinal importance than the papacy or purgatory, it is arguable that Melanchthon's later view of salvation effectively undermines, if it does not indeed overthrow, Luther's theology.

[37] 'Quandoquidem omnia quae eveniunt, necessario iuxta divinam praedestinationem eveniunt, nua est voluntatis nostrae libertas', *OM* 21. 93.

[38] 'Cum in conversione exoriendum sit a verbo Dei, certe id audiendum est, et cum verbo Dei efficax est Spiritus sanctus, erigens et adiuvans corda, cum fide nos sustentamur. Nec otiosi indulgeamus diffidentiae aut allis vitiis contra conscientiam, nec conturbemus Spiritum sanctum, sed assentiamur verbo Dei et obsequamur Spiritui sancto. In hac lucta sentiemus voluntatem, repugnantem diffidentiae et aliis vitiis non esse otiosam. Hoc ipsum monet Paulus inquiens 2 Cor. 6 [:11], Adhortamur, ne frustra gratiam Dei accipiatis. Vult audiri Evangelium, vult nos assentiri et obsequi, non indulgere contra conscientiam impietati. Praeterea Luc. 11 [:13] dicitur: Dabit Spiritum sanctum petentibus. Non inquit aspernantibus, conturbantibus et repugnantibus. Vult igitur luctari nos cum infirmitate nostra; Vult agnoscere peccata et quaerere liberationem, non retinere ea contra conscientiam, non igitur est otiosa voluntas', *OM* 21. 761.

[39] 'Caussam igitur reprobationis certum est hanc esse, videlicet peccatum in hominibus. . . . Nam verissima est sententia, Deum non caussam peccati nec velle peccatu. . . . Econtra vero recte dicitur, caussam electionis esse misericordiam in voluntate Dei, qui non vult perire totum genus humanum, sed propter Filium colligit et servat Ecclesiam. . . . Nam ideo electi sumus, quia efficimur membra Christi', *OM* 21. 127. Although Melanchthon is here referring to our knowledge of election as based upon prior incorporation into Christ, his synergism and his consequent failure to base election upon an objective decree suggest that election is also ontically based upon incorporation into Christ by faith.

THE REFORMED HERITAGE

As well as the Lutheran theology emerging from Wittenberg, the English Reformers were also exposed to the other major branch of Reformation thought: Reformed theology. Unlike Lutheranism, Reformed theology in the sixteenth century was not dominated by the thought of a single theologian. Thus, in attempting to give a brief outline of those aspects of Reformed thought which are of most relevance to an understanding of the English Reformation, one cannot simply focus on the impact of one particular character. Indeed, it is difficult to give a precise and comprehensive definition of such a broad movement and so, for the purposes of this study, Reformed thought can probably be most helpfully characterized in terms of its differences with Lutheranism.

The most substantial difference between the two movements was that of Eucharistic doctrine: while the Lutherans held that Christ was present in the Eucharist according to his humanity, the Reformed argued that his presence there was only spiritual, that is, according to his divinity. This disagreement led to the rift between Lutheran and Reformed theology which was symbolized, and indeed formalized, by the failure of Luther and Zwingli to reach agreement on the Eucharist at the Colloquy of Marburg in 1529.

In addition to this issue, there were a number of other areas where differences were apparent. For example, the Reformed generally placed greater emphasis on the sovereignty of God and less upon justification by faith alone. They had perhaps a greater sense of the role of the community in Christian faith than was characteristic of the rather individualistic approach of Luther. Also, they had a characteristically greater concern for good works than Luther, as evidenced in their less radical separation of law and gospel and their adoption of the idea of the third use of the law.

These observations are all generalizations. However, in the case of the English Reformers, we can isolate two particular areas in which Reformed thought was of particular importance: sacramental theology; and a greater emphasis on salvation as regeneration than was typical of the Lutheran tradition.

Sacraments as Covenant Signs

The Reformed understanding of the sacraments cannot really be understood apart from the notion of covenant, a concept which was to play an increasingly important role in Reformed theology, especially in the later sixteenth and seventeenth century. However, even in the early days of the Reformation, the idea performed a significant function within theological structures, offering a convenient aid to the understanding of salvation.

Broadly speaking, early notions of covenant can be divided into those which are unilateral and those which are bilateral.[40] The unilateral covenant idea stresses that God in his grace has unilaterally committed himself to giving man salvation as a gift. Thus, the emphasis is upon salvation as a gift. The bilateral scheme stresses that God and man are bound together in a salvific covenant which places certain obligations upon each party. Thus, the emphasis is upon mutuality. Despite the obvious difference, these two understandings of covenant should not necessarily be understood as mutually exclusive: some theologians, notably Calvin, combined both the unilateral and bilateral understandings in a single theology.[41]

Reformed thinkers developed their doctrine of salvation on the basis that both Old and New Testaments represented a substantial unity around the God's one covenant which both articulated God's promise of salvation to man and defined the relationship between God and man. Thus, one clear sign of Reformed influence on, for example, William Tyndale, is his increasing use of the idea of covenant as a soteriological motif.

This partiality for the idea of covenant also co-ordinated well with the Reformed understanding of sacraments. On the basis of the covenant unity of both Old and New Testaments, the Reformers were able to argue that sacraments fulfilled identical functions under both dispensations. Thus, they drew

[40] This helpful distinction is made by R. W. A. Letham in his Ph.D. diss. 'Saving Faith and Assurance in Reformed Theology from Zwingli to the Synod of Dordt'. However, Letham does regard the two groups as mutually exclusive, a position not borne out by close theological analysis: see J. R. Beeke, *Assurance of Faith*, 44–5. For the development of covenant in the early sixteenth century, see K. Hagen, 'From Testament to Covenant in the Early Sixteenth Century', *SCJ* 3 (1972), 1–24.

[41] See A. Hoekema, 'The Covenant of Grace in Calvin's Teaching', *Calvin Theological Journal* 2 (1967), 133–61; also R. A. Muller's similar observations on Bullinger and later covenant thought, *Christ and the Decree*, 41.

a close link between the roles of circumcision and the Passover in the Old Testament and those of baptism and Eucharist in the New. Both operated as signs of God's one promise of salvation in Christ; the difference was that the former looked forward, and the latter back, to Christ.

On this basis, the Reformers were able to argue for the validity of infant baptism: it was not performed in order to cleanse from original sin, as the Western Augustinian tradition (including Luther) argued, but because God's promise of salvation also embraced children within the covenant: the promise was to Abraham and his seed; as Abraham's male children had been circumcised, so Christian children should be baptized. This was the position advocated by Zwingli in opposition to the anabaptists.[42] Furthermore, in the matter of the Eucharist, the Reformed rejected the physical presence of Christ's humanity, emphasizing instead the symbolic function of the elements in pointing the believer to the spiritual reality rather than physically providing him with it.[43] It is faith in Christ, in the promise of salvation in him, which is the decisive factor. On this basis, Zwingli interpreted the eating in John 6 as referring to faith, not the physical eating involved in the Eucharist.[44]

Sacramental theology is not central to this study. However, it does provide the clearest evidence that Reformed theology, and not just Lutheranism, made a significant impact on English thought at a very early stage in the Reformation. In fact, four of the five English Reformers rejected the Lutheran view of the sacraments, preferring instead interpretations which reflect a Reformed understanding. As this is true even of the earliest Reformers, Tyndale and Frith, we know for certain that Lutheran theology never had a monopoly of influence in England. This, of course, immediately raises a question of great relevance to this study: the extent to which Reformed theology influenced their doctrines of salvation.

Salvation

For Luther, justification by faith in Christ was the *central dogma* of his doctrine of salvation. Reformed theologians, however,

---

[42] See Z VI. i. 48. 13–15. For the relationship between covenant and baptism in Zwingli, see Stephens, *The Theology of Huldrych Zwingli*, 206–11.
[43] Ibid. 188.   [44] Ibid. 235.

tended to place a less exclusive emphasis on the imputation of an extrinsic righteousness and to emphasize instead the actual change which salvation wrought within the believer's life.

There are a number of reasons for this shift in emphasis. Unlike Luther, all the other major Reformers were deeply influenced by Erasmian Humanism, and it is arguable that this background gave them a much greater concern for the practical outworking of the Christian life. Whereas Luther's torments of soul had led him to focus on the individual's status *coram Deo*, before God, other Reformers balanced this with a stress on how the believer was to appear before men. That positive exposure to Erasmian Humanism did lead to such an emphasis is nowhere more clearly demonstrated than in the thought of Melanchthon: despite being a leading Lutheran, his development of the third use of the law, amongst other things, demonstrate a significant shift away from the emphasis of Luther.

Theologically, this differing emphasis can be seen in the fact that the Reformers' had a greater concern for the subjective renewal wrought by the Holy Spirit in salvation than was characteristic of Luther.[45] For example, Zwingli's doctrine of salvation emphasizes renewal and regeneration rather than alien justification.[46] Oecolampadius too, steeped in Erasmianism, stressed the practical, moral aspects of the Christian faith.[47] This emphasis is most clearly expressed in the writings of Martin Bucer, one of the major early Reformed theologians, who combined a doctrine of justification by imputed righteousness with a parallel emphasis upon outward righteousness before the world.

Bucer uses the term 'justification' in a loose manner, referring to both the believer's justification before God by imputed righteousness and justification before men by imparted righteousness.[48] The two types of justification are inextricably linked, bound together by a rigorous doctrine of predestination: if God predestines someone for salvation, he is also predestining him for conformation with God's will and will thus predestine

---

[45] For a survey of this subject, see A. E. McGrath, 'Humanist Elements in the Early Reformed Doctrine of Justification', *ARG* 73 (1982), 5–20.

[46] See Stephens, *The Theology of Huldrych Zwingli*, 155–69.

[47] See E. G. Rupp, *Patterns of Reformation* (London, 1969), 45.

[48] The best discussion of Bucer on justification is that of W. P. Stephens, *The Holy Spirit in the Theology of Martin Bucer*, 49–100.

the means to this end.[49] This sanctification process is also 'justification' according to Bucer's terminology, and thus corresponds to what would later be referred to as 'sanctification'.[50]

Bucer's position, incorporating the imputation doctrine of Luther and the impartation doctrine of Zwingli, represents typically Bucerian mediation between theological poles. However, he must not be misunderstood as teaching justification by works in a Catholic sense. Primary justification is by imputation; but predestination ensures that this will be evidenced in the performance of good works. Thus, Bucer is able to set the Lutheran doctrine within a framework which underlines the need for good works: if someone is not performing good works, one can infer that they are thus not justified before God.

This different emphasis in the formulation of salvation is important for an understanding of the English Reformation. As we have seen, all five of the Reformers were educated at the hands of either Humanists or Reformers who were steeped in Humanism. It is therefore perhaps to be expected that their approach to the doctrine of salvation will have been shaped by this background.

SUMMARY

The English Reformers had two distinctive Reformation traditions upon which they could draw in the development of their theology: the Lutheran; and the Reformed. The former, dominated by the figure of Luther himself, stressed that justification by faith, with its various implications for the understanding of the cross, law and gospel, and predestination, lay at the very heart of the Church's proclamation. This emphasis led Luther to focus on the imputation of righteousness rather than upon the need of the believer to perform good works. He understood good works as the inevitable result of justification, but his major concern was always the righteousness of faith, not deeds. This was expressed most clearly in his understanding of the radical opposition of law and gospel.

[49] See Stephens, *The Holy Spirit in the Theology of Martin Bucer*, 98–100; McGrath, 'Humanist Elements', 13.

[50] In this context, see McGrath's rather strange criticism of Stephens: 'Humanist Elements', p. 13 n. 39.

Luther's colleague, Melanchthon, exhibited a greater concern for good works than his mentor, and also recoiled from some of the more difficult areas of Luther's doctrine. In the writings of Melanchthon, Lutheranism was modified: justification was explicitly understood as a forensic concept; the law was understood as having a third, positive use; and double predestination was abandoned in favour of a synergistic understanding of salvation.

The Reformed tradition distinguished itself from Lutheranism primarily in terms of its Eucharistic doctrine, where the elements were primarily understood in symbolic terms and were closely linked to the understanding of the Bible in terms of a single covenant.

In addition to the sacraments, the Reformed tradition can also be distinguished from the position of Luther in terms of its greater emphasis on actual righteousness as a vital part of the Christian life. This view was best expressed in the early Reformation by Martin Bucer who did not reject the Lutheran understanding of justification, but balanced the emphasis on imputation with a secondary emphasis upon impartation and undergirded the whole scheme with a rigorous doctrine of predestination.

Such then, was the immediate theological background of the English Reformation. In the detailed examination of texts which follows, it will become clear that the English Reformers drew positively on both traditions, Lutheran and Reformed, in their efforts to develop truly biblical theologies.

PART TWO

The Reformers under Henry VIII

4

William Tyndale

TYNDALE'S matriculation at Wittenberg in 1524 signalled his decisive break with the Catholic Church. For the remaining twelve years of his life, he devoted himself to his principal task of translating the Bible. However, he also produced a steady stream of theological tracts dealing with various aspects of the Christian faith, and it is in these that his doctrine of salvation receives its fullest expression. His two earliest works were written as aids to understanding the scriptures. *The Cologne Fragment* (1525), is all that survives of Tyndale's first attempt to translate the New Testament into English. It consists of a prologue, based on Luther's 1522 New Testament preface, a list of the New Testament books, and the first twenty-one chapters of Matthew's Gospel with marginal notes. Of these, it is the prologue which gives most insight into Tyndale's theological standpoint, and this contains a consistent emphasis on the New Testament as teaching that man is saved by faith in the gospel. This same theme is taken up in his next work, *The Prologue to Romans* (1526). This work is an explanation of Romans and is once again heavily dependent upon Luther, being in part a translation of the latter's *Introduction to Romans* (1522).[2] Again, man's salvation is the dominant theme.

The year 1528 saw the publication Tyndale's two most important theological treatises, *The Parable of the Wicked Mammon*, and *The Obedience of a Christian Man*.[3] Both works were written

---

[1] I have adopted the tripartite division of Tyndale's career used by W. A. Clebsch. This provides a useful framework for studying his writings and facilitates interaction with Clebsch's work. However, the division is artificial and should not be overemphasized.

[2] See Clebsch, p. 145.

[3] The publisher was John Hoochstraten of Antwerp: see Mozley, *William Tyndale*, p. 123.

to refute Catholic objections to justification by faith alone. *The Mammon*, probably based upon a Lutheran original,[4] is an exposition of the parable of the corrupt steward (Luke 16) and is aimed at disproving Catholic claims that justification by faith undermines the need for good works. *The Obedience* rebuts the charge that the doctrine leads to anarchy, and asserts the need for everyone to submit to those in authority in all matters which do not involve disobedience to the word of God.

What is clear from each of these writings is that man's salvation was by this time occupying a central place in Tyndale's thinking. His theology of salvation falls into two parts: the objective aspect, dealing with the need of man, election, and the redemptive work of Christ; and the subjective aspect, dealing with conversion, justification, and the problem of the believer's assurance. A close examination of Tyndale's writings reveals that both aspects are intimately related.

The Objective Basis of Salvation

The emphases in Tyndale's soteriology depend to a large extent upon his doctrine of fallen man. This doctrine is expressed in *The Fragment* (1525) in the following terms:

The Fall of Adam hath made us heirs of the vengeance and wrath of god, and heirs of eternal damnation. And hath brought us into captivity and bondage under the devil. And the devil is our lord and our ruler, our head, our governor, our prince, yea and our god. And our will is locked and snet faster unto the will of the devil than could an hundred thousand chains bind a man unto a post.[5]

In this passage, Tyndale clearly interprets the Fall as having a twofold effect upon man: it brings him under the wrath of God; and it brings his moral will into bondage to Satan. However, Tyndale consistently emphasizes the latter, while tending to ignore the former. The idea that man is morally guilty before God and that this guilt needs to be removed does not play a significant role in his theology. Instead, he focuses attention upon man's moral will. For example, in *The Prologue* (1526), Tyndale refers to the Fall only in that it renders man incapable of fulfilling the law.[6] Then, in *The Mammon* (1528), Tyndale makes several references to the fallenness of man, but this is

---

[4] Trinterud, 'A Reappraisal', 31.   [5] *NT* 25. 9.   [6] *Works* 1. 500.

always related to discussions of man's consequent inability to fulfil the law. He does not mention the idea of God being angry with man because of his moral guilt.[7]

Tyndale's approach to the Fall is thus centred on man, not God, and emphasizes its actual existential results in the consequent bondage of man's moral will. Therefore, for Tyndale, the basic problem in the salvation of man is not his objective guilt before God, but his bondage to sin and to Satan. This emphasis is reflected time and again throughout Tyndale's doctrine of salvation.

This moral bondage binds man's will to sin and thus prevents him from initiating his own salvation. This implies that the initiative for saving an individual must lie within the will of God, and thus raises the whole question of Tyndale's attitude to the doctrines of election and predestination.[8]

It is important to note that Tyndale rarely speaks in terms of an order of salvation. His interest lies more in the existential effects of salvation than in its objective foundations. He does make occasional references to election, which he defines as the act of God in eternity by which a certain portion of mankind were chosen for salvation in Christ.[9] However, he only mentions the doctrine in one of two contexts: when he needs to underline that salvation is by grace, which he defines as the free favour of God;[10] or when he asserts that man's will is bound, preventing the individual from initiating his own salvation.[11] Tyndale demonstrates both of these functions in his comment upon Rom. 9, 10, and 11 in *The Prologue*:

In the ninth, tenth, and eleventh chapters he treateth of God's predestination; whence it springeth altogether; whether we shall believe or not believe; be loosed from sin, or not be loosed. By which predestination our justifying and salvation are clean taken out of our hands, and put in the hands of God; which thing is most necessary of all. For we are so weak and so uncertain, that if it stood in us, there would of a truth be no man saved; the devil no doubt would deceive us.[12]

---

[7] Ibid. 47, 76, 81, 83, 86, 89, 111. Cf. *The Obedience* (1528), *Works* 1. 183; also *NT* 25. 2. The last passage is translated from Luther: see *WA (DB)* 6. 4. 3–11.

[8] Previous scholars have characterized Tyndale's theology as strongly predestinarian: see Trinterud, 'The Origins of Puritanism', 40; D. D. Wallace, *Puritans and Predestination: Grace in English Protestant Theology, 1525–1695* (North Carolina, 1982), 11–12.

[9] *Works* 1. 65. [10] Ibid. 65, 77; *NT* 25. 7.

[11] *Works* 1. 80, 89. [12] Ibid. 504–5.

Here, Tyndale regards predestination as necessary for salvation because the doctrine of man's inability demands it. He does not introduce the doctrine because of theological considerations, such as the sovereignty or immutability of God, but makes it a consequence of his doctrines of grace and anthropology. Therefore predestination does not function as a theological axiom but is rather a derivative of previously established doctrines which it in turn supports.

Tyndale's treatment of election as the logical consequence of other doctrines is reflected in the caution with which he handles the subject. He never indulges in speculation and stresses that God's choice of one and not another is hidden and not to be enquired into. However, he does not develop a doctrine of reprobation to parallel that of election.[13] Nor does Tyndale speculate concerning the extent of election: he uses the word 'elect' only to refer to a category of people, not a quantity. When he does discuss election, he always links it with the actual application of salvation to the believer by the Holy Spirit in time.[14] In this way, he draws attention away from election as an abstract decree of God, and emphasizes the effects of election within time.

However, while he introduces election as a consequence of other doctrinal considerations, Tyndale still draws upon the

[13] 'Now may not we ask why God chooseth one and not another; either think that God is unjust to damn us afore we do any actual deed. . . . God will be feared, and not have his secret judgments known', Wallace (p. 12) sees Tyndale as here implying the doctrine of reprobation. However, Tyndale's statement is ambiguous. It could mean that God damns individuals through non-election rather than through positively selecting them for damnation. The difference is subtle, but important. Perhaps if Tyndale does hold to double predestination, one might expect him to develop further the idea of God possessing both a hidden and a revealed will in order to deal with exegetical problems raised by the doctrine, as do Luther and Barnes. In fact, Tyndale places a single-minded emphasis upon the revealed will of God and can even assert that God is only that which he has revealed himself to be: see *Works* 1. 160. Møller, who correctly regards Tyndale as paying little attention to predestination, argues that this is indicated by the fact that he treats the subject only in those works most dependent upon Luther: see 'The Beginnings of Puritan Covenant Theology', 52. However, Tyndale does not develop the doctrine along Lutheran lines. Luther and Barnes both emphasized God's hidden will in order to provide a basis for the doctrine of double predestination: for Luther, see Ch. 3; for Barnes, see Ch. 6.

[14] The link between election and the work of the Holy Spirit is so close in Tyndale's thought that at times he appears to equate the two: '[God's] Spirit breatheth where he listeth, and maketh the ground of whose heart he lusteth fruitful, and chooseth whom he will at his own pleasure, and for no other cause known unto any man', *Exposition of the First Epistle of John* (1531) in *Works* 2. 181.

biblical teaching in order to provide the concept with its content. For example, he stresses that election is from eternity. This idea is not necessarily demanded by his position but is part of the biblical teaching on the subject. While not pointing to any specific verse in this context, Tyndale expresses the idea in terms very similar to those contained in Eph. 1. In these same passages, he also emphasizes that election is 'in Christ', another example of doctrinal content which is biblical, not logical in origin.[15] Thus, the biblical teaching does influence his formulation of the doctrine.

This reference to 'in Christ' leads us to Tyndale's assertion that redemption is objectively accomplished by Christ and that salvation thus has a Christocentric base. This is clear from his assertion that the man who seeks heaven by his own works is devaluing the blood of Christ.[16] His doctrine of Christ as Redeemer reflects the emphases of his anthropology. He bases its necessity not so much on man's guilt before God as on the need to free man from his bondage to sin. In *The Fragment* (1525), he translates a passage from Luther which emphasizes that Christ overcame the Devil and freed man from bondage to sin.[17] Christ's work is thus the basis for the restoration of

[15] 'In Christ' is taken by Tyndale to mean 'on account of Christ', thus drawing a close link between his doctrines of election and justification. P. A. Laughlin sees election as forming part of an *ordo salutis* in Tyndale's theology, and uses this as a framework within which his soteriology is analysed: 'The Brightness of Moses's Face: Law and Gospel, Covenant, and Hermeneutics in the Theology of William Tyndale', unpubl. Ph.D. dissertation (Emory University, 1975), 69–89. This approach is problematic. While it is true that Tyndale does refer to an *ordo salutis*, this is only when summarizing salvation in order to emphasize that it originates in God's grace: see *Works* 1. 89. Apart from this, he never uses the *ordo* as a framework to develop his own doctrine. Thus, the adoption of this *ordo* as an analytical framework tends to over-systematize Tyndale's thought. Smeeton refers to election as the logical point to start any discussion of Tyndale's soteriology (*Lollard Themes*, 124). While it may be the logical place to start, it is certainly not that chosen by Tyndale and implies that his thought was structured in a far more systematic manner than was actually the case. Such an approach can lead to distortions of emphasis. Furthermore, the logical structure of the *ordo* rather than Tyndale's own statements can become the determining factor in interpretation. For example, Laughlin places great emphasis upon the relationship between election, justification and ultimate salvation, leading him to argue that Tyndale does not believe a truly justified man can fall from grace ('Moses's Face', 78). In fact, while Tyndale does argue for an unbreakable link between election and final salvation, he does allow that a justified man can finally fall away. See *The Prologue to Galatians*, 1534 in *Works* 1. 513.

[16] *Works* 1. 65.

[17] *NT* 25. 2–3. Cf. *WA (DB)* 6. 2. 23–4. 11.

man's moral abilities, as shown in the following passage of *The Mammon* (1528):

Health is power or strength to fulfil the law, or keep the commandments. Now he that longeth for that health . . . is blessed in Christ, and hath a promise that his lust shall be fulfilled, and that he shall be made whole.[18]

However, while Christ's work provides the basis for this restoration, Tyndale does not elaborate on how this is done. Because he fails to emphasize the guilt of man before God, he consequently places little emphasis upon the God-ward aspects of Christ's work. As a result, his theology of atonement is extremely vague. Indeed, the notion of appeasing God's wrath is mentioned only once in *The Fragment*, and then only in passing.[19] Reference is made to Christ's blood making satisfaction for sin, but this is not explicitly related to God's anger.[20] More often Tyndale speaks of Christ's merits in general as putting away sin and earning salvation.[21] In this way, the cross does not play the central role in Tyndale's theology that it does in that of Luther. Also, Tyndale tends to refer not to faith in Christ, but to faith in the promises, placing emphasis upon God's mercy without setting this within a Christological context. This heightens the subjective emphasis of his doctrine of salvation by failing to stress its objective accomplishment.

Overall, Tyndale's references to Christ as Redeemer show that he regards salvation as having been objectively accomplished by Christ but they do not provide detail as to how he believes this has been done. More importantly, his lack of emphasis upon the God-ward aspects of this redemption and his stress upon the healing effects derived from Christ's work reflect the concerns expressed in his anthropology: salvation is concerned more with man's moral inability than with his guilt before God.

---

[18] *Works* 1. 79.
[19] *NT* 25. 10. D. B. Knox notes that Tyndale does not develop any clear doctrine of atonement, but does not attempt to explain this or link it to the emphases in Tyndale's doctrine of fallen man: see *The Doctrine of Faith in the Reign of Henry VIII* (London, 1961), 5–6.
[20] *NT* 25. 5; *Works* 1. 48, 66.
[21] *NT* 25. 4, 10; *Works* 1. 52, 72.

The Subjective Appropriation of Salvation

Tyndale provides a summary of his understanding of the Christian's conversion in *The Fragment* (1525):

When Christ is this wise preached, and the promises rehearsed . . . then the hearts of them which are elect and chosen begin to wax soft and to melt at the bounteous mercy of God and the kindness showed of Christ. For when the evangelion is preached, the spirit of God entereth into them which God hath ordained and appointed unto eternal life, and openeth their inward eyes, and worketh belief in them. When the woeful consciences taste how sweet a thing the bitter death of Christ is, how merciful and loving God is through Christ's purchasing and merits, they begin to love again and to consent to the law of God, how that it is good, and ought to be so, and that God is righteous which made it.[22]

All the major strands of Tyndale's theology of conversion are here. At times, he does refer to the convicting power of the law in terms as strong as those used by Luther,[23] but his general emphasis in conversion is on man's realization of the love of God, not his conviction of sin.[24] This love of God is expressed in the promises of God's mercy, which are received in faith, here referred to as the 'belief'. When these promises are believed, they bring peace, as opposed to the law of God, which brings death and damnation.[25] The promises refer to the work of Christ, the benefits of which are appropriated by the believer through faith in them.[26]

In this emphasis on faith and the contrast between law and gospel, we can clearly discern the impact of Lutheran thought upon Tyndale. However, Tyndale develops his thought in a way which reveals significant differences in emphasis from that of Luther. Tyndale is careful to make a close connection between faith and the activity of the Holy Spirit. Indeed, at times he speaks of faith itself bringing the Spirit.[27] Elsewhere, however, he is careful to stress that faith is a work of God's Spirit within

[22] *NT 25*. 10–11.
[23] Ibid. 4.
[24] Ibid. 7; *Works* 1. 65. Conviction of sin is still a presupposition of conversion (see the reference to 'woeful consciences' above), but Tyndale never emphasizes it as central.
[25] Ibid. 46–8, 65.
[26] Ibid. 52.
[27] Ibid. 31, 65. Cf. Robert Barnes, Chapter Six.

the believer and not an act of man's free will.[28] Fallen man
cannot exert faith of his own strength.[29]

According to Tyndale, the presence of the Spirit within the
believer has a fourfold effect: first, he frees man from bondage
to the Devil. This is significant as it once again underlines the
fact that Tyndale's understanding of salvation relates primarily
to man's moral being, not to his guilt before God. Secondly,
he assures man of the love of God towards him. Thirdly, he
makes man return this love. Finally, he causes man to demonstrate this love in the performance of good works. These works
are performed not in order to merit salvation, but because man
has already been freely given salvation. Works are thus the
result of the ontological change effected by the Spirit, as
demonstrated by Tyndale's continual use of the biblical analogy
(of which Luther was so fond) of the tree and its fruit: good
works are the natural fruit of a good nature.[30] They are also
the spontaneous response of man to the love of God.[31]

This analysis of the Spirit's work possesses both logical and
theological strength. Logically, Tyndale makes works the inevitable result of faith: true faith always results in the reciprocation
of love which is demonstrated by good works.[32] Theologically,
all the elements in this process are undergirded by the activity
of the Spirit. This helps emphasize that both faith and its fruits
are the work of God, not man.[33]

---

[28] *NT 25.* 89.   [29] Ibid. 47.   [30] Ibid. 56, 113.

[31] 'And when the gospel is preached unto us, we believe the mercy of God; and in
believing we receive the Spirit of God, which is the earnest of eternal life, and we are
in eternal life already, and feel already in our hearts the sweetness thereof, and are
overcome with the kindness of God and Christ; and therefore love the will of God, and
of love are ready to work freely; and not to obtain that which is given us freely, and
whereof we are heirs of eternal life', ibid. 65.

[32] Tyndale (ibid. 53, 121) is careful to distinguish assent to the objective truth of the
gospel from true saving faith. In his *Answer to More* (1531), he calls the former 'story
faith' (*Works* 3. 197). Such faith lies within the power of natural man and does not lead to
good works. True faith, on the other hand, is supernatural in origin, involves personal
trust in the promises and manifests itself in good works. Cf. ibid. 1. 280; 2. 146; 3. 197. In
his reply to Tyndale, More accused him of deriving the distinction between story-faith
and true faith from Melanchthon, who employs it in the 1521 edition of the *Loci*: see
The Complete Works of St. Thomas More, 8. 741; *OM* 21. 162. J. A. R. Dick sees Luther as
supplying the substance of the idea, with Melanchthon merely supplying the terminology: see 'A Critical Edition of William Tyndale's *The Parable of the Wicked
Mammon*', unpubl. Ph.D. dissertation (Yale University, 1974), pp. xliv–xlv.

[33] It has been argued that Tyndale's pneumatology is his most original contribution to Reformation theology. See D. D. Smeeton, 'The Pneumatology of William

While the Spirit realises these works in the believer, Tyndale points the believer to Christ as their pattern. He speaks of the believer following in the steps of Christ, an idea which is present in the *Enchiridion* of Erasmus.[34] This is a sign of Humanist influence upon Tyndale. Elsewhere, he argues that the believer is to be to his neighbour what God in Christ is to him: merciful.[35] Furthermore, as Christ did not do his works in order to merit heaven, neither must the believer: on the contrary, he does such works because he is already heir of heaven.[36]

Tyndale clearly regards conversion primarily as an ontological change effected by the Spirit resulting in the production of good works motivated from love to God. As such, conversion rectifies the major result of the Fall: man's moral bondage. However, regenerate man does not perform works quite as easily as the above might suggest: he still retains his fallen nature to a certain degree, and this evidences itself in a tendency towards sinning. Tyndale describes this sinful disposition with the terms 'the old Adam', and 'the flesh'.[37] This sinful tendency is involved in a continual struggle with man's new, spiritual nature. Tyndale describes

Tyndale', *Pneuma: The Journal of the Society for Pentecostal Studies* 3 (1981), 22–30; also *Lollard Themes*, 255. Augustine too emphasizes the role of the Spirit in producing good works, as shown in the following criticism of the Pelagian concept of grace in his *Opus Imperfectum contra Julianum*, 2. 146: 'Hoc est occultum et horrendum virus haeresis vestrae, ut velitis gratiam Christi in exemplo ejus esse, non in dono ejus, dicentes, quia per ejus imitationem fiunt justi, non per subministrationem Spiritus sancti, ut eum imitentur adducti', *PL* 44. 1202.

[34] *Works* 1. 62. This is a fundamental aspect of the Christology of the *Enchiridion*, as expressed in the fourth rule: see *Enchiridion Militis Christiani* (Cambridge, 1685), 129–39.

[35] *Works* 1, 73. The idea is reminiscent of that of Luther, and perhaps shows that the ethical aspect of Tyndale's Christology have Lutheran as well as Humanist roots: see *WA* 7. 66. 23–8. However, for Luther the concept of Christ serving as an ethical example is not emphasized. When Luther points to Christ as an example to be followed, it is generally in terms of suffering and the cross and is subordinated to Christ's work as Redeemer: see M. Lienhard, *Luther: Witness to Jesus Christ*, trans. E. H. Robertson (Minneapolis, 1982), 108–9, 198; also I. D. K. Siggins, *Martin Luther's Doctrine of Christ* (Yale, 1970), 161–4. In Tyndale, however, the idea is mentioned as parallel to the work of redemption and has more in common with the Christological thought of Augustine and Humanists such as Erasmus than with Luther. Indeed, both Augustine and Erasmus recommend Christ as an example of love and mercy: see J. Burnaby, *Amor Dei: a Study of the Religion of St. Augustine* (London, 1938) 168–9; P. I. Kaufman, *Augustinian Piety and Catholic Reform: Augustine, Colet, and Erasmus* (Macon, 1982), 122–4.

[36] *NT 25*, 11–12.

[37] In *The Obedience of a Christian Man*, published in the same year (1528), he defines 'flesh', as referring to all in man that is not of God, echoing the position of Luther: see *Works* 1. 139.

this conflict from both human and divine perspectives. From a human perspective, he emphasizes that it is the responsibility of man to subdue this old Adam through a combination of prayer and good works. This is to be maintained until man is wholly Spirit; that is, until he is no longer subject to the assaults of the old Adam.[38] Thus the goal of salvation is the total sanctification of the believer. From the divine perspective, Tyndale explains this gradual overcoming of the old Adam in terms of the activity of the Holy Spirit. The saved man is analogous to the barrel of meal in Matt. 13: 33. The Spirit is the leaven, which works through the meal until the whole is thoroughly leavened. Thus total sanctification is the ultimate result of the presence of the Holy Spirit as leavening is the consequence of the presence of leaven.[39]

In treating the subject in this twofold fashion, Tyndale is able to affirm the responsibility of man in the process while avoiding legalistic or man-centred overtones through his stress on the work of the Spirit. Furthermore, by pointing to total sanctification as both the goal and inevitable result of salvation, he reveals an aspect of his doctrine that has great significance for his understanding of justification.

The concept of justification is intimately connected with the concept of righteousness.[40] According to Tyndale true righteousness is the perfect fulfilment of the law 'from the ground of the heart'.[41] Thus, outward conformity to the law is not sufficient in itself. In fact, no-one has this righteousness perfectly, except for Christ, and thus Christ's righteousness must form the starting point for justification.

In relating Christ's righteousness to the believer, Tyndale does not develop an explicit doctrine of imputation. However,

---

[38] 'there abideth and remaineth in us yet of the old Adam . . . against whom we must fight and subdue him, and change all his nature by little and little, with prayer, fasting and watching, with virtuous meditation and holy works, until we be all together Spirit', *Works* 1. 113. By making good works a primary means of the mortification of sin, Tyndale reveals an emphasis somewhat different from that of Luther. The latter sees mortification primarily in terms of the old Adam being continually crucified by the law: see Althaus, *The Theology of Martin Luther*, 269.

[39] '"The kingdom of heaven," saith Christ, "is like leaven, which a woman taketh and hideth in three pecks of meal, till all be leavened." The leaven is the Spirit, and we the meal, which must be seasoned with the Spirit by a little and a little, till we be throughout spiritual', Works 1. 113.

[40] See Ch. 3.

[41] *NT* 25. 8.

he is careful to emphasize that justification is on account of Christ's merits, a position which he establishes at the very start of *The Mammon*, pointing to Rom. 1: 16–17, the passage which had caused Luther so much anguish of soul, as the biblical basis.[42] Elsewhere, he speaks of Christ as working reconciliation between God and man and that Christ is the believer's righteousness.[43] Indeed, in a remarkably graphic passage, he even goes as far as to express the concept of justification in terms of union with Christ whereby his works become the believer's works in the sight of God.[44]

The shape of Tyndale's doctrine is profoundly influenced by what he regards as the purpose of justification. This is that the believer should be made actually righteous.[45] While he is clear in his affirmation that this justification is on account of faith alone,[46] in both *The Fragment* and *The Mammon* Tyndale tends to emphasize the actual righteousness that results from the new birth rather than the objective righteousness of Christ:

[When converted we] consent to the law, and love it inwardly in our heart, and desire to fulfil it, and sorrow we because we cannot; which wish (sin we of frailty never so much) is sufficient till more strength be given us; the blood of Christ hath made satisfaction for the rest.[47] The promises, when they are believed, are they that justify; for they bring the Spirit, which looseth the heart, giveth lust to the law, and certifieth us of the good-will of God unto usward. If we submit ourselves unto God, and desire him to heal us, he will do it, and will in the mean time (because of the consent of the heart unto the law) count us for full whole, and will no more hate us, but pity us, and love us as he doth Christ himself.[48]

---

[42] *Works* 1. 46–7.

[43] Ibid. 95.

[44] 'by thy good deeds shalt thou be saved, not which thou hast done, but which Christ hath done for thee; for Christ is thine, and all his deeds are thy deeds. Christ is in thee, and thou in him, knit together inseparably. Neither canst thou be damned, except Christ be damned with thee: neither can Christ be saved, except thou be saved with him', ibid. 79.

[45] Ibid. 126.

[46] 'By faith are we saved only in believing the promises. And though faith be never without love and good works, yet is our saving imputed neither to love nor unto good works but unto faith only.' *NT* 25. 8.

[47] Ibid. 7; cf. *Works* 1. 76.

[48] Ibid. 52; see also p. 76. These quotations are clearly not consistent with Clebsch's claim that *The Mammon* contains 'a single-minded emphasis upon faith': see Clebsch, p. 152.

In these passages justification is based both on the righteousness of Christ and also on that which the believer possesses as a consequence of his new birth. While the latter is only perfect when viewed as an eschatological reality, its deficiency in this life is made up for by the righteousness of Christ. Tyndale's doctrine of justification therefore has a strong proleptic dimension where account is taken of the eschatological reality of man's perfect righteousness. Justification is based upon the objective work of Christ, but also takes account of the work of the Spirit in the new creation. In this incorporation of actual righteousness into the doctrine of justification, we can clearly discern the outworking of Tyndale's emphasis upon the freeing of man's will as the primary constituent of salvation.

Both of these aspects of justification are to be found in the theology of Luther. Nevertheless, for Luther, it is justification on account of Christ that is placed at the centre of his theology.[49] Tyndale's soteriology is throughout concerned with the actual effects of salvation upon a man's being rather than with salvation as an objective accomplishment. This is reflected in his doctrine of fallen man and Christ's redemptive work. The same is true in justification, where Tyndale emphasises the new birth and mentions Christ's merits as a basis for this. His ethical emphasis in justification places his thinking much closer to that of Augustine and Humanism than that of Luther.[50]

The Problem of Assurance

Before leaving discussion of Tyndale's early teaching on salvation, there is one further aspect that demands attention as it leads to significant developments in his later thought: the problem of assurance. Tyndale characterizes the relationship between faith and work as one that is based upon love to God. This love is itself a response to the prior love of God for the believer, which is understood through faith. Thus, love to God, arising from the assurance of God's love, is the cause of works. However, in *The Mammon* (1528), Tyndale also refers to works as the primary means of assurance of God's love towards the individual:

---

[49] See Ch. 3.
[50] See E.-W. Kohls, 'The Principal Theological Thoughts in the *Enchiridion Militis Christiani*.' in *Essays on the Works of Erasmus*, edited by R. L. DeMolen (Yale, 1978), 73; A. E. McGrath, 'Humanist Elements', 6–7.

Thou canst never know or be sure of thy faith, but by the works: if works follow not, yea, and that of love, without looking for any reward, thou mayest be sure that thy faith is but a dream . . . and not justifying.[51]

This idea that works constitute a primary basis for assurance introduces a tension into Tyndale's definition of the causal relationship between faith and works: to make works a basis for assurance effectively negates this relationship.

Tyndale himself does not appear to have been aware of the problem and so makes no attempt either to harmonize the two concepts or to explain how they relate to each other.[52] There would appear to be only two reasons why he might need to develop this line of thought: first, he may have wished to deal with the pastoral problem of lack of assurance; secondly, he may have wanted to maintain emphasis upon the need for good works.

As to the first, there is no hint in Tyndale's works that this is the reason for the idea. Nowhere does he say that a soul troubled about his eternal destiny should look to see if he is doing good works in order to gain assurance. On the contrary, Tyndale elsewhere characterizes weak faith as having only little love for the law and thus producing hardly any good works.[53] Therefore, we can discount this as the motive behind his thinking on this issue.[54]

---

[51] *Works* 1. 60.

[52] None of the secondary studies appear to be aware of the problem either.

[53] See *Works* 1. 57; cf. ibid. 2. 7.

[54] In later theology the so-called practical syllogism was introduced in order to provide a framework for a works-based assurance. This should not be seen as a later example of what is here present in Tyndale who is not developing the concept in order to deal with lack of assurance. Barth sees the idea as originating in the theology of Calvin but undergoing considerable development at the hands of Beza: see *CD* 2. 2, 335–40; R. A. Muller too finds the idea present in a cautious form in Calvin, as does G. C. Berkouwer: see Muller, *Christ and the Decree*, 25–7; Berkouwer, *Divine Election*, 288–90. Others deny that Calvin taught such a doctrine: see W. Niesel, *The Theology of John Calvin*, trans. H. Knight (Philadelphia, 1956), 178–9. R. T. Kendall explicitly follows Niesel, apparently unaware of the views of Barth and Berkouwer, and blames the development of the practical syllogism on theological innovations, particularly that of limited atonement: *Calvin and English Calvinism to 1649* (Oxford, 1979) 28, 33–4 (where he argues that it was Beza who developed the idea). Kendall's argument is that universal atonement is vital as an objective basis of assurance: if it is limited, then a Christian cannot be sure that Christ has died for him and therefore seeks for *signs* of election. Kendall's thesis lacks logical coherence because he argues for a limitation of Christ's priestly intercession. Therefore, it is immaterial whether the atonement is universal or not: the key question for assurance becomes, not 'Did Christ die for me?', as with limited atonement, but 'Is Christ interceding for me?'. The problem is merely

Therefore, we are left with the second explanation: that Tyndale introduces the idea in order to maintain the need for good works.[55] This conclusion is borne out by his actual application of the idea because he uses it not to assure weak consciences but to prevent presumption. Thus, at times, he can speak of assurance as coming only through works and not being part of faith at all.[56] It appears then that Tyndale introduces a works-based assurance as a means of maintaining emphasis upon works.[57]

Two further general conclusions can be drawn at this point. The first involves Tyndale's theological method. His failure to harmonize his doctrine of a works-based assurance with the causal relationship between faith and works demonstrates that consistency is not a major concern in his formulation of doctrine. Instead, he is willing to subordinate logical consistency in order to maintain emphasis upon the ethical aspects of the Christian life. Indeed, this tension leaves the way open for increased emphasis upon works in the future.

The second conclusion is closely related to the first: by basing assurance upon works, Tyndale once again demonstrates his tendency to place his major emphasis upon the subjective

shifted from Calvary to the right hand of God! The real problem for objective assurance is the tension created by the classic Augustinian model of salvation where there is a tension between God's revealed will and his hidden will, as theologians such as Barth and Berkouwer have pointed out. As for Calvin, his comment on 1 John 2: 3 points towards the basic structure of the practical syllogism, but he is emphatic that this is not to be used as a simple logical process in isolation from the believer's faith whereby works would effectively become the basis for faith: see *OC* 55. 310–11. For Beza, see his *Catechismus Compendiarius* [*Tractationes Theologicae* (Geneva, 1570–82), vol. 1, p. 690], where he declares that good works are 'huius [verae] fidei indicium'. This idea is not allowed to eclipse the notion of assurance based upon the the inner witness of the Spirit: '[tuam electionem] cognosces, partim ex Spiritu adoptionis intus clamante; partim etiam ex eiusdem Spiritus vi et efficacia in seipso.' *Tractationes Theologicae*, vol. 1, p. 200.

[55] A further element in this matter of works-based assurance concerns Tyndale's tendency to point the believer to the promises without also referring him explicitly to the objective basis of these promises in Christ. The result is that God's acceptance of the individual is apparently based upon God's merciful character and not upon Christ's objective work. This, in turn, leads to an emphasis upon the believer's intrinsic merits rather than upon the atonement. This is entirely consistent with Tyndale's general vagueness concerning the means whereby salvation was accomplished by Christ.

[56] See the previous quotation. This passage gives clear indication that Tyndale's doctrine is not intended to comfort the doubting conscience. Not only must the believer be doing works, he must be doing them from love. How he knows that this is his motive is not clear, but clearly the works themselves are insufficient evidence for this.

[57] However, it must be remembered that Tyndale regards works as the result of the Holy Spirit's activity, and so avoids the error of Pelagianism.

effects of salvation within the believer. His overriding concern is with the practical outworkings of Christianity, and this concern with morality flavours all aspects of his doctrine, even to the point of introducing stark tensions into his thought.

Summary

Tyndale's early soteriology is based upon his perception of fallen man's predicament as not fundamentally one of moral guilt but one of bondage to sin. This concern is reflected both in his formulation of the work of Christ as overcoming the Devil and the bonds of sin, and in his description of conversion which is seen primarily in terms of the regenerating work of the Holy Spirit. While he regards justification by faith as the foundation of Christian salvation, his emphasis is always upon the subjective effects of this, such as the Christian's love of the law and his subsequent efforts to fulfil the commands. He deals with doctrines such as election primarily as necessary derivatives of other doctrines and not as axioms which shape his overall position. He conceives of justification itself as possessing a strong proleptic dimension and bases assurance upon the believer's good works. Thus, throughout his soteriology, there is a continuous ethical concern which is far more pronounced than that in Luther. In this concern, reflected in the stress upon regeneration, it is possible to see the continuing influence of Humanist thought at work upon Tyndale as he develops a doctrine of salvation akin to that of contemporary Reformed theologians.

TYNDALE IN MID-CAREER: 1530–2

From 1528 to 1530 Tyndale had been occupied with translating parts of the Old Testament. Then, between 1530 and 1532, he wrote six theological works, none of which was specifically devoted to the doctrine of salvation. However, there are sufficient references to this theme to allow for an accurate assessment of his views during this period.

Translating the Bible remained Tyndale's priority, and in 1530 he published an English version of the Pentateuch. This was prefaced by a brief outline of the difficulties he had experienced in his attempt to find a sponsor for a translation of the scriptures. He also included brief introductions to each book, outlining their contents and significance. In the same year, he also published *The Practice of Prelates* in which he attempted to demonstrate from history that the papacy was nothing but a corrupt, power-hungry institution which had usurped the role of the temporal authorities.

In 1531 he published no less than four works, three of which were related directly to the Bible. *A Pathway to the Holy Scriptures* was a revision edition of the prologue to the *Cologne Fragment* (1525). While retaining much of the original text, Tyndale added a significant new section which dealt with the nature and purpose of works. *The Prologue to Jonah* was Tyndale's introduction to the one other Old Testament book which he had translated, an introduction which was actually longer than the book itself. In this, he outlined the book's contents, its relevance for his readers, and a few theological principles to help with interpretation and application. His third book, *The Exposition of 1 John*, was essentially an expanded paraphrase of the New Testament letter, accompanied by relevant application. It seems probable that this work had a Lutheran model.[58] Finally, 1531 also saw the publication of *The Answer to More*, a point-by-point reply to Sir Thomas More's *Dialogue Concerning Heresies* (1529). As one might expect, in this work Tyndale touches on most of the areas in dispute between the Reformers and the Catholics.

Salvation

The manner in which Tyndale generally discusses salvation is very similar to his approach in earlier works. Once again, his approach is characterized by an emphasis upon its effects rather than its objective foundations. For example, he seldom refers to an order of salvation founded on God's election. In *The Answer* he does refer to God's choice of man as the ultimate cause of salvation.[59] However, he makes no reference to reprobation and moves straight on to describe the actual application and

---

[58] See Rupp, *English Protestant Tradition*, 51. Clebsch (p. 170) remarks that modern writers dismiss *The Exposition* as one of the least valuable of Tyndale's works. This may be true with respect to content. However, it is reasonable to assume that his choice of book would have been influenced by his perception of the importance of its subject matter. Thus, his choice of 1 John, with its emphasis upon love and obedience to the commandments, implies that major concerns of his earlier theology were still of great importance to him in 1531.

[59] *Works* 3. 35.

effects of salvation. Later in the same work, he criticises More's rejection of predestination as asserting free will and therefore denying that salvation is a gift of God.[60] Thus it is clear that Tyndale still discusses predestination and election only as concepts which safeguard God's grace.

For the unconverted man, Tyndale still regards law and gospel as in opposition, and identifies them as the two keys given to the Church by Christ.[61] However, this aspect of his thought does not receive much attention; instead, Tyndale is more concerned with the dynamics of the Christian life and thus he tends to describe conversion in terms almost identical to those employed in his earlier works. For example, in *The Pentateuch* (1530) and *1 John* (1531), he outlines conversion in the following terms:

And when this testament [the gospel] is preached and believed, the Spirit entereth the heart, and quickeneth it, and giveth her life, and justifieth her. The Spirit also maketh the law a lively thing in the heart; so that a man bringeth forth good works of his own accord, without compulsion of the law . . . but of the very power of the Spirit, received through faith.[62]

When a true preacher preacheth, the Spirit entereth the hearts of the elect, and maketh them feel the righteousness of the law of God, and by the law the poison of their corrupt nature; and thence leadeth them through repentance, unto the mercy that is in Christ's blood; and as an ointment healeth the body, even so the Spirit, through confidence and trust in Christ's blood, healeth the soul, and maketh her love the law of God . . .[63]

All of the key elements of Tyndale's earlier position are again expressed here: conviction by the law; the work of the Spirit; and love to the law. Underlying this is once again the idea that man's problem is fundamentally one of his moral being not his guilt. This leads to the characteristic emphasis upon salvation as an ontological change whereby the sinful nature is healed. Indeed, in no work of this period does Tyndale proceed to develop the idea of man's guilt or of Christ's objective work; the result is a doctrine of salvation which is once again overwhelmingly concerned with its subjective effects.

---

[60] Ibid. 140.   [61] Ibid. 1. 416; 2. 282.
[62] Ibid. 1. 417.   [63] Ibid. 2. 183–4.

The manner in which these effects are produced is also fundamentally the same as in the earlier period: the Holy Spirit applies salvation to the individual, and causes love towards God. This love then provides the motivation for good works, which are performed in order to demonstrate love to God. This leads Tyndale to make two remarkable statements. The first is from *The Answer*, the second from *1 John*:

And we affirm that we have no free-will to prevent God and his grace, before grace prepare ourselves thereto; neither can we consent unto God before grace be come. For until God hath prevented us, and poured the Spirit of his grace into our souls, to love his laws, and hath graven them in our hearts . . . we know not God as he is to be known, nor feel the goodness or any sweetness in his law.[64]

Love is the instrument wherewith faith maketh us God's sons, and fashioneth us like the image of God, and certifieth us that we so are.[65]

In both passages, salvation is seen in terms of moral transformation. In the first, Tyndale identifies grace with the Holy Spirit. Such an identification originated in Augustine and was developed during the Middle Ages.[66] Salvation thus becomes the result of the infusion of the Spirit. In the second passage, adoption is seen as the result of love causing man to be fashioned into the image of God. In both cases, one can discern the concept of a proleptic justification underlying Tyndale's theology. This is particularly clear in the second passage which virtually states that faith saves because it causes love to God.[67] As in his earlier writings, Tyndale is again structuring his doctrine in a way that underlines the actual moral transformation of the believer.

---

[64] *Works* 3. 174. Tyndale here appears to be attacking the medieval teaching that man could merit the initial infusion of grace through his own efforts. This, the position of the *via moderna* was the position Luther reacted so vigorously against: see Ch. 3.

[65] *Works* 2. 200.

[66] Calvin criticizes Augustine for his failure to distinguish carefully between grace and the work of the Spirit in regeneration: see *Institutes* 3. 11. 15. The ambiguity in Augustine's doctrine is discussed in an article by L. D. Sharp, 'The Doctrines Of Grace in Calvin and Augustine', *EQ* 52 (1980), 84–96. The importance of the idea of the infusion of grace to Aquinas' doctrine of justification is made clear in *Summa*, 1a2ae 113, 6.

[67] When one considers the fact that Tyndale does not discuss faith except as it relates to the existential effects of salvation (i.e. love and its consequences), it is arguable that faith is itself instrumental as regards love. Certainly, the lack of emphasis upon faith's object, Christ, seems to make faith only necessary in so far as it produces the response of love in the believer.

Finally, it is important to notice that Tyndale sees this salvation as being the same in both Old and New Testaments. The first quotation above is taken from *The Pentateuch* and is referring to the Old Testament. For Tyndale, the New Testament, in terms of the gospel of Jesus Christ, has existed from the beginning of time and is contained in both Old and New Testament scriptures. Thus, he is able to describe Deuteronomy as 'very pure gospel' because it preaches faith and love, and asserts a specific relationship between faith, love to God, and love to one's neighbour.[68] The importance of the unity of the Testaments is that Tyndale can now draw on both in formulating his doctrine of salvation, and this could possibly lead him to infuse Old Testament elements into his doctrine of salvation.

The overall framework of salvation in these writings is the same as that expressed in Tyndale's earlier works. He introduces election only to underline grace, and rarely discusses the other objective aspects of salvation, such as God's wrath and Christ's propitiation. Instead, he focuses upon the moral bondage of man, not his guilt, and sees salvation as an actual release from this bondage which is effected by the Holy Spirit. As a consequence, man loves God and performs good works. This was Tyndale's position in his earliest writings, and remains so here.

The Role of Works

It is in Tyndale's understanding of the nature and function of works that W. A. Clebsch claims to discern a significant shift in his theology towards legalism.[69] However, a close examination of Tyndale's thinking on this subject reveals that, while there is greater emphasis upon works in this period, his position is still fundamentally consistent with that of his earlier writings.

The Pathway (1531) is essentially a reprint of the prologue to *The Cologne Fragment* (1525), but contains a certain amount of new material. The major part of this consists of a section on the use of good works, which Tyndale regards as threefold:

Our deeds do us three manner of service. First, they certify that we are heirs of everlasting life. . . . And secondarily, we tame the flesh

---

[68] This comment on Deuteronomy is interpreted by Clebsch as a sign of Tyndale's growing legalism and his increasing distance from Luther. In fact, Tyndale's statement merely echoes Luther's own verdict upon the book: see *WA (DB)* 8. 32–4.

[69] See Clebsch, pp. 154–74.

therewith, and kill the sin that remaineth yet in us; and wax daily perfecter and perfecter in the Spirit therewith. . . . And thirdly, we do our duty unto our neighbour therewith, and help their necessity unto our own comfort also, and draw all men unto the honour and praising of God.[70]

The basic outlines of all three of these functions were present in *The Mammon* (1528), and only the first, that of works as a basis for assurance, was not already present in the original text of *The Fragment*. Thus, in making this statement, Tyndale is not revealing a radical break with his earlier position. The fact that he chooses to add this passage to the original 1525 text perhaps indicates an increased emphasis upon works in his theology and a broader understanding of the Christian life, but it cannot be described as a 'new understanding' of the value of works.[71] Tyndale is simply reaffirming that deeds are essential to the believer.[72]

However, Tyndale does now place more emphasis upon works as an outward sign of inward justification before God. For example, in referring to salvation in *The Pentateuch* (1530), he argues that believers in ancient Israel were 'justified' in a twofold fashion:

The new testament was ever, even from the beginning of the world. For there were always promises of Christ to come, by faith in which promises the elect were then justified inwardly before God, as outwardly before the world by keeping of the law and ceremonies.[73]

Tyndale's application of the word 'justified' to outward works in this context leads Clebsch to term the idea 'double justification'.[74] This is misleading, as Tyndale's thinking here bears no resemblance to what is usually meant by the term, whereby

---

[70] *Works* 1. 23–4.

[71] See Clebsch, p. 167.

[72] Clebsch points to the function of works as providing assurance for the believer and help to his neighbour, and thus characterizes them as 'acts of enlightened self interest' (p. 167). Such characterization is unfair, ignoring the basic principle that Tyndale regards the motive for works as love to God, not love to self, as has been demonstrated above. Cf. *Works* 1. 441. Clebsch also claims that Tyndale now advocates a view that regards the Christian life as one of increasing perfection. In fact, Tyndale has always regarded works as directed towards one's neighbour and as increasing in perfection as the believer continues in faith. Indeed, this idea shapes his entire thinking on justification: it is no innovation.

[73] *Works* 1. 417.

[74] See Clebsch, pp. 166–8.

man's relationship with God is based in part upon his works.[75] This is not Tyndale's meaning here, as demonstrated by the following passage in *The Answer* (1531):

And when Paul saith, 'faith only justifieth'; and James, that 'a man is justified by works and not by faith only'; there is a great difference between Paul's *only* and James's *only*. For Paul's *only* is to be understood, that faith justifieth in the heart and before God without help of works, yea, and ere I can work; for I must receive life through faith to work with, ere I can work. But James's *only* is this wise to be understood; that faith doth not so justify, that nothing justifieth save faith: for deeds do justify also. But faith justifieth in the heart and before God; and the deeds before the world only, and maketh the other seen: as ye may see by the scripture [Rom. 4].[76]

It is clear from this passage that Tyndale is not referring to true double justification but is emphasizing that works are derived from, and declare before the world, the prior justification of the sinner by faith before God. This position is entirely consistent with his earlier statements concerning the inseparability of faith and love and his proleptic construction of the doctrine of justification.[77] Such emphasis upon outward works as testifying to prior justification by God through faith is a common element amongst early Reformed thinkers and Tyndale's loose use of the word 'justification' echoes that of Martin Bucer.[78] While Luther does refer to the idea that outward works testify to prior justification by faith alone before God,[79] Tyndale uses the idea in order to deal with the problem of interpreting the difficult passages in James, a problem which Luther solved simply by denying the importance of the letter's teaching.[80] This points away from Lutheran influence in this matter and towards that of Reformed thinkers. Reformers such as Bucer followed Augustine's interpretation of James and stressed that

[75] See H. Küng, *Justification: The Doctrine of Karl Barth and a Catholic Reflection*, trans. by T. Collins *et al.* (London, 1981), 219; D. Fenlon, *Heresy and Obedience in Tridentine Italy: Cardinal Pole and the Counter Reformation* (Cambridge, 1972), 53–61.

[76] *Works* 3. 202.

[77] Clebsch's misunderstanding of this idea of a twofold justification is central to the theological difference which he claims exists between Tyndale and Frith. It will be discussed in more detail in Ch. 5.

[78] See Ch. 3.

[79] *WA* 2. 145–52.

[80] *WA (DB)* 7. 388.

the works referred to in James 2 were a consequence, and not a cause, of justification. It is to this tradition of interpretation that Tyndale belongs.[81]

Further evidence of Reformed influence upon Tyndale's doctrine of works is evident in his teaching on merit. In the following extract from *The Pathway* (1531), Tyndale reproduces a section of the original prologue with significant additions (which have here been italicized):

By faith we receive of God, and by love we shed out again. And that must we do freely, after the example of Christ, without any other respect, save our neighbour's wealth only; and neither look for reward in the earth, nor yet in heaven for *the deserving and merits of* our deeds, *as friars preach; though we know that good deeds are rewarded, both in this life and the life to come.*[82]

A few pages after this statement, Tyndale refers to heaven as 'the reward of well-doing' while cautioning that this is not to be the motive for good works.[83] Clebsch interprets these statements as signalling a dramatic departure from Tyndale's earlier position. In 1525, he claims, the first passage allowed no reward for deeds.[84] In fact, this is not strictly accurate. All that the passage said was that the believer was neither to 'look for reward in the earth nor yet in heaven for our deeds'. This is primarily a statement concerning the motivation for good works, and not a specific denial that they do merit something in the after-life. All that can be safely said is that Tyndale did not make his position on this matter clear in 1525.

Clebsch also claims that by mentioning reward, and making heaven the 'reward of well doing', Tyndale effectively makes desire for reward the motive for good works despite his claims to the contrary. However, the first reference to heaven, followed as it is by reference to the preaching of the friars, could well be intended as a corrective to the errors of Catholic opponents rather than a surreptitious attempt to motivate his

---

[81] See Augustine, *De Fide et Operibus*, PL 40. 211. This passage is used by Bucer to deal with the same issue of faith and works in *Enarratio in Epistolam ad Romanos* (Strasbourg, 1536), 232–3. See also *The Common Places of Martin Bucer*, trans. D. F. Wright, (Appleford, 1972), 159; Stephens, *The Holy Spirit in the Theology of Martin Bucer*, 56; *The Theology of Huldrych Zwingli*, 160.

[82] *Works* 1. 20.

[83] *Works* 1. 22.

[84] See Clebsch, p. 167.

readers. The second instance, where heaven becomes the reward of well doing, still does not mean that salvation is merited by good works in a strict sense. However, it does support the interpretation of Tyndale's doctrine of justification as proleptic whereby man is justified on account of his new birth which will lead to increasing perfection in this life and absolute perfection in the next. This points to the influence of Augustinian thought on this matter, which may have been obtained directly or mediated through the Reformed tradition via the writings of men such as Bucer. It certainly indicates an affinity with the position on merit adopted by Reformed thinkers.[85] It is also consonant with the inseparability of faith, love, and works in Tyndale's theology, where the presence of one implies the presence of all. On this basis, works could be said to merit heaven in that they presuppose faith and the new birth. Whatever the case may be, the introduction of the concept does not automatically reveal a rejection of an earlier position, as Tyndale had not previously committed himself on this question.

As regards the function of works, Tyndale's statements indicate that he is developing and applying his previous theology rather than repudiating or undermining his earlier position. If any change at all is to be discerned, it is in his emphasis: his additions to the prologue of *The Fragment* and his elaboration of the declaratory nature of works indicate that ethical considerations are still a primary concern in his theology. However, this now brings us to the question of the nature of the works themselves: what exactly constitutes a good work?

In his earliest works, Tyndale provided three principles for good works: the law; love; and the example of Christ. In reality, these three were one, as both the law and the example of Christ were reflections of love to God. It is the claim of Clebsch that this middle period of Tyndale's career is marked by an increasing emphasis upon the law as the guide of the Christian's life.[86] Central to this, according to Clebsch, is Tyndale's study of the Old Testament. However, an examination of Tyndale's theology reveals that his study of the Old Testament served only to reinforce rather than to repudiate his earlier position.

[85] See J. Rivière, 'Mérite.' in *Dictionnaire de théologie catholique* 10: 647; Stephens, *The Holy Spirit in the Theology of Martin Bucer*, 55–61.
[86] See Clebsch, pp. 155–9.

Tyndale's major treatment of the relationship of the Old to the New Testament occurs in *The Practice of Prelates* (1530), where he is discussing the problem of Henry VIII's divorce from Catherine of Aragon. The fundamental difference he sees between the two Testaments is that the Old looks forward to Christ, while the New actually reveals him. Tyndale divides the Old Testament legislation into three types of law: ceremonial; judicial; and natural. Tyndale regards the ceremonial laws of the Jews as pointing forward to Christ, and thus abrogated by his coming. These are now replaced by the preaching of the gospel and by the sacraments of baptism and the Eucharist.[87] Also abrogated are the judicial laws of Israel, relevant only in the social context of ancient Israel. Their underlying principle, that of maintaining a stable society, still applies, but the detailed content is no longer binding.[88]

The last category, that of natural law, refers to those parts of the law which pertain to faith and love. For Tyndale, this embodies absolute truth and applies to all nations at all times.[89] This is significant for Tyndale's doctrine of salvation. He describes justification under the Old Testament as based upon the gospel and thus as being substantially identical to justification under the New Testament. This involved justification before God by faith, which is declared before men by obedience to the ceremonial, judicial, and moral precepts of the law. Now, after the coming of Christ, the ceremonial and judicial aspects of the law have been abrogated, but the natural law is still binding. Thus, the natural law remains normative for outward Christian conduct under the New Testament dispensation.[90]

However, while this assertion of testamental unity provides an Old Testament foundation for Tyndale's ethical emphasis, it does not mark a radical break with his earlier theology. He regards the natural law as embodied in the decalogue, but he insists that this is to be interpreted and applied on the basis of

[87] *Works* 1. 423. Tyndale here refers to Old Testament sacrifices and New Testament sacraments as 'tokens' and 'signs', a clear indication that he has come under the influence of Reformed theology. In *The Answer* (1531) he mentions both Zwingli and Oecolampadius with approval in connection with the Eucharist.

[88] *Works* 1. 324.

[89] Ibid. 324–5.

[90] 'We be under the law to learn it, and to fashion our deeds as like it as we can; but not under the damnation of the law that we should be damned', ibid. 2. 159.

love. Thus he makes the precepts of the decalogue subordinate to love and does not argue for their application in terms of a simplistic litcralism.[91] By establishing the priority of love, he presents the role of law in the Christian life in the same terms as in 1525 and 1528.[92]

Tyndale also points to Christ as example. He does not place great emphasis upon this concept in these writings, and when he does, he links it closely to the law of God. He says that Christ is an example of how works should be performed, that is, naturally and perfectly.[93] He also refers to following 'after the footsteps of Christ', which he places in apposition to 'in the law of God', showing the practical identity of the two ideas.[94] Thus, Christ is the perfect example of law in action, and therefore the perfect example for the Christian to emulate.

For Clebsch, Tyndale's understanding of the role of the law in the Christian life reveals his fundamental rejection of Luther's position. While it is true that Tyndale's frequent references to the love of the law are very un-Lutheran, his actual concept of Christian ethics is fundamentally identical with that of Luther. While Luther can speak of the decalogue as no longer having relevance for the believer, he can also speak of it as the highest expression of the natural law. This Luther understands as love to God and to one's neighbour, which is identical with the view of Tyndale.[95] While there is an ambiguity in Luther's position in terms of his ambivalent position on the decalogue, it is clear that he is happy to regard it as normative for Christian behaviour when it is interpreted in terms of love.[96] This position is identical to that of Tyndale.

From this, it is clear that Tyndale's view of the normative principle for good works remains fundamentally the same as in his earlier writings. Both the law and Christ provide good

[91] This is seen most clearly in his references to the Sabbath: 'And as for the Saboth, a great matter, we be lords over the Saboth; and may yet change it into the Monday, or any other day, as we see need; or may make every tenth day holy, if we see a cause why', ibid. 3. 97. This was clearly too much for the editor of the Parker Society edition who describes this reference in the index as Tyndale's 'lax doctrine'. Cf. ibid. 2. 325. Sabbatarianism was, of course, considered by early Protestants, such as Tyndale, to be a Catholic doctrine, smacking of legalism.

[92] 'To love is not painful: the commandments are but love, therefore they be not grievous; because love maketh the commandments easy', ibid. 208.

[93] Ibid. 151.   [94] Ibid. 332.

[95] *WA* 16. 380, 390.   [96] See Ch. 3.

guidelines for conduct, but the major principle underlying the law, and thus Christ's own activities, is love. Tyndale's study of the Old Testament leads him to assert that the natural law is binding on all in terms of ethics. However, his interpretation of this primarily in terms of love, and not in terms of a literalist application of the decalogue, means that his position on this matter is continuous with earlier statements on the requirements of the law.

Summary

During the years 1530–2, Tyndale repeats the same basic ideas about salvation as he did earlier in his career, stressing the importance of regeneration through the Holy Spirit. He does place an increased emphasis upon works as an outward demonstration of inward justification, but this is not made at the expense of compromising his earlier position on justification by faith only; rather, this emphasis is fundamentally continuous with the proleptic orientation of his doctrine of justification. While he now explicitly allows for the reward of good works in the after-life, his earlier silence on the issue prevents dogmatic conclusions as to whether this marks a change in his position. It certainly underlines the continuing ethical concern of his theology, and places him closer to Bucer and early Reformed thinkers than to Luther.

Concerning the normative principle for works, Tyndale maintains the same position as earlier, seeing the law in terms of the commandments to love God and one's neighbour as providing the fundamental guide for the Christian's conduct. This is basically the position of Luther, although Tyndale's expression of the idea contains none of Luther's ambivalence concerning the role of the law.

LATER CAREER: 1533–6

Little is known about Tyndale's life immediately prior to his arrest. During this period, he wrote five works which reveal significant developments in his thought. The first was his *Exposition upon the Fifth, Sixth, and Seventh Chapters of Matthew* (1533). As the title suggests, this work is an exposition of the Sermon on the Mount and was probably based upon a Lutheran original.[97] Bible translation still remained Tyndale's priority, and he published an edition of the New Testament in 1534, along with prefaces and marginal notes. In the same year, he also produced a second edition of the Pentateuch. In this edition, Tyndale included revisions of the prologue, and the preface to Genesis. Only the Genesis translation was slightly altered; the other four books were, in fact, remaining copies of the 1530 edition bound in with the new material.[98]

In addition to these biblical works, Tyndale wrote two other tracts. The first, a commentary upon the will of William Tracy, was found among his papers, along with the similar work by John Frith, after his execution in 1536. The second, *A Brief Declaration of the Sacraments* was also published posthumously. Both works give clear indication of the influence of Reformed patterns of thought upon Tyndale's theology particularly with reference to his sacramental thought.[99]

The writings of this period reveal a new emphasis in Tyndale's theology on God's covenant. This concept dominates all areas of his thinking, from hermeneutics to the sacraments. However, the covenant concept is, in fact, the flowering of principles implicit even in his earliest writings.

Development of the Covenant Motif

As early as 1525, Tyndale makes reference to the idea of a testament in a passage translated from Luther's *Preface*:

This evangelion . . . called the new testament. Because that as a man when he shall die appointeth his goods to be dealt and distributed after his death among them which he nameth to be his heirs. Even so Christ before his death commanded and appointed that such evangelion . . . should be declared and there with to give unto all that believe all his goods, that is to say his life . . . his salvation.[100]

In this sense, Tyndale uses the word 'testament' as analogous to a man's last will and testament. As such it is a unilateral arrangement, created and executed by God and not dependent upon or inclusive of man's response. However, three years later

---

[97] Mozley, *William Tyndale*, 241; Trinterud, 'A Reappraisal', 37–9.
[98] See Clebsch, p. 181.
[99] *Works* 1. 349.
[100] *NT* 25. 2–3.

he is to use the term to mean something very different, as shown in the following passage from *The Mammon* (1528):

> Our mind, intent, and affection or zeal, are blind; and all that we do of them, is damned of God: and for that cause hath God made a testament between him and us, wherein is contained both what he would have us to do, and what he would have us ask of him. See therefore that thou do nothing to please God withal, but that he commandeth; neither ask any thing of him, but that he hath promised thee.[101]

This statement has been taken to indicate that Tyndale's later concept of covenant is already present under the guise of testament as early as 1528. Clearly Tyndale is not using the word in the same way as in 1525 as he now refers 'testament' to the obligations of man, not to a unilateral arrangement centred on Christ. Indeed, he even calls this arrangement a covenant in the marginal notes.[102]

However, it is important to understand this passage in its original context. Tyndale has just been discussing the nature of good works and how man's own view of what is good cannot be relied upon because his moral sense has been blinded by the Fall. It is at this point that he makes the above statement concerning God's testament: the testament contains what man should do for God and what he should ask of God; that is, it supplies man with the moral knowledge which he lost at the Fall. Thus, testament here is not primarily an expression of the soteriological relationship between God and man but a principle regulative of man's conduct. Of course, this regulative aspect is a fundamental element of his mature covenant concept, but his later development of the doctrine stresses the mutuality of man's works and God's saving activity. Here, Tyndale does not actually relate the testament to God's salvation of the individual or make man's works into one half of a covenantal relationship between God and man. Thus, while his use of the word testament has undergone change between 1525 and 1528, he has still not fully developed his mature covenant concept.

---

[101] *Works* 1. 105–6.
[102] 'God hath made an everlasting covenant with us that we should go no more astray after our good intent', ibid. 105.

It is in *1 John* that Tyndale makes his first reference to an arrangement between God and man which approximates to that which he later describes with the term covenant:

[God] hath made an appointment betwixt him and us, in Christ's blood; and hath bound himself to give us what ever we ask in his name ... and that he will be a father unto us, and save us both in this life and in the life to come, and take us from under the damnation of the law, and set us under grace and mercy, to be scholars only to learn the law; and that our unperfect deeds shall be taken in worth, yea and though at a time we mar all through infirmity, yet if we turn again, that shall be forgiven us mercifully.[103]

Although he uses the term 'appointment', Tyndale here expresses all the major elements of his later concept of covenant. God and man are seen as bound together: God is obliged to be a father to his people; and they are bound to obey the law to the best of their ability. In this way, the appointment combines both the 1525 promissory understanding and the 1528 ethical understanding of testament. The whole arrangement is built upon the prior love of man for God and underwritten by Christ's blood.[104] Thus, the appointment is not only a principle regulative of Christian conduct; it is also an expression of the soteriological relationship between God and man, a clear development from the idea of testament in 1528.

Thus, a development in Tyndale's thinking can be traced in the early years from testament as analogous to a will to testament as regulative of man's conduct. Then, in 1531 he describes the relationship between God and man in terms of an

[103] Ibid. 2. 166.

[104] Clebsch misses the important point that love is the foundation of the appointment by explaining Tyndale's meaning here by the use of an inappropriate metaphor: 'God was the master and man the apprentice, but the obligation bound the one as it bound the other. The apprentice, totally undeserving when taken into the master's service, by his work put the master under stipulated obligations', Clebsch, p. 172. God, however, has bound himself to be a *father*, not a *master*. The master-apprentice relationship is based on commercial considerations, not love. Clebsch has not only interpreted, rather than expounded Tyndale's meaning; he has also imported connotations into the discussion which are absent from Tyndale's own metaphor. The problem with metaphors is that they can be used not merely to illustrate a truth, but as an authoritative explanation of the mechanics of that truth: see F. Lyall, 'Of Metaphors and Analogies: Legal Language and Covenant Theology', *SJT* 32 (1979), 1–17; 'Metaphors, Legal and Theological', *Scottish Bulletin of Evangelical Theology*, 10 (1992), 94–112. On affiliation, not commercialism, as the basis for Tyndale's covenant concept, see M. McGiffert, 'William Tyndale's Concept of Covenant', *JEH* 32 (1981), 167–84.

appointment, embodying both aspects of the earlier under-standings of testament.[105]

Tyndale's Mature Covenant Theology

In discussing Tyndale's theology, it is vitally important that we never lose sight of the fact that he considered his most important role to be that of making the Bible comprehensible to his fellow countrymen. While this made scripture translation his overwhelming priority, it also made him concerned that those who could then read the Bible should do so in a correct and edifying manner. For this reason, a significant number of his writings are concerned either with expounding the Bible or with outlining principles of biblical interpretation. It is in this context of concern for biblical hermeneutics that Tyndale's covenant concept must be understood. This is made abundantly clear in the following comment in Tyndale's preface to his 1534 edition of the New Testament:

The right way, yea, and the only way to understand the scripture unto salvation, is that we earnestly and above all things search for the profession of our baptism, or covenants between us and God.[106]

From this statement we learn not only that the covenant is fundamental to understanding scripture, but also that it is inti-mately related to baptism and that it is an arrangement between man and God. The reference to salvation indicates that this covenant idea links the issue of biblical interpretation to the salvific relationship between God and man. Thus it is clear that while the covenant provides a useful key for interpreting the Bible, it has the added bonus of articulating the nature of man's salvation.

While Tyndale uses the plural 'covenants' when referring to the content of scripture, he regards all of them as part of the one great covenant, which he describes in the following terms:

The general covenant, wherein all other are comprehended and included, is this: If we meek ourselves to God, to keep all his laws, after the example of Christ, then God hath bound himself unto us, to

---

[105] It is interesting that Tyndale's transition from the concept of 'testament' to that of 'covenant' reflects a general tendency in Reformed theology in the early decades of the sixteenth century: see Hagen, 'From Testament to Covenant in the Early Sixteenth Century'.
[106] *Works* 1. 469.

keep and make good all the mercies promised in Christ throughout all the scripture.[107]

Man and God are therefore bound together by the covenant which contains obligations for both. God's part in the covenant is that he is to fulfil for man all those things which he objectively accomplished through Christ. This is, of course, what Tyndale has always regarded as God's part in salvation. Man's duty is to keep all of God's laws. The actual application of law in this context is exactly the same as in earlier writings: Christ is proposed as an example to be followed; and, immediately after this quotation, the law is defined as the decalogue which is itself comprehended in love to God and to one's neighbour.[108] If one does the latter, then one fulfils the decalogue and all other laws. Thus, Tyndale understands the normative principle for the Christian's ethical conduct in the same terms as he has understood it from his earliest writings.

Both parts of the covenant, God's saving of man because of Christ, and man's obedience to God's law, are ideas which have been fundamental to Tyndale's doctrine of salvation since 1525. The difference now is that these ideas are now set within a covenant framework, and this raises a new question concerning the relationship between salvation and works: is the relationship covenantal or contractual?

Broadly speaking, a contractual understanding of covenant makes God's saving action conditional upon man's activity, and bases the whole scheme upon the idea of commercial transaction. In fact, an examination of Tyndale's covenant doctrine shows that he does regard God's action as dependent in some sense upon man's works, but that this takes place within a familial, not a commercial, framework.

That salvation is conditional upon man's works is clear from the passages concerning the covenant already quoted. Indeed, Tyndale even uses the very word 'condition' in this context in *Exposition* (1533):

all the good promises which are made us throughout all the scripture, for Christ's sake, for his love, for his passion or suffering, his blood-

---

[107] Ibid. 470; see also ibid. 403. Tyndale, like other early covenant theologians but unlike those later, does not construct a two covenant scheme.

[108] 'And he that loveth his neighbour, in God and Christ, fulfilleth these two; and consequently the ten; and finally all the other', ibid. 470.

shedding or death, are all made us on this condition and covenant on
our party, that we henceforth love the law of God, to walk therein,
and to do it, and fashion our lives thereafter . . .[109]

This passage clearly makes God's saving of the individual conditional upon the prior commitment of the believer to love the
law and to strive to fulfil it. Taken in isolation, this certainly
supports the interpretation that Tyndale's theology is one of
contract. Indeed, such an interpretation is strengthened by the
connection he draws between baptism and salvation. Baptism is
analogous to circumcision, and initiates the individual into the
covenant community. It also places him under the obligations
of the covenant, as Tyndale explains in *The Sacraments*:

So now by baptism we be bound to God, and God to us, and the
bond and the seal of the covenant is written in our flesh; by which
seal or writing God challengeth faith and love, under pain of just
damnation: and we (if we believe and love) challenge . . . all mercy,
and whatsoever we need; or else God must be an untrue God.[110]

Baptism places man under the obligation to believe and love.
When this is done, then man can claim mercy; if it is not done,
then man stands condemned. Again, the covenant is defined in
a strongly conditional manner.

However, before concluding that this reflects a contractual
understanding, it is necessary to place Tyndale's covenant idea
within its wider context. In *Exposition* (1533), he is careful to
reject the notion that the works merit salvation in a strict sense
by using a significant metaphor:

Take an ensample of young children, when their father promiseth
them a good thing for the doing of some trifle, and, when they come
for their reward, dallieth with them, saying: 'What, that thou hast
done is not worth half so much: should I give thee so great a thing for
so little a trifle?', they will answer: 'Ye did promise me: ye did say
so!' . . . But the hirelings will pretend their work, and say, 'I have
deserved it: I have done so much, and so much, and my labour is
worth it.'[111]

Two things emerge from this passage. The first is that Tyndale
does not regard works as meriting salvation in a strict sense.
The believers plead the promises as the basis for their reward,

---

[109] *Works* 2. 6.   [110] Ibid. 350.   [111] Ibid. 89–90.

and not the intrinsic value of their own works: the reward they receive is out of all proportion to their own efforts.

Secondly, the whole context of this arrangement is that of a family. The term contract is hardly suitable in this context, as it implies an exchange of goods within an arrangement based upon commercial considerations; Tyndale, on the other hand, regards the God–man relationship as based upon love, and upon familial principles, as is reflected by this passage. The idea of the family was the image used in Tyndale's earlier expression of the covenant idea as appointment in *1 John* (1531). Indeed, this is the only analogy Tyndale ever uses with reference to the relationship between God and man.[112] Therefore, it is illegitimate to impose the language of commerce upon his conception of this relationship. Tyndale never uses such language himself, and to do so is to import ideas alien to his thinking.

This family relationship is, of course, the result of the prior act of God in salvation. In *The Testament* (1535–6), Tyndale ascribes the application of salvation and its subsequent effects to the Holy Spirit who frees the believer from bondage to Satan and gives power to love and fulfil the law.[113] It is within the context of this salvation that the conditions of the covenant must be understood. In other words, initiation into the covenant by adoption is the work of God; however, once the believer is adopted, then the conditions become operative.[114]

It is clear from this that Tyndale's view of the covenant cannot accurately be described as contractual. He rejects the idea that the works merit salvation in any intrinsic way. More importantly, he bases his conception of the covenant upon the prior establishment of the familial relationship between God

---

[112] For other examples of familial imagery in this context, see ibid. 138, 167, 193; and 3. 81, 198.

[113] Ibid. 276.

[114] Cf. the comment of John Murray on the Abrahamic covenant, *The Covenant of Grace: a Biblico-Theological Study* (London, 1954): 'It is not quite congruous . . . to speak of these conditions as conditions of the covenant. For when we speak thus we are distinctly liable to be understood as implying that the covenant is not to be regarded as dispensed until the conditions are fulfilled and that the conditions are integral to the establishment of the covenant relation. And this would not provide a true or accurate account of the covenant.' While discussing Tyndale's political thought, W. D. J. Cargill Thompson makes the point that an agreement which involves mutual obligation does not mean that it is a contract but merely that it articulates the dynamics of a relationship: see 'The Two Regiments', 29–30.

and man. This relationship originates in the unilateral act of God in salvation, and is founded upon love, not commercial considerations. As a relationship founded on love and initiated by regeneration through the Holy Spirit, Tyndale's covenant concept is consistent with his earlier formulation of the relationship between God and the believer. Nevertheless, his concept is definitely conditional. If the purpose of the conditions is not to initiate salvation, then they must have relevance for the Christian life subsequent to conversion. In this context, the covenant can be seen as fulfilling two related roles. The first is that of encouraging the believer to produce good works. Earlier, in *The Mammon* (1528), Tyndale himself interpreted the conditional statements in the Bible as fulfilling just this purpose:

The scripture speaketh as a father doth to his young son, Do this or that, and then I will love thee: yet the father loveth his son first, and studieth with all his power and wit to overcome his child with love and with kindness, to make him that which is comely, honest, and good for itself. A kind father and mother love their children even when they are evil, that they would shed their blood to make them better, and to bring them into the right way.[115]

If scripture speaks in conditional terms in order to encourage the believer to produce good works, then it seems reasonable to hold that this is one reason for Tyndale speaking in the same manner. For Tyndale, salvation is seen in terms of a transformation of man's moral being, and justification has a strongly proleptic dimension. Good works are of the essence of the Christian life, and Tyndale has never regarded them as an optional extra. Indeed, several earlier statements speak of God regarding the believer as righteous if he is striving to fulfil the law. The covenant concept does not introduce the idea of works as a condition of salvation; rather, it provides a convenient framework within which to underline this ethical imperative: it is to make the sons of God obedient rather than the obedient into the sons of God.[116]

---

[115] *Works* 1. 107.

[116] The covenant has implications not only for Tyndale's doctrine of salvation but also for his sociological thought, as it serves to express the basic structure of society, and defines the relationship that exists between parent and child, master and servant, king and subject: see J. M. Mayotte, 'William Tyndale's Contribution to the Reformation in England', unpubl. Ph.D. dissertation (Marquette University, 1976), 83–92.

The second function of the covenant in salvation is as a basis for man's assurance. It is not only man who is bound by the covenant, but God as well. The covenant is not only an expression of the ethical imperative of the Christian life; it also expresses the obligation of God to save those who turn to him and love the law. Tyndale makes it clear that this is one of the reasons behind the establishment of the covenant in the following quotation from *The New Testament* (1534):

God hath promised and bound himself to us, to shew us all mercy, and to be a Father almighty to us, so that we shall not need to fear the power of all our adversaries.[117]

The covenant is therefore a revelation of God's mercy and the regulative principle of his dealings with man. The man who believes in God and loves the law can have full confidence that God will save him because God has willingly bound himself so to do. Once again, this idea introduces no new content into Tyndale's thinking. He regarded works as a basis for assurance from at least 1528, and all that he is really doing here is setting this works-based assurance within a covenantal framework.

The fact that Tyndale does not change the substance of his soteriology when he introduces the concept of covenant raises the question of why he develops the idea, and where he derives it from. Some scholars have pointed to the influence of Reformed thinking on his theology and have thus reasoned that Tyndale's covenant is the result of contact with the works of Zwingli, Oecolampadius, or Bullinger.[118] However, nothing certain is known about which Reformed works Tyndale may

---

[117] Works 1. 470.

[118] See Baker, *Heinrich Bullinger and the Covenant*, 209; Trinterud, 'The Origins of Puritanism', 40; R. L. Greaves, 'John Knox and the Covenant Tradition', *JEH* 24 (1973), 30; 'The Origins and Early Development of English Covenant Thought', *The Historian*, 31 (1968), 26–7; McGiffert, 'William Tyndale's Conception of Covenant', 181; Møller, 'The Beginnings of Puritan Covenant Theology', 51. Only McGoldrick attempts to demonstrate that the doctrine may have had Lutheran roots by quoting at second-hand the translation of a passage from Luther's work *Against Latomus*, which does indeed sound as if it could have been written by Tyndale. The original Latin reads: 'Quia pepigit deus pactum iis, qui sunt hoc modo in Christo, ut si pugnent contra seipsos et peccatum suum, nihil sit damnationis', *WA* 8. 114, 30–2; see McGoldrick, p. 132. However, Luther never develops the idea to form the central element of his theology, and he never makes works into the primary source of assurance, both characteristics of Tyndale's covenant scheme. While McGoldrick has shown that his idea of covenant is not necessarily incompatible with Luther's theology, Tyndale's

have read.[119] Furthermore, while Reformed influence is undeniable, especially as regards sacramental theology, it is evident
from the above that the major strands of Tyndale's covenant
thought were present in his thinking from an early stage.[120]
Therefore, it is not necessary to look beyond Tyndale's own
writings for the basic framework of the covenant. He may well
have adopted the term as a result of reading Reformed literature, but its principles are rooted within his own thinking.[121]
What is certain is that the idea of covenant enabled him to
express his doctrine of salvation through a motif which
provided readers of the Bible with a simple device for understanding the scriptures. This fact, above all else, would have
recommended the idea to him.

Summary

Tyndale's covenant theology emerges late in his career, but it
pulls together various theological strands that have been present
in his thinking from the late 1520s. It provides a useful hermeneutical key to unlocking the scriptures, but soteriologically
it serves to emphasize that God's relationship with man is
based upon love and upon mutual obligation. That it is based
upon love means that it cannot be correctly described as a contract, as its conditions do not function in terms of commercial
contract. That it is based upon mutual obligation indicates that

sacramental views point clearly to some kind of Reformed influence upon his thinking.
However, the statement of G. H. Greenhough that 'Bullinger, Bibliander, Bucer, and
Peter Martyr were propagating the same covenant theology that Tyndale was making
plain in England' is based upon far too simplistic an interpretation of Reformed
covenant theology and is thus far too sweeping a claim: see his article 'The Reformers'
Attitude to the Law of God', *Westminster Theological Journal* 39 (1976), 86.

[119] Clebsch points out that there is no positive evidence upon which to base
dogmatic conclusions concerning the origins of Tyndale's covenant thought: see
Clebsch, p. 199. Strehle points to the medieval aspects of Tyndale's covenant conception but regards Tyndale's sacramental theology as giving decisive indication of
some kind of Reformed influence: see *Calvinism, Federalism, and Scholasticism*, 324–8.

[120] Indeed, Tyndale may well have been influenced by his early reading of the
Enchiridion of Erasmus in this matter, as this work refers to baptism in terms of an
ethical pact: 'Etenim qui cum vitiis pacem iniit, cum Deo in baptismate percussum
foedus violavit') *Enchiridion Militis Christiani*, 43. This is similar to Tyndale's own
view: see *Works* 1. 350.

[121] The concept has several features to recommend it to Tyndale: not only is it a
biblical term for the relationship between God and man, but it also emphasizes the
unity of the two Testaments around the one way of salvation. Therefore it provides a
key for understanding scripture, which was, after all, the main concern of his career.

it is continuous with Tyndale's earlier stress upon the need for the believer to bring forth works and the use of these works as a basis for assurance. The covenant concept unifies these various concerns in a single idea. It does not introduce new substance into Tyndale's theology. The origins of Tyndale's concept are impossible to identify, although it seems more likely that they lie in Reformed theology rather than in Lutheranism.

CONCLUSION

From his earliest doctrinal writings, Tyndale's soteriology is structured towards maintaining the ethical dimension of Christianity. He regards the primary purpose of salvation to be the freeing of man's will and not the putting away of man's moral guilt. Indeed, the latter concept plays little part in his theology. As a result, his doctrine of the atonement is vague, and his emphasis falls more upon the subjective activity of the Holy Spirit within the believer than upon the objective work of Christ.

Tyndale's ethical concern also emerges in his preoccupation with the law and with works. Love for the law is fundamental to his scheme. The law, interpreted not literally but in terms of love, is normative for the Christian's conduct. In the matter of works, Tyndale argues that they flow from the believer's response of love to God's salvation and can therefore be used as an outward sign of inward justification. However, he allows his concern for ethics to override his consistency by making works not simply an assistance to, but the primary basis of, assurance. The tension this creates in his theology is not resolved by Tyndale, and leaves the way open for legalistic misconstruction of his thought.

In terms of development, there is no reason to see in Tyndale's later theology a rejection of his earlier position. His thought was always strongly ethical in orientation, and the most significant development, the covenant concept, is entirely continuous with his early position and merely gathers together various strands of his thought. There is development, certainly, but no basic change of substance.

The origins of Tyndale's thought clearly lie in both Humanism and Lutheranism. There is no evidence to suggest that he embraced the theology of the Reformation before 1524, and even after coming to Wittenberg, the distinctive ethical emphases of Humanism continued to shape his theology. The impact of Lutheranism did not lead him to reject his earlier concerns, but rather to set them within a new conceptual framework. This is indicated by Tyndale's extensive use of Luther's own writings, and by his stress upon justification by faith as the essential foundation of the Christian life. Later in his career, Tyndale was clearly subject to Reformed influences, but there is nothing in his thought, not even his view of the law that is necessarily inconsistent with Lutheranism. However, significant areas of Luther's theology, such as God's wrath against man's objective guilt, are absent from that of Tyndale.

It is therefore incorrect to characterize Tyndale as either Lutheran or Humanist, as if the influence of Luther precludes that of Erasmus. He borrowed from both, and if the influence of either had been absent, his thought would have been very different. He was a theologian who used the concepts of Luther in order to establish the ethical concerns of Humanism, and, as such, his overall position is closer in emphasis to the theology of men such as Bucer than to that of Luther.

5

John Frith

EARLY WRITINGS

FRITH'S earliest works consist of two translations of Lutheran tracts. It is impossible to know which was published first, but it appears that they were both produced in 1529. *Patrick's Places* is a translation of a short tract by the Scottish martyr, Patrick Hamilton.[1] According to Frith, the work 'entreateth exactly of certain common places, which known ye have the pith of all divinity'.[2] It consists of six sections on law, gospel, faith, hope, charity, and works. His other work, *The Revelation of Antichrist*, was published under the pseudonym of Richard Brightwell. It consists of three sections: *An Epistle unto the Christian Reader*, *The Revelation of Antichrist*, and *Antithesis Between Christ and the Pope*. Only the first of these was Frith's own work. *The Revelation* and *Antithesis* are translations of Luther's *Concerning Antichrist* (1521) and Melanchthon's *Suffering of Christ and Antichrist* (1521). The work as a whole is an attempt to contrast the work and salvation wrought by Christ with the work and teaching of the Pope. The underlying concern in both this work and *Patrick's Places* is the doctrine of justification by faith.

Law and Gospel

In *Patrick's Places* discussion of the law precedes that of the gospel, pointing towards the Lutheran nature of the treatise.[3]

---

[1] Hugh Watt argues that the form of *Patrick's Places* indicates that the tract is not a translation of Hamilton's original theses but a conflation of these and notes on the actual disputation. No original text has been found: see H. Watt, 'Hamilton's Interpretation of Luther, with Special Reference to "Patrick's Places"', in *Patrick Hamilton: First Scottish Martyr of the Reformation*, 28–36. The text of Frith's translation is in John Knox, *History of the Reformation of Religion within the Realm of Scotland*, ed. W. C. Dickinson, 2 vols. (London, 1949), vol. 2, 219–29.
[2] *Work*, 76.   [3] Cf. Melanchthon, *Loci Communes* (1521), *OM* 21. 82–227.

The purpose of the law is to command good and forbid evil.[4] This is seen most clearly in the decalogue, which can be summed up in love to God and to one's neighbour. However, man is not capable of keeping these commandments. Neither tract contains any detailed explanation of why man is not capable of doing so. In *An Epistle* Frith refers to Adam's eating of the apple as bringing condemnation on his posterity, but he does not elaborate upon the existential effects of the Fall on man's moral capabilities.[5] In Frith's earliest works, man's impotence is simply assumed.

Because man is incapable of fulfilling its demands, the law takes on a wholly negative role. The purpose of the law is to demonstrate to man that he is sinful, that he cannot save himself, and that he must therefore look outside himself for his salvation.[6] As such, the law must precede the gospel and drive a man to despair of himself before he can be saved.[7] Thus, in describing the role of the law as it relates to the unconverted man, Frith adopts a thoroughly Lutheran position.[8]

As the law condemns, so the gospel saves. For Frith, the gospel is equated with Christ. At the start of *An Epistle* he points out that the name Jesus itself means saviour,[9] and the entire discussion of salvation in these two tracts is conducted in terms of Christ and his work. As with Tyndale, Frith sees redemption as the result of Christ's objective work. One aspect of this is Christ's objective fulfilment of the law on behalf of man.[10] The other aspect is his death, the payment of the penalty merited by man's sin. Unlike Tyndale, however, Frith places great emphasis upon the element of atonement in Christ's death and does give some detail as to how this relates to redemption. Indeed, it is this aspect of Christ's work to which most attention is devoted in the two tracts. In *Patrick's Places*, there are twenty-four statements given which are said to summarize the gospel. Of these, ten refer to Christ's death or to his pacification of the Father. The other fourteen consist of vague statements to the effect that Christ is a saviour but do not explain how he is such.[11]

[4] See Dickinson, p. 220.   [5] See Russell, p. 464.
[6] See Dickinson, p. 221   [7] See Russell, p. 461.
[8] The idea is clearly Lutheran in origin, but it is Augustine whom Frith quotes as support for his case, using passages from Letter 167 (to Jerome) and *Confessiones*: PL 33. 739; 32. 796.
[9] See Russell, p. 460.   [10] Ibid. 462.
[11] See Dickinson, pp. 221–2.

Therefore, it is clear that Hamilton sees the death of Christ as the single most important element in redemption. That this is also true of Frith is indicated by his emphasis upon atonement in *An Epistle*. He expresses this doctrine in the following passage:

God hath given us eternal life, and this life is in his Son, which was made our beast, bearing our sins upon his own back, made obedient unto the death, offering up our iniquities (as a sacrifice) unto his Father, being our mediator and atonement between his Father and us. . . . So that sin hath no power over us, nor can condemn us; or our satisfaction is made in Christ, which died for us that were wicked, and naturally the children of wrath even as well as the other.[12]

From this passage it is clear that Frith sees Christ's atonement as lying at the heart of the gospel. Elsewhere in the tract, he mentions that in Christ God punished sin in the flesh and it is through this act that we are saved.[13] Related to this are his references to the wrath of God against sin and against sinners.[14] Indeed, Frith consistently links the concept of the sinner's guilt, implicit in the idea of God's wrath against sin, with Christ's work of atonement. Thus, Frith frames this doctrine in terms of different theological emphases from those of Tyndale, who stresses not man's guilt so much as his moral bondage to sin.

Faith and Works

Law and gospel are antithetical in salvation. The law demands that man should do something that he cannot do. The gospel, on the other hand, requires that man believe in Christ. It is this belief in Christ, this faith, that saves.

Frith always speaks of faith as belief in a person. Tyndale sometimes speaks of faith as trust in Christ, but more often emphasizes that it is belief in the promises. He has no clearly defined doctrine of atonement, and frequently fails to link God's promises of mercy with the work of Christ. Sometimes, therefore, he appears to base salvation upon the merciful character of God rather than upon the work of Christ.

There is no such ambiguity in Frith's work: faith is belief in Christ.[15] While this includes belief in those promises given in

---

[12] Russell, p. 462.   [13] See Russell, p. 460.
[14] See Dickinson, pp. 222, 223; Russell, pp. 461, 462, 463.
[15] See Dickinson, p. 224; Russell, p. 459.

Christ, Frith never discusses the promises outside the context of Christ's work. However, it is not enough simply to believe that Christ is Saviour: the devils do that and tremble; they understand the atonement which he wrought upon the cross, but they are damned.[16] True faith, on the other hand, is a gift from God and is not within the natural powers of fallen man.[17] As such, it differs radically from mere historical faith:

It is not therefore sufficient to believe that he is a Saviour and Redeemer, but that he is a Saviour and Redeemer unto thee; and this canst thou not confess, except thou knowledge thyself to be a sinner, for he that thinketh, himself no sinner, needeth no Saviour and Redeemer.[18]

Faith therefore involves the believer accepting his own sinfulness before God and then trusting that he is saved solely for the sake of Christ. In this manner, true faith is distinguished from a mere intellectual assent to the truth of the gospel. The distinction is the same as that drawn by Luther.[19] It is also similar to that made by Tyndale and Barnes.

Frith's emphasis upon Christ embraces both the believer's conversion and subsequent life. Faith saves because it effects the union of the believer to Christ. Salvation has been objectively accomplished by Christ, and it is as the believer is united to him, and continues in union with him, that this salvation becomes a subjective reality. Frith quotes Eph. 2: 4–9 and Rom. 7: 4 in support of this.[20] That God loves sinners only through Christ and in Christ is the key to Frith's whole doctrine of salvation. It is true that he does not elaborate this doctrine to include the Lutheran idea of the glorious exchange of righteousness and sin between Christ and the believer, but his doctrine is no less centred on Christ.[21]

Combined with the idea that salvation is by faith alone is Frith's unequivocal assertion that works cannot and do not

[16] See Russell, p. 460.
[17] See Dickinson, p. 223; Russell, p. 462, where Frith quotes Eph. 2: 8.
[18] Russell, p. 460.   [19] See Althaus, *The Theology of Martin Luther*, 230.
[20] See Russell, pp. 462, 465.
[21] Ibid. 460, 462, 464, 466. This is another point of contrast with the theological emphases of Tyndale. Tyndale's doctrine of salvation is centred in the presence of the Holy Spirit within the believer. This reflects his concern with the effects of salvation and is indicative of the more subjective orientation of his theology than that of Frith: see Ch. 4.

save. Indeed, Frith accuses those who try to justify themselves by their works of making themselves into Christs.[22] Faith is the fundamental prerequisite to the performance of good works, and no work done without faith is good.[23]

For Frith, the fundamental purpose of salvation, as expressed in Rom. 7: 4, is that man should bring forth good works as the fruits of his faith. Thus Frith, like Tyndale, exhibits ethical purpose in the construction of his doctrine of salvation. In *Patrick's Places*, Hamilton uses the biblical analogy of the tree and its fruit, and this provides the basis for Frith's understanding of the position of good works in the life of the Christian.[24] He describes the means whereby the believer is enabled to perform such works in the following passage which is permeated with imagery drawn from Romans:

But ye, dear brethren, are made dead as concerning the law, by the body of Christ, that ye should be coupled to him that is risen again from death, that we should bring forth fruit unto God; for when we were under the law, the lusts of sin which were stirred up reigned in our members, to bring forth fruit unto death. But now we are delivered from the law, and dead from it, whereunto we were in bondage, that we should serve in a new conversation of the Spirit, and not in the old conversation of the letter.[25]

Once again, Frith's thought is clearly constructed around Christ. In this passage, the believer's union with Christ provides the foundation for the practical morality of the Christian life. This is because in Christ the believer has died to the law and been raised to new life, and is now dead to the law. In

---

[22] See Dickinson, p. 228.

[23] Ibid. 225; cf. *WA* 7. 60, 23–9.

[24] 'XIII: He that hath the faith, is just and good. And a good tree bringeth forth good fruit. Ergo, all that is in faith done pleaseth God.' Dickinson, p. 223. Clebsch makes the following comment on this article: 'In order to view the document [*Patrick's Places*] in a form true to the original, the reader of more modern works must rely on the title and preface from Foxe and on the body of the work from Knox, or else Hamilton's and (presumably) Frith's theological conviction that "all that is in faith done pleaseth God" will read "he that hath faith is just and good"—a substantial variation', *England's Earliest Protestants*, 84–5. As N. T. Wright notes, both phrases occur in all editions of the work, which is not surprising as they form two parts of a syllogism. There is no 'substantial variation' between the two ideas, as the syllogism and the tree analogy demonstrate. Both ideas are also entirely consistent with the Lutheranism that Clebsch himself regards Frith as espousing: see *WA* 7. 59, 37–60, 29.

[25] Russell, p. 465.

dealing with this, Frith employs the Augustinian/Lutheran distinction of the Letter and the Spirit. In opposition to those exegetes who followed Origen in identifying the Letter with the literal sense and the Spirit with allegorical sense(s), Frith follows Luther in referring the former to the law which kills and the latter to the grace of the gospel which gives freedom from the law.[26] This freedom from the law is not the basis for antinomianism but rather the basis for bringing fruit forth unto God. In *Patrick's Places*, faith is emphasized as the basis of two other virtues: hope and charity. Hope refers to the life to come, and derives from faith. Charity derives from both, and has reference towards one's neighbour:

Charity is the love of thy neighbour. The rule of charity is to do as thou wouldst were done unto thee: for charity esteemeth all alike; the rich and the poor; the friend and the foe; the thankful and the unthankful; the kinsman and stranger.[27]

Charity is the basis of the decalogue, and thus Frith's understanding of the law is in fundamental agreement with that of Luther and Tyndale.[28] He also agrees with them on the basis for love towards God and towards one's neighbour: this is the realization through faith of all that God in Christ has endured for the sake of sinners.[29] However, he does differ from Tyndale in the manner in which he expresses the ethical activity of the believer. The idea of following in Christ's footsteps occurs in *Patrick's Places* as it does in Tyndale's works. Unlike Tyndale, however, Frith does not talk here of the believer loving, or striving to fulfil, the law. Instead, he refers only to the believer as being dead to the law. It is arguable that the difference is slight, in that both men hold substantially to the same ethical principle, that of love to God and to one's neighbour. However, Frith's terminology ensures that a clear distinction between law and gospel is maintained, a distinction which Tyndale's language tends to blur. As such, the tone of Frith's language is closer to that of Luther than is that of Tyndale.

While faith causes a change in man's moral being, and leads him to perform works of love, it does not make man instantly perfect. The believer carries around within him the remnant of

[26] See Russell, p. 465; cf. *WA* 7. 653, 35–654, 8.
[27] Dickinson, p. 226.
[28] See Dickinson, p. 220; for Tyndale, see Ch. 4.
[29] See Dickinson, p. 228.

his sinful nature which strives continually against the new man. For this reason, Frith argues, it is necessary for the believer to pray continually to God for forgiveness and for the power to be righteous:

We know that as long as we live in this world, we carry about with us the old man of sin, which (without he be by continual diligence suppressed and mortified) besiegeth the new man with his venom and concupiscences. . . . Since then we cannot be without this old man of sin . . . yet let us do our diligence, calling for the Spirit of God, that this concupiscence reign not in our mortal body, ever knowledging, with a mild heart, our iniquities to our Father which is in heaven, for he is faithful and just to remit us our sins, and to purge us from all iniquity, through the blood of Jesus Christ his Son.[30]

In this passage, Frith characterizes salvation in terms of two elements: the remission of sins and the purging of the believer. Both of these are to be fundamental in his later attack upon the doctrine of purgatory. It is clear even at this early stage in Frith's career that he conceives of salvation not simply as a matter of dealing with sin in an objective sense, but also as leading to an actual purging of the believer through the Spirit of God.

Summary

Frith develops his early soteriology in terms of a basic law–gospel opposition. The law condemns, while the gospel gives life. Frith identifies Christ as the gospel, and makes him the centre of his soteriology. He regards God's righteous wrath against sin as the decisive element in the work of Christ, and so emphasizes the cross as a propitiatory sacrifice and as the focus of Christ's redemptive work. In so doing, he advocates an understanding of the atonement which is both more detailed than and somewhat different from that of Tyndale.

Salvation is appropriated through faith, which is the gift of God. Frith describes faith in terms more Christocentric than those of Tyndale, speaking more often of belief in Christ himself rather than of belief in the promises associated with him. Faith effects a union of the believer with Christ, and out of this union flow good works, motivated by the love that flows from belief in Christ. These works are to be directed towards one's neighbour in his need.

[30] Russell, pp. 465–6.

FRITH BEFORE IMPRISONMENT

Before his imprisonment, John Frith wrote two original treatises. The first of these, *A Disputation of Purgatory*, was published in 1531 was Frith's first major polemical work, an attack upon the Catholic doctrine of purgatory. The work consists of a preface and three major sections. Each of these replies to a different advocate of the doctrine of purgatory: in the first, Frith replies to John Rastell, who argued for purgatory with rational arguments in his *New Book of Purgatory* (1530); in the second, Frith refutes the attempt made to establish the doctrine by Thomas More, who used texts of scripture to prove his case in the book *The Supplication of Souls* (1529); and in the third section, he attacks the patristic evidence for the doctrine presented by John Fisher in his anti-Lutheran work, *Confutation of Lutheran Assertions* (1523).

Frith's second work, a commentary on *Tracy's Testament*, was found among the papers of William Tyndale after the latter's arrest. The tract was probably written some time after Frith's last return to England in July 1532, but before his arrest in October of that year. Tyndale too wrote a commentary on William Tracy's will, and thus Frith's work is important because it offers an opportunity for a direct comparison of the theological approaches of the two men.

The Development of the Doctrine of Purgatory

In selecting purgatory as the subject for his first polemical treatise, Frith would appear to have made an unusual choice of doctrine for debate. After all, did not Luther himself refer to purgatory as a 'trifle' compared to the bondage of man's will?[31] However, in order to understand Frith's choice, it is necessary to have some knowledge of the history of the doctrine of purgatory. Such knowledge reveals that Catholic teaching on this matter had important implications for the doctrine of salvation, and that in striking at such teaching, Frith was able to expound his own soteriological convictions.

The doctrine of purgatory has its roots in the patristic era, although it was not defined in any systematic way until medieval

---

[31] This well-known remark occurs at the close of *De Servo Arbitrio*: *Studienausgabe* 3. 355.

times. Augustine, in *The Enchiridion*, ch. 69, refers to the idea of a purification for some believers after death, the length of which will be determined by the degree to which they have loved.[32] Later, in *The City Of God* 21:13 he is slightly more specific, allowing for a time before the final judgement when sins unremitted in this life can be purged away.[33] Gregory the Great (*c*.540–603) also refers to this kind of idea in *Dialogues*, 4, stating that purgatory is where man's 'lesser' sins are burned away, using 1 Cor. 3: 12–15 as biblical support for his position.[34]

The difference between the purgatory advocated by Augustine and Gregory and that developed by the scholastic theologians lay in the fact that the patristic writers discussed purgatory primarily in terms of eschatology; it was not until Peter Lombard (*c*.1100–59) that the doctrine became linked to the idea of penance. Lombard's argument, *Sentences* 4: 21, was that for a venial sin to be remitted it had to be both repented of and abandoned by the believer. Because it was not possible for every sin in this life to be dealt with in such a way, some venial sins would have to be remitted after death in purgatory.[35] While Lombard utilizes the sayings of Augustine and Gregory, he goes further than they did by providing a dogmatic foundation for their statements in the doctrine of penance.

In his commentary on Lombard's *Sentences* 4: 21, Thomas Aquinas (1225–74) deduces purgatory from the reference in 2 Macc. 12: 46 concerning prayers for the dead. As there is no need to pray for the dead in heaven, and it would be useless to pray to those in hell, the reference must be to purgatory.[36] The punishment is twofold: the withholding of the beatific vision, and the punishment of the body by fire.[37] Thus purgatory is partly retributive and partly purifying. However, as eternal life is the end result, purgation is ultimately a positive process. Aquinas is, however, concerned to maintain salvation by grace. Obviously, if man's sufferings in purgatory earn the remission of his sins, then salvation is no longer by grace. In order to avoid such a conclusion, therefore, Aquinas makes a distinction between the guilt pertaining to a sin and its required punishment. The former can be remitted only by an act of God's grace.[38]

---

[32] See *PL* 40. 265. [33] Ibid. 41. 728. [34] Ibid. 77. 396.
[35] Ibid. 192. 896–7. [36] *Scriptum super Sententiis* 4. 21. 1. 1.
[37] Ibid. 20. 1. 1. [38] *De Malo*, 7. 12.

Thus purgatory is concerned with the punishment of sin and not the remission of guilt.

In the later Middle Ages, purgatory became linked with the treasury of merits and then with the concept of indulgences. In the bull *Unigenitus* of Clement VI, issued in January, 1343, the treasury of merits was made the basis for indulgences, and this was extended and applied to souls in purgatory by the bull *Salvator noster* of Sixtus IV in August 1476.[39] It was this doctrine that provoked Luther to draw up his Ninety-Five Theses, although it was not until 1530 that he rejected the idea of purgatory outright.[40]

Zwingli, however, opposed the doctrine from an early stage. It was attacked in both the *Articles* of 1523 and in the *Commentary on True and False Religion* (1525).[41] In both works he rejected the doctrine on exegetical grounds.

This brief historical survey clearly reveals that the doctrine of purgatory touched on areas of crucial importance to Reformation debate, especially in its relation to salvation where it had implications regarding the nature of sin, the efficacy of Christ's work on the cross, the application of this to the believer, the motivation for good works, and the idea of merit. In the light of this, Frith's choice of purgatory as a subject for a treatise is understandable. The doctrine had received extensive treatment at the hands of English Catholics and no doubt Frith saw his treatise as a means of helping his fellow countrymen to realize the errors which underpinned and reinforced the doctrine.[42] More importantly, however, Frith undoubtedly saw the subject as lending itself to a positive exposition of his own doctrine of salvation.

[39] B. J. Kidd, *Documents Illustrative of the Continental Reformation* (Oxford, 1911), 1–4.

[40] Luther's Ninety-Five Theses were motivated not by opposition to the doctrine of purgatory, but by opposition to the notion that remission of sins could be purchased for money: see Bainton, *Here I Stand*, 81.

[41] See Zwingli, Z III, 855–67.

[42] It is also possible that Frith's background in Lollardy may have influenced his choice of purgatory as a topic for debate. While Wyclif and early Lollards do not appear to have been greatly exercised by the doctrine, by 1462 discussion of purgatory was not uncommon. As the doctrine took on more importance as a subject of debate in the Reformation, it is likely that Lollards continued to discuss the doctrine: see A. Hudson, *The Premature Reformation* (Oxford, 1988), 309–10. Frith's tract would therefore have been a timely contribution to the debate.

Frith's 'Two Purgatories'

Frith's concept of the two purgatories is fundamental to his doctrine of salvation. He expounds this idea in the preface to *A Disputation* in order to demonstrate that such a doctrine renders the Catholic purgatory obsolete. Instead of a place of purification in the after-life, Frith declares that there are two purgatories: the word of God; and the cross of Christ. He defines the purgatory of the word as follows:

God hath left us two purgatories; one to purge the heart and cleanse it from the filth which we have partly received of Adam, (for we are by nature the children of wrath, Ephes. 2) and partly by adding thereto by consenting unto our natural infirmity. This purgatory is the word of God, as Christ saith, (John 15) Now are ye clean for the word which I have spoken unto you. This purgation obtaineth no man but through faith, for the unfaithful are not purged by the word of God, as the Scribes and Pharisees were nothing the better for hearing his word, but rather the worse, for it was a testimony against them unto their condemnation. And because we receive this purgation only through believing the word, therefore is the virtue of this purging applied also unto faith; for Peter saith, (Acts 15) That the Gentiles' hearts were purged through faith, that is to say, through believing the word. And what word is that? verily the preaching that Christ's death hath fully satisfied for our sins, and pacified for ever the Father's wrath towards us etc. This faith purifieth the heart, and giveth us a will and gladness to do whatsoever our most merciful Father commandeth us.[43]

Three important aspects of Frith's thought are contained in this passage: the centrality of Christ; the importance of faith; and the existential effects of salvation.

The centrality of Christ is emphasized by Frith's identification of him and his death with the saving word of God. In *Tracy's Testament*, he argues that Christ's person is essential to salvation because of the task he is to fulfil in redemption, that of mid-dealer between God and man. Essential to this office is the fact that Christ is both human and divine. Were he not so, he would not be able to act as intermediary: if he were mere man, he himself would require to be saved, but as God-man he is able to merit salvation and communicate it to others.[44]

---

[43] See Russell, p. 90.
[44] Ibid. 249, where Christ is described as 'mid-dealer' between God and man.

However, Christ's incarnation does not in itself accomplish salvation. Frith points to Heb. 9: 22 as proof that the shedding of blood is necessary in order for there to be remission of sins. Thus, it was necessary for Christ to die in order to accomplish salvation.[45] Frith is also careful to link Christ's death to his doctrine of God. Rastell argued that God's omnipotency means that he might forgive sin without any satisfaction being made, if he so desired.[46] Frith rejects this by asserting that God's omnipotency must be seen in terms of his essential righteousness. He argues that no one attribute of God can be regarded as independent from the others as all are carefully balanced in relation to each other. Thus, it is impossible for God's omnipotency to act in a way that contradicts his righteousness. This righteousness has been offended by sin and must be satisfied before sin can be remitted.[47] This satisfaction is found in the blood of Christ alone, which Frith specifically links to the pacification of God's wrath:

But the whole cause of the remission of our sins, and of our salvation, is the blood of Christ, which hath fully counterpoised the justice of God the Father and hath pacified his wrath towards us that believe.[48]

By making God's righteousness the decisive factor in Christ's work of atonement, Frith reveals his difference from Tyndale. Tyndale is vague on atonement, focusing on the significance of Christ's death as God's basis for freeing the will and not as the propitiation of God's wrath. This reflects his general emphasis upon the subjective aspects of Christianity. Frith, however, formulates his doctrine of atonement primarily in terms of objective theological truth. As a result, the necessity for the atonement is defined more clearly in his theology than that of Tyndale, and emphasis is placed upon the objective aspects of Christ and his work rather than subsequent subjective effects within the believer.

---

[45] See Russell, p. 117.

[46] It appears that the idea underlying Rastell's statement here is that of the dialectic between God's absolute power and his ordained power which was a standard element of the theology of the *via moderna*: see A. E. McGrath, *The Intellectual Origins of the European Reformation* (Oxford, 1987), 77–85.

[47] 'If God have an absolute justice, then cannot his absolute power prevail until his absolute justice be fully counterpoised.' Russell, p. 130.

[48] Russell, p. 124.

The second important aspect of Frith's view of the word as purgatory is the role which he ascribes to faith. For the word to be effective, it must be received by faith. Frith states this clearly in *Tracy's Testament*:

This death of the merciful Lord cannot profit me, except I receive it through faith; and therefore he reckoneth right well that the faith in Christ is all his merit, I mean the faith that worketh through charity, that is to say, faith formed with hope and charity, and not the dead historical faith which the devils have and tremble.[49]

There are two aspects of this passage that merit further enquiry: the way in which Christ's death profits the believer; and the use of the term 'formed' with reference to faith.

Frith allows that although the believer will always see himself as a sinner, once he has received the word by faith, he is righteous before God because God will not impute his sins to him:

in our own sight, we find ourselves sinners. . . . But he maketh us blessed and righteous, and imputeth not our sins unto us.[50]

That Frith believed that salvation involved the non-imputation of sin is clear, but it is not quite so clear as to whether he held to the related doctrine of the imputation of Christ's righteousness. Clebsch denies that Frith does, but he fails to discuss the central passage in this matter.[51] This occurs when Frith is answering More's objection that, if the prayers of saints cannot profit the believer, then neither can those of Christ. In responding to this, Frith constructs a series of antitheses between Christ and Adam. The tenth of these reads as follows:

10: Through Adam, Adam's sin is counted our own. 10: Through Christ, Christ's righteousness is reputed unto us for our own.[52]

Frith's thought here appears to be similar to that contained in his earlier concept of union with Christ, whereby the believer is united to Christ by faith. Then, Christ deals with God on man's behalf, and man is thus saved by virtue of this union. Such an interpretation appears to do justice to Frith's own paralleling here of Adam and Christ, where the whole foundation of the antitheses is that God deals with man in terms

---

[49] Ibid. 251.   [50] Ibid. 118.
[51] See Clebsch, p. 115.   [52] Russell, p. 179.

either of Adam or of Christ. Frith does not develop the idea of imputation elsewhere and neither does he refer to Christ receiving man's sins in exchange for his righteousness. It seems reasonable to regard the above quotation as a reference to the results of Frith's earlier concept of union with Christ rather than as a significant development in his theology.[53]

The second point of interest concerns Frith's use of the term 'formed faith'. Indeed, his use of the phrase is in contrast with the attitude of other Reformers who rejected the term as part of scholastic sophistry.[54] Seen in this light, Frith does appear to be making something of a concession to his Catholic opponents. However, in actual fact it probably indicates little more than a desire to, communicate his ideas using Catholic language in order to avoid unnecessary debate about terminology and to focus instead upon theological content. Such an interpretation is strengthened by the fact that he describes false faith as historical, not unformed faith. To use the term unformed faith would probably involve conceding too much to his opponents. Implicit in the formed/unformed distinction is the idea that it is the form (i.e. love) that makes the difference between the faith which saves and that which does not.[55] In his discussion of faith in the *Loci*, Melanchthon rejected the scholastic distinction on the grounds that faith without love was imaginary and hypocritical. It was not the result of the Holy Spirit's work and thus bore no relation to true faith. Therefore, use of the scholastic distinction would serve only to blur the radical difference between that faith which is from the Spirit and that which is only intellectual assent.[56] Therefore, in adopting the term 'formed' without its antithesis, 'unformed',

---

[53] McGrath comments that the 'parallelism between Adam's sin and Christ's righteousness is evidently constructed on the basis of Augustinian presuppositions, rather than those of later Lutheranism.' *Iustitia Dei*, 2. 227 n. 8. He gives no indication of what he means by 'Augustinian presuppositions' and ignores the idea of union with Christ that Frith expounded earlier. Thus, in arguing against the idea that Frith holds to the later Lutheran idea of imputation, he would seem to be both refuting an interpretation of Frith that no scholar has ever advocated and failing to set Frith's thought here within the larger context of his theology.

[54] e.g. Melanchthon, *OM* 21. 160, where he expresses his utter contempt for the various scholastic distinctions in the matter of faith.

[55] See Vos, *Aquinas*, 32.

[56] See *OM* 21. 161–2. Frith's use of the term 'historical' suggests the influence of Melanchthon.

Frith is conceding as much as he can to his opponents without obscuring the fundamental uniqueness of true, saving faith.

Throughout his discussions of faith, Frith is concerned to emphasize that it has inevitable existential implications for the believer. By leading to hope and love, faith effects a fundamental change in the believer's outlook. This is the third aspect of the first purgatory: not only does the word received by faith lead to the remission of sin, it also changes man's will and gives him a desire to obey God. Frith's thought here is similar to that of Tyndale, although the latter devotes more attention to this theme, seeing the renewal of the will as the central aspect of redemption. There are also differences of emphasis in their respective formulations of this doctrine. While Tyndale focuses on the work of the Holy Spirit in freeing the believer's will, Frith, with a characteristically Christ-centred approach, emphasizes faith in Christ as purifying the heart and thus leading to good works. Another difference is that Tyndale speaks of the will being loosed, implying that its bondage was the result of sin and that this is rectified by redemption. This understanding is closer to that of Augustine than that of Luther. Frith, however, does not speak of the will being loosed, only of God giving man a new will that desires to do as God commands. There is just a hint here that Frith is closer than Tyndale to Luther on this issue. However, these differences should not obscure the fact that both men agree that justification by faith leads to love of God and the consequent performance of good works.

In his development of the idea of the word as the first purgatory, Frith points to three important aspects of his soteriology: the doctrines of the person and work of Christ, which are constructed in relation to theological considerations; the centrality of faith in apprehending the benefits of Christ's objective work; and the existential change wrought in man which flows directly from faith. However, Frith also argues for a second purgatory: the cross of Christ.

Because the believer retains much of his old, sinful nature, God has appointed a second purgatory to help him in overcoming this moral imperfection:

Nevertheless, because our infirmity is so great, and our members so weak and frail that we cannot eschew sin as our heart would, and as our will desireth; therefore hath God left us another purgatory, which is Christ's cross: I mean not his material cross that he himself died on, but a spiritual cross, which is adversity, tribulation, worldly depression, etc. And this is called the rod or scourge of God, wherewith he scourgeth every son that he receiveth, that we remember his law, and mortify the old Adam and fleshly lust, which else would wax so rebellious that it would subdue us, reign in us, and hold us thralled under sin.[57]

Frith clearly indicates here that the Christian life involves striving for actual righteousness, and that salvation is no mere legal fiction. While the first purgatory is primarily concerned with man's state before God, this second concept involves man's actual moral being. Sin is to be beaten down within the believer through suffering, suffering which finds its archetype in the agony of Christ upon the cross. While Christ's person and work point to the uniqueness of his suffering, the fact that Christ did suffer provides a paradigm for the believer. As Christ triumphed over sin in an objective sense upon the cross of Calvary, the believer must overcome his own sin through the spiritual cross of suffering. It is through this suffering that Christ's once-for-all triumph over sin is actualized within the believer.

The affinities with Luther's theology at this point are obvious. Luther too argues for Christ's death as both a once-for-all event whereby sin was conquered, and as an example, prescribing the way of the Christian as the way of suffering. These sufferings are appropriated by faith and form part of the believer's union with Christ. Indeed, they are actually a revelation of God's special love towards the believer. While Luther's expression of this doctrine frequently refers to the idea of Christ within the believer, a point not brought out by Frith, the two men are nevertheless in substantial agreement here.[58]

In the concept of the two purgatories Frith provides a comprehensive and thoroughly christocentric foundation for man's redemption in terms of both his status before God and his moral being. He holds firmly to the idea that it is only Christ who has merited redemption by appeasing God's wrath, and it is only as we are united with him through faith that he can act as mid-dealer for us with God the Father. He also regards faith as giving man a desire to do God's bidding, and argues that this

---

[57] Russell, pp. 90–1.
[58] See Althaus, *The Theology of Martin Luther*, 211–18.

will is aided by suffering, which mortifies the old man. He describes this suffering in terms of a spiritual cross, and this idea is very similar to that of Luther whereby the believer is to actualize Christ's victory over sin within his own life. Indeed, in his twofold emphasis upon the word of God and the cross of Christ, Frith's doctrine of the two purgatories clearly suggests the strong impact of Luther's thought upon his theology.

The Role of Works

Having emphasized so strongly that salvation has been objectively accomplished by Christ, Frith has to deal with the accusation that his doctrine undermines the need for good works. In responding to this, he points out that, while his doctrine does preclude certain incorrect motives for doing good works, it also establishes firm and correct reasons for the Christian to live a good life.

Frith regards the main error concerning the motive for doing good works to be the belief that they merit salvation. He rejects this on two counts: first, it is in effect a rejection of the idea that only Christ has merited salvation for man; secondly, it contradicts the whole concept of predestination:

Christ is given thee freely, and with him hast thou all things. He is thy wisdom, righteousness, hallowing, and redemption. . . . By him art thou made inheritor of God and fellow heir with Christ. . . . This is freely given thee with Christ before thou wast born, through the favour and election of God, which election was done before the foundations of the world were cast. . . . Now wert thou very fond and unkind, if thou thoughtest to purchase by thy works the very thing which is already given thee.[59]

Thus predestination precludes any notion that works can merit salvation. Salvation has already been given to individuals before even the world was created, and therefore before the performance of good works. The use of predestination in such an axiomatic manner might seem to suggest that Frith is a strong predestinarian. Certainly it is undeniable that Frith is here expressing the view that salvation is predetermined. However, like Tyndale, he leaves the doctrine undeveloped in terms of reprobation and the extent of election. Functionally too he

[59] Russell, pp. 137–8.

does not develop the doctrine or use it in other contexts as a theological axiom: it serves only to underline his contention that works are not to be done in order to merit heaven. In this context, the doctrine is not a matter for speculation, but simply something to be accepted.

A second incorrect reason for doing good works is that of fear. Rastell argued that to deny purgatory is to remove the threat of punishment for sin from believers and encourages them to be less diligent in doing good works. Frith is contemptuous of such a position, and replies that it is not fear that should motivate the believer but love towards God.[60] Thus, it is love, not fear or desire of gain, which provides the correct motive for works.

Having dismissed these false motives, Frith summarises his view of the necessity of good works in the following passage:

Peradventure thou wilt say unto me, shall I then do no good works? I answer, Yes. Thou wilt ask me, Wherefore? I answer, Thou must do them, because God hath commanded them. Thou wilt say, For what intent hath he commanded them? I answer, Because thou art living in this world, and must needs have conversation with men, therefore hath God appointed thee what thou shalt do to the profit of thy neighbour, and the taming of thy flesh.[61]

Here Frith indicates that it is God's will which is the decisive factor in making works necessary, and that this should, in itself, be sufficient. However, he does not stop here but points to the rational basis for God so doing: it is because man still lives in society and has to relate to others; and because he is still sinful and needs to mortify his flesh. The latter idea is closely related to Frith's concept of the second purgatory: it is the believer's duty to actualize Christ's conquest of sin in his experience. As such, Frith's statement simply reaffirms his position.

The former idea affirms that, viewed teleologically, works are not performed for God's benefit, but for the benefit of our neighbours. This is the same basic position which was advocated in *Patrick's Places* (1529). The idea is expressed in terms very

[60] See Russell, p. 119. Cf. Augustine's thought in Letter 145: 4: 'Inimicus . . . justitiae est, qui poenae timore non peccat: amicus autem erit, si ejus amore non peccat; tunc enim vere timebit peccare. Nam qui gehennas metuit, non peccare metuit, sed ardere', *PL* 33. 594.
[61] Russell, p. 137.

close to those of Luther who also stressed that man's relationship to his fellow men in this world necessitated that he direct his good works towards them.[62] In the above quotation, Frith echoes this position.[63] For both men, the motive for these works is to be the believer's love towards his neighbour, which is itself the result of justification by faith. Indeed, both Luther and Frith also regard God's gracious dealings with man in salvation as the paradigm for the believer's dealings with his neighbour: when God sent Christ to redeem man, he acted out of unconditional love and with no thought for personal gain; therefore, man must be similarly motivated when he performs good works. In this way, the believer is said to be a Christ to his neighbour, a phrase found in Luther and adopted by Frith.[64] For Frith, the ultimate purpose of these works is that our neighbours should be brought to glorify God.[65]

Frith also places the necessity of works within the framework of a twofold satisfaction. Satisfaction to God is found only in the blood of Christ, but that to our neighbours is found in dealing with them as God deals with us. If a man has offended us, we are to forgive him; if we have stolen anything, we are to return it. This idea leads Frith to talk of works in a manner which is very similar to the conditional covenant scheme of Tyndale:

[62] *WA* 7. 64, 14–23.

[63] Frith expresses the single purpose and motivation of works in the following passage: 'Therefore must thou do thy works with a single eye, having neither respect unto the joys of heaven, neither yet to the pains of hell; but only do them for the profit of thy neighbour, as God commandeth thee, and let him alone with the residue', Russell, p. 138.

[64] 'Igitur sicut proximus noster necessitatem habet et nostra abundantia indiget, ita et nos coram deo necessitatem habuimus et misericordia eius indiguimus: ideo sicut pater coelestis nobis in Christo gratis auxiliatus est, ita et nos debemus gratis per corpus et opera eius proximo nostro auxiliari et unusquisque alteri Christus quidam fieri, ut simus mutuum Christi et Christus idem in omnibus, hoc est, vere Christiani', *WA* 7. 66, 23–8; 'And so are they [works] both profitable for thy neighbour, and also a testimony unto thee, by the which men may know that thou art the right son of thy heavenly Father, and a very Christ unto thy neighbour: and even as our heavenly Father gave his Christ unto us, not for any profit that he should have thereby, but only for our profit, likewise thou shouldest do all thy good works, not having respect what commodities thou shalt have of it, but ever attending, through charity, the wealth and the profit of thy neighbour', Russell, p. 137. Tyndale also refers to Christ as the pattern for works, but his emphasis is not upon the motivation of God the Father in sending Christ, but upon Christ's motivation in performing his various acts of mercy while living on earth. Thus, Tyndale's approach is closer to that of Erasmus than to that of Luther.

[65] See Russell, p. 137. This idea is implicit in the quotation from Luther in the previous note. It is also present in the thought of Tyndale, *Works* 1. 24.

God forgiveth no man which had offended his neighbour, unless that he make satisfaction unto his neighbour, if he be able; but if he be not able, yet is he bound to acknowledge his fault unto his neighbour, and then is thy neighbour bound, under the pain of damnation, to forgive him, so that God never forgiveth until thy neighbour be pacified in case the crime extend unto thy neighbour.[66]

In this statement, Frith makes God's forgiveness of the sinner dependent upon the sinner's forgiveness of his neighbour. However, Frith does not express this idea using the covenant motif, nor does he place any great emphasis upon the idea in his theology as whole. References to the relationship between works and forgiveness as being conditional are rare in his writings, and he does not follow Tyndale into making works a basis for assurance. Instead, he chooses to place most stress upon Christ and faith. Nevertheless, the above quotation does reflect a desire to maintain the absolute necessity of good works in the believer's life. This points to the inaccuracy of Clebsch's simplistic distinction between Frith and Tyndale in terms of a single-minded emphasis upon faith as opposed to a single-minded emphasis upon morality. Frith may emphasize faith, but this is not to the complete exclusion of works.

The idea of twofold satisfaction lies behind Frith's assertion of a twofold justification in *Tracy's Testament* (1532). Clebsch claims that this document reveals a theological breach between Frith and Tyndale which is so great that it probably accounts for the fact that the latter did not publish the work.[67] This difference, according to Clebsch, concerns the notion of double justification.

There are several problems with Clebsch's approach. His use of the term 'double justification' is itself thoroughly misleading, as it automatically implies substantial similarity between the doctrine expounded by Tyndale and that doctrine commonly understood by the term. This latter was expounded by

---

[66] Russell, p. 129.

[67] See Clebsch, p. 107. There is absolutely no corroborative evidence for such a claim. Tyndale and Frith remained on good terms until the latter's death in 1533, as evidenced by their surviving correspondence: see *Work*, 492–8. The fact that Tyndale did not publish Frith's work may mean little more than he had not had an opportunity so to do, or that he intended to publish it along with his own commentary. Either of these propositions is more likely than the interpretation of Clebsch, as it will become clear that the alleged theological breach did not actually exist.

Catholic theologians such as Contarini, Morone, and Pole at the Council of Trent. These men asserted a doctrine whereby both Christ and man's works provided formal bases for justification.[68] Thus, the term carries certain technical connotations, and so it is necessary first of all to prove that such terminology is applicable in the case of Tyndale before it can be legitimately used to characterize his position. If this is not done, then concepts alien to his thought will immediately be imposed upon his theology.

In the case of Tyndale, works are said to justify only in the sense that they declare outwardly that inner justification appointed by God, accomplished by Christ and applied by the Holy Spirit without reference to prior works performed by man. While Tyndale does use the term 'justify' with reference to works, it is in the context of attempting to reconcile the apparent contradiction in the use of the word by Paul and James. Such an explanation was used by other Reformed theologians at this time in order to deal with this same problem. Tyndale's use of the word 'justify' with reference to works cannot be taken to imply that his theology is substantially that of Catholics, such as Contarini, nor that his view of justification by faith alone is at all compromised by such language;[69] rather, it reveals an attitude to the Letter of James which distances him from Luther's view of the same book and places him closer to Reformed theologians who were concerned to emphasise the ethical imperatives of the Christian life.

Having indicated that it is misleading to describe Tyndale's doctrine as double justification, it is now necessary to assess whether there is nevertheless a fundamental difference between him and Frith in this area. In fact, the question can be answered in the negative simply by referring to *Tracy's Testament*. The very work which Clebsch claims proves that a difference exists in fact demonstrates that both men hold to the same basic doctrine. The key passage reads as follows:

Out of this fountain [i.e. faith] spring those good works which justify us before men, that is to say, declare us to be very righteous, for before God we are verily justified by that root of faith; for he searcheth the heart, and therefore this just judge doth inwardly justify

---

[68] See Küng, *Justification*, 219.   [69] This is the claim of Clebsch, p. 94.

or condemn, giving sentence according to faith; but men must look
for the works, for their sight cannot enter into the heart, and therefore they first give judgment of works. and are many times deceived
under the cloak of hypocrisy.[70]

Here, Frith uses the very language of Tyndale in describing
the function of works: they act as a justification before men in
that they reveal the reality of that faith which is itself invisible
to mortal eyes. Clebsch's own use of this passage is interesting as
he quotes only 'men must . . . of hypocrisy' and comments that:

Justification before men was therefore a dubious matter, not to be
shown forth by good works which might easily deceive; God alone
determined, granted, and knew the justification of sinners. So Frith
stood with Luther as late as 1532, while his cohorts abroad were
moving toward Osiander and Bucer and the Rhineland theologians
on this critical point.[71]

By quoting only part of the passage, Clebsch misses the crucial
statement on justification before men. Then, in the above
comment, he effectively reverses Frith's actual meaning, implying that the passage is a rejection of the notion of justification
found in the works of Tyndale. In fact, in the passage used by
Clebsch, Frith is simply pointing out that our knowledge of
another's justification must be based upon his outward deeds
as we cannot see into the heart, but that such knowledge is not
perfect as deeds can be deceptive. In other words, Frith is
advocating the same doctrine as Tyndale, and simply warning
that a man might well be outwardly justified by his works
before men without being inwardly justified by faith before
God. Clebsch's claim of a breach is therefore without any
foundation and distorts the thought of both Tyndale and Frith.

Summary

In the controversy over purgatory, Frith formulates his
soteriology in terms of a twofold purgation of the believer: by
the word, through faith; and by the cross of suffering. The
word is concerned with the objective work of Christ. Again,

---

[70] Russell, p. 253.
[71] Clebsch, p. 109. Clebsch does not provide any exposition of the teaching of
Osiander or Bucer on 'double justification' and gives no references to the works of
either in order to provide a foundation for this sweeping claim.

God's wrath against sin is made the decisive factor in Christ's sacrifice. Through faith, the believer is counted righteous through the non-imputation of his sins. Through suffering, the believer gains in actual righteousness. In stressing both the objective and subjective dimensions of salvation, Frith is expressing thoughts continuous with his earlier theology and similar to the position of Luther.

Frith also stresses that works are essential to the believer. These are to be motivated by love, not by thoughts of punishment or of earning heaven thereby. He underlines the need for works by adopting a scheme involving a twofold satisfaction: as Christ's work on the cross made satisfaction to God, thus the believer's good works make satisfaction towards his neighbour. Indeed, Frith is so concerned to stress the necessity of works that, in discussing this scheme, he can even adopt the conditional language so typical of Tyndale in order to make his point. However, unlike Tyndale, Frith does not then proceed to make works a primary basis of assurance.

In describing the function of works within the Christian life, Frith adopts the same concept of justification before men as Tyndale uses. This involves no compromise of his earlier theology, although it is perhaps the clearest indication so far of the influence of Reformed thinking upon Frith. It also points to the fundamental similarity, not opposition, between the views of Tyndale and Frith on the role of works in this instance.

FRITH IN PRISON

Although Frith was confined to the Tower for the last year of his life, this did not prevent him from composing a series of theological works. While all of these must have been composed in late 1532 or 1533, it is impossible to establish a comprehensive relative chronology for them. In *A Bulwark Against Rastell*, Frith refutes an attempt by Rastell to answer his earlier work on purgatory. As such, he covers much of the same ground as the earlier treatise, although this time he managed to convince his opponent of the truth of his case.[72] *A Letter to the Faithful* is a brief pastoral letter written to encourage fellow

---

[72] See Clebsch, p. 109.

Christians who were facing persecution for their beliefs. *A Mirror to Know Thyself* was written at the request of a friend and consists of an attempt to demonstrate that the practical Christian life rests upon a correct understanding of God's grace. In the course of the work, Frith gives his most extensive discussion of predestination. *A Declaration of Baptism* is Frith's only writing devoted to the subject of baptism. He proposes a view of baptism that is non-sacramental in essence, stressing the obligations which the sacrament imposes upon the recipient rather than the objective reality of the ordinance itself. *A Christian Sentence* was written at the request of a friend who desired a summary of Frith's views concerning the Eucharist. In it, he asserts that belief in transubstantiation is not essential to salvation, and argues that believers feed spiritually on the body of Christ. Finally, *Answer to More on the Sacrament* is Frith's attack upon the arguments that Sir Thomas More lodged against *A Christian Sentence*. Frith covers similar ground to the earlier work, but provides more extensive evidence for his position in terms of arguments from scripture, Christology, and patristic sources.

Frith is primarily concerned with salvation only in *A Mirror*, although he deals with various aspects of faith and works in the course of his sacramental writings. This provides a natural division in his writings and forms a convenient framework for studying his thoughts on salvation during this period.

Salvation, Self-Knowledge, and Predestination

For Frith, self-knowledge is fundamental to man's salvation. He describes the idea that self-knowledge is the essence of wisdom as the teaching of the 'philosophers to whom God had inspired certain sparkles of truth'.[73] While he is not specific about the philosophers to whom he is referring, the idea was common in classical times. The inscription 'Know Thyself' was written above the oracle's sanctuary at Delphi, pointing those who came seeking knowledge to the essence of true knowledge. The idea also underlies the thinking of Socrates' declaration that a wise man knows that he knows nothing.[74]

The motif entered Christian thinking with Clement of Alexandria's statement in *Pedagogus*, that to know oneself was

[73] Russell, p. 265.   [74] Plato, *Apologia*, 23. B.

the greatest and the most beautiful of disciplines.[75] The idea was also developed by Augustine and thus passed into the Western theological tradition.[76] During the Reformation, Zwingli used the idea at the start of his *Commentary on True and False Religion*, expressing the notion that true discussion of religion must start by acknowledging God and understanding man.[77] Later, Calvin used the concept in the opening paragraphs of his *Institutes*.[78]

In the early English Reformation, both Tyndale and Barnes mention self-knowledge, but they refer the idea to man's realisation that he is a sinner through seeing the demands which the law makes upon him. This is not the same understanding of the concept which Frith expresses. He regards self-knowledge as the foundation of all wisdom. According to Solomon, Prov. 1: 7, fear of God is the beginning of wisdom, and Frith argues that such fear presupposes knowledge of self. This knowledge concerns man as he relates to God in terms of both his sinfulness and his creatureliness.

The fundamental element of self-knowledge is the understanding that every good gift comes from God. Frith asserts this at the outset of the treatise, giving James 1: 17 as his proof-text. These good gifts do not relate only to salvation but also to existence itself. At the end of the work, Frith recounts the story of a shepherd who praised the Lord for making him into a man rather than a toad.[79] The purpose of the story is to underline Frith's previous assertion that man is God's creature, and God could have made him into whatever he wished.[80]

The effect of this basic premise is to set the whole treatise within the context of God's sovereignty and to point to God's grace in creation. However, Frith also wishes to emphasize the grace of God in salvation. It is not only the good gifts of life in general which God gives, but also those that have significance for the soul. Frith's discussion of salvation is therefore again based upon God's sovereignty: it is God's sovereign choice to save man, and this choice is motivated solely by mercy.[81] Christ is both the instrumental cause and the revelation of this salvation, which consists of predestination, election, vocation and

---

[75] *PG* 8. 556.
[76] See, for example, *Soliloquy* 2. 1. 1, *PL* 32. 886.
[77] See Z III. 640.
[78] See *OC* 1. 27 (1536); 2. 31 (1559).
[79] See Russell, p. 279.
[80] Ibid. 278.   [81] Ibid. 266.

justification.[82] Significantly, he does not discuss God's sovereignty in terms of an abstract power which renders man as little more than a plaything in the hands of almighty God. Instead, he refers the idea to God's mercy in both creation and salvation. As such, sovereignty functions as that which undergirds God's grace rather than something which stands in opposition to it. This is reflected in Frith's extreme caution in his formulation of the doctrine of predestination.

Self-knowledge therefore consists of the realization that both man's existence and his salvation are the result of God's mercy worked out through his sovereign will. Man obtains this self-knowledge from two sources. The first is scripture, which explicitly testifies that all good things in general come from God, and the second is the revelation in Christ, in whom God shows man his merciful salvation.[83] This point is interesting, as it demonstrates once again the Christocentric emphasis so characteristic of Frith's theology. Rather than building his argument upon his anthropology, Frith is instead pointing to Christology as the clearest proof of salvation by grace. Frith regards salvation as summed up in God's gift of Christ. Christ was given freely out of mercy and therefore proves that salvation itself is the gift of God.

This emphasis upon God's free grace in salvation leads Frith to give his fullest discussion of the doctrine of predestination. Like Tyndale, he does not approach the subject directly but through his understanding of salvation by grace. Therefore, he does not take any abstract doctrine of God's sovereignty as the starting point for his discussion. Indeed, Frith develops the doctrine of God's sovereignty only as far as is necessary to support his view of God's mercy and grace. His handling of predestination is marked throughout by a reverent caution.

Frith's doctrine of predestination is framed in terms of three main concerns: that God's election of individuals is not based upon foreseen merits; that God's election is based upon his own sovereign grace; and that God's will in election is inscrutable and not to be investigated. Each step is supported by a quotation from St Augustine. It is indicative of his caution in this matter that he chooses not to elaborate upon any of these quotations.

---

[82] See Russell, p. 266.   [83] Ibid. 266–7.

In arguing that God does not elect on the basis of foreseen merits, Frith quotes Augustine's comment on John 15: 16:

St. Austin saith, Some man will affirm that God did choose us, because he saw before that we should do good works; but Christ saith not so, which saith, Ye have not chosen me, but I have chosen you; for, (saith he,) if he had chosen us because he saw before that we should do good works, then should he also have seen before, that we should first have chosen him, which is contrary to the words of Christ, and mind of the Evangelist.[84]

This passage clearly indicates that Frith regards election as based upon the free choice of God. It is interesting that he does not choose an argument based upon man's inability to do good in order to establish his point but once again refers salvation to Christology. This is continuous with his earlier statement that God's grace in salvation is revealed by God's free gift of Christ.

In the second element of his argument for predestination, Frith again borrows a quotation from Augustine, this time referring to the very nature of grace. Grace cannot be grace unless it is free and unmerited, and therefore it cannot be dependent upon foreseen merits.[85] Again, Frith is constructing his understanding of predestination in reference to theological, not anthropological, considerations, making the God of grace his starting point.

The final paragraph on predestination consists of a brief summary of the whole doctrine, with a warning from Augustine that the matter is not to be a subject for speculation:

And this are we sure of, that whomsoever he chooseth, them he saveth of his mercy; and whom he repelleth, them of his secret and unsearchable judgment he condemneth. But why he chooseth one, and repelleth the other, enquire not, saith St. Austin, if thou wilt not err. Insomuch that St. Paul could not attain to the knowledge thereof, but cried out, Oh! the depth of the riches and wisdom of the knowledge of God, how unsearchable are his judgments, and how incomprehensible are his ways![86]

There are several important elements in this quotation. The first is the matter of double predestination. This passage is the

---

[84] Ibid. 267.   [85] Ibid.   [86] Ibid. 268.

only indication we have that Frith may have held to the doctrine. It is possible that Frith's use of the term 'repelleth' is intended to convey something more than the idea of God simply passing over those he is not to save. Certainly this gains some support from the fact that Frith ascribes the cause of this reprobation to God's secret will rather than simply to man's own sin. However, Frith's warning against speculation is perhaps a sign that he wishes to leave the question open rather than affirm a dogmatic stance on this matter. Like Tyndale, Frith does not develop the idea of God's hidden will as an important theological concept in the manner of Luther and Barnes, and his concern is almost exclusively with God's revelation.

This concern is reflected in the second point of interest in the passage: the doxological use of predestination. Predestination is not a doctrine that is meant to frighten man; rather, it is something to draw out his praise and wonder at God's wisdom. This point is continuous with Frith's earlier introduction of the sovereignty of God as that which undergirds God's mercy. While allowing for the existence of those whom God does not elect, Frith is careful to point away from the dark shadow which this might cast over the doctrine of salvation to the glorious nature of the God of grace himself. Unlike Barnes, who uses the distinction between God's hidden and revealed wills to emphasize the drama of faith, Frith avoids placing emphasis upon the negative aspects of the idea. Instead, he points the believer to God's wisdom and thus gives predestination a positive function, underscoring that salvation is all of grace and eliciting praise for the unfathomably wise God.

Frith's teaching on predestination is non-speculative and practical, as it leads the believer to doxological praise of God's grace. This practical dimension of self-knowledge is very important to Frith, and he devotes almost three-quarters of his treatise to the practical implications of realising that all good things come from God. The primary point that he makes is that God's gifts place man under an obligation to use them for good. In a manner not dissimilar to Tyndale's covenant scheme, Frith argues that knowledge of God and salvation is not something to boast about, but rather a 'chargeable office'.[87]

---

[87] See Russell, p. 269.

While salvation is a free gift of God, Frith, like Luther, can also describe it as something that costs the individual clearly in terms of inevitable trouble and persecution. It also obliges him to love and help others. If a believer sees his neighbour perishing because of his ignorance of the gospel, then he is bound to instruct him in the true knowledge of God. Indeed, in a passage which speaks as clearly as any in Tyndale of the believer's obligations, Frith states the following:

[If I] espy my neighbour in danger of the pit, then am I nevertheless bound to lead him from it. . . . And the law of God and nature bindeth me thereto, which chargeth me to love my neighbour as myself, and to do unto him as I would be done to.[88]

In his identification of the law of God and the law of nature with the obligation to love one's neighbour, Frith is reaffirming his commitment to the Lutheran interpretation of the role of law in the believer's ethical conduct which Tyndale too advocates. While it is true that Frith does not use this as a basis for developing a covenant scheme or for making works the primary basis for assurance, it is clear that he regards salvation as involving distinct moral obligations. Indeed, if the believer neglects these obligations, he risks being rejected by God. For this reason, the believer is to make his calling sure by exercising himself in mortifying his sin and in performing good deeds.[89] In stating this, Frith is allowing that works do play a secondary role in assurance, although he does not develop the idea to the same extent as Tyndale does. However, in the matter of the necessity for good works, he and Tyndale are in fundamental agreement.

A further practical result of self-knowledge is that it humbles man to realize that he possesses nothing of any value except what has been freely given to him by God. This is the source of the believer's motivation for good works and prevents his thought from being interpreted as justification by works: works are man's humble and grateful response to God's salvation.[90] However, Frith does not allow this idea of response to undermine the believer's own responsibility, and he stresses that without good works there can be no perseverance:

[88] Ibid. 270.   [89] Ibid. 271.   [90] Ibid. 277.

And since all our goodness cometh of him, we must again be thankful unto him and keep his commandments; for else we may fear lest he take his gifts from us, and then shall we receive the greater damnation.[91]

Frith's use of the word 'must' in the above quotation under-scores man's moral responsibility. Furthermore, by allowing that the believer can fall from grace, Frith destroys any notion that faith implies election and this effectively prevents the possibility of any definite knowledge of God's predestination in this life. He is not prepared to formulate a doctrine of predestination which could in any way be construed as weakening man's moral obligation.

In his work on self-knowledge, Frith is concerned to demonstrate that his view of salvation provides a firm foundation for practical morality. He asserts that salvation is the free gift of God in Christ, and undergirds this by a cautious development of the doctrine of predestination. He then proceeds to delineate the manner in which this should affect the believer's life. In doing this, he emphasizes works as the responsibility of the believer while also pointing out that they are also the natural response of a humble and grateful conscience. In so doing, his treatise exhibits a practical concern similar to that of Tyndale.

Salvation and the Sacraments

Frith's sacramental writings, particularly those dealing with the Eucharist, are not primarily concerned with salvation. However, they do provide important insights into two particular areas which have a direct bearing upon salvation: the nature of saving faith; and the ethical concern of his theology.

Frith wrote both *A Christian Sentence* and his *Answer to More* primarily to counter the idea that belief in the dogma of transubstantiation is necessary for salvation.[92] This also formed one of the articles for which he was ultimately condemned.[93] He bases his rejection of the necessity of belief in transubstantiation not primarily on exegesis of Christ's words of institution, but on the nature of salvation itself. It is not Christ's presence in the bread that saves, but his presence in

---

[91] Russell, p. 277. Frith then underlines this point by giving three examples of gifts that can be ungratefully received and consequently taken away.
[92] Ibid. 324; *Work*, 478.
[93] Russell, p. 451.

the heart.[94] In asserting this, Frith is not so much concerned to deny that Christ is physically present in the Eucharist, although he is to do this later, but to argue that such presence is not important to salvation. To prove this, he refers to the Old Testament saints who were saved in the same manner as later believers and yet existed before Christ's incarnation or the institution of the Eucharist.[95] Such, he argues, could not possibly have been saved by belief in Christ's corporal presence in the Eucharist or by feeding upon the same. Instead, they fed on Christ spiritually by faith in the promises of salvation through the Christ who was to come. By analogy, it is this spiritual feeding which is also important for those believers who live after Christ.[96]

Frith's argument at this point reveals several important aspects of his thought. As in his earlier use of scholastic terminology with reference to faith, we see here a desire to meet his opponents half way: he does not initially reject the content of their Eucharistic doctrine but calls into question the function which they ascribe to it. As with his attack on purgatory, it is only after he has demonstrated that the Catholic dogma is unnecessary that he then attempts to show that it is also erroneous.

Underlying this approach is the conviction that it is not assent to dogma which saves, but a vital spiritual relationship with Jesus Christ. This latter is founded on faith in the salvation which is wrought in him. Thus, Frith is underlining his earlier christocentric emphasis by making the person of Christ, and not Church dogma, the main focus of salvation for the individual. Secondly, he is allowing his earlier argument for faith as trust in Christ rather than assent to dogmatic propositions to inform other areas of his theology. It is too easy in a polemical context to replace true faith in Christ with belief in particular doctrines in order to discredit one's opponents. This is a position that Frith's consistent focus on Christ prevents him from adopting, but which constitutes the basic error of his opponents.

In dealing with the nature of the sacraments, Frith first expounds a general sacramental theory within which baptism and the Eucharist are to be understood. He defines the sacraments in general terms as signs of holy things or outward signs

[94] Ibid. 324.   [95] Ibid. 325.   [96] Ibid. 326.

of invisible grace.[97] More specifically, he argues that there are three elements to every sacrament: the sign (water, bread, wine), the signification, and the faith in God's word without which the sacrament has no meaning for the individual.

The signification of both the Eucharist and baptism is the same: the prior reception of God's grace by the one receiving the sacrament. Frith is careful to emphasize that the sacrament itself does not convey grace to the individual. He also emphasizes that the Spirit of God is not tied to the sacraments in such a way that he must work where the signs are present and cannot work where they are absent.[98] Instead, grace is given to the individual prior to the sacrament:

the sacraments are given to be an outward witness unto all the congregation, of that grace which is given before privately unto every man.[99]

Thus the sacraments are the corporate declaration of individual salvation. However, Frith's stress upon the universal nature of grace underlying the sacraments causes a serious tension in his theology of baptism. Baptism, as a sacrament, is a sign of prior grace given by God to the recipient. In the case of those of the age of discretion, this is according to their faith in Christ. Thus, an adult baptismal candidate is asked if he has faith in Christ. In the case of infants, however, this grace is given according to promise.[100] This is where the problem in his theology occurs.

Frith argues that baptism, like circumcision, is a sign of election. However, he regards election as the free decision of God, and in no way tied to the sacraments. Therefore he is unwilling to identify the baptized congregation with the company of the elect. Indeed, as he himself points out, many who receive both sacraments prove ultimately to be godless and

[97] *Work*, 286. The second definition is also that used by Augustine in *De Civitate Dei* 10. 5 (see *PL* 41. 441), but both definitions occur together in Peter Lombard's *Sentences* 4. 1 (*PL* 191. 839) and Aquinas, *Summa* 3a. 60, 1–2. It is therefore possible that Frith's definition has a scholastic source.

[98] See Russell, p. 285.

[99] Ibid.

[100] Frith gives no specific text to support this idea, but presumably it is Acts 2: 39 that lies behind his thinking here. Later, he draws an analogy with circumcision in order to justify the baptism of infants, and so it is dear that his understanding of baptism is derived from the unity of salvation he sees between the two Testaments. This position is the same as that of Zwingli: see Z VI. i. 48. 13–15.

reprobate.[101] In view of this, Frith emphasizes baptism as a sign of membership of the visible congregation which is a mixture of both elect and reprobate.[102] Furthermore, because such a doctrine of election divorces grace as an objective reality from the sacraments, Frith does not describe the sacrament in terms of what it offers to the believer. Instead, he stresses the obligation under which baptism places its recipient:

a Christian man's life is nothing else save a continual baptism, which is begun when we are dipped in the water, and is put in continual use and exercise as long as the infection of sin remaineth in our bodies, which is never utterly vanquished until the hour of death. . . . And thus is Paul to be understood (Gal. 3) where he saith, 'All ye that are baptised into Christ, have put Christ on you'; that is, you have promised to die with Christ as touching your sins and worldly desires past, and to become new men, or creatures, or members of Christ. This have we all promised unto the congregation, and it is represented in our baptism.[103]

Thus, baptism has become a sign not so much of objective grace but of the promise by the individual that he will become a Christian.[104] Frith continues the passage by emphasizing that it is man's duty to have faith, maintaining his stress upon man's responsibility. Such an understanding is very similar to that of Tyndale, and shows Frith's concern not to allow any element of his theology to undermine the idea of man's own responsibility in spiritual matters.[105]

---

[101] See Russell, pp. 284–85.

[102] See Russell, p. 287; cf. Zwingli, Z VI. i. 170. 17–171. 14

[103] Russell, p. 290.

[104] R. E. Fulop argues that, for Frith as for Luther, baptism and the objective work of Christ are inseparable: see his 'John Frith and His Relation to the Origins of the Reformation in England', unpubl. Ph.D. diss. (University of Edinburgh, 1956). In actual fact, Frith places surprisingly little emphasis upon Christ's objective work in his treatment of baptism.

[105] N. T. Wright comments that 'baptism [for Frith] is based, not on the faith of the individual, but on the election of God which precedes faith, and therefore on the promise of salvation to all who are elect' (*Work*, 50–1). This is not quite an accurate statement of Frith's position. Rather, because actual election is hidden, it can be no basis for the baptism of children. The warrant for paedobaptism lies in the promise of election to believers' children. Frith's argument is that, if election is hidden, it cannot be used to prove the non-election of individual children and thus cannot be used to limit the scope of the promise of election. Thus it is the promise of election, not election itself, that provides the basis for paedobaptism: see Russell, p. 286. Zwingli uses exactly the same argument against the anabaptists: Z VI. i. 178. 27–179. 5. The general similarity

Summary

Frith uses the classical idea of self-knowledge in order to introduce discussion of the doctrine of predestination. His treatment of this topic is set within the context of God's sovereignty, but the emphasis is always upon God's grace and mercy. His actual formulation of predestination is marked by the same caution as Tyndale demonstrated, and Frith uses Augustine, not Luther, as his mentor in this matter. While stressing that God's sovereign will is the decisive factor in election, Frith does not commit himself on the question of predestination. This underlines the doxological purpose of the tract as a statement concerned with God's grace towards man. Frith also manages to give the doctrine an ethical slant by arguing that perseverance is dependent upon good works. Thus he prevents any abstract notion of predestination from undermining man's responsibility and presents an understanding of the doctrine very similar to that of Tyndale.

In dealing with the sacraments, Frith argues that faith is belief in the person of Christ, not in dogma, in this particular case transubstantiation. He also discusses baptism which is presented not so much as an objective offer of grace by God but as the recipient's public commitment to living the Christian life. Thus, as in the case of predestination, Frith underlines man's responsibility in salvation.

CONCLUSION

Frith's doctrine of salvation can be summarized in terms of the idea of the two purgatories. The first purgatory, that of the word, involves the forgiveness of sins by God. This has been obtained by Christ who has satisfied the wrath of God in his sacrifice upon the cross. In making God's righteous wrath the decisive factor in determining the nature of the atonement, Frith differs from both Tyndale and Barnes in developing a clear doctrine of propitiation.

This forgiveness is appropriated by the individual through faith. Faith is primarily a trust in Christ as personal saviour,

between the two men on the subject of baptism suggests the influence of Zwingli upon Frith in this matter. This has been missed by G. W. Locher in his survey of Zwingli's influence in England: see *Zwingli's Thought: New Perspectives* (Leiden, 1981), 355–6.

and not adherence to specific dogmas. Such a definition of faith, combined with the doctrine of atonement, ensures that Frith's doctrine of salvation is fundamentally Christocentric.

The second purgatory is that of the cross of suffering, which follows faith in Christ and is an aid to sanctification. This reveals Frith's practical concern in his theology, in that salvation embodies not simply remission of sins but also growth in holiness. In general, Frith sees works as flowing from the love caused by faith. He does not place as much emphasis on the law as Tyndale, although their basic ethical positions are identical. However, while Frith can speak in conditional terms, using the same concept of works as an outward sign of justification, he does not make works a primary basis of assurance and maintains a more single-minded stress upon faith. In later works he does develop his predestinarian and baptismal doctrines in a manner that serves to emphasize the individual's responsibilities, but he never adopts the strong ethical position of Tyndale. On the issue of predestination, Frith develops a cautious doctrine, following the thought of Augustine closely, and introducing the idea only to underline God's grace and mercy. He is uncommitted on the question of reprobation.

It is difficult to draw firm conclusions concerning Frith's development. His output is comparatively small covering a wide number of topics over a period of only five years. In terms of his influences, however, we are on firmer ground. While he was initially a Humanist, like Tyndale, the shape of his soteriology reveals that Lutheranism had a greater impact upon him than upon his colleague. In his objective view of atonement, the substance of his two purgatories' doctrine, his Christocentricity and his choice of language in the realm of ethics, he shows a clear debt to Luther. However, Reformed influence can also be discerned in his attitude to the Letter of James and his sacramental theology. There are several echoes of Zwingli's position in his discussion of baptism. Augustine too provides the basic substance of his doctrine of predestination. Thus, it would be incorrect to use the blanket term of 'Lutheran' to describe him. He is, rather, a theologian subject to various influences each of which contributes to his overall position.

6

Robert Barnes

THE THEOLOGY OF BARNES'S FIRST *SUPPLICATION*

WHEN Barnes first came to prominence as an advocate of reform, it seems likely that his theology was closer to that of Catholic Humanism than to that of Luther.[1] However, when he came to write *A Supplication*, his theology had undergone considerable change, as had the political climate. England was in a state of some tension. Wolsey had been dismissed and indicted in 1529, and the crisis of the king's divorce was still building, focusing the conflict between the Catholic Church and the State. The state was now openly challenging the authority of the Church, using its powers to bring actions of *praemunire* against eight bishops and seven clergymen in 1530 for giving money to Wolsey. The accusations were dropped after bribes were given, but not before the charges had been broadened to include all the clergy. Meanwhile, on the Continent, Charles V was increasing his control over Rome, preventing Clement VII from granting Henry the divorce he desired, as Catherine of Aragon was Charles's aunt. All of this indicated that the Church's power was becoming an irritant to Henry VIII and that England was thus heading towards an ecclesiastical crisis.[2]

Even from the brief summary above it is clear that the movement of political events from this point would have important repercussions for the theological climate. The points at issue in the political world were the authority of the Pope and of the Catholic Church. If these were rejected by Henry in the matter of his divorce, then perhaps they might be thrown off safely by the English in the more strictly theological area of doctrine.

---

[1] See Ch. 2.
[2] Dickens, *The English Reformation*, 149–50.

In 1531, however, it was far from clear which direction events would take.

It was in this climate of uncertainty that Barnes took up his pen. If the evangelical faith were to stand any chance of Henry's patronage, Barnes realized that he would have to demonstrate that it presented no threat to the interests of the king, especially as regards civil obedience, and that it would be even more amenable to the monarch's ideas of Church and State than Catholicism. It is this concern that sets the tone, although not the content, of the first edition of *A Supplication*. There are long, bitter polemics against the bishops, whom Barnes is concerned to identify with the powers that oppose the king and foster corruption in government. However, all of this is woven around a set of themes that have far more relevance to theology than to politics.

Theologically, Barnes probably had two major motives for writing. First, he was concerned to vindicate himself against the charge of heresy. From 1526 to 1529 Barnes had been confined, and from 1529 he had been in exile. He was probably homesick, and, with More as chancellor, the only chance of a safe return would have been with a royal pardon. This explains why the treatise opens with a long section on the articles for which he was originally condemned in order to show the unfairness of his treatment at the hands of the bishops. It also explains why the sole focus of his hatred is the Catholic Church and its theologians. Probably Barnes felt that such attacks would commend him to a king who was committed to clipping the wings of the ecclesiastical establishment.

Secondly, there was a more general theological reason for writing. That Barnes was a well-known figure in English Protestantism is demonstrated by the visit he received from the Lollards even before he first travelled to Wittenberg. Now, after studying at the centre of the Reformation, he would no doubt have realized that, although absent in the body, he could be of great use to his homeland through the medium of the printed word. *A Supplication* offered him a way in which to place a compendium of Reformation theology into English hands. No doubt this was why he chose to write in English, as Latin would have suited Henry but restricted the general usefulness of the treatise. He could not have known whether the work would have any impact upon the king, but its broad scope made it far more useful to others than a mere personal appeal to the king would have done.

The work itself consisted of three basic divisions: a direct personal appeal to the king; a critical assessment of the charges of heresy brought against Barnes; and ten theological common places. Of these, the sections relevant to Barnes's doctrine of salvation are: *that only faith justifieth before God*; and, *that free will of man after the fall of Adam can do nothing but sin.*

Justification by Faith Alone

While the concepts of justification and the will of man are inextricably related, Barnes chooses to treat the two in separate essays. His approach is to address the problem of justification first and the will second. While the reverse order might appeal because of its obvious logic (i.e. with justification by faith flowing from the doctrine of fallen man), it is more faithful to Barnes's own emphasis and method to treat them in the same order in which he did.[3]

It is important to realize that Barnes's tract on justification has a primarily negative purpose whereby his first concern is to reject the notion that works play any part in justification. It is only after this foundation has been established that he proceeds to the positive aspects of the doctrine. The essay is fundamentally a polemic against the perceived Catholic position.

One final preliminary comment concerns the importance of the doctrine for Barnes. He regards it as the central theological concern of the apostle Paul, and as the underlying principle of the scriptures. For Barnes therefore the doctrine is the necessary foundation for any correct understanding of the Christian faith.[4] In this matter, Barnes reveals his clear affinity with Luther,

---

[3] In his dissertation on Barnes, Charles Anderson points out that Barnes's theology is not developed systematically, but rather in opposition to various false doctrines, and that to treat his work as systematic theology would lead to distortion: see 'The Person and Position of Dr. Robert Barnes', 190–1. However, he does not fully follow his own advice, treating Barnes's arguments in his sections on justification and on the will under two headings, 'Justification by Faith' and 'The Christian Life'. In these sections he quotes indiscriminately from both essays of Barnes, thus presenting the Reformer's arguments for justification as flowing logically from his anthropology. While this is true, it is not how Barnes himself presents his arguments, and Anderson completely ignores the very important argument from Christology, which is what Barnes himself chooses to place at the forefront of both essays.   [4] *1531* 1. a; *1531* xlviii. b.

and this is no doubt why he chose to deal with justification before discussing the bondage of the will.

Methodologically, Barnes's first concern is to establish the authorities upon which his argument is to be based. These are the scriptures and the Fathers. From here he moves to a consideration of the doctrine's relationship to Christ and the gracious nature of justification, a correct understanding of which precludes justification by works. Finally, in the course of refuting his opponents' interpretation of key passages of scripture, he gives a more positive affirmation of the relationship between saving faith and good works.

The argument of the essay begins with a statement concerning Christ and his work. Barnes quotes, Matt. 1: 21, 1 Cor. 1: 30, and Isa. 54: 8b, all texts which he interprets as displaying the comprehensiveness of Christ's role in salvation: 'Christ is nothing else but a saviour, a redeemer, a justifier, and a perfect peace maker between God and man.'[5] If Christ is such an all-sufficient saviour, the result is that 'we need of nothing but of him only' and works are precluded from justification from the outset.[6] This approach is interesting not only because it reveals the strongly Christocentric nature of Barnes's thought, but also because it provides a point of contrast with the approach of Tyndale. Tyndale's Christology is vague, and he tends to emphasize Christ's work as an example rather than as an objective accomplishment of redemption. His arguments for justification by faith are built primarily upon man's moral inability rather than upon objective Christological considerations. In contrast, Barnes's approach is closer to that of Frith who emphasizes the central role of the person of Christ in salvation.

This emphasis upon the role of Christ leads Barnes to elaborate upon the relationship of the historical Christ to salvation. Indeed, both the historical person of Jesus and the theological significance of Christ are united in a manner which underlines the Christocentric nature of salvation. This close union arises from the fact that Christ's incarnation, his entry into history, was for the sole purpose of achieving reconciliation between God and man. In emphasizing this, Barnes lays the foundations for his view of saving faith: faith in Christ involves not simply

---

[5] *1531* xxxviii. b.   [6] Ibid.

the acceptance of his historicity or even of his divinity, but belief in the purpose and effects of his incarnation. To deny any of these effects, even if one accepts the orthodox teaching concerning his person, is the act of an antichrist. This is expressed in a passage addressed to the bishops:

You grant that he was born, but you deny the purpose; you grant that he is risen from death, but you deny the profit thereof, for he rose to justify us. You grant that he is a saviour, but you deny that he is alonely the saviour. . . . Say what you will, if you give not all and fully and alonely to one Christ, then deny you Christ and the Holy Ghost, and St. John doth declare you to be contrary to Christ.[7]

To be orthodox concerning Christ's person, but not his effects is therefore not even a half-way faith, but a complete repudiation of Christianity because such belief implies that something other than Christ is required for reconciliation to be achieved. Therefore the entire basis for justification by faith alone is undermined. Once again, Barnes is stressing the Christ as the basis of justification.

The thought of Barnes here is clearly identical with that of Luther, as expressed in *The Freedom of the Christian Man*, who stresses that Christ must be preached not only as objective truth, but also as subjective reality.[8] For Barnes, as for Luther, there is no opposition between the objective truth of Christ and the believer's faith in him. In this respect, Barnes's thought displays a Christocentric emphasis which is closer to that of Frith than that of Tyndale. In their treatment of the content of faith, both Barnes and Frith generally speak of the person of Christ; Tyndale, on the other hand, generally speaks of faith in terms of God's promises to be merciful and can even omit any mention of Christ. This contributes to the overall moral emphasis in Tyndale's writings.

It is interesting that there is perhaps just a hint of independence from Luther in Barnes' choice of biblical text to emphasize the exclusivity of Christ. He chooses to use Rev. 5,

---

[7] *1531* xxxix. a–b.

[8] 'Non esse satis nec Christianum, si Christi opera, vitam et verba praedicemus historico more, ceu res quasdam gestas, quas nosse satis sit ad vitae formandae exemplum. . . . Oportet autem, ut eo fine praedicetur, quo fides in eum promoveatur, ut non tantum sit Christus, sed tibi et mihi sit Christus, et id in nobis operetur, quod de eo dicitur et quod ipse vocatur', *WA* 7. 58, 31–4, 38–59, 1.

in paraphrase form, where the scriptures declare that there is no-one in heaven or on earth found worthy to open the Book except for the Lamb. The point made by Barnes is simple enough: if the angels and the elders acknowledge the Lamb alone as worthy, then 'have you found them whom they could not find?'[9] Again, the emphasis is upon the Christological basis for justification by faith alone. However, it is interesting that Barnes uses Revelation to make such a point, when there are plenty of other texts from other parts of the scripture that would have done just as well. This suggests that he holds the book in higher esteem than does Luther, who, while mellowing in his attitude to the book during his career, never regards it as possessing great authority.[10]

Barnes's emphasis upon Christ as achieving redemption for man raises the question of how he understands Christ to have accomplished this. Like Tyndale, Barnes is frustratingly vague concerning the precise manner in which salvation was objectively accomplished, and he generally assumes it as fact instead of trying to explain it. Considering his alleged close affinity with Luther, there is a noticeable lack of emphasis upon the cross. While he does refer occasionally to the Lamb shedding his blood,[11] and to Christ as 'making satisfaction',[12] these are little more than passing comments which are not elaborated. Perhaps most significant of all is the omission of any mention of the cross in the list of Christ's acts and effects.[13] While it is true that reference is made to Christ rising for our justification, this is little more than a quotation of Rom. 4: 25 and need not imply that Barnes is centring his theology of redemption in Calvary.[14]

To some extent, this lack may be the result of the problem in hand: the subjective appropriation of redemption. However, even this is firmly grounded upon its objective accomplishment in Christ, a fact which Barnes is not slow to emphasize, as the first section of the essay clearly demonstrates. Nevertheless, Barnes does not attempt to develop a doctrine of atonement

---

[9] *1531* xxxix. b.   [10] Althaus, *The Theology of Martin Luther*, 84–5.
[11] *1531* xxxix. b.   [12] *1531* liv. b–lv. a.
[13] *1531* xxxix. a–b.
[14] This lack of emphasis on the death of Christ is not noticed by McGoldrick, who regards Barnes as following Luther in his stress upon the death of Christ. No evidence for this position is offered: see McGoldrick, pp. 110, 115.

in relation to the doctrine of God as, for example, Frith does. Instead, he expresses no clear doctrine of God's righteousness or of his wrath, and consequently does not proceed to construct a doctrine of propitiatory atonement. This significant point has been overlooked by those eager to equate his theology with that of Luther.[15]

Thus, justification by faith alone is established from the outset as a fact arising from the nature of Barnes's Christology, whereby salvation is objectively accomplished in the person of Christ.[16]

Having done this, Barnes now turns his attention to the nature of grace. The essence of grace for Barnes, as for Luther, is that of a freely given gift: 'What call you by his grace? If it be any part of works, then it is not of grace.'[17] Grace is the unmerited favour of God: if anything is done by man to deserve it, it ceases to be grace. This idea is reflected in the definitions Barnes gives of justification, which all point to the passivity of man in the process. At one point, he defines justification simply as the remission of sins acquired through faith.[18] Elsewhere, he goes further and, in commenting on Rom. 4: 4, declares that it involves the imputation of righteousness.[19] In both cases, justification is the act of God arising from himself and not solicited by any action of man, and is therefore all of grace.

In view of the lack of the idea of imputed righteousness in Tyndale and Frith, it is worth considering the statement of Barnes that justification involves the imputation of righteousness. Is this righteousness the righteousness of Christ, or is it that of the believer considered proleptically? The statement itself reads as follows:

I pray you, what good works doth the wicked man? Mark also how he saith that righteousness is imputed unto him. Ergo, it is not deserved. For that that is deserved is not imputed of favour, but it must be given of duty.[20]

---

[15] For Luther on atonement, see Althaus, *The Theology of Martin Luther*, 203.

[16] The fact that Barnes regards justification by faith alone as primarily dependent upon Christology is important, as this is also his position in 1534 and thus casts immediate doubt upon Clebsch's claim of a shift in his basic position.

[17] *1531* xl. b.

[18] 'Again, the same thing that purchaseth us remission of sins doth also purchase justification; for justification is nothing but the remission of sins', *1531* xlvii. b.

[19] *1531* xliii. a.

[20] Ibid.

While this statement could be interpreted as teaching the imputation of righteousness, two considerations require us to be somewhat cautious. First, it is important to realize that Barnes's concern in this context is not with the content of justification as such, but with God's grace in salvation. This is reflected in his choice of metaphors in this section which are employed to highlight the motive, rather than the action, of God.[21] In view of this, it is dangerous to argue that Barnes held to the Lutheran concept of imputation from this text alone.

Secondly, Barnes does not develop the idea of union with Christ. This is the concept that underlies Luther's use of the marriage metaphor in *The Freedom of a Christian Man* and its notion of the joyful exchange of righteousness and sin between Christ and man.[22] This concept is important as it contains the seeds from which the later doctrine of imputation grew.[23] While Barnes does refer once in the essay to the relationship between Christ and the believer as a marriage, this is actually in an acknowledged quotation from St Bernard which is used to highlight Christ's unconditional love for the believer and is not used in the way employed by Luther. One scholar interprets this lack as a sign of independence from Luther in terminology.[24] However, while that is certainly true, it is also true that Barnes reference to imputation in 1531 is not set within the same context as in Luther.[25] As a result of these considerations, it is just not possible to reach firm conclusions on Barnes's doctrine of imputation based on this isolated statement.

[21] e.g. *1531* xlviii. a, where Barnes compares salvation to being appointed to the king's council, where the choice lies in the king's favour not in the individual's merits. This metaphor is perhaps unsuited to its theological purpose, as one would assume that the king would select ministers whom he would consider to be competent. However, no doubt Barnes intended this passage as much as a flattering compliment to the king as a theological statement. The second image (*1531* 1. b) is that of a king freely pardoning a thief, which is well-suited both for its theological and political purpose.

[22] See Ch. 3.

[23] McGrath, *Iustitia Dei* 2, 14.

[24] N. H. Fisher, 'Robert Barnes and the English Reformation', unpubl. MA diss. (Birmingham University, 1950), 253.

[25] McGrath argues that Barnes's position in 1531 is ambiguous, but that in 1534 he makes an unequivocal statement concerning imputation: see *Iustitia Dei* 2, 99. The passage in 1534 to which McGrath refers occurs in *1534* xliii. a. This certainly is an unequivocal statement of the doctrine, but it occurs in the summary of the chapter. The implication, therefore, is that Barnes did hold to this doctrine in 1531, and that the 1534 statement marks a clarification, rather than a development, of his position.

In dealing with the concept of justification, Barnes starts with its objective foundations in Christology and in the grace of God. From here he turns to the problem of the subjective appropriation of this justification.

Saving Faith and Good Works

While justification by faith alone is the central thesis and continual theme of the whole of the essay, it is not until folios lviii. b and lix. a that Barnes actually addresses the problem of the nature of faith itself. It has already been seen that faith's object is Christ not simply as a historical or even as a theological truth in the objective sense, but Christ in his significance for the individual on a personal level. This is emphasised by Barnes as he describes the process of the redemption of particular believers:

The very true way of justification is this: first cometh God for the love of Christ Jesus and alonely of his mere mercy, and giveth us freely the gift of faith whereby we do believe God and his holy word, and stick fast by the promises of God, and believe that though heaven and earth and all that is in them should perish and come to nought, yet God shall be found true in his promises: for this faith's sake be we the elect children of God.[26]

Two aspects of this passage are particularly interesting. The first is the light it sheds upon the content of faith. The definition of faith in this passage is reminiscent of Luther in its emphasis upon believing God as he has revealed himself in the promises, no matter what the believer's outward condition may be. Barnes uses this idea of the paradox of faith to distinguish it from false faith. He argues elsewhere that even pagans are able to achieve a propositional belief in God by using their natural powers of reason, but that such faith does not save. True faith is trust in God and in his revelation. It is not simply to accept that God is a heavenly Father; it is to believe that he is *my* heavenly Father. Such faith is heavenly in origin, and comes as a gift of God, not the result of man's own reason.[27] It involves the believer committing himself to God, casting himself upon God, and trusting that God will save him as promised no matter what his outward circumstances. The emphasis upon

---

[26] *1531* lviii. b–lix. a.   [27] *1531* xlix. a.

trust as the distinctive of true faith is similar to the distinction between the kinds of faith made by Tyndale and Frith. However, Barnes's language is far more dramatic, stressing the paradoxical dimension of faith. In so doing, he remains closer than Tyndale or Frith to the language of Luther. Indeed, later in the treatise he is to follow Luther by linking the content of faith to the idea of double predestination, declaring that faith is believing that God has saved you even though he has predestined so many to damnation.[28]

The second interesting aspect of the passage is the light it sheds upon the centrality of faith in Barnes's thought. The passage ends with a remarkable statement whereby election is apparently made dependent upon faith. This is an apparent contradiction of the logic of Barnes's position, whereby faith is given through the sovereign, unmerited act of God and thus logically given only to those who God has decided shall receive it. It also contradicts Barnes's own explicit teaching that God has chosen some to salvation and some to damnation before the foundation of the world.[29] As a result of these considerations, Barnes's statement here cannot be interpreted as a theological axiom, but rather as an expression of the importance which he ascribes to faith. His theology is not ultimately concerned with speculative notions of God's being or action, but with the reality of a salvation that is appropriated through faith. Therefore, it is faith, not election, that Barnes sees as the central element in the individual's salvation. In making election apparently dependent upon it, Barnes is refusing to allow anything either to obscure the centrality of faith or to undermine the need for the individual to exercise such faith. Like Luther, Barnes regards it as the essence of salvation and is prepared to sacrifice theological consistency to emphasize this.[30]

Thus, in the third phase of Barnes's argument, redemption is shown to be subjectively appropriated by faith, where the definition of faith is built upon the foundations of his Christology and his view of grace. Faith is made the work of God alone, and this excludes once more the idea that man takes any active

---

[28] *1531* xciiii. b.

[29] See reference in n. 28.

[30] Barnes's inversion of the order of faith and election provides an interesting comparison with similar sayings in Tyndale: see *Works* 1. 31, 65.

part in the initiation of salvation. Finally, Barnes's inversion of the order of faith and election reveals the importance he places on the former in the matter of salvation.

In emphasizing both the objective basis of salvation in Christ's work and God's grace, and its subjective appropriation by the believer through God's gift of faith, Barnes has carefully precluded any notion of a justification involving works. However, in order to avoid accusations that he teaches antinomianism, he goes on to emphasize that works are not an optional extra for the believer but an essential accompaniment of salvation. The basis for this is found in the impact faith has upon the believer, an impact which leads both to a change of the individual's status and to practical results in the subsequent good works:

Finally, of a fleshly beast it maketh me a spiritual man; of a damnable child it maketh me a heavenly son. Of a servant of the devil it maketh me a free man of God's, both delivered from the law, from sin, from death, from the devil, and from all misery that might hurt me. My lords, this is the faith that doth justify, and because it is given from heaven in to our hearts by the Spirit of God, therefore it can be no idle thing.[31]

According to this passage, it is faith that leads man to do works. This is interesting, as it marks a significant difference in emphasis from Tyndale and Frith. The former always emphasizes the role of the Spirit in regeneration and man as a new creation. Therefore, he places less stress upon faith as the source of works and more upon the subjective activity of the Spirit and upon the idea of love. Frith, while laying less emphasis upon the Spirit, also centres his theology of works in the notion of love, not faith. There is no fundamental contradiction between Barnes and the other two in this matter, but it is evident that Barnes again places faith at the centre of his theology by making it the immediate cause of the Christian's moral activity rather than simply part of a causal sequence. While Tyndale and Frith emphasize the believer's change in being in regard to works, Barnes emphasizes his change in status.[32]

---

[31] *1531* xlix. b.

[32] N. H. Fisher goes so far as to declare that Barnes regards justification as involving the impartation of real righteousness: 'Robert Barnes and the English Reformation', 255. His argument does contain some truth, in that justification is inseparable from the subsequent change of being in man, and is the basis for actual

Barnes characterizes these good works in the same manner as does Luther, and, for that matter, Tyndale and Frith: they are acts which honour God and help one's neighbour.[33] Their actual function within the Christian life is clarified by Barnes's use of two analogies. The first refers to Christ, who is the supreme example of one who performed works without any personal need of doing so.[34] This concept of Christ as example is possibly a sign of the Humanist influence upon Barnes's thought in this area, although the idea is present in the works of Luther.

The second analogy is the biblical example of the tree and the fruit. Make the tree good, and the fruit will automatically be good.[35] Thus, Barnes restates the position on the relationship between faith and works adopted by Martin Luther. Later on in the essay, Barnes elaborates this idea, indicating that works are a sign of inward justification:

the works of the law be no cause of justification, but alonely an outward testimony . . . that the law is fulfilled inwardly in their consciences afore God.[36]

This statement is an expression of that doctrine which Clebsch terms 'double justification'. According to Clebsch, Barnes does not advocate this idea until the 1534 edition of *A Supplication* and then its introduction reveals a fundamental shift from his position in 1531.[37] However, it is clear from this passage that Barnes already regards works as an outward sign of justification before God in 1531. Therefore, the repetition of this idea using different terminology in 1534 cannot be described as a substantial change.

righteousness. However, it is important to a correct understanding of Barnes on this issue not to confuse justification with actual righteousness. He generally defines justification as the remission of sins, which involves a change in status. However, Fisher implies that Barnes sees justification primarily in terms of a change of being. In fact, this change of being is dependent upon the prior change of status and is thus related to, but still distinct from, justification. At worst, Barnes is guilty of unclear terminology, probably because his vocabulary does not include the technical terms of regeneration and sanctification. Had it done so, there is no doubt that he would have employed them to describe the freeing of the believer from sin, and his subsequent growth in holiness. If one keeps in mind Barnes's actual definition of justification, along with his rejection of works as playing any part in that justification, then it is clear that Fisher's interpretation cannot be accepted.

[33] See *1531* xlix. b.
[34] Ibid.
[35] See 1531 xlix. b–l. a.
[36] *1531* liii. b.
[37] See Clebsch, p. 68.

Having established that works are an essential accompaniment to justification, Barnes proceeds to dismiss those professors who do no good works. Works are a sign of faith in an individual, and therefore their absence is a sign of lack of faith. However, Barnes is not advocating that the individual should look to his own works as a sign of his justification. On the contrary, works are the believer's grateful response to his free justification by God:

therefore those men that will do no good works because they be justified alonely by faith be not the children of God nor the children of justification, and of that is this a sure and evident token; for, if they were the very true children of God, they would be the gladder to do good works because they are justified freely. Therefore should they also be moved freely to work, if it were for no other purpose nor profit but alonely to do the will of their merciful God that hath so freely justified them.[38]

There is only one proper motive for good works: they are the free and unconditional response to the love of God in justifying the sinner.[39] Unlike Tyndale, Barnes does not weaken this position by allowing works a primary role in assurance. This point will be of significance when the edition of 1534 is examined to see if it shows signs of shift towards a greater emphasis upon the role of works.

Barnes has so far established that justification, as based upon the exclusive role of Christ and upon God's free grace, excludes works. He has then proceeded to argue that to interpret this as a rejection of good works is a false dichotomy. Works are essential because faith brings about a change of being as well as of status and inspires good works for the honour of God and the aid of fellow man. However, he now turns those parts of scripture that seem to allow works a formal role in the actual justification of man. Of these, the most important is the Letter of James. Barnes's attitude to this book changes between 1531 and 1534, and it is this shift in position which forms the crux of Clebsch's argument that the later Barnes totally compromises his commitment to justification by faith alone.

[38] *1531* l. b.

[39] This is reflected in the image Barnes uses to describe this. He likens the believer's attitude to God to that of a thief pardoned by a king. For him to return to his stealing would be a total rejection of the king's mercy, and he would ultimately pay the price: see *1531* l. b.

The Letter of James

In dealing with those problematic verses in James which appear to teach justification by works, Barnes offers three lines of attack. The first, and the simplest, is that the epistle is of doubtful canonicity, and that the Church has always doubted its authority.[40] Secondly, he claims that it cannot be canonical because it is a flat contradiction of the principle of justification by faith alone. Thirdly, and somewhat paradoxically, he is willing to allow for its hypothetical canonicity. If that is so, he argues, the letter does not contradict the principle of faith alone. It is the last two arguments that are of importance in this study.

Earlier on in the essay, Barnes has stated that the doctrine of justification by faith alone is to be the basic hermeneutical principle by which all interpretation is to be judged. Barnes initially introduces this idea in order to defend his selective use of the Fathers: he accepts their teaching when they are in agreement with Rom. 4: 5, and rejects it when they are not, because 'this is the place whereby other places must be expounded'.[41] If the normative principle of justification by faith is now applied to James, Barnes can either reject the letter on the grounds that it contradicts this principle or subordinate the letter's interpretation to Rom. 4: 5. In fact, he is to do both. First, he declares boldly that 'I have invincible scriptures to prove that it cannot be St James.'[42] The first of these concerns James's statement that Abraham was justified by works when he offered his son Isaac as a sacrifice. This, according to Barnes, is a flat contradiction of Moses' statement in Gen. 15: 6 that Abraham's faith was credited to him as righteousness. As Barnes points out, this was before Isaac was born, and long before he was offered to God.[43] He then lists other scriptures where Abraham is explicitly stated to have been justified by faith apart from works. Similar treatment is given to James's statement concerning Rahab, where Heb. 11: 31 is seen to contradict and to override what he has to say. In this context, Barnes is following the arguments proposed by Luther in his

[40] 'If I denied this epistle to be Saint James, you could not prove it by the authority of the church, for she hath always doubted of it', *1531* lii. b.
[41] *1531* xliiii. b.
[42] *1531* lii. b.
[43] *1531* lii. b–liii. a.

own preface to James.[44] The whole discussion at this point neither adds to nor subtracts from Barnes's previous statements upon justification; rather it underlines his conviction that justification by faith alone is to be the normative principle for evaluating scripture.

However, Barnes now proceeds to discuss the teaching of the letter on the hypothetical basis that it is canonical. This is done ostensibly, to provide a common basis for debate with his opponents.[45] It is most surprising that Barnes feels obliged to concede so much, considering his recent claim to be able to refute James with 'invincible scriptures'. In fact, in the light of what follows it seems that Barnes himself is not totally convinced either way concerning the letter's canonicity. This point is of immense importance when judging the difference between his approach to the letter in 1531 and 1534.[46]

The exposition of James that Barnes chooses to use is that of Augustine and is very simple, drawing a distinction between works that are performed before justification and those performed after. If a life-long sinner truly believes just before he dies, then he will be saved because his faith has saved him, not his merits; but, if a man is justified and then lives for some time, how can he help but do good works? When Paul refers to justification by faith alone, he is thus referring to the fact that no works precede justification; when James speaks of justification involving works, he is referring to those works which are the consequence of prior justification.

In light of what has been noted previously concerning Barnes's view of the necessity and inevitability of works in the life of the justified man, it is surprising that he is so tentative, almost reluctant, in proposing this explanation of Augustine. Possibly he is still not convinced that Augustine was correct concerning James and feels that the letter might possibly teach justification

---

[44] *WA (DB)* 7. 388. Luther's attitude to James is encapsulated in his marginal comments on James 2: 24: 'Daß der Mensch durch die Werke gerecht wird. Das ist falsch!' Luther underlines the point with characteristic humour in his comment on James 3: 1: 'Unterwinde sich nicht jedermann. Ei! wenn du es doch auch beobachtet hättest.'

[45] 'But notwithstanding all these things, I will grant you this epistle to be of authority that you may have something to dispute with', *1531* liii. b.

[46] Clebsch fails to note that Barnes does allow for the hypothetical canonicity of the letter in 1531, and thus does not realise the hint of difference with Luther over the letter which appears implicit in Barnes's use of Augustine's interpretation: see Clebsch, p. 66.

by works, or perhaps he is unwilling to disagree publicly with the opinions of Luther. Whatever the reason, the crucial point is that Barnes's rejection of James is far from emphatic in 1531; indeed, he outlines an interpretation of the letter which allows for the hypothetical canonicity of James but which does not contradict his own view of the relationship between justification by faith alone and good works. In this matter one can possibly discern the influence of his patristic learning leading him towards deviating from the views of Luther.

The Bondage of the Will

In his essay on justification, Barnes has established that justification is subjectively appropriated by faith, which is itself a gift of God's grace. Now he turns from the theological to the anthropological aspects of salvation in order to show that faith is necessary as a gift not simply because that is how God has chosen to operate but because the very nature of fallen man demands it. That the doctrine of man's will is the key to a correct theology is vigorously asserted by Luther in the conclusion to *The Bondage of the Will*.[47] Barnes's agreement with this sentiment is shown by the fact that he devotes a whole section of his treatise to the subject, and by the polemical vigour with which he expounds the doctrine. Moreover, it is generally held by scholars that Barnes does no more than reproduce the arguments of Luther as laid out in the *The Bondage of the Will*.[48] However, a careful examination of Barnes's argument reveals his adherence to the position of Luther is not as uniform as has been suggested.

The essay opens with Barnes carefully defining exactly what it is he intends to examine:

In this article will we not dispute what man may do by the common influence given him of God over these inferior and worldly things, as what power he hath in eating and drinking . . . but here will we search what strength is in man of his natural powers, without the spirit of God, for to do or to will those things that be acceptable unto God.[49]

---

[47] See *Studienausgabe* 3. 355.
[48] C. Anderson, 'Robert Barnes on Luther', in *Interpreters of Luther*, ed. J. Pelikan (Philadelphia, 1968) 50; Clebsch, p. 71; McGoldrick, p. 105.
[49] *1531* lxxxi. a.

In making this distinction, Barnes is following Luther's approach in *The Bondage of the Will* but the relationship between the two men upon this point is not quite as simple as might first appear. In the first place, Luther shows extreme reserve in allowing the term 'free will' to be used at all, and would rather that it should be completely abolished. Indeed, when he allows that it may be used in non-spiritual matters, it is a concession and not a reflection of his own beliefs. Barnes never shows any such reserve in his use of the term.[50]

The second point is that Barnes's differentiation between man's bondage in matters of salvation and freedom concerning earthly pursuits contains none of the tensions inherent in Luther's own use of the distinction. Unlike Luther, Barnes does not build his argument on the axiom of God's immutability with its implications of absolute determinism.[51] It has been argued that the Lutheran concept of immutability is present in Barnes's formulations concerning the will of God,[52] but the relevant reference occurs in a passage discussing why sinners will not turn to God of their own unaided will. The point Barnes is making is that sinners cannot act in a way inconsistent with their sinful nature. Thus the immutability being referred to is that which means a creature cannot of his own strength change his moral nature from bad to good. This is not the same as arguing deductively from the immutability of God to a doctrine of determinism.[53] In fact, such an argument, axiomatic to Luther's position in *The Bondage of the Will*, is never used by Barnes in his discussion of the will. This means that the tension present in Luther's work is absent from that of Barnes. Barnes omission of such a fundamental aspect of *The Bondage of the Will* reveals a significant departure from the argument of Luther. Failure to notice this has been an important factor in the simplistic identification of the substance of the essays of the two men.

Having defined the point at issue, Barnes moves into the main body of the argument. As in his treatment of justification, his first argument is based upon the relationship of Christ to

[50] *Studienausgabe* 3. 210.   [51] See Ch. 3.
[52] Anderson, 'The Person and Position of Dr. Robert Barnes', 198. Cf. 'Robert Barnes on Luther', 49.
[53] *1531* xciii. a–b.

salvation. The text he uses is John 15: 5–6, which he expounds as meaning that man can do nothing worthwhile towards his own salvation unless he already has Christ 'in him'.[54] This is the logical development of the exclusive role of Christ in salvation which was established in his essay on justification. This indicates that he sees the bondage of man's will as flowing in one respect from the nature of Christ's role in salvation. While this text is dealt with by Luther in *The Bondage of the Will*, it is examined because he believes it has been misinterpreted by Erasmus, and not because it forms a fundamental part of his own positive argument against free will.[55] While the influence of Luther's interpretation of this passage on Barnes cannot be discounted, Barnes himself chooses to quote Augustine as his authority.[56] This, and its primary place in his argument, indicate that Barnes's theology is not being shaped only by the theology of Luther.

Having argued for the bondage of the will in terms of the Christological nature of salvation, Barnes now turns to his previous conclusions regarding the relationship between man and works in order to formulate a second conclusion regarding the power of the will. To begin with, he refers to the analogy of the tree and the fruit (Matt. 7. 16), and to the statement of Christ concerning the pharisees (Matt. 12: 34). The point is the same as that made earlier with regard to justification: an evil man cannot perform good deeds.[57] According to Barnes, sin affects the whole of man's being. This leads him to take issue with the Scotist distinction between man's lower and higher faculties, where it is only the former, the fleshly desires and not the will, which are regarded as profoundly affected.[58] In opposition to this, Barnes adopts the same position as Luther in asserting that it is the whole man who is corrupted and that there is no good left within him:

For all that is in man, heart, soul, flesh, and bone, etc., with all their works, is but flesh except the Spirit of God be there.[59]

---

[54] *1531* lxxxi. b–lxxxii. a. [55] *Studienausgabe* 3. 316–22.
[56] *1531* lxxxiii. b–lxxxiiii. a. [57] See *1531* lxxxiii. a–b.
[58] 'But here Master Duns' men will make a distinction, and say that flesh is taken here for fleshly desires only and voluptuousness, and not for the desires of the soul, nor for the election of the will', *1531* lxxxiiii. b. Cf. Calvin, *Institutes* 2. 2. 3 for a similar criticism of Scotus.
[59] *1531* lv. a.

Thus unregenerate man is not a kind of duality where one part of him wishes to pursue one course of moral action while another desires differently: his whole being is corrupt and aims to sin.[60] It is clear from this that Barnes's anthropology dovetails neatly into his belief that salvation is by grace: man is incapable of initiating any move towards God because there is nothing within him to motivate him in such a direction.

It is at this point in the argument that Barnes introduces a concept important both for understanding his view of the will and for evaluating the influence of Luther upon him. This concerns the role of the Fall, and is introduced by a quotation from the *Enchiridion* of Augustine.[61] To this quotation, Barnes adds the following comment of his own:

How think you by this, you defenders of free will? Doth he not clearly say that man hath lost his free will by sin? And can no more do unto goodness than a dead man can do to make himself alive again. Yea, he can do nothing but delight in sin. Call you that a freedom? Call you that *bonum conatum*? Call you that a preparing to grace?[62]

The point of Barnes's argument here is that man lost his free will through the Fall. In order for man to have been able to lose it, however, he must first of all have possessed it. The implication of this statement is that Barnes believes that man had free will prior to the Fall. Such an idea is important because it contradicts the doctrine taught by Luther and places him much closer to the thought of Augustine.[63] Even the title of this section, *That free will of her own strength can do nothing but sin*, is suggestive of the Augustinian idea of captive free will. His selection of the quotation from Augustine and his subsequent commentary on the passage where he argues that man's bondage

[60] Luther makes substantially the same point in *De Servo Arbitrio*, although his particular opponent is, of course, not Scotus but Erasmus: see *Studienausgabe* 3. 310.

[61] See *1531* lxxxiii. b–lxxxiiii. a. The original reads: 'Quid enim boni operatur perditus, nisi quantum fuerit a perditione liberatus? Numquid libero voluntatis arbitrio? Et hoc absit: nam libero arbitrio male utens homo, et se perdidit et ipsum. Sicut enim qui se occidit, utique vivendo se occidit, sed se occidendo inon vivit, nec se ipsum poterit resuscitare cum occiderit: ita cum libero peccaretur arbitrio, victore peccato amissum est liberum arbitrium, a quo enim quis devictus est, huic et servus addictus est (2 Pet. 2: 19). Petri certe apostoli est ista sententia: quae cum vera sit, qualis, quaeso, potest servi addicti esse libertas, nisi quando eum peccare delectat?', *PL* 40. 246–7.

[62] *1531* lxxxiiii, a.

[63] This point has not been noticed in other studies of Barnes's thought. For the differences between Augustine and Luther on this matter, see the discussion in Ch. 3.

is the result of the Fall all point away from Luther and towards Augustine as the major influence in this matter. Furthermore, the absence of any argument based upon the immutability of God enables Barnes to follow Augustine's thinking at this point without creating tensions within his theology. This is in contrast to Luther, whose necessitarian argument forces him to a tacit rejection of Augustine's view that it is the Fall which deprives the will of freedom. Barnes's omission of the immutability of God as a basic premise in his discussion of free will is no mere cosmetic difference but has far reaching theological implications.

Such a radical difference in approach raises the question of why Barnes does not follow Luther in a point so basic to the latter's argument. There are three possible solutions to this problem: he is either unaware of Luther's position or does not appreciate its significance; he is aware of Luther's position and its significance but rejects it; or his methodological approach precludes him from stating the Lutheran doctrine.

The first answer, that Barnes is unaware of Luther's precise thinking at this point, or at least unaware of its significance, is the least likely of the three. Barnes knew Luther personally, had read his works, and had studied under him. Thus it is unlikely that when he comes to write on the subject of man's will he is not fully conversant with Luther's approach to the subject. It is of course possible that he did not grasp the full significance of the doctrine of divine immutability for Luther's argument. For example, Zwingli read Luther and interpreted him in such a way as to confirm his own Humanist convictions without initially appreciating the novel elements of Luther's theology.[64] Tyndale too appears to have been an admirer of Luther at a time when his own convictions were basically those of an Erasmian. However, Erasmus's reply to Luther, *Hyperaspistes*, concentrated upon refuting the doctrine of divine immutability, and, if Barnes read this work, he would most certainly be aware that this doctrine was fundamental to Luther's argument. Nevertheless, it cannot be proved that Barnes read the *Hyperaspistes* and so it is just possible that he was unaware of Luther's position.

The second explanation, that Barnes rejects Luther's argument at this point, is more plausible. It is possible that his training in

---

[64] See Stephens, *The Theology of Huldrych Zwingli*, 45–6.

the classics led him to associate Luther's argument from divine immutability with pagan ideas of determinism. Indeed, Luther does quote Virgil in support of his position, which Barnes never does. However, there is no indication that Barnes disapproves of Luther on these grounds, and, if he does so, it is surprising that he follows Luther in the matter of double predestination. Alternatively, it is possible that Barnes feels that this part of Luther's argument was very weak and vulnerable to the criticisms of Catholic opponents. Therefore, when he comes to write on the subject himself, he finds that a return to the doctrine of Augustine avoids the tensions inherent in Luther's argument. Furthermore, it has the added polemical advantage of enabling him to claim, as he does, that he is only following the teachings of Augustine and is therefore truly Catholic in maintaining a strongly anti-Pelagian view of the will.

The third possibility is that Barnes's method prevents him from stating the doctrine in the terms used by Luther. This is because his self-imposed method involves supporting doctrinal propositions with quotations from patristic sources whose authority is accepted by his opponents. This means that his argument will generally contain only those elements which he can find in, or at least plausibly extract from, patristic authors. It might be argued against this that Barnes explicitly subjects the Fathers to the authority of scripture, and is also not afraid to quote scripture on its own in the course of the argument. However, his general practice, even when quoting scripture, is to find an exposition of the text in the patristic sources. This reflects his stated concern both to meet his opponents on a common ground of authority and to demonstrate that Reformation doctrine is a recovery of the teaching of the early Church. As a result, his presentation of the subject of the bondage of the will is constructed primarily around quotations from Augustine, and therefore reflects the general pattern of Augustine's thinking upon the subject. Since Augustine does not develop the idea of divine immutability as the basis for the bondage of the will, this might therefore be the reason why it is omitted by Barnes.

It would most certainly be incorrect to see the last two explanations of Barnes's apparent deviation from Luther on this issue as mutually exclusive alternatives. While Barnes's method certainly influences his presentation of theological issues, he is prepared to introduce elements that are distinctively Lutheran, such as his formulation of double predestination. He is also willing to prefer the views of Luther to those of Augustine, as in his interpretation of Pharaoh's hardening. Thus, there is no reason to believe that Barnes does hold to Luther's view of immutability but does not mention it merely because of methodological constraints. It is therefore reasonable to interpret Barnes's silence on the matter as a tacit rejection of Luther's position.[65] It is thus clear that in the matter of man's loss of free will, Barnes follows Augustine rather than Luther in allowing that man's will is in bondage as a result of the Fall not of his status as a creature.

The Problem of the Law

Having asserted that fallen man cannot turn to God through his own strength and volition, Barnes now faces the same problem posed by Erasmus to Luther: if man cannot obey the commands of the law, why did God issue them?

In approaching this problem, Barnes chooses not to address the purpose of the commandments directly, but first of all to establish a doctrine of God upon which to build his argument. From this position, he addresses the subject of the commandments as it is raised in particular scriptural passages used by the opposition.

The first point that Barnes makes is that an infinite qualitative difference exists between God and man, which means that man has no right to question the reason for which God does things. To do so is the act of 'blind, presumptuous and damnable reason'.[66] The second point, closely related to the first, is that the commands are grounded in the being of God, who is essential goodness, and that they are framed with reference to this, not to the needs of man. Discussion of the commandments is therefore to be theocentric. As a result, the question, 'Why does God give commands if man cannot fulfil them?', is

[65] Those who wish to maintain that Barnes himself does hold to Luther's argument might find some support in his statement regarding the Fall on fol. xci. b: 'Now was it not free for him to use this tree after his own will but after the commandment of God; and what power he had by his free will to keep this commandment the effect did declare'. The implication seems to be that the Fall was outside the sphere of man's free will. However, the hint is too slight to base any decisive argument upon it.

[66] *1531* ixxxvi. b.

irrelevant, because God's giving of commands has nothing to do with the ability of man. If he wills to command something, that is a sufficient reason.[67]

However, the commands do concern man because they are addressed to him, and so Barnes is forced to relate them to his anthropology. He regards their function as being twofold. First, they are to subdue the pride of man by revealing to him his own inability:

> Thy maker knoweth that they be impossible for thee. He knoweth also thy damnable and presumptuous pride that reckonest how thou canst do all things that be good of thine own strength without any other help; and, to subdue this presumptuous pride of thine, and to bring thee to knowledge of thine own self, he hath given thee his commandments; of which thou canst not complain, for they be both righteous and good.[68]

So the law is to show man his pride and inability, bringing about self-knowledge.[69] However, Barnes does not stop here but proceeds to argue that condemnation through the law leads to positive results:

> But now wilt thou ask, What remedy? No remedy but this only, to confess thy weakness, to confess thy pride, to knowledge thy unableness, to grant that these commandments be lawful, holy and good, and how thou art bound to keep them, and to give laud and praise to God for them.[70]

This passage follows the basic Lutheran argument that the law shows man his weakness over against Erasmus' view that the commands imply man's ability to fulfil them. However, Barnes never uses the extremely negative language which Luther employs in his treatment of the law, and this suggests a possible difference between the thought of the two men. Indeed, in this passage there is in fact much positive language used to describe the law. For example, the idea of the law eliciting praise to God

---

[67] See *1531* lxxxvi. b–lxxxvii. a.

[68] *1531* lxxxvii. a.

[69] The idea of the law as bringing self-knowledge to man is common also to Tyndale and Frith. In his prologue to the New Testament of 1525, Tyndale makes the following comment: 'The law . . . was given to bring us unto the knowledge of ourselves', *NT 25*. 4. Frith too devotes a whole tract to self-knowledge, which is defined as the realization that all good comes from God, and in which the demands of the law play an important part: see Russell, pp. 263–79.

[70] *1531* lxxvii. b.

is a concept foreign to Luther's way of thinking, and this difference is made even more dramatic by the fact that Barnes makes no reference either to Christ or to the gospel promises in this context. There is a possible hint here that, while Barnes is pursuing a characteristically Lutheran theme, i.e. that the commands do not imply natural ability, he is, in fact, deviating in terms of emphasis from a strictly Lutheran position on the nature of the law's relationship to man.[71] Indeed, his more positive statements in this context are reminiscent of those made by Tyndale.

Barnes's formulation of his position involves the use of both Augustine and Luther. First, he initially appears to adopt the position of Augustine, rather than Luther, as regards the ability of regenerate man to fulfil the commands: as the commands subdue pride and elicit praise to God, man turns to God and asks him for the strength to be able to fulfil the law. Barnes supports this idea with a quotation from Augustine's *On Grace and Free Will*.[72] That Barnes apparently agrees with the sentiments expressed by Augustine is underlined by his own comments on the quotation:

But St. Augustine saith they [the commandments] be impossible, and therefore they be given that we should know our weakness and also ask the strength to fulfil them; for faith by prayer doth obtain strength to fulfil the impossible commandments of the law.[73]

In stating that regenerate man is given the strength to fulfil the law Barnes appears to be closer to the position of Augustine than to that of Luther. However, it is at this point that his approach becomes confused by a reversion to a more thoroughly Lutheran stance when he turns to Ecclus. 15: 14–17:

[71] Anderson argues that this positive view of the law is similar to that held by Melanchthon and Calvin: see 'The Person and Position of Dr. Robert Barnes', 206. It is certain that the latter is not the source on purely chronological grounds, and, while Melanchthon is a possibility, there is no positive evidence to prove this. McGoldrick, in his discussion of the law in Barnes's theology makes no mention of the more positive approach adopted by the Englishman, and implicitly identifies his view with that of Luther. This is another example of his simplistic over-identification of the theologies of the two men: see McGoldrick, pp. 128–35.

[72] See *1531* lxxxvii. b–lxxxviii. a. The quotation from Augustine is: 'Magnum aliquid Pelagiani se scire putant, quando dicunt, "Non juberet Deus, quod sciret non posse ab homine fieri." Quis hoc nesciat? Sed ideo jubet aliqua quae non possumus, ut noverimus quid ab illo petere debeamus', *PL* 44. 900.

[73] *1531* lxxxviii. b.

God himself made man from the beginning, and left him in the hand of his own counsel. If thou wilt, thou shalt keep the commandments; and to perform faithfulness is of thine good pleasure. He hath set fire and water before thee: thou shalt stretch forth thy hand unto whichsoever thou wilt. Before man is life and death; and whichsoever he liketh, it shall be given him. [Revised Authorized Version]

This passage was of key importance to the argument employed by Erasmus in his *Diatribe* and it is dealt with in detail by Luther. Barnes's own exposition of the passage follows closely that of Luther and is obviously dependent upon him. For example, both men refer the verses to man's creation task of being Lord of all creatures, and not to the freedom or otherwise of his will.[74] Secondly, they both interpret the commands not as implying man's ability but as demonstrating his subjection to God because God both gives him instructions concerning how he is to govern and restricts his freedom by forbidding him to eat the fruit of the tree of the knowledge of good and evil.[75] Thus far, Barnes has clearly followed the reasoning of *The Bondage of the Will*. However, at this point in his work, Luther goes on to expatiate on the concept of the two kingdoms, that which is earthly, where man is in charge, and that which is spiritual, where God makes the rules. Barnes, however, departs from the flow of Luther's argument in *The Bondage of the Will* at this point and makes the following statement concerning the Fall:

Now was it not free for him to use this tree after his own will but after the commandment of God, and what power he had by his free will to keep this commandment the effect did declare.[76]

---

[74] '"Deus constituit hominem ab initio" hic de creatione hominis loquitur, nec adhuc quicquam vel de lib(ero) arb(itrio) vel de praeceptis dicit', *Studienausgabe* 3. 240; '"God from the beginning did make man." These words be open of the creation of the first man. "He left him in the hands of his own counsel." These words make nothing for free will, for where is nothing commanded him to do but alonely here is signified that man is made lord over all creatures, to use them at his pleasure', *1531* xci. a–b.

[75] '"Adiecit mandata (et) praecepta sua." Ad quid adiecit? nempe ad consilium (et) arbitriu(m) hominis et ultra illam constitutione(m) dominij humani super res alias, Quibus praeceptis ademit homini dominiu(m) una parte creaturaru(m) "puta arboris scientiae boni et mali" ac potius non liberum voluit', *Studienausgabe* 3, 240; '"He did add his commandments and his precepts." In these words is there no power given unto him, but here be given him commandments whereby he must be ordered and ruled. . . . Wherefore, by these commandments was there part of his free domination and lordship that he had over the inferior things taken away, as where God commanded him that he should not eat of the tree of knowledge both of good and evil', *1531* xci. b.

[76] *1531* xci. b.

Here Barnes is apparently going beyond Augustine and coming very close to Luther's position whereby the Fall is not the result of the choice of man's free will. This appears to contradict his close adherence to Augustine's understanding of the Fall in the earlier part of this essay, and constitutes the nearest approach he makes to the necessitarian position of Luther. However, it is not necessary to regard this as a contradiction if one interprets Barnes as meaning not that God determined that man should fall, but that pre-Fall man himself was designed to live in communion with God and to rely upon God's strength to fulfil his allotted tasks. This explanation ties in well with Barnes's underlying definition of free will as the ability of man to make choices. It also points to a synthesis of the view of Augustine and Luther, adopting the former's positive view of the law and the latter's belief that a command does not imply natural ability.

Further evidence of Barnes's fundamental agreement with Augustine concerning the law is his emphasis on the role of the Holy Spirit in enabling man to fulfil the commandments. Significantly, the Christological emphasis, which was so evident in the essay on justification and at the start of this work, is completely absent from discussion of man's abilities in respect of the law. There is no emphatic contrast of the law and the gospel; rather, the justified man actually receives, through the Holy Spirit, the ability to fulfil the law.[77] In this respect, Barnes' thinking is very similar to that of Tyndale, who also emphasized the role of the Holy Spirit in this context.[78]

---

[77] 'For the Spirit of God is not given us to give commandments, but for to give us strength to fulfil and righteously to understand those things that be commanded us. By the commandment is declared that we ought to do, and also they show our weakness and imbecility that we might learn to seek for a greater strength and greater help than is in us', *1531* xcii. b.

[78] While Tyndale and Barnes both have more positive views of the law than Luther, their views are not identical Tyndale uses the law as the basis for his covenant scheme, a scheme which not only has relevance for the ethical dimension of the Christian life, but which provides the fundamental hermeneutical key to understanding the scriptures. Barnes, however, while agreeing with Tyndale concerning the believer being enabled to fulfil the law, though not perfectly, does not use this as the basis for covenant theology. Rather his interpretation of the commands flows from his doctrines of God and man, and 'faith alone' still provides the key to the scriptures. He does not develop the idea of a covenant founded upon the promises and commands, and does not make works a primary source of assurance. It is arguable that the difference between the two men on this issue is purely terminological, but it does reveal a difference in emphasis and in interpretation of the scriptures, in the latter of which Barnes is much closer to Luther than is Tyndale.

There are several explanations for this difference with Luther over the role of the law. It is possible that Barnes's Humanist background left him with a concern for practical morality that makes him unwilling to reject outright the law as a positive guide for the Christian. It is also possible that he has noticed the ambivalence in Luther's own position on the law and that he has chosen to adopt the more positive aspects of the latter's doctrine while rejecting the more extreme position expressed, for example, in the heat of the free will controversy.[79] When one remembers that Barnes's own view of good works is that they are done for God's glory and for the profit of one's neighbour, the difference between him and Luther is virtually reduced to one of terminology. Another explanation is that Barnes is deliberately following Augustine's view of the law, as evidenced by his extensive use of Augustine's works in the discussion. It is impossible to tell whether it is one or all of these factors which influences Barnes here. All that can be said with certainty is that Barnes is not adopting the extreme position concerning the law which Luther advocates in *The Bondage of the Will*.

Before leaving the subject of the law, it is worth looking briefly at Barnes view of Scotus, against whose doctrine of the will the treatise is directed. The precise doctrine that Scotus held concerning the will is a matter of debate down to the present day. McSorley provides a useful summary of Catholic views of Scotus, some of which interpret him as semi-Pelagian, others as Augustinian. McSorley's own conclusion is that Scotus is guilty only of unclear terminology.[80]

Barnes himself appears to have been aware of Scotus' ambiguity on this point,[81] but, in the interest of his own anti-medieval polemic, he chooses to interpret him as a semi-Pelagian. Having quoted Scotus' views concerning self-preparation for grace, he makes the following observation:

[79] For the ambivalent nature of Luther's view of the law, see Ch. 3.

[80] See McSorley, p. 169. Much of the ambiguity probably arises from the fact that Scotus' doctrine of the will arises from his philosophical presuppositions and not primarily from his interpretation of biblical texts: see L. D. Roberts, 'Indeterminism in Duns Scotus' Doctrine of Human Freedom', *The Modern Schoolman* 51 (1973), 1–16.

[81] 'Duns, being wrapped between carnal reason and the invincible scriptures of St. Paul, cannot tell whether he may grant that the will of God is alonely the cause of election or else any merits of man preceding afore; he concludeth that both the opinions may be defended' *1531* xcv. b.

This is ten times worse than the Pelagians' sayings, for they grant that man must needs have a special grace to perform his good purpose, and Master Duns saith that man may perform his attrition of his natural power; yea, and this attrition of congruence is a disposition to take away mortal sin without any special grace.[82]

It is not the purpose of this study to evaluate the accuracy of Barnes's interpretation of Scotus, which is largely irrelevant to the understanding of Barnes's own thinking on the matter. However, the above outburst aimed against Scotus is significant because it has a close parallel in *The Bondage of the Will*, except that there it is aimed against the view of Erasmus.[83] In fact, this passage in Barnes is possibly the closest verbal following of Luther's argument in the whole treatise and decisively proves his textual dependence upon the latter.

In his treatment of the law, Barnes adopts a position that combines both Augustinian and Lutheran elements. He avoids the more extreme statements of Luther, and describes the law in language that is characteristically more positive than the latter. His emphasis is not simply upon the role of the law in convicting of sin and revealing man's impotence, but also upon the link between the law and the practical morality of the believer's life.

Predestination

Having established that the commands do not imply that fallen man has the ability to fulfil them, Barnes now has to deal with those texts which appear to imply that man can turn to God using his natural power. The major text he deals with in this connection is Matt. 23: 37, where Christ weeps over the impenitence of Jerusalem, a text with which Luther also deals in *The Bondage of the Will*. Barnes's interpretation of this passage provides important insights into his theology:

---

[82] *1531* lxxxix. a.

[83] 'Deinde quod hac hypocrisi gratiam Dei longe vilius (et) aestimamus (et) emimus quam Pelagiani. Hi enim non esse aliquod pusillum in nobis asserunt, quo gratiam consequamur, sed tota, plena, perfecta, magna (et) multa esse studia (et) opera, Nostri vero minimum (et) fere nihil esse, quo gratiam meremur. Si igitur errandum est, honestius illi errant (et) minus superbe, qui gratiam Dei magno constare dicunt, charam (et) preciosam habentes, quam ij, qui parvo (et) pusillo eam constare docent, vilem (et) contemptibilem habentes', *Studienausgabe* 3. 338.

First must we consider that there are two manner of wills in God: one is called his godly will or his secret or inscrutable will, whereby that all things be made and ordered, and all things be done. Of this will no creature hath knowledge what he ought thereby to do or not to do, for, as St. Paul saith, it is inscrutable, and therefore it is sufficient for us to know thereof alonely that there is an inscrutable will. The other will in God is called a declared and a manifested will. The which is declared and given to us in Holy Scriptures. This will was shown unto us to the uttermost by our Master Christ, the Son of God, and therefore is it lawful, and also all men are bound to search to know this will and for that consideration was it manifested unto us. This will doth declare what every man is bound to do and what every man is bound to fly. And by this will is offered unto every man those things that be of salvation, and by this will God will have no man damned. Now he that will know this will must go to our Master Christ in whom, as St Paul saith, be all treasures of wisdom and science. So that he will show us as much as is necessary for us to know, and as much as the Father of heaven would we should know.[84]

Having established such a distinction, Barnes then interprets Matt. 13: 37 as having reference to the revealed will of God: God, as revealed in Christ, desired that Jerusalem be saved, but, in terms of his hidden will, he had determined that this should not be so. Christ did all he could to convert the Jews, but God had blinded them.[85]

The distinction itself has its origin in the scriptures, and, from the time of Augustine, it became part of the theological vocabulary for dealing with problems raised by predestination. As we noted earlier, the concept is a central part of Luther's argument in his controversy with Erasmus.[86] In *The Bondage of the Will*, Luther deals with Matt. 23: 37 but only mentions the revealed aspect of God's will in this context. However, Barnes's tract is shorter and thus he concentrates more theological arguments into the treatment of fewer texts. His argument is entirely consonant with the position of Luther. Both men stress God's revelation in Christ, showing an identical christocentric emphasis and guarding against a speculative treatment of the concept of predestination. Thus it is clear that Barnes is closely following Luther in this matter.

[84] *1531* xcii. b–xciii. a.
[85] *1531* xciii. a–b.
[86] For further discussion of this distinction and its dogmatic problems, see Ch. 3.

Barnes's assertion that it is ultimately God who is responsible for men not turning to Christ because he blinds them, takes him beyond the single predestination of Augustine to the double predestination of Luther. It also raises the obvious question: how can God justly condemn men for doing what they cannot avoid, especially if it is he who hardens their hearts? The question is very similar to that concerning the purpose of commands, and Barnes answers it in a similar fashion. First of all, however, he introduces the Lutheran distinction between the necessity of immutability and the necessity of compulsion: God does not compel men to sin in an external-mechanical way that violates the orientation of their will; rather, he operates in accordance with their will.[87] This is a further example of Barnes's adoption of Lutheran concepts in dealing with this area of theology. Then, as with discussion of the commandments, he returns to the doctrine of God, asserting that by his very nature God cannot will something which is unjust. Therefore none of his acts can be described as unjust.[88] Out of this flows Barnes's view of the nature of faith which is clearly borrowed from Luther:

Moreover, thou believest that God is righteous, that God is wise, and that God is merciful. Now faith is of those things that do not appear, nor that can be proved by exterior causes. Hold thee fast to this faith, then all thy fleshly reasons be afoiled. For, when God saveth so few men and damneth so many, and thou knowest no cause why, yet must thou believe that he is merciful and righteous. This is faith, which, if it could be proved by exterior causes, then were it no need to believe it.[89]

[87] 'But it standeth in that that [*sic*] all thing that he will or will not is at his own will and is not thereto constrained but willeth it freely without any compulsion, and yet he cannot choose, no, nor will not choose so to will or so not to will. So that there is a necessity immutable, but not a necessity of compulsion or coaction', *1531* xciii. b. Cf. *Studienausgabe* 3. 206–7.

[88] *1531* xciiii. a–b.

[89] *1531* xciiii. b. Cf. 'Altera est Quod fides est rerum non apparentium, Ut ergo fidei locus sit, opus est, ut omnia quae creduntur, abscondantur, Non aut(em) remotius absconduntur, quam sub contrario obiectu, sensu, experientia. . . . Hic est fidei summus gradus, credere illum esse clementem, qui tam paucos salvat, tam multos damnat. . . . Si igitur possem ulla ratione comprehendere, quomodo is Deus sit misericors (et) iustus, qui tantam iram (et) iniquitatem ostendit, non esset opus fide', *Studienausgabe* 3. 206. It is strange that O. T. Hargrave fails to notice that Barnes's statement at this point is simply a reiteration of the Lutheran view of the matter. This leads him to compare Barnes to Ochino, who makes similar statements concerning faith, without apparently realizing that they may both be drawing independently from Lutheran sources: see 'The Doctrine of Predestination in the English Reformation', unpubl. Ph.D. diss. (Vanderbilt University, 1966), 17, 64.

In proposing such a definition of faith, Barnes effectively side-steps any speculative notion of predestination, and instead places the doctrine at the centre of Christian experience, inasmuch as it is a fundamental aspect of God and something to be accepted in faith. Indeed, it can only be accepted by faith because it contradicts reason.

Having asserted that predestination is a truth, Barnes now proceeds to establish his case from the scriptures. He has approached the subject through his anthropology, and has employed the idea primarily as a means of interpreting Matt. 23: 37. As such, the doctrine has fulfilled the function of undergirding his doctrine of grace in the light of man's impotence and has not been used as a theological axiom. It is only after this that Barnes proceeds to provide the doctrine with an explicitly biblical basis.[90]

Any discussion of election must start by attempting to define its cause. It is upon this issue that Barnes and his opponents disagree: they see foreseen merits as the cause; Barnes sees the sovereign will of God as the only cause. The example Barnes uses to illustrate this is that of Jacob and Esau, the former of whom was elect, and the latter reprobate, before they were even born. To the objection that God predestined them according to their foreseen merits or demerits, Barnes quotes Rom. 9: 15 as upholding the sovereignty of God's merciful choice in this matter.[91]

To make his point yet more emphatically, Barnes now turns to the case of the hardening of Pharaoh's heart. This is an interesting choice, as both Augustine and Luther interpret this passage in different ways. This difference facilitates a comparison between their respective positions and that of Barnes.

To a large extent, Barnes's exposition of the incident is simply an application of the theological principles he has developed so far, but there is some new material. First of all, Barnes rejects the argument that God is merely passive in the process and

---

[90] In his study of Barnes, McGoldrick places predestination at the start of his discussion of Barnes's soteriology: see McGoldrick, p. 110. Such a position is misleading, as it distorts Barnes's own emphasis: predestination is not the starting point for his discussion of salvation, but its terminus beyond which it is not possible for man's thoughts to penetrate. It flows from, and serves to undergird, previous statements concerning the relationship between God and man in salvation.

[91] *1531* xcv. b.

that Pharaoh's hardening is simply the result of God's permissive will allowing him to sin. This view was advocated by Origen, Jerome and the Catholic Glosses, all of which are criticized by name, revealing that Barnes is not frightened of criticizing the Fathers when he feels they are incorrect.[92] Against this view, Barnes argues strongly for the natural grammatical sense of the words, which demands that God took an active role in the process.[93] Luther too stresses the simple sense of the words, but does so with far more brevity.[94] Having refuted this interpretation on grammatical grounds, Barnes now turns to what he sees as the correct understanding, which is to be found through an application of his earlier conclusions concerning the relationship between man and grace. When Adam fell, all mankind fell with him, and so all men are by nature evil. However, by grace God has made some men good. Thus every man is either an evil man, according to nature, or a good man, according to grace.[95] All men are also moved by God, as he is their creator.[96] Now, Barnes is able to acquit God of being responsible for moral evil by using the same idea that underlies the concept of the necessity of immutability (i.e. that God works in each man according to his nature).[97] The analogy he uses for this is the same as that employed by Luther, and presumably taken directly from him: that of the good workman using the bad saw. As the resulting cut is poor because of the tool and not because of the poor skill of the workman, so evil acts are the results of man's moral corruption and not the direct acts of God.[98]

This much of the argument could be deduced from what has gone before, but Barnes adds one more element: it is the nature of natural man to be hardened by the things of God. When the word is preached, as it was through Moses to Pharaoh, the

---

[92] *1531* xcvii. a.
[93] *1531* xcvii. a–xcviii. b.
[94] *Studienausgabe* 3. 280–1.
[95] *1531* xcviii. b.
[96] *1531* xcviii. b–xcix. a.
[97] *1531* xcix. a.
[98] 'A man doth saw a block with an evil saw, the which is nothing apt for to cut well, and yet must it needs cut at the moving of the man though it be never so evil. For the man in moving doth not change the nature of the saw. Nevertheless, the action of the man is good and cunningly done but the cutting of the saw is after his nature', *1531* xcix. a. Cf. Luther: 'Vitium ergo est in instrumentis, quae ociosa Deus esse non sinit, quod mala fiunt, movente ipso Deo, Non aliter quam si faber securi serrata (et) dentata male secaret', *Studienausgabe* 3. 278.

natural man is made harder and harder against it.[99] Thus, the hardening of Pharaoh is based upon his nature but is effected by God through the preaching of the gospel.[100] It is in this way that God can be said to harden the heart of Pharaoh, and, Barnes adds, those of the contemporary bishops.[101] In this matter, Barnes again shows himself in line with Luther's interpretation of the passage, as opposed to that of Augustine who interprets the hardening as the result of persistent sin and thus makes the cause of reprobation man's own intrinsic qualities and not the extrinsic decision of God.[102]

Of course, it might well be objected that Barnes does not deal with the reason why God does not alter the will of Pharaoh. For Barnes this is a question which must be left to the hidden will of God. Predestination is not a matter for speculation or which can be penetrated by the use of reason: his only concern is to show that it is a fact of revelation, and it is the task of faith simply to accept it as such.

In his treatment of predestination, Barnes develops his doctrine in a far more complex manner than either Tyndale or Frith. While they both allow for the distinction between God's

[99] 'Wherefore when God the author of goodness doth anything or saith anything unto them [wicked men], then are they more and more, sorer and sorer, contrary unto God and all his works', *1531* xcix. b. Cf. 'Haec ipsa irritatio impiorum [i.e. Euangelion], cum Deus illis contrarium dicit aut facit, quam vellent, est ipsorum induratio (et) ingravatio. Nam cum per sese sint aversi ipsa naturae corruptione, tum multo magis avertu(n)tur et peiores fiunt, dum ipsorum aversioni resistitur aut detrahitur', *Studienausgabe* 3. 279.

[100] 'When the blessed word of God is preached unto them that be wicked, to whom God hath given no grace to receive it, then they are nothing amended, but more indurated and all ways harder and harder, and the more the word of God is preached, the more obstinate are they', *1531* xcix. b. Cf. 'Sic indurat Pharaonem, cum impiae (et) malae eius voluntati offert verbum (et) opus quod illa odit, vitio scilicet ingenito (et) naturali corruptione', *Studienausgabe* 3. 280.

[101] 'After this manner was the heart of Pharaoh indurated when the word of God was declared unto him by Moses and he had no grace to receive it, then the more Moses laboured in the word, the more sturdier was he in withstanding of it and all ways harder and harder. . . . What need we to go into Egypt to fetch an example of this: look of our bishops', *1531* xcix. b–c. a.

[102] Augustine treats this matter in *De Gratia et Libero Arbitrio*: 'Nam invenimus aliqua peccata etiam poenas esse aliorum peccatorum: sicut sunt vasa irae, quae perfecta dicit Apostolus in perditionem (Rom. 9: 22): sicut est induratio Pharaonis, cujus et causa dicitur, ad ostendendam in illo virtutem Dei (Exod. 7: 3, and 10: 1).' *PL* 44. 906); 'Fixum enim debet esse et immobile in corde vestro, quia non est iniquitas apud Deum (Rom. 9: 14). Ac pere hoc quando legitis in Litteris veritatis, a Deo seduci homines, aut obtundi vel obdurari corda eorum, nolite dubitare praecessisse mala merita eorum, ut juste ista paterentur', *PL* 44. 909; cf. *PL* 44. 910–11.

will as hidden and as revealed, they do not use this concept as a means of interpreting difficult passages of scripture. Instead, they emphasize; that it is God's revelation that is important, and that man must look no further than sin for the cause of any individual's reprobation. Thus they are fundamentally single predestinarians and do not follow Luther in this matter. Indeed, by advocating double predestination and by linking this to his doctrine of faith, Barnes is easily the most vigorous predestinarian of the three. However, like Tyndale and Frith, he develops the doctrine as the consequence of other related doctrines and does not use it as axiomatic in the formulation of his theology.[103]

Summary

Barnes's essay on justification begins by establishing the objective aspects of the doctrine. Christ is an all-sufficient saviour, and so to believe that man can contribute to his salvation in any way is a denial of Christ. Grace is the basis for salvation, which, by its very nature is free and unmerited. This precludes the idea that salvation may be earned. The exact details of how this salvation was achieved by Christ are not developed, and Barnes does not appear to have a clear doctrine of atonement. Salvation itself is appropriated through faith, faith which is not simply belief in objective doctrine but belief that God is who he has revealed himself to be: the heavenly Father of the believer. Such faith is not attainable by rational enquiry and is a gift from heaven. In describing faith, Barnes follows the language of Luther much more closely than either Tyndale or Frith. Once the believer has received faith, two things happen: he is justified, in that he has his sins remitted, and he starts to do good works as a grateful response to God's grace. Good works are therefore an essential for the believer, and, although Barnes is clearly undecided concerning the Letter

[103] In view of Barnes's vigorous statement of double predestination compared to the more reserved approaches of Tyndale and Frith, it is surprising that D. D. Wallace mentions him only very briefly in his study of English predestinarianism and makes no mention of his doctrine. Wallace gives more extensive treatment to Tyndale and Frith and his characterization of these two men as strong predestinarians is misleading and very much an exaggeration: see Wallace, *Puritans and Predestination*, 9. Pp. 8–13 are devoted to Tyndale and Frith. It is arguable that his passing over of Barnes results from Wallace's interest in the influence of Rhineland theologians upon English thought, but Barnes's writings show that Rhineland influences were not alone in making predestination important to English theology.

of James, he is able to offer an interpretation that allows for the book's hypothetical canonicity and yet does no violence to his view of justification by faith alone.

Barnes's treatment of the will is continuous with that of justification, and, as in the former essay, he takes Christ as his starting point. He then proceeds to argue that man's will has become enslaved to sin as the result of the Fall. In this matter, he agrees with Augustine and implicitly rejects the Lutheran notion that man's will is bound because of God's immutability. In dealing with the commands, he uses language that is more positive than that of Luther in the same context, and allows for regenerate man's ability to obey the law with the help of God. Finally, in dealing with predestination, Barnes develops this doctrine in order to undergird his doctrine of salvation by grace and to provide a key for interpreting difficult passages of scripture. He uses Lutheran concepts in this context, such as the distinction between God's will as hidden and as revealed, and advocates an unequivocal double predestination. This is a position not adopted by either Tyndale or Frith.

THE *SUPPLICATION* OF 1534

Unlike the earlier edition, this work was printed in London, indicating that Barnes was no longer an exile. In fact, he had returned to England in 1532 under a safe-conduct from Cromwell, and from then until his fall from favour he was to be used frequently on diplomatic missions. Therefore, the need for self-vindication was not so great as it had been, although the second edition does retain the section on the articles, and includes an additional record of Barnes's actual trial. However, the overall tone of the work is different. At a minor level, many polemics against the bishops are omitted, or toned down by replacing the accusatory 'you' with the more sympathetic 'we'. At a more serious level, many changes reflect the shift in the political scene. All passages that might have cast doubt upon the Royal Supremacy, such as the entire chapter *That men's constitutions bind not the conscience* are omitted.[104] Other chapters

---

[104] The changes concerning the political aspects of the treatise are discussed in W. D. J. Cargill Thompson, 'The Sixteenth-Century Editions of A Supplication unto King Henry the Eighth by Robert Barnes, DD: a Footnote to the Royal Supremacy',

omitted are those on the lawfulness of scripture in the vulgar tongue, on receiving the sacrament in both kinds, and on the idolatry of honouring images and praying to saints. In place of these, the new edition includes the account of Barnes's trial already mentioned, and an essay on the error of clerical celibacy. The chapter on the Church is a reply to Sir Thomas More, then in the Tower.

The significance of these revisions for Barnes's doctrine of salvation is limited to his views on justification, as he makes no significant changes to his essay on the will. However, even in the matter of justification it is important to realize that the omission or addition of entire sections does not necessarily imply any change in theology; they may simply reflect those issues which Barnes considered of importance to the Church at the time he was writing. However, when parts of reprinted essays are either omitted or changed dramatically in the second edition, it is safe to assume that there is an important reason for this. In the case of those matters relating to politics, the change can be seen as the result of the broader political climate. However, as the broader religious context was still conservative and hostile to the fundamentals of the Reformation, a change in theological content may well indicate a corresponding change in Barnes's own theology. It is on such alterations that Clebsch builds his case that Barnes moves to a more works-centred doctrine of justification in the 1534 edition.

Justification by Faith Alone

Clebsch's argument concerning the shift in Barnes thinking on justification concentrates upon the latter's revision of his comments upon the Letter of James. However, these revisions must be set within the context of the broader changes in the two editions. As these other changes occur in the text before James is discussed, such an approach does no violence to the flow of Barnes's argument.

Transactions of the Cambridge Bibliographical Society 3 (1960), 133–42. Clebsch's argument concerning Barnes's development hinges on textual variations between the 1531 and 1534 editions of the treatise. In light of this, it is incredible that J. E. McGoldrick can attempt a refutation of Clebsch using John Foxe's 1572 edition of the work which is, in fact, a conflation of the two earlier editions. If Clebsch is to be answered, the original texts must be used.

Various parts of the 1531 treatise are omitted in the 1534 edition. In 1531 Barnes started his discussion of justification with a statement of the authorities upon which he was to base his argument, i.e. the patristic authors subject to scripture. He also defined the nature of antichrist as one who did not necessarily deny the historical reality of Christ, but who denied his significance. The whole section was aimed at the bishops, and so in the changed climate of 1534, Barnes must have considered it wise to omit this passage. Polemic against the bishops remains, but it is more concise and restrained. It would be futile to argue that the omission of this passage also indicates that Barnes has come to reject the idea that belief in Christ is inseparable from belief in his effects. Other passages expressing this thought remain intact.[105] The reason for omission cannot therefore have been theological.

Two further large passages are omitted, both of which contain little but polemical application of Barnes's doctrine to the bishops and are not theologically significant.[106] Apart from the section on James, the only other areas of omission concern single words or minor sentences which do not alter the substance of what is said.

In terms of additions, the majority of changes are very minor: words or sentences that simply expand upon what has already been said. However, there are several which are more important. The first is a passage which argues that Christ himself introduced no new law or works for justification, but simply reaffirmed the decalogue, by which no man is justified. This argument presents no new theology; rather it simply uses the 1531 theology to refute a new objection, that Paul condemns only the works of the old law, not those of the new. Clebsch argues that Barnes's identification of the Sermon on the Mount with the law of the Old Testament reveals a shift in his theology towards legalism.[107] In fact, it does no such thing. Barnes specifically identifies both the decalogue and the Sermon on the Mount as teaching that love to God and to one's neighbour is the only way of fulfilling the law. This is the position which he advocated in 1531, and is the same as that of Luther. His whole argument is in fact framed to counter the allegation that works

---

[105] e.g. *1534* xxxii. b (=*1531* xxxix. a).   [106] *1534* xli. b and xlv. a.
[107] See Clebsch, pp. 65–6.

under the New Testament help in justification.[108] To underline this point, Barnes ends the passage with an unequivocal statement of the difference between Christ and Moses, and of the objective accomplishment of salvation by the former:

The law is given through Moses, but grace and verity came by Jesus Christ. He is the giver of grace and mercy, as all the prophets testifieth, and not another Moses. And therefore to purchase us favour, he died on the cross. And so did not Moses, but he commandeth us to do this and do that. But Christ saith, Hang thou on my doing, and believe thou that I have done for thee, and not for me.[109]

It is doubtful if even Luther could have expressed himself with less ambiguity on the matter. It is also interesting to note that emphasis on the objective side of justification seems rather to have increased than decreased in this edition. The passages which emphasize the exclusive role of Christ in justification and which formed the start of his discussion in 1531 are all retained, showing that Barnes's doctrine in 1534 is built upon the same conceptual foundation as earlier. Furthermore, in the above passage we see Barnes for the first time making an explicit link between the death of Christ with the purchase of redemption. If Clebsch's thesis is correct, one would have expected an increase in emphasis upon the subjective aspects of the doctrine. Instead, Barnes's thought is, if anything, heading in the opposite direction.

The other two major additions are a paragraph on the justification of Abraham, used in a continuation of the above argument that justification is without the law,[110] and an explicit statement that it is only Christ who justifies. This latter is interesting because Barnes allows that works do have a glory and a reward, but he denies that this has anything to do with justification, even when considering those works done in faith. That honour belongs to Christ alone.[111] This passage in itself is sufficient to refute Clebsch's claim that Barnes teaches that works play any role in justification.

---

[108] *1534* xxxiii. b–xxxiv. a.

[109] *1534* liv. a.

[110] *1534* xxxiv. b.

[111] 'No manner of works, whether they be in faith, or out of faith, can help to justify. Nevertheless, works hath their glory and reward. But the glory and praise of justification belongeth to Christ only', *1534* xxxv. b.

Thus, apart from the treatment of James, the essay on justification is theologically the same as that in the earlier edition. The arguments concerning the all-sufficiency of Christ, free grace as the basis of salvation, faith as the gift of God, justification as remission of sin leading to freedom from sin, and the necessity of producing works resulting from the new nature, all remain intact. If anything, the objective basis of justification in Christ is expressed with greater clarity and emphasis in 1534 than in 1531. Thus, the theological framework with which Barnes approaches the Letter of James is identical to that of 1531. It would therefore be most surprising to discover that his treatment of this book reveals any major shift in his theology.

The Letter of James: Clarification or Compromise?

In dealing with James in 1531, Barnes adopted a somewhat ambiguous stance: on the one hand, he argued that the book was a plain contradiction of justification by faith alone, and thus non-canonical; on the other hand, he cited the interpretation of Augustine, who referred the idea of justification in James to works that followed actual justification before God. Thus works held a sacramental significance. Clebsch fails to notice that the second of these two arguments is present in 1531, and sees Barnes consequently as unequivocal in his rejection of the Letter of James.[112] Barnes may have said that he rejected James out of hand, but his inclusion of Augustine's argument in 1531 suggests that he was not as certain about the letter's authority as he might have liked to appear.

In 1534, Barnes entirely rewrites this section. Significantly, he omits the rejection of the letter's canonicity, starting instead with the identical argument from Augustine that was present in the earlier edition.[113] Clearly, Barnes has now come to accept that this interpretation is correct. He proceeds to justify this position by expounding its hermeneutical basis: in scripture, obscure passages are to be expounded with reference to those places whose meaning is clear. Paul has always been held in

---

[112] See Clebsch, p. 66.

[113] 'St. Augustine, willing to save the estimation of this epistle, doth declare, how that St. Paul doth speak of works that go before faith, and St. James speaketh of works that follow faith', *1534* xl. b. Cf. *1531* liii. a.

higher esteem by the Church than James (although, Barnes now allows, the latter is an accepted authority), because he teaches justification by faith better than anyone.[114] Thus, Barnes's hermeneutical principle of justification by faith remains basic to his approach in 1534 as in 1531, and James is to be interpreted in the light of Paul. As a result, Barnes argues that James cannot be teaching justification by works and that his statements must be understood in their context. James is actually writing against antinomians and is therefore simply stressing the same thing which Paul emphasizes elsewhere: that Christians must do good works.[115] This is no more than that which Barnes himself teaches in both editions of *A Supplication* when he likens justification and good works to a tree and its fruit. There is no special emphasis upon works here which was not already present in 1531. The only shift in position is that Barnes now accepts that the Letter of James is canonical and does not contradict Paul, a view about which he was doubtful in 1531. While this may indicate a change in his view of the scriptural canon, Barnes's interpretation of what James actually means does not introduce anything into his soteriology which was not present in the first edition of the work.

Barnes now applies this idea to James's reference to Abraham using the same language as Tyndale:

[Abraham's] faith was declared [through his offering of Isaac], and had a great testimony afore all the world, that it was a living, and a perfect, and a right shapen faith, that Abraham had. So that his inward faith declared him afore God, and his outward works afore the world, to be good and justified.[116]

In this passage, Clebsch once again manages to find that doctrine of 'double justification' which he claims compromised the theology of the English Reformers.[117] In fact, Barnes's thought is identical with that of Tyndale and Frith in this regard: works simply declare to the world that the believer is indeed justified before God. Barnes's theology contained this idea in 1531, and all that is new here is his use of the term 'justify' in this context. All that he is doing is paralleling the function of works before

---

[114] *1534* xl. b.   [115] *1534* xl. b.
[116] *1534* xli. a. Cf. Tyndale on Abraham, *Works* 1. 526.
[117] See Clebsch, pp. 66–8

men with that of faith before God   in such a way as to bring
out the active, moral results of justification by faith alone. It is
not a shift from his earlier theological position.

CONCLUSION

It will be clear from what has been said above that it is
inaccurate simply to classify Barnes as a Lutheran and nothing
more. If being a Lutheran means placing justification by faith
at the centre of all theology, then Barnes was undoubtedly such
a one. However, this blanket term hides those areas in which
Barnes's emphasis, and even his doctrine, differed from that of
Luther. There is certainly a Christological emphasis common
to both men, but Barnes does not develop the idea of imputation to any significant degree. Instead, he is rather vague
about the precise content of justification. Nor does he propose
any detailed idea of propitiation and tends to see Christ's work
in general as the centre of his redemptive work.

Concerning works, Barnes is clear that they do not earn
salvation, but his view of the law is somewhat ambivalent. While
arguing that commands do not imply ability, he nevertheless
points the believer to the law as something he should strive to
obey. In this manner, he seems to offer a view of the law which
combines both Augustinian and Lutheran elements.

His Augustinianism is again apparent in his deviation from
Luther over the Fall. For Barnes, the Fall is the result of
Adam's free choice. He does not use Luther's argument from
immutability as a decisive element in his anthropology, and
thus avoids the apparent determinism of the latter. Nevertheless,
Barnes is heavily indebted to Luther. In his emphasis upon the
radical nature of faith, double predestination, and the exposition
of Ecclus. 15: 14–17 and the hardening of Pharaoh's heart,
Barnes follows Luther's argument in *The Bondage of the Will*
very closely. In advocating double predestination, Barnes shows
none of the reserve of Tyndale or Frith and places the doctrine
at the very heart of his soteriology.

However, despite his affirmation of double predestination,
there is a great concern throughout his writings for practical
morality. He does not express the ethical imperative of the
Christian life using the conditional framework of Tyndale, and

does not make works a basis for assurance. Instead, his emphasis is consistently placed upon the transforming nature of faith from which good works flow. However, this stress is never allowed to obscure the centrality of faith.

As regards his development, it seems that even in 1525 Barnes was still fundamentally a Humanist reformer, and that it is not until he had arrived at Wittenberg that there is any evidence of his views becoming more radical. As for the argument of Clebsch that he shifts his ground concerning justification between 1531 and 1534, this has been shown to be entirely without foundation as his soteriology and anthropology remain unchanged in this period. The only real change in this matter is his view of the Letter of James, which he comes to accept but interprets in a way consistent with the faith only principle. If there is any development here it is in his view of the canon, not soteriology.

Of the three Reformers studied in this section, Barnes is undoubtedly the closest to Luther both in form of expression and basic approach, but there are important areas of difference with the Reformer concerning the Fall and the law which reveal the influence of Augustine and of the concerns of Humanism upon his theology.

CONCLUSION TO PART TWO

UNITY AND DIVERSITY

Detailed study of Tyndale, Frith, and Barnes reveals that any attempt to categorize them with such blanket labels as 'Lutheran', 'Humanist', or 'Reformed' is doomed to failure. The theological background of each is too complex to be dealt with so simplistically. Luther, Erasmus, and the emerging Reformed theology of the Upper Rhineland each helped to shape their respective theologies.

First, it is clear that not one of these three men came to Reformation theology without a previous thorough grounding in Humanism. It was only after they had distinguished themselves as Humanist scholars that they came under the influence of Reformation thought. That this background exerted a formative influence on all three men can be seen in the high regard they each had for the Fathers of the Church, as opposed to the contempt they expressed for the scholastic theologians. It is also evident in the concern which they each had for the production and distribution of the vernacular Bible. Furthermore, Humanism also gave them a lasting concern for the practical, moral dimension of the Christian life.

While their initial reforming activities were shaped by their Humanist convictions, all three men were profoundly influenced by continental Lutheranism. Tyndale and Barnes both studied at Wittenberg, while Frith's earliest published works were translations of tracts by Luther, Melanchthon, and Patrick Hamilton, a Scottish Lutheran. The extent to which each followed Luther is a complex question, and reveals differences between their respective positions. All three accepted justification by faith as fundamental. However, Frith was the only one who, in his doctrine of the two purgatories, came close to developing a Lutheran theology of the cross. He was also the only one to develop a clear doctrine of the atonement based upon God's righteous wrath against sin. Barnes's position on the atonement was vague, while Tyndale tended to focus upon the work of Christ as the means of freeing man's will rather than as the means of dealing with his moral guilt. Barnes was the only one to develop a doctrine of double predestination. He was also alone in his statement of the Lutheran idea of imputation, although this concept does not play a significant role in his theology. However, in arguing for the bondage of man's will, Barnes did not use the argument from God's immutability which was axiomatic to Luther's own position. Furthermore, all three men allowed the law a more positive role in the Christian life than did Luther. Indeed, when looked at in these terms, the English Reformers, in their interpretation of Luther, can be said to be as remarkable for what they altered or omitted as for what they wholeheartedly adopted.

While it is impossible to prove that they were influenced by specific Reformed theologians, certain aspects of their theology clearly suggest Reformed influence. It is perhaps most obvious in the writings of Tyndale and Frith, as both rejected the Lutheran position on the Eucharist, a position maintained by Barnes. Tyndale's emphases upon the Holy Spirit and upon the idea of covenant both reveal close similarities with the concerns of Reformed theology, and almost certainly indicate its influence upon him. Frith's theology of baptism is very close to that of Zwingli. However, in the matter of double justification, the affinity of all three with Reformed thought is evident. All three reject Luther's position on the Letter of James, preferring the Augustinian interpretation of James's use of the term 'justify', whereby he is regarded as applying the term to works after conversion. Such works declare before men the prior justification of the believer before God by faith. This position, with its loose definition of 'justification', was also adopted by Reformers such as Bucer, and does not necessarily undermine the Lutheran notion of justification by faith alone. It is used by Tyndale, Frith, and Barnes as a means both of explaining the apparent contradiction between Paul and James, and of articulating their ethical concern by clarifying the relationship between faith and works. Clebsch's claims that this doctrine implies salvation by works and that it was held by Tyndale and Barnes but not by Frith are incorrect. The first claim is based upon a fundamental misunderstanding of the idea of double justification, while the second is based upon a misreading of Frith's own writings

While each of the Reformers has his own particular emphases in soteriology, these should not obscure their fundamental unity. The three men are united in their attempt to maintain two basic principles: the doctrine of justification by faith, and the need for the believer to perform good works. Each has a different approach to relating faith to works. Tyndale emphasizes regeneration by the Holy Spirit as a consequence of faith. This leads the believer to perform good works by his own volition. Tyndale reinforces the moral dimension of his theology by making works a source of assurance and by developing the idea of a bilateral covenant. It is in this context, and not in the context of a works-based salvation, as Clebsch incorrectly claims, that his covenant idea must be understood. Neither Frith nor Barnes uses the covenant motif in such a manner or develops a doctrine of works-based assurance. Instead, they emphasize that works are motivated by the believer's love for God. However, these differences do not undermine the fundamental unity of the three men. They all three regard faith in Christ as the only means of justification, and love to God and to one's neighbour as the essence of the law and therefore normative for Christian conduct. On these two issues they are in substantial agreement with each other and with the continental Reformers, both Lutheran and Reformed. No wedge can really be driven between them on the essential points of salvation.

For Tyndale, Frith, and Barnes, the central soteriological dogma was justification by faith, and it was this truth which they sought to establish. While they did deal with other doctrines, such as predestination, this was only in order to support the concept of justification by faith alone. However, with the advent of the Reformation under Edward VI, when the Reformers were no longer outlaws and Reformation teaching was officially accepted, the battle for justification by faith was effectively won and it became the accepted teaching of the Anglican Church. Therefore, the focal point of debate inevitably shifted away from this doctrine to other matters. In the realm of soteriology, disputes were to erupt amongst those who held the doctrine of justification by faith but disagreed about the overall framework within which this justification took place: was faith grounded in God's eternal election or in the individual's decision in time? Thus, the doctrine of predestination, while not a source of tension amongst English Reformers under Henry VIII, became the cause of a number of acrimonious disputes under Edward VI and Mary. Thus, we shall find that, in Part Three, it is election, and not justification by faith, which emerges as the major soteriological issue of the years 1548 to 1556.

The Reformers under Edward VI and Mary

7

John Hooper

HOOPER'S WRITINGS

While John Hooper has traditionally been regarded as a proto-puritan English mouthpiece for the ideas of Heinrich Bullinger, a close examination of what Hooper actually wrote suggests that such a view needs to be considerably modified.[1] His writings, however, present a number of problems which could obscure a correct understanding of his thought. First, he was not a systematic thinker or accomplished prose stylist: his writings are often rambling and repetitive. Therefore, a work-by-work analysis of his entire output would probably emulate these same faults and shed little light on his thought. However, a purely thematic approach would scarcely be any better: Hooper's doctrine of salvation was, to a large extent, hammered out in the heat of controversy; divorcing statements from their historical context could therefore lead to a basic misunderstanding of Hooper's motivation in writing.

As a result of these considerations, Hooper's thought on salvation is best approached through those treatises which take this as a central theme. Such an approach allows for the omission of irrelevant ramblings and for the treatment of key themes within their historical and polemical contexts.

---

[1] See F. J. Smithen, *Continental Protestantism and the English Reformation* (London, 1927), 81–4; Letham, 'Saving Faith and Assurance', 245–7. The most thorough statement of the Bullinger–Hooper thesis is that of W. M. S. West in his doctoral thesis and subsequent articles. G. W. Locher has recently argued that Hooper's dependence on Zwingli and Bullinger has been overstated, but his arguments are based on the radical position Hooper adopted in the vestment controversy and not on study of the texts: see *Zwingli's Thought*, 365. As will become clear, a close reading of Hooper's works reveals a source for his doctrine which could never have been suggested by the kind of stance he took over vestments.

The three relevant treatises for any study of Hooper's doctrine of salvation are: *A Declaration of Christ and His Office* (1547); *A Declaration of the Ten Holy Commandments* (1549, 1550); and *A Godly Confession and Protestation of the Christian Faith* (1550). Close examination of each work in turn reveals surprising evidence about the relationship of Hooper's theology to continental patterns of salvation.[2]

A DECLARATION OF CHRIST AND HIS OFFICE

This tract is the earliest of Hooper's extant works and was published at Zurich in 1547. It is a discussion of the relationship between Christology and personal salvation and therefore deals with both the objective work of Christ and the application of this to the believer.

Christ and Salvation

Hooper starts his discussion of the work of Christ with a general statement concerning the importance of Christ to personal salvation. From here, he moves to a detailed examination of the various functions which Christ fulfils in his capacity as saviour.

Because the major problem facing man is his loss of perfection and eternal life, his greatest concern must be to know how he can regain his pre-Fall position before God. God himself has provided the solution to this, a solution to which he first pointed in the prot-evangel of Gen. 3. This promise referred to the Seed, Christ, in whom is encompassed the whole of salvation.[3] Thus, the chief task of man must be to seek to know all he can about Christ, and then to act in a manner consistent with this knowledge. Only in this way will the salvation of the

---

[2] A fourth work, *A Brief and Clear Confession of the Christian Faith*, allegedly published in 1550, is not by Hooper. Not only is it stylistically unlike Hooper's other works, it also contains a view of predestination which fundamentally contradicts that expressed in *A Godly Confession*. Furthermore, there is no historical evidence to suggest that Hooper was the author. For a full treatment of these issues, see West, 'A Study of John Hooper', 21–28; D. S. Ross, 'Hooper's Alleged Authorship of *A Brief and Clear Confession of the Christian Faith*', *CH* 39 (1970), 18–29. Ross suggests that the author is Jean Garnier, minister of a French church in Strasbourg.

[3] Gen. 3: 15 is an important text for Hooper's doctrine of Christ. In a later work on Christology, *A Lesson of the Incarnation of Christ*, which he wrote in order to refute anabaptist rejections of the doctrine of Christ's humanity, Hooper sees this text as providing the fundamental proof that Christ had to assume human flesh: see *LW*, p. 5.

individual be accomplished.[4] Salvation is therefore intimately related to Christ.

After a brief statement on the person of Christ, affirming his eternal nature, his equality with the Father, his twofold nature, and the basic facts of his earthly and heavenly ministry, Hooper moves to a discussion of the offices of Christ.[5] These offices he divides into two main categories: those referring to his role as priest; and those referring to his role as king.[6] These two main divisions are then subdivided in order to allow for detailed discussion of separate aspects of his work.

By dividing the offices of Christ into two, those of priest and king, Hooper stands in the mainstream of Reformation theology before Calvin. For example, Luther regarded the concept of anointing inherent in the title 'Christ' as placing him in line with both the priests and kings of the Old Testament. Both Bullinger and Melanchthon also adopted this twofold distinction, and it was not until Calvin that the idea of the threefold office of Christ became standard for Reformed theology, although the concept had existed before him.[7]

Hooper finds his authority for this division in two different considerations, one purely biblical, the other a combination of biblical teaching and secular political philosophy. He regards Christ's priesthood as clearly taught in Heb. 5: 5–6, which refers to the Father's public witness to his Son at Jesus' baptism, and to the Old Testament prophecy concerning the priesthood of Melchizedek in Ps. 110: 4.[8] Thus, Christ's priesthood is the fulfilment of Old Testament prophecy, and an office bestowed upon him by the Father.

However, the basis for Christ's kingship is not found in explicit verses of scripture but in the actual functions he performs for the Church: the government and protection of his people. These roles, Hooper argues, are those of the king, and so Christ must be king of the Church.[9] For his authorities, he refers not only to scripture, but also to Aristotle's *Politics* and to Justinian's *Institutions*. Thus, Hooper bases Christ's title of king upon the analogy of his biblical tasks with the structure of secular society and not upon his role as the anti-type to Old Testament kings.

---

[4] *EW* 15.   [5] *EW* 16–19.   [6] *EW* 19.
[7] See J. P. Baker, 'Offices of Christ', in *NDT*, 476–7.
[8] *EW* 19.   [9] See *EW* 18.

That Hooper is prepared to use Aristotle in order to support this aspect of theology is not necessarily to be equated with a secret respect for medieval theological method which was full of Aristotelian concepts. In fact, Reformers often used Aristotle because of their Humanist respect for classical literature.[10] However, it is also clear that Hooper's use of Aristotle here does not involve the infusion of pagan elements into the content of his theology: it is the Bible which defines the actual functions of Christ which happen to correspond with Aristotle's definition of the role of a king.

Christ's Priesthood

Having established this twofold division in the work of Christ, Hooper now moves on to discuss in detail the precise elements of his priesthood and kingship. Only the former has relevance for Hooper's doctrine of salvation as the latter refers to the external government of the Church. He divides Christ's priestly work into four distinct categories: teacher; intercessor and blesser; sacrifice; and sanctifier. This fourfold division points to the influence of Bullinger.[11] He defined Christ's priestly work in exactly the same fourfold manner as Hooper and his influence upon him in this work is hardly surprising, as it was both composed and published in Zurich in 1547. By then, this division of the work of Christ was already part of the confessional framework of the Zurich Church.[12] Thus, Hooper's treatise is an English expression of Zurich theology.

[10] Thus, the wish of Melanchthon to produce a pure Greek text of Aristotle arose from a desire to show how he had been misused by scholastic theologians and formed 'part of a humanist anti-scholastic offensive': see H. A. Oberman, *Masters of the Reformation* (Cambridge, 1981), 59.

[11] Later in this Chapter, Hooper will be shown to be heavily dependent upon Melanchthon for much of his theology. However, Melanchthon is not an influence here as he refers sanctification to Christ's role as king: see *OM* 21. 920 and 1087.

[12] *Orthodoxa Tigurinae Ecclesiae ministrorum Confessio* (Zurich, 1545), 46a. T. H. L. Parker comments on the identity of Hooper's view of Christ's priesthood with that of Bullinger, but the only reference he gives for Bullinger is to Decade 4: 7, which was not published until 1550. Parker acknowledges that this rules out Hooper's dependence on this particular sermon, and he apparently leaves the question of influence open: see his introduction to *A Declaracion of Christe and His Offyce* in *English Reformers* (London, 1966), 187–8. However, the fact that the *Confessio* contains a firm statement of the twofold office is proof that this concept was firmly established in Bullinger's theology by 1545.

Hooper initially addresses Christ's first role as the perfect teacher.[13] The law of God is perfect, and tells man all he needs to know concerning his duty towards God and towards his fellow man.[14] This law received its pre-eminent exposition in the teachings of Christ, and thus all doctrine is to be judged by the standard of Christ's word.[15] Many good Church Fathers erred in allowing too much authority to the traditions of men, and even Luther was mistaken in his view of the Lord's Supper.[16] It is only as men follow the precise teaching of Christ that they can hope to attain to the whole truth. This teaching was not simply verbal but involved the example of the life that Christ lived:

He that will conform his knowledge unto the word of God, let him likewise convert his life withal, as the word requireth, and as all the examples of Christ and his gospel teacheth; or else what will he do with the doctrine of Christ, which only teacheth, and sufficiently teacheth, all verity and virtuous life?[17]

In this passage Hooper draws a close link between the concept of knowledge and the practical morality of the Christian: knowledge of God demands an ethical response and should lead to a transformation of the individual's life. Knowledge is a key theme throughout Hooper's theology. At the very start of this treatise, he emphasized that it is the responsibility of the believer to 'know perfectly' the means of salvation.[18] Indeed, the fact that Hooper discusses Christ's role as teacher before any of his other priestly functions indicates the importance of the idea of knowledge and learning to his doctrine of salvation. While he does not state that Christ's roles are ranked in order of relative importance, the order is none the less suggestive and points to a soteriology which underlines the ethical demands of Christianity. This link between knowledge and morality is made explicit in later writings in which Hooper emphasizes ignorance as the fundamental cause of sin. The idea that emerges from these emphases is that salvation consists primarily of true knowledge of God.

The second priestly role of Christ is to make intercession for his people and to bless them.[19] This intercession 'only sufficeth', and this was the same for the Old Testament as it is

---

[13] *EW* 25. [14] *EW* 26. [15] *EW* 26.
[16] *EW* 29. [17] *EW* 33. [18] *EW* 15. [19] *EW* 33.

for the New.[20] Thus, the two Testaments can be regarded as a unity in terms of their relationship to Christ's priesthood. Any notion of praying to saints undermines the uniqueness of Christ's role as the sole mediator between God and man, a fact underlined by Hooper in several pages of polemic.[21]

In discussing Christ's work, Hooper relates the objective aspects of this intercession to his role as teacher and example. He emphasizes that Christ is the sole mediator and that it is therefore necessary to approach God through Christ alone. However, he also stresses that Christ's life of continuous prayer is a paradigm that the believer should follow.[22] Thus, Hooper is again underlining the practical applications of his Christology.

The intercession of Christ is based upon his death. The death of Christ was the purpose of his coming to earth, and his incarnation was instrumental to this end.[23] The incarnation and death of the Son of God were the fulfilment of the Old Testament sacrifices which pointed forward to Christ. Like these sacrifices, Christ's death revealed both God's mercy and his justice: mercy, in sending his Son in order to redeem all those who would believe in him; and justice, in refusing to redeem a single individual until Christ, by his sufferings, had endured the wrath of God against sin.[24] Finally, Hooper points to the importance of the death of Christ for theology by stating that a true understanding of this doctrine leads to correct views of both justification and the Eucharist.[25]

In making such a statement, Hooper is linking the subjective reality of personal justification to the objective work of Christ. He defines this justification in the following terms:

Saint Paul, when he saith that we be justified by faith, Rom. 3, 4, 5, he meaneth that we have remission of sin, reconciliation, and acceptation into the favour of God. So doth this word *justify* signify, Deut. 25, *hisdich*, where as God commandeth the judge to justify, quit, and absolve the innocent, and to condemn and punish the person culpable.[26]

---

[20] *EW* 34.   [21] *EW* 35.   [22] *EW* 34–5.

[23] *EW* 48.   [24] *EW* 48–9.

[25] *EW* 49. In terms of Eucharistic theology, Hooper sees a correct view of the satisfaction wrought by Christ's death as precluding the Roman notion of sacrifice: 'Et nullum a morte Christi esse sacrificium propitiatorem credimus ac confitemur; hoc est, a morte et praeter mortem Christi nullum tale esse sacrificium vel opus, quod iram et indignationem Dei erga peccatum placare, atque illius gratiam in remissionem peccatorum peccatoribus impetrare possit', *LW* 500.   [26] *EW* 49.

This definition is very similar to that provided by Melanchthon in the *Loci*. He too uses the triplet of remission, reconciliation, and acceptation, and also refers to the legal connotations of the term.[27] Later, in his discussion of election, Hooper uses translated passages of the *Loci* at key points in his argument. Thus, he clearly possessed knowledge of, and respect for, Melanchthon's work. While there is no verbatim translation in this treatise, the similarities between the two men in the definition of justification are clearly suggestive of the influence of Melanchthon.

In his formulation of justification, Hooper is concerned to emphasize the inseparability of justification and regeneration and yet to avoid any confusion of the two. In order to do this, he stresses that remission of sin is obtained only through sorrowing for sin and total dependence upon Christ:

And although with this remission of sin he giveth likewise the Holy Ghost to work the will of God, to love both God and his neighbour, [yet] notwithstanding the conscience, burdened and charged with sin, first seeketh remission thereof. For this thing the conscience laboureth and contendeth in all fears and terrors of sorrow and contrition. It disputeth not, what virtues it bringeth, wretched soul, to acclaim this promise of mercy; but forsaking her own justice, offereth Christ, dead upon the cross, and sitting at God's right hand.[28]

In this passage, Hooper makes the giving of the Holy Spirit simultaneous with the remission of sins. Thus, the justified believer has also undergone a fundamental change in his being whereby he now works the will of God. However, this regeneration is not a cause of justification, as justification is based upon Christ's merits alone.

This passage of Hooper has a striking parallel in the *Loci*, where Melanchthon argues for the same approach, and even refers to the role of the Holy Spirit in the same context. Indeed, Hooper's statement even contains various precise English equivalents of Latin words used by Melanchthon.[29] While not

---

[27] 'IUSTIFICATIO significat remissionem peccatorum et reconciliationem seu acceptationem personae ad vitam aeternam. Nam Hebraeis Iustificare est forense verbum. . . . Sumpsit igitur Paulus verbum iustificandi ex consuetudine Hebraici sermonis pro remissione peccatorum et reconciliatione seu acceptatione', *OM* 21. 742.

[28] *EW* 50.

[29] 'Quanquam autem, ut antea dixi, cum Deus remittit peccata, simul donat Spiritum

conclusive, this lends increased strength to the idea that Hooper is using the *Loci* as his textbook as he writes these passages. It certainly reveals a basic similarity in their thinking.

Hooper sees the necessity for Christ's merits as deriving from anthropological considerations: fallen man is sinful, and not able to fulfil the law; therefore, he cannot merit salvation for himself. Christ is thus the divine response to man's predicament. His merits are the cause of salvation, and man's faith is the means whereby this is appropriated.[30] Hooper illustrates this idea by referring to Christ's interview with Nicodemus in John 3, where he expounds the incident of Moses and the bronze serpent. Moses set up this serpent so that those children of Israel who had been bitten by the snakes could be cured; in similar fashion, God has set up Christ as a means whereby sin might be cured. The children of Israel were restored to health by looking towards the serpent. This is analogous to the role of faith, by which we look to Christ and are healed of sin.[31] Hooper then decisively rejects the idea that works play any part in obtaining remission of sins, either before or after justification.[32]

Hooper regards the fact that justification is based upon the merits of Christ alone as the foundation of correct Christian conduct. If salvation depended upon man's efforts even in part, then he could never be certain that he was accepted by God and could not pray or act in faith. In short, he could not live life as a Christian. Therefore, it is important to understand the nature of justification, as such understanding will naturally lead to correct Christian living.[33] Here once again we see Hooper referring to the related themes of correct knowledge and correct morality.

Hooper's concern for practical morality and individual holiness is apparent throughout his treatment of Christ's priestly

sanctum inchoantem novas virtutes, tamen mens perterrefacta primum quaerit remissionem peccatorum et reconciliationem: de hac angitur, de hac dimicat in veris pavoribus, non disputat, quae virtutes infusae sint, quae etsi comitantur reconciliationem, tamen nequaquam iudicandum est, nostram dignitatem aut munditiem caussam esse remissionis peccatorum', *OM* 21. 742.

[30] *EW* 51.
[31] *EW* 52–6.
[32] 'This example of Nicodemus declareth, that neither the works that go before justification, neither those that follow justification, deserve remission of sin', *EW* 56.
[33] *EW* 56–7. John Bradford makes a similar objection to the idea of a works-based justification: see *Writings* 2. 130–1.

office: he is always careful to link knowledge of the gospel not simply with believing but also with acting; he points to Christ as an example to be emulated; he highlights the relationship between remission of sins and regeneration through the Holy Spirit; and he emphasizes the connection between justification, assurance, and correct Christian living. All of these aspects of Christ's work point towards his role as the sanctifier of his people, which Hooper summarizes as follows:

He [Christ] is not only holy himself, but maketh others holy also. . . . This sanctification is none other but a true knowledge of God in Christ by the gospel, that teacheth us how unclean we are by the sin of Adam, and how that we are cleansed by Christ.[34]

Once again, Hooper refers to the idea of knowledge, this time in terms of sanctification. However, this sanctification is not simply to be regarded as a mere intellectual quality. There is a strong emphasis in Hooper's theology upon the actual holiness of the believer. This is reflected in his earlier coupling of knowledge with moral obligation. He also stresses that contrition is as necessary after coming to Christ as it was before, and that the believer must continue to pray for strength and wisdom to follow God against the world and the flesh.[35] The justified man must follow the example of past saints and bring forth the fruits of justification, or else he is not truly justified.[36]

It is clear from these statements that Hooper's doctrine of salvation embodies not only the concept of gracious salvation on account of Christ, but also ethical responsibilities for the believer. Hooper embodies both of these elements in the following statement:

For as God hath bound himself by his promise to be our God and helper for Christ; so hath he bound man by his commandment to be his servant, and in his word to follow Christ, and in Christ God, for the commandment's sake, until such time as the end wherefore man was made be obtained, which is eternal felicity, and man restored and made like unto the image of God, as he was at the beginning; full of justice, obedience, and love towards his Creator and Maker.[37]

---

[34] *EW* 71.   [35] *EW* 57.   [36] Ibid.

[37] *EW* 86. This idea of a bilateral arrangement between God and man is also central to Hooper's sacramental theology, indicating the Reformed roots of his theology: e.g. see *EW* 136, 196. In later works, Hooper refers to this arrangement with the term 'contract'.

This passage points to the fundamentally practical purpose of man's redemption: that man should be restored to the image of God, which Hooper defines in terms of moral qualities. The arrangement between God and man is formulated with this end in view. It is also entirely consistent with Hooper's Christological construction of salvation. Christ is central to both parts of the contract: his work forms its objective foundation; and his teaching and example define the ethical conduct which the contract requires. Thus, the concept unites the two basic aspects of Hooper's Christology: Christ as the objective basis for salvation; and Christ as the teacher and ethical example to be followed.

It cannot be proved that Hooper was definitely influenced by another Reformer in this matter, but the most likely source is his friend and teacher, Bullinger, whose covenant doctrine involved a similar bilateral arrangement between God and man, as did that of Tyndale.[38] Melanchthon too regarded salvation as a mutual arrangement between God and man which could be terminated if man failed to fulfil his part.[39] The concept certainly articulates Hooper's own desire to combine the idea of gracious salvation with the need to perform good works, and refers both of these concerns to the work of Christ.

Summary

In *A Declaration of Christ and His Office*, Hooper presents a Christological doctrine of salvation. He regards Christ as fulfilling two offices: priesthood and kingship, of which the former is directly relevant to soteriology. Hooper defines the separate functions of this priesthood as teaching, interceding and blessing, sacrificing, and sanctifying. This fourfold division follows that used by Bullinger in, for example, the *Confessio* of 1545.

Hooper links the idea of salvation to knowledge of God, and this knowledge to ethical responsibilities. This is reflected in the priority he gives to Christ's role as teacher. This teaching consists

---

[38] For Bullinger, see *De Testamento seu Foeder . . . Expositio* (Zurich, 1534); Baker, *Heinrich Bullinger and the Covenant*; Møller, 'The Beginnings of Puritan Covenant Theology', 48; Strehle, *Calvinism, Federalism, and Scholasticism*, 134–49. For Tyndale, see Ch. 4. Tyndale also articulates substantially the same idea as Hooper, but he refers to this as a 'covenant'. Hooper, however, uses only the term 'contract' and this suggests that Tyndale is not the source of his concept.

[39] *OM* 21. 775.

of both precept and example. Christ's intercession and sacrifice provide the objective basis for man's justification, but Hooper is careful to stress that justification cannot be separated from regeneration and ethical reformation. In discussing these points, Hooper's language is close enough to that of Melanchthon in the *Loci* to suggest the influence of the latter. Finally, he expresses both the idea of gracious redemption and the need for good works in terms of a bilateral arrangement between God and man. This arrangement is Christocentric because Christ's death and intercession are the basis for redemption, while his conduct and teachings define the ethical standards to be followed.

A DECLARATION OF THE TEN HOLY COMMANDMENTS OF ALMIGHTY GOD

This treatise, first published in 1549 and republished in 1550, is of importance to the understanding of Hooper's soteriology not only because it constitutes his most thorough discussion of the law and its place in the Christian's life, but also because it contains his most detailed treatment of the subject of election and predestination. This latter is not dealt with in the main body of the text but in the preface, a fact which can be related to the contemporary theological climate.

The Polemical Background

By 1550 Hooper's views on predestination had brought him into conflict with fellow Reformers. In the preface to the second edition of *A Declaration of the Ten Holy Commandments*, he declares that the first edition was roundly condemned by certain individuals who regarded John Calvin's doctrine as normative in this matter.[40] It is perhaps ironic that the man now often seen as a proto-Puritan was actually regarded with suspicion in his own lifetime by those who looked to Geneva for theological inspiration. Little is actually known of the details of the controversy, but enough can be inferred from a series of letters addressed to Bullinger to discern the substance of the disagreement. The first letter is one from John ab Ulmis, dated 30 April 1550, where he refers to Hooper and Bartholomew

---

[40] *EW* 269–70.

Traheron,[41] observing that 'it is wonderful how very far they disagree respecting God's predestination of men'.[42] That the controversy dragged on is apparent from a second letter to Bullinger, dated 31 December 1550, where ab Ulmis refers to complaints made by Traheron concerning Hooper 'respecting his books, and also some letters formerly addressed in common to both, not having been returned to him'.[43] From the last remark it seems that the dispute between the two men probably involved a certain level of personal animosity as well, but this is not to imply that the theological difference was not serious. It is not clear from these letters what the nature of this difference was, but this missing piece is supplied by a letter from Traheron to Bullinger, dated 10 September 1552. It appears that there was another controversy about predestination in this year, and Traheron was anxious to obtain firsthand the views of leading continental Reformers in order to strengthen his own case.[44] The relevant passage is worth quoting in full as it sheds light upon the influences at work upon English theologians at this time:

I am exceedingly desirous to know what you and the other very learned men, who live in Zurich, think respecting the predestination and providence of God. If you ask the reason, there are certain individuals here who assert that you lean too much to Melanchthon's views. But the greater number among us, of whom I own myself to be one, embrace the opinion of John Calvin as being perspicuous and most agreeable to holy scripture. And we truly thank God that that excellent treatise of the very learned and excellent John Calvin against Pighius and one Georgius Siculus should have come forth at

[41] Bartholomew Traheron was born *c.*1510. Orphaned at an early age, he was brought up by the Protestant, Richard Tracy, son of William Tracy whose will formed the basis of tracts by both Tyndale and Frith. Having studied at both Oxford and Cambridge, he then went abroad, first to Zurich in 1537, and then to Strasbourg in 1538. In 1539 he was recruited by Thomas Cromwell, but after the latter's fall, Traheron was again forced abroad. In 1548 he appeared in Geneva, where he studied under Calvin and became a firm adherent of the Reformer's doctrine. He returned to England later in the same year, and in the following years was engaged in controversy over predestination with John Hooper. When Mary acceded to the throne, he again fled abroad, this time to Frankfurt. He died at Wesel in 1558.

[42] *OL* 406.

[43] *OL* 426.

[44] Hargrave suggests that this dispute took place during the discussions then in progress on the formulation of the Edwardian Articles: see 'The Doctrine of Predestination in the English Reformation', 39.

the very time when the question began to be agitated amongst us.
For we confess that he has thrown much light on the subject. ... We
certainly hope that you differ in no respect from his excellent and
most learned opinion.[45]

This passage shows that Calvin's views already had vociferous
exponents in England at the time, although the claim to be in
the majority is perhaps dubious. The fact that Traheron was
writing to Bullinger also indicates that the latter's views were
also considered to be important by English theologians.

This letter provides important hints concerning the details
of the disagreement between Traheron and Hooper. While it is
true that this letter is written several years after the original
dispute, and that Calvin's *Concerning the Eternal Predestination
of God* was not published until 1552, Traheron imbibed
Calvinist doctrine while he was resident at Geneva in 1548. It
was aspects of this doctrine that were the source of his disagreement with Hooper.

Traheron was far from satisfied with Bullinger's reply to this
letter, and his critique of its content reveals much about his
own thought. It was Bullinger's unwillingness to place sin and
the Fall within the decretive will of God, leaving them rather
as results of God's permissive will, that most displeased him.
In opposition to this, Traheron advocated a more causal view
which allowed a positive connection between sin and God's
predetermination.[46] It is almost certain that this issue was the
source of tension between Hooper and Traheron in 1550.
Internal evidence in the text suggests that Hooper is writing
specifically to refute absolute predestination and its implications. Furthermore, in 1549 Hooper wrote a letter to Bullinger
in which he criticized anabaptists for holding a view of predestination involving two wills in God.[47] That Hooper made such

---

[45] *OL* 325.

[46] 'I cannot altogether think as you do. For you so state that God permits certain
things, that you seem to take away from him the power of acting. We say that God
permits many things, when he does not renew men by his Spirit, but gives them up to
the dominion of their own lusts. And though God does not himself create in us evil
desires, which are born with us; we maintain nevertheless, that he determines the
place, the time, and mode [of bringing them into action], so that nothing can happen
otherwise than as he has before determined that it should happen', *OL* 326.

[47] 'They [the anabaptists] maintain a fatal necessity, and that beyond and besides
that will of his which he [God] has revealed to us in the scriptures, God hath another
will by which he altogether acts under some kind of necessity', *OL* 66–7. This is

a comment indicates that this was an area of controversy in 1549, and his opponent may well have been Traheron: the reference to anabaptists may simply have been a device designed to discredit the idea.[48] What is certain, however, is that Hooper only treats predestination in the context of a dispute within English theology.

Grace and Predestination

The discussion of grace and predestination occurs in the preface of *A Declaration* and is not referred to in the main text which is an exposition and application of the decalogue. Hooper does not approach the subject of predestination directly but first defines the relationship between God and man. Only when this is done does he then apply his findings to areas which relate to predestination.

Hooper starts the preface by drawing an analogy between the relationships that exist between men and that which exists between God and man. As a man to man relationship, or contract as Hooper calls it, requires a set of principles upon which the two parties are mutually agreed, so does that between God and man. In the latter case, these are provided by the content of the decalogue, which contains the promise of God to be a Father to his people, and defines the obedience demanded of man as a consequence.[49] This contract scheme, based on promise and obedience, is the same as that which he advocated in *A Declaration of Christ and His Office*.

This contract between God and man provides the basis of Hooper's approach to the decalogue. However, before he can proceed to the main discussion of the law, it is necessary for

probably a reference to the distinction between God's will as hidden and as revealed. It seems that Hooper is slightly confused here, as the idea of two wills in God does not demand that God himself 'works under some kind of necessity' which would imply that God's will was not free but subject to something else. It is also worth noting the stress here upon God's will as revealed, as this emphasis is repeated in the close relationship which Hooper draws between faith and election. Election for Hooper can never be conceived of in a way that places it outside of, or in opposition to, God's revealed will.

[48] There does not appear to be any evidence for associating English anabaptism with such a doctrine of absolute predestination: see G. H. Williams, *The Radical Reformation* (London, 1962), 403. Hooper himself had continual trouble with anabaptists but this was over the doctrine of the incarnation. His treatise, *A Lesson of the Incarnation of Christ* (1549), was written as a refutation of their doctrine of the celestial flesh of Christ: see *LW* 1–19.

[49] *EW* 255.

him to demonstrate how it is that God and man are brought into such a relationship in the first place. If this was strictly analogous to a contract between men, then the idea would be essentially commercial whereby the contract itself was the self-contained basis of the relationship. In the matter of salvation this would imply to a doctrine of justification by works. This is not the case in Hooper's theology, but he is aware that his statements thus far are tending towards such a conclusion. Therefore he points out that the mutual love of God and man, and not any commercial consideration, provides the foundation for the contract. This love presupposes the prior reconciliation of the two parties.[50] However, such a reconciliation must take into account the condition of fallen man: fallen man has nothing but hatred for God and his commands. Unless this situation can be overcome, a contract between God and man is a contradiction in terms. Thus, any such relationship can originate only in the unilateral love of God, not man. This love finds nothing in fallen man to motivate it, and so must be moved solely by the mercy of God.[51] Therefore, the peace between God and man is not based upon commercial considerations but upon the unilateral mercy of God; and the contract is not the means of effecting reconciliation but a framework within which the previously reconciled parties can articulate their mutual love.

Up to this point, the contract has been discussed without any reference to Christ, but Hooper is concerned that God's mercy is not devalued. He avoids this by stressing the Christological aspect of the contract: he interprets the promises made to Adam and Abraham as having reference to Christ. If on the one hand man deserved nothing but sin, then Jesus, on account of his perfect life, deserved nothing but God's blessing.[52] In this way, the contract is seen as being mediated through Christ. If commercial concepts are to be applied to the idea, then they must only be applied to the work of Christ who earns salvation through his obedience and his death upon the cross.[53]

This objective work of Christ has significance for man because of Christ's relationship to the human race. Hooper

---

[50] *EW* 255–6.   [51] *EW* 257.   [52] Ibid.

[53] Ibid. That Christ's work provides the very foundation of the contract is not noticed by West in his treatment of Hooper. He regards Hooper as making the death of Christ simply the confirmation of the contract, and thus there appears a Christological gap in his exposition of the Reformer's theology: see 'Origins', 257–8.

finds the basis for this relationship in the paralleling of Adam and Christ in Rom. 5:

But as God accounted in Adam's sin all mankind, being in his loins, worthy of death; so he accounted in Christ all to be saved from death.[54]

It is important to notice that Hooper considers the effect of both Adam's sin and Christ's redeeming work as universal in scope. This is to be a key element in Hooper's formulation of the doctrine of reprobation. Secondly, this second Adam Christology leads Hooper to point to the Christocentric nature of salvation: as God dealt with humanity in the person of Adam, so he now deals with humanity in the person of Christ. All of God's promises are made to Christ, and it is only as man is united to him that he is saved.[55] However, it is at this point that a fundamental difference between Christ and Adam emerges: the idea of being 'in Adam' is seen in biological terms, as indicated by the term 'in his loins';[56] however, there is no corresponding phrase in Hooper's reference to all being 'in Christ'. Indeed, if the union was biological, then this would imply that the whole of humanity would be redeemed and thus lead to a doctrine of universalism. This conclusion is unacceptable to Hooper, and it is in this context that he turns to discuss how it is that certain men are not saved.

From the parallelism of Christ and Adam, Hooper concludes that God's grace is universal in scope and promised to all men. The first promise of grace was given to Adam after he had sinned; thus, as all mankind participated in the sin of Adam, all mankind received the promise of salvation through Christ. All men are therefore children of promise.[57] In the light of such emphasis on the universality of God's grace, it is not the reality of salvation but the reality of damnation which is problematic. Therefore, it is to the problem of reprobation, not election, that Hooper first addresses himself.

---

[54] *EW* 257.

[55] 'All these promises, and other that appertained unto the salvation of Adam and his posterity, were made in Christ and for Christ only, and appertained unto our fathers and us, as we appertained unto Christ. . . . And as the Devil found nothing in Christ that he could condemn, John 14, likewise now he hath nothing in us worthy damnation, because we be comprehended and fully inclosed in him', *EW* 257–8. The concept of union with Christ is central to the soteriology of John Bradford: see Ch. 8.

[56] *EW* 258.   [57] *EW* 258–9.

By making the universal grace of God in Christ his starting point, Hooper frames his discussion of predestination in theological, not anthropological, terms. Thus, his approach is different from that of Tyndale for whom predestination was necessary primarily in order to demonstrate how impotent man could be saved. For Hooper, the problem of predestination derives from the need to reconcile two scriptural truths: that God's grace extends to all; and that some are nevertheless damned. He expresses this concern, and points towards a solution in the following passage:

If all then shall be saved, what is to be said of those that Saint Peter speaketh of, 2 Pet. 2, that shall perish for their false doctrine? And likewise Christ saith, that the gate is strait that leadeth to life, and few enter, Matt. 7. Thus the scripture answereth, that the promise of grace apperteineth unto every sort of men in the world, and comprehendeth them all; howbeit within certain limits and bounds, the which if men neglect or pass over they exclude themselves from the promise in Christ: as Cain was no more excluded, till he excluded himself, than Abel; Saul than David; Judas than Peter; Esau than Jacob. . . .[58]

Thus, while Hooper maintains the potential universality of the promise of grace, he accepts that this is actually contained within certain limits. It is the responsibility of man to observe these limits because ignoring them will lead to exclusion from the promise. Man's rejection of the gospel is therefore the formal cause of his damnation.

It is interesting that Hooper lists examples to support his doctrine. This list arguably raises more questions than it answers. For example, it is scarcely convincing to cite Judas as demonstrating self-exclusion from the promise without attempting to deal with John 17: 12, a verse which appears to speak of his damnation having been predetermined in order that scripture might be fulfilled. However, in view of the controversial context, it is possible that the list represents examples cited by Traheron in support of his own case, and that Hooper is simply casting them back at his opponent. That such is the case is suggested by the fact that Hooper now turns to a discussion of Rom. 9: 13, 'Jacob have I loved, Esau have I hated'. This is a central text for the doctrine of predestination, and would almost

[58] *EW* 259.

certainly have been used by Traheron in his own arguments. It is probably a desire to strike at the heart of Traheron's position that leads Hooper to deal with this passage.

Hooper offers two interpretations of the passage. First, he accepts that the passage appears to teach that the election and reprobation of Jacob and Esau respectively were prior to their love and hatred for God. Nevertheless Hooper rejects such a view. Instead, he argues that the threat against Esau was analogous to that made by Jonah against Nineveh [Jonah. 3: 4]. It was only as Esau rejected the gospel that he became reprobate. Significantly, Hooper does not deal with Rom. 9: 11 or 16 which would appear to contradict his interpretation.[59]

Secondly, having first argued that the threat was conditional, Hooper now proceeds to deny that the threat actually referred to the eternal blessedness of Esau as an individual at all. Instead, he declares that it applied to the temporal promised land, and that its fulfilment occurred in the descendants of Esau when his inheritance was made desolate. Hooper then argues that Rom. 9 must be seen in the context of chapters 3, 4, and 5 of the same letter. Paul's purpose is not to construct a doctrine of predestination but to remove any confidence that the Jews may have had in their carnal lineage.[60]

It is possible that Hooper's interpretation of Rom. 9 is framed first as a rejection of Traheron's position, whereby he refutes the idea that God's sentence of reprobation exists prior to Esau's sin; and then as an assertion of his own view, which regards Rom. 9 as removing the Jew's carnal confidence. This idea is supported by the fact that his first interpretation is not an exegesis of the passage, but rather a rejection of a predestinarian interpretation based upon a prior rejection of predestinarianism as a whole. What is certain is that Hooper sees Esau's reprobation as the result of his own sin and not of God's predetermination. Thus, reprobation is the result of self-exclusion from the promise of grace.[61]

---

[59] *EW* 259.   [60] *EW* 260.

[61] Hooper's interpretation of Esau's reprobation in Rom. 9 does not appear to have derived from either Bullinger or Melanchthon. While both see the passage as destroying the Jews' confidence in their carnal lineage, they do not make God's pronouncement of reprobation against Esau conditional upon his response to the gospel: see Bullinger, *In Pauli ad Romanos Epistolam Commentarius* (Zurich, 1533), 120b–121b; *In omnes Apostolicas Epistolas, Divi videlicet Pauli XIIII. et VII. Canonicas Commentarii* (Zurich, 1537), 79–80; *OM* 15. 474, 682–3.

Hooper summarizes his doctrine of reprobation in the following passage:

The cause of rejection or damnation is sin in man, which will not hear, neither receive the promise of the gospel; or else, after he hath received it, by accustomed doing of ill he fall either in a contempt of the gospel, will not study to live thereafter, or else hateth the gospel, because it condemneth his ungodly life, and would there were neither God nor gospel to punish him for doing of ill. This sentence is true, howsoever man judge of predestination: God is not the cause of sin, nor would not have man to sin. Ps. 5, *Non Deus volens iniquitatem tu es*, that is to say, 'Thou art not the God that willeth sin.' Hos. 13, it is said, 'Thy perdition, O Israel, is of thyself, and thy succour only of me.'[62]

This passage is of great importance because it has a close parallel in the *Loci* of Melanchthon, and the close similarities between the two make it obvious that Melanchthon is the source of the substance of Hooper's statement.[63] Such similarities with the *Loci* were apparent in *A Declaration of Christ and His Office*, but here they are even closer. This use of Melanchthon demonstrates that previous assessments which regard Hooper as the disciple of Bullinger present an inadequate picture of the influences which helped to form his theology. However, there is a possibility that Hooper's dependence upon Melanchthon was noticed by his contemporaries. In his letter to Bullinger, Traheron refers to 'certain individuals here who assert that you lean too much to Melanchthon's views'.[64] While the tone of the passage would imply that these 'certain individuals' were critical of Bullinger, it is possible that they simply argued that his views were akin to those of Melanchthon, and that the qualitative judgement is Traheron's own interpretation. If this is the case, this passage may be a veiled reference to Hooper: his use of Melanchthon may well have been noticed, and he may have attempted to defend his position by arguing that he was not deviating significantly from the doctrine of Bullinger. Alternatively, the fact that Hooper, a pupil of Bullinger, used Melanchthon may have led 'certain individuals' to conclude that Bullinger held similar beliefs concerning predestination. These ideas cannot be proved, but they do offer interesting and plausible interpretations of Traheron's comment.

---

[62] *EW* 264.   [63] *OM* 21. 915 (quoted in Ch. 3, n. 39).   [64] *OL* 325.

Theologically, the quotation from the *Loci* is consistent with the overall structure of Hooper's soteriology. Once again he defines the cause of reprobation as man's sin. The idea of the contract undergirds his thinking here: man must continue to shun sin and love the gospel after he is saved or else he will lose his salvation. There is also an indication of the religious motive which underlies Hooper's formulation of reprobation: the desire to absolve God from any responsibility for sin.[65] It is evident from Traheron's letter to Bullinger that the former made a positive connection between God's will and sin, and that he was disappointed when Bullinger failed to agree with him. This was almost certainly one of the areas of Traheron's teaching with which Hooper disagreed most strongly. There is, however, a second error which Hooper wishes to avoid:

It is not a christian man's part . . . to say, God hath written fatal laws, as with the Stoic, and with necessity of destiny violently pulleth one by the hair into heaven, and thrusteth the other headlong into hell.[66]

While attacking fatalism, a statement such as this does not necessarily imply a rejection of eternal predestination: Bradford too expresses an identical concern while also advocating the doctrine of an eternal decree of particular election. Bradford makes a careful distinction between compulsion and necessity: all things happen by necessity, but not by compulsion. Compulsion implies that some external force compels man to a certain course of action against his will, whereas God works out his purposes by necessity but without violating the will of his creatures.[67] However, in the above passage Hooper uses the idea of necessity as Bradford would use that of compulsion. Nowhere does he distinguish between the two. The reason for this is that he has no need to do so: he does not develop a doctrine of an eternal decree nor any concept of absolute predestination, and thus the problem of the relationship between God's predetermination and man's will does not arise. Furthermore, in the context of the controversy with Traheron, it is most likely that the above statement should be read as a thinly veiled criticism of the Calvinistic doctrine of predestination. It is clear that

[65] This is also a fundamental concern in Bradford's doctrine of election and predestination: see Ch. 8.
[66] *EW* 263.   [67] *Writings* 2. 212–13.

Hooper interprets such doctrine as leading to the consideration of salvation and damnation purely in terms of God's will, abstracted from the reality of the individual's faith or sin. Hooper regards such a position as ignoring the scriptural teaching concerning the heinousness of sin and the necessity of faith, and thereby undermining the imperatives of Christianity.[68]

Throughout his treatment of reprobation, Hooper does not allow that God in any way predetermines either sin or individual damnation. This is apparent from his interpretation of Rom. 9 as teaching conditional reprobation and from his emphasis on the fact that sin is the only cause of damnation. While his doctrine of reprobation is thus formulated in order to avoid making God the cause of sin and undermining the imperatives of the Christian life, his doctrine of election is developed in opposition to the error of Pelagianism. It is important, he declares, that the Christian does not ascribe salvation to his own will as to do so would extenuate the effects of original sin.[69] Thus, he does not build his doctrine of election as a parallel to reprobation in terms of the same underlying concerns; rather, he constructs his view of election with reference to the nature of salvation in Christ:

The cause of our election is the mercy of God in Christ, Rom. 9. Howbeit, he that will be partaker of this election must receive the promise in Christ by faith. For therefore we be elected, because afterward we are made the members of Christ. Eph. 1, Rom. 8. Therefore, as in the justification or remission of sin there is a cause, though no dignity at all, in the receiver of his justification; even so we judge him by the scripture to be justified, and hath remission of his sin, because he received the grace promised in Christ: so we judge of election by the event or success that happeneth in the life of man, those only to be elected that by faith apprehend the mercy promised in Christ. Otherwise we should not judge of election. For Paul saith plainly, Rom. 8, that 'they that be led by the Spirit of God are the children of God;' and that 'the Spirit of God doth testify with our spirits that we are the children of God.' Being admonished by the scripture, we must leave sin, and do the works commanded of God: or else it is a carnal opinion, that we have blinded ourselves withal, of fatal destiny, and will not save us. And in case there follow not in our knowledge of Christ amendment of life, it is not lively faith that we have, but rather a vain knowledge and mere presumption.[70]

---

[68] *EW* 263–4.   [69] *EW* 263.   [70] *EW* 264–5.

As with his summary of reprobation, Hooper bases this passage too upon a similar statement in Melanchthon's *Loci*.[71] He again relates the idea of election to union with Christ which is effected through faith, and thus focuses attention on both the christocentric nature of salvation and the crucial importance of faith. Such a position guards against abstract speculation. Hooper underlines this by emphasizing that election can be known only through its concrete results in the lives of men.

Hooper does not link the idea of election to the concept of a decree of particular election. Indeed, to do so would undermine his emphasis upon the universal nature of God's grace in Christ and also point towards a determinist view of salvation of the kind which he has rejected. The decisive focal points of his doctrines of election and reprobation are not abstract but personal and existential (i.e. faith and sin respectively). This raises the problem of the origin of faith: does it originate partly or even wholly in man's will; or does it derive entirely from God?

Hooper's doctrines of election and reprobation are built upon different foundations: election is based upon God's decision, in the face of man's inability, to bring about redemption through Christ; reprobation is based upon man's failure to heed the gospel and to fulfil his moral responsibilities. In the former, it is God who is the cause, in the latter it is man, and each reflects Hooper's desire to be faithful to particular aspects of the Bible's teaching. However, it is legitimate at this point to ask if Hooper's doctrine can be described as synergistic. When writing this tract, Hooper was engaged in controversy against Calvinist doctrine which he equated with fatalism and which he considered as detrimental to the imperatives of Christianity. Perhaps such objections to Calvinist predestinarianism arose

[71] 'Econtra vero recte dicitur, caussam electionis esse misericordiam in voluntate Dei, qui non vult perire totum genus humanum, sed propter Filium colligit et servat Ecclesiam. Hoc vult Paulus, cum 9. cap. [:15] ad Rom. citat dictum: Misereor, cuius misereor. Negat propter legem, propter praerogativam generis, homines electos esse, ut fiat illustrius, propter Filium electam et conditam esse Ecclesiam; sed tamen in accipiente concurrere oportet apprehensionem promissionis seu agnitionem Christi. Nam ideo electi sumus, quia efficimur membra Christi. Ergo ut in iustificatione diximus, aliquam esse in accipiente caussam, non dignitatem, sed quia promissionem apprehendit, cum qua Spiritus sanctus simul est efficax, ut Paulus inquit, Fides ex auditu est; ita de electione a posteriore iudicamus videlicet haud dubie electos esse eos, qui misericordiam propter Christum promissam fide apprehendunt nec abiiciunt eam fiduciam ad extremum', *OM* 21. 915–6.

because he himself held to a synergistic doctrine of salvation. His use of Melanchthon, who did hold such a view, is a possible indication that this was indeed the case. Moreover, the doctrine of Bullinger, Hooper's friend and mentor, has not been above suspicion of tending towards synergism.[72] Thus, this question of synergism is of great relevance to an understanding of Hooper's writings on predestination.

Hooper makes no robust statement on predestination, in terms of decrees of election and reprobation, which would preclude synergism from the outset.[73] D. D. Wallace concedes that Hooper is cautious in dealing with predestination, but he considers that his argument for Hooper's predestinarianism is safe because of a single quotation regarding the election of particular individuals before the foundation of the world.[74] However, this statement is from *A Brief and Clear Confession*, which W. M. S. West has demonstrated, beyond reasonable doubt, was not written by Hooper at all. While in prison, Hooper did sign a document which referred to an eternal election of part of the human race, but this was a joint statement which was signed by, among others, Bradford and Sandys. It is not known who was responsible for the predestinarian clause, and Hooper's signature may not be at all significant. The purpose of the tract was to present a united front in the face of the Catholic reaction. It is quite possible that Hooper disagreed with the predestinarian clause but felt that its mild tone and its minor role in

[72] See Baker, *Heinrich Bullinger and the Covenant*, 29; Berkouwer, *Divine Election*, 191–4; Muller, *Christ and the Decree*, 45. These scholars see apparent ambiguities in Bullinger's doctrine, but conclude that he did not hold a synergistic position. The similarity between Hooper and Bullinger in stressing that election is known only in Christ can be seen by comparing Hooper's statement on election with article 10 of the *Confessio Helvetica* (1566), quoted by Karl Barth, *CD* 2. 2, p. 62. However, unlike Hooper, Bullinger also argues for an absolute decree which, as Barth argues, stands behind the Christological reference and is surely decisive for his doctrine of election: see *CD* 2. 2, p. 65.

[73] This contrasts sharply with Bradford's use of the decree as axiomatic to his discussions of salvation: see Ch. 8.

[74] See *Puritans and Predestination*, 18. The quotation reads as follows: 'I believe that the Father in Jesus Christ his Son through the Holy Ghost hath elected and chosen those that are his own, according to his good will, before the foundations of the world were laid, whom he hath predestinate unto eternal life', *LW* 25. If Hooper had written this, it would mark a significant development in his thought. That he is alleged to have published this in the same year as the second edition of the work on the decalogue is another indication that it is probably not from his pen, as the ideas on predestination are clearly dissimilar.

the statement should not prevent him from identifying with his fellow prisoners.

If Hooper's failure to advocate a predestinarian decree does not preclude the possibility of synergism, it does not necessarily imply that he did hold such a doctrine.[75] Nevertheless, a positive case can be made on several grounds for arguing that Hooper's theology is at least synergistic in tendency. First, there are his repeated declarations concerning the need for the individual to turn to God.[76] Of course, such statements reflect the teaching of the New Testament and need not imply synergism as they refer to the duty, not to the ability, of man. Only the most rigid hyper-Calvinist would object to such.[77]

Secondly, and more important, are the various references to the fact that God does not operate against man's will. For example, Hooper declares that it is not true that God 'with necessity of destiny violently pulleth one by the hair into heaven, and thrusteth the other headlong into hell'.[78] On the surface, this may appear to indicate that Hooper is denying the idea of election and reprobation through God's sovereign predestination. However, the statement is immediately followed by an appeal to 'ascertain . . . by the scripture, what be the causes of reprobation, and what of election'. These, Hooper then proceeds to argue, are sin and faith in Christ respectively. In context, therefore, this statement is an objection to a formulation of the doctrines which divorces them from existential considerations.

Nevertheless, Hooper does tend to allot man's will a decisive role in salvation through his emphasis on man's rejection of grace. While it is true that man sins because of original sin, Hooper always points towards actual sins as the cause for indi-

---

[75] The modern theologian G. C. Berkouwer rejects the concept of equally ultimate decrees of election and reprobation. He also refuses to accept that God is the cause of sin or that his hidden will can in any way contradict his revelation. Nevertheless, his work also represents one of the most brilliant recent attacks on synergism: see his *Divine Election*.

[76] e.g. *EW* 413, 421.

[77] In the nineteenth century, the Baptist preacher C. H. Spurgeon, whose favourite theologians even included the famous 'hyper' John Gill, was himself accused of Arminianism because he preached a general call to repentance: see I. H. Murray, *The Forgotten Spurgeon* (Edinburgh, 1973), 44–66. It is interesting that Baptist hyper-calvinism still objects to a general call but on the basis that man is impotent to respond, not because of a double decree.

[78] *EW* 263.

vidual reprobation. This does not mean that Hooper's doctrine is necessarily synergistic, but it does focus attention upon the actions of the individual in time as the decisive element in salvation or damnation.

Hooper's comments on John 6: 44 also point towards an incipient synergism within his thought:

John 6 saith, 'No man cometh unto me, except my Father draw him.' Many men understand these words in a wrong sense, as though God required in a reasonable man no more than in a dead post, and marketh not the words that follow: *Omnis qui audit a Patre et discit, venit ad me*; that is to say, 'Every man that heareth and learneth of my Father cometh to me.' God draweth with his word and the Holy Ghost; but man's duty is to hear and learn, that is to say, receive the grace offered, consent unto the promise, and not repugn the God that calleth. God doth promise the Holy Ghost unto them that ask him, and not to them that contemn him.[79]

This passage is again based upon a similar statement in the *Loci*, and thus indicates Melanchthon's pervasive influence on Hooper's doctrine in this area.[80] Its content is also central to an understanding of Hooper's doctrine of salvation and demonstrates once again the close relationship between faith and union with Christ: only those who listen to God's voice are drawn to Christ. This is entirely consistent with Hooper's other statements that God does not force man to heaven. However, Hooper also draws a close link here between the activity of God in salvation and that of man: God draws by the word and Spirit; man hears and learns. The key word in the passage is 'duty', an accurate translation of 'oportet' in the *Loci*. This clearly denotes man's responsibility to believe the gospel. While the problem of synergism does not relate to man's responsibility but to his ability, there are several indications that this passage does indeed imply a synergistic view of salvation. First, the overall tone of the passage points to an understanding

[79] *EW* 265.

[80] 'Sic cum Ioan. 6[: 44] dictum esset, Nemo venit ad me, nisi Pater traxerit eum; sequitur statim: Omnis, qui audit a Patre et discit, venit ad me. Orditur Deus et trahit verbo suo et Spiritu sancto, sed audire nos oportet et discere, id est, apprehendere promissionem et assentiri, non repugnare, non indulgere diffidentiae et dubitationi', *OM* 21. 926. Melanchthon is apparently using Chrysostom's gloss on the text at this point, and so it is possible that Hooper is doing the same. However, his dependence on the *Loci* in other parts of this treatise makes this unlikely.

of salvation as a co-operative process between God and man where God's part is to offer the gospel, and man's part is to accept it. Secondly, the passage is borrowed from a section of the *Loci* which constitutes one of Melanchthon's major statements upon synergism. If Hooper wished to distance himself from such a doctrine, it is most surprising that he chose such a passage to support his position against Calvinist attacks.

It is true that Hooper makes no statement which can be regarded as an unequivocal declaration of synergism. However, his emphasis upon God's universal grace, the decisive role of the human will in reprobation, and his use of Melanchthon all point in this direction. Taken together, all these pieces of evidence strongly suggest a Melanchthonian view of the roles of God and man in salvation. As we examine his doctrine of the law and the model of redemption in *A Godly Confession*, we will find further evidence to support this conclusion.

Salvation and Law

The emphasis upon man's responsibility in the preface points towards the central purpose of *A Declaration of the Ten Holy Commandments*, which is to expound role of the law in the life of the Christian. This is linked to Hooper's doctrine of election because the decalogue forms part of man's obligation in the bilateral arrangement which articulates the relationship between God and man subsequent to the latter's reconciliation through Christ. Both Bullinger and Melanchthon regarded the law as defining the believer's ethical obligation to God.[81] However, as in the preface, it is from Melanchthon that Hooper borrows much of the substance of this section.

In the main body of the work, Hooper deals with the law under several headings. First, he defines what the law is; secondly, he discusses its applications; and thirdly, he indicates how man should regard the law. Finally, he expounds each of the individual commands. This last section is little more than a series of long and tedious applications of the law to specific situations, and has no relevance for an understanding of Hooper's doctrine of salvation.

For Hooper, the whole of scripture is simply an extended exposition of the law. Thus, the teaching of the prophets,

[81] See Bullinger, *De Testamento* 17b; *OM* 21. 719.

apostles, and Christ himself is one in subject matter.[82] Such a statement is entirely consistent with his view that Christ is the only means of salvation in both Testaments: Christ and the law are both parts of the one contract between God and man. By emphasizing that Christ's preaching is also essentially that of the decalogue, Hooper underlines this testamental unity.

Hooper gives the following general definition of the law:

[The law is] a certain doctrine, shewing what we should do, and what leave undone, requiring perfect obedience towards God, and advertising us that God is angry and displeased with sin.[83]

Hooper supports this definition by referring to Matt. 22, Exod. 20, Deut. 6; 28: 15, and Matt. 25: 41. In an identical context in the *Loci*, Melanchthon quotes Matt. 22: 37 and 39, Exod. 20: 17, and Matt. 25: 41.[84] It is arguable that these are key verses for defining the law and likely to feature in any such discussion. However, the order in which they occur in Hooper's treatise is similar to that in the *Loci*. Furthermore, there is a similarity in argument. Both Hooper and Melanchthon move immediately from this general definition to a clarification of the difference between the laws of men and those of God: while both require external obedience, God's law also demands internal obedience.[85] This close similarity, coupled with the evidence of dependence upon the *Loci* in other parts of this work, indicates that Hooper is also following Melanchthon's arguments at this point.

Hooper gives three main reasons for man's deviation from the law:

From this right line and true regle of God's word man erreth divers ways: sometime by ignorance, because he knoweth not or will not know, that only the express word of God sufficeth. . . . The second

---

[82] 'And whatsoever is said or written by the prophets, Christ, or the apostles, it is none other thing but the interpretation and exposition of these ten words or ten commandments', *EW* 271.

[83] *EW* 273.

[84] See *OM* 21. 685. In the original text, Hooper refers only to Matt. 22 and Exod. 22 as chapters, without giving a verse. The marginal notes, not inserted until the edition of 1588 [i.e. over 30 years after the death of the author] give verses 34 and 1 respectively. While these verses do fit the context, the evidence points towards Hooper following the *Loci* at this point and thus it seems legitimate to disagree with the marginal notes.

[85] *EW* 273–4; cf. *OM* 21. 685–6.

way . . . is many times the power and authority of this world: as we
see by the bishop of Rome . . . who giveth more credence and faith
unto one charter of Constantinus than to all the whole Bible.
Another erreth by mistaking of the time, making his superstition
far elder than it is.[86]

Ignorance is the underlying theme in each of these reasons for
sin. It is perhaps significant that Hooper does not refer to the
Fall and man's subsequent impotence in this context. This
reflects a general pattern in his writings: he is continually
stressing the need for reform on both a corporate and individual
level, but he never balances this with a similar emphasis upon
man's inability to reform himself. Such an imbalance is consistent with the synergistic tendency within his theology.

The stress on ignorance in this context parallels a similar
emphasis on knowledge in *A Declaration of Christ and His Office*.
In that work, Hooper stressed that the believer's duty is to
know Christ and to act in accordance with such knowledge. In
this work, he refers man's disobedience to his ignorance. Thus,
there appears to be a basic relationship in Hooper's theology
between ignorance and sin, and knowledge and salvation. Salvation therefore demands the impartation of such knowledge and
when Hooper expounds the work of Christ, he places his role
as teacher, one who imparts knowledge and dispels ignorance,
at the forefront of his discussion. The same emphasis occurs in
this treatise, where the only mention of Christ in his discussion
of the definition of the law is as teacher of the decalogue.

Having argued that sin is the result of ignorance, Hooper is
careful to affirm that, whatever else the law is for, it is not
meant to show man how to be justified by works:

It is well known by the places afore rehearsed, that the law of God
requireth an inward and perfect obedience unto the will of God: the
which this nature of man, corrupted by original sin, cannot perform,
as St. Paul proveth manifestly in the seventh and eighth chapter to
the Romans. There remaineth in man, as long as he liveth, ignorance
and blindness, that he knoweth not God nor his law, as he ought to
do, but rebelleth by contumacy against God.[87]

This passage is very similar to the opening of the section on
the uses of the law in the *Loci*.[88] Once again this suggests that

---

86 *EW* 25–76.   87 *EW* 281.   88 See *OM* 21. 716.

Hooper is consciously following the arguments of Melanchthon. It also represents a clear statement of the results of the Fall. While emphasizing that the Fall has left man corrupted and unable to achieve the perfection needed to save himself, it is not an unequivocal statement that man is entirely impotent. Hooper only states that man cannot fulfil the law perfectly, and that man in himself does not naturally know God as he should. Again, Hooper characterizes, man's predicament in terms of innate ignorance and not moral bondage. All that Hooper has actually rejected is the notion that man can save himself by his own efforts; he has not precluded the idea that man can co-operate with God in the initiation of his salvation. Indeed, the presence of an almost identical statement in Melanchthon's *Loci* indicates that the thought here is consistent with a synergistic view of salvation.

Hooper ascribes three specific uses to the law: to preserve society; to convict of sin; and to show Christians the works they should do. Hooper describes the first use of the law as civil and external, given for the preservation of the commonwealth. The two verses he uses to support this are 1 Tim. 1: 9 and Deut. 19: 19–21. While there is no exact translation of Melanchthon, the parallel in argument and content is close enough to suggest that Hooper is once again following the argument of the *Loci*.[89]

Hooper's treatment of the second use of the law, its role in conviction of sin, also appears to derive from the *Loci*. First, he points to the law as damning and terrifying sinful man, using as his texts Rom. 1 and 7; then he goes on to emphasize, that the law's function is positive, leading to Christ, as shown by Rom. 11 and Gal. 3.[90] All these thoughts follow closely those of Melanchthon on this same subject, and read as a summary of the latter's argument.[91] However, while Melanchthon devotes two long paragraphs to this matter, Hooper completes his treatment of the subject in two sentences. This is further indication of the lack of emphasis in Hooper's writings upon the

---

[89] Cf. *EW* 282 and *OM* 21. 716–17.

[90] 'The second use of the law is to inform and instruct man aright, what sin is, to accuse us, to fear us, and to damn us and our justice, because we perform not the law as it is required, Rom. 1 and 7. Howbeit the law concludeth all men under sin, not to damn them, but to save them, if they come to Christ. Rom. 11, Gal. 3', *EW* 282.

[91] *OM* 21. 717–19.

moral impotence of man. He is far more concerned with practical applications of the law to the ethical lives of Christians.

The first two uses of the law apply to non-Christians as much as to Christians. However, the third use of the law is peculiar to those who are born again, in that it is 'to shew unto the Christians what works God requireth of them'.[92] Again, the idea is present in Melanchthon, although this time there is no paralleling of words and verses.[93] This function of the law outlines man's duties in the contract between God and man, and thus provides the basis for Hooper's extensive application of individual commandments to the Christian life.

Summary

Hooper wrote this work while engaged in controversy with Bartholomew Traheron over the nature of predestination. He objected to the latter's Calvinist notion of eternal election and reprobation, and his assertion that God was in some way the cause of sin.

Hooper argues that the believer is reconciled to God through Christ and is subsequently bound to keep believing the gospel and performing good works. This concept of contract is probably derived from Bullinger and is based upon the prior reconciliation of God and man through Christ. Hooper rejects any notion that either reprobation or election can be known other than in sin and faith respectively, and does not formulate any doctrine of an eternal decree. Christ's grace, like Adam's sin, extends to all, but if individuals refuse to believe the gospel and persist in sin, then they will be damned.[94] This is the manner in which reprobation is to be understood. Election, on the other hand, occurs when men do not reject God's grace in Christ. This formulation clearly suggests a synergistic view of salvation, an interpretation supported by Hooper's constant use of Melanchthon throughout his discussion of predestination.

In his discussion of the law, Hooper advocates a threefold use: to preserve society; to convict of sin; and to guide Christian behaviour. The third use defines man's obligations in the

---

[92] *EW* 282.

[93] *OM* 21. 719.

[94] Hooper does not deal in this work with the reason why specific individuals do not reject God's grace. This aspect of his soteriology will be examined in the next section.

contract with God. This section again reveals close similarities with Melanchthon's *Loci.*

A GODLY CONFESSION

A Godly Confession and Protestation of the Christian Faith was published by John Day in 1550, in which year it went through two editions. Its compact size and comprehensive scope would undoubtedly have made it a useful handbook of doctrine.

The work is a miniature systematic theology, presenting the single most comprehensive statement of Hooper's theology which we possess. He declares that he wrote the work primarily in order to combat both heretical and negligent ministers. In the preface to the work, he also expresses the hope that the treatise will establish his catholicity, teach king and council their duty, and call men to repentance. Thus, he does not intend the work simply as a statement of doctrine but also as an aid to practical reform in Church, State and personal lives.[95]

For the student of Hooper's theology the work is highly important because, as a mini-dogmatics, it reveals his theological method and emphases in a more strictly systematic manner than his other thematic, controversial, or expository works. The work itself consists of a series of brief sections on the cardinal elements of the faith. The general pattern followed is that of the Apostles' Creed, whose statements Hooper quotes as summaries of cardinal doctrines.[96]

The *Confession* starts with the doctrine of creation, covering both God, who is eternal and uncreated, and the angels and man, created within time. Thus, at the outset the two basic components necessary to theological discussion are affirmed: the existence of God; and the existence of man.

Having dealt with creation, Hooper then proceeds to discuss the God revealed in the Bible, a God who exists in Trinity. God's Trinitarian nature is discussed in terms of its ontology. Hooper affirms that God is three persons who are equal and of

---

[95] *LW* 66–9.

[96] The other *Confession* ascribed to Hooper also follows the pattern of the Apostles' Creed, adding further strength to the case against his authorship as well as the doctrinal differences, it seems unlikely that Hooper would produce two entirely different works based upon the same framework in the same year. Bradford too uses the Apostles' Creed as a framework for a general statement of his theology: see *Writings*, 1, 140–8.

one substance. The main emphasis of this section falls upon the action of the Trinitarian God in redemption. Indeed, this provides the framework for Hooper's entire treatment of the subject in this work.

After discussing creation and redemption, Hooper closes the *Confession* with brief statements on his view of the Church, in terms of its two marks, word and sacrament, followed by a summary of the obedience owed by a subject to his sovereign.[97] Thus, in this work, Hooper covers all areas from creation to ethics.

Creation and Fall

Before turning to the subject of redemption, Hooper outlines what makes redemption necessary: the Fall.

According to Hooper, creation was perfect because it arises from an act of God. As God himself is perfect, so must his acts be. For this reason, the origin of the Fall must not be ascribed in any way to God, because that would be to imply that he was imperfect in some way. Instead, the Fall must be seen as the result of man's being deceived by the Devil. It is this deception which leads to the Fall and thus to man's need of redemption.[98]

In his brief treatment of the Fall, Hooper is consistent with his earlier statements on sin in *A Declaration of the Ten Holy Commandments* where he refused to link sin in any way to the will of God. It is also significant that Hooper links the notion of the Fall and sin to man's ignorance. According to Hooper, it was man's ignorance that led him to be deceived by the devil.[99] It is therefore not surprising that he moves immediately from making this point to discussing the knowledge of God.

The Knowledge of God

In *A Declaration of Christ and His Office*, Hooper emphasized that the knowledge of God is the supreme concern of the individual's life. Then, in *A Declaration of the Ten Holy Commandments*, he contrasted the ideas of knowledge/salvation and ignorance/

[97] In the other *Confession*, three marks of the Church are advocated: word, sacrament, and discipline. This shows a marked divergence from Hooper's *Godly Confession*.
[98] *LW* 70–1.
[99] '[Man] fell into this ruin . . . by ignorance, and by craft of the devil deceived', *LW* 70–1.

sin. This same contrast is used again here in order to characterize those who are saved and those who are lost:

I believe all the people of the world to be either the people of God, or the people of the devil. The people of God be those that with heart and mind know, worship, honour, praise, and laud God after the doctrine of the prophets and apostles. The people of the devil be those that think they worship, honour, reverence, fear, laud, and praise God, any other ways besides or contrary to the doctrine of the prophets and apostles.[100]

This passage reflects the general emphasis upon knowledge in Hooper's soteriology and Christology. It is perhaps surprising that he does not mention the doctrine of Christ along with that of the prophets and apostles, as elsewhere he equates all three. However, instead of stressing the Christological aspect of this knowledge, Hooper points instead to the Bible, stressing that this contains all true knowledge of God.[101] He then proceeds to define this knowledge in terms of doctrine. For example, the Bible teaches us that God is a trinity and that he is both Creator and Redeemer. In so doing, Hooper is equating true *saving* knowledge of God with true *doctrinal* knowledge of God.

This marks a significant divergence from the position of the earlier English Reformers. For them, salvation was appropriated through faith. They defined faith primarily as trust in Christ. Of course, if the term 'Christ' is not to be emptied of its content, then the concept of trust in Christ must rest upon a certain doctrinal understanding of his person and work. However, Tyndale, Frith, and Barnes emphasized the fiduciary aspect of saving faith and were careful to point to the essential difference between this and mere assent to doctrine. Hooper, however, does not make such a clear distinction. In *A Declaration of Christ and His Office*, he characterizes the difference between saving and non-saving knowledge of God in terms of the moral activity the believer undertakes as a result of this knowledge.[102] While he does state that true faith involves trust as well as correct knowledge of God, this is an isolated statement.[103] The whole thrust of his soteriology, with its emphasis upon man's ignorance, leads to a stress on the doctrinal rather than the fiduciary aspects of faith.[104]

---

[100] *LW* 71.   [101] Ibid.   [102] *EW* 33.   [103] *EW* 51.
[104] This is clear from the following passage which occurs at the end of *A*

The Trinitarian Structure of Redemption

God's act of grace in redemption is one in which all three persons of the Trinity are involved. Hooper is careful to stress that the decision to redeem man was taken by Father, Son, and Holy Spirit:

I believe that the mercy of the Father, the Son, and the Holy Ghost, pitied and had compassion upon Adam and the lost man, and was provoked to ordain the Son of God, to debase and humble himself unto the nature of man, and also to become man, to redeem and save the lost man.[105]

This passage emphasizes that redemption is the merciful response of the whole Trinity to man's plight. Unlike Bradford, Hooper does not discuss this decision to redeem man in terms of an eternal decree which embraces only a portion of the human race.[106] Instead, he uses the general term 'lost man' to refer to the objects of redemption, and gives no hint that this redeeming work of Christ is deliberately limited in its intent. Hooper's failure to do this is a clear indication that his theology is fundamentally non-predestinarian in structure.

Having established the origin of redemption, Hooper turns to the means whereby that redemption is objectively achieved. This is through the second person of the Trinity, Jesus Christ. He does not use the framework of Christ's roles as priest and king in order to expound the work of Christ in this treatise. Instead, he discusses the redemption purchased by Christ in terms of a second Adam Christology: Christ undoes all the

---

Declaration of the Ten Holy Commandments: 'Although thou canst not come to so far a knowledge in the scripture as other that be learned . . . yet mayest thou know, and upon pain of damnation art bound to know, the articles of thy faith; to know God in Christ, and the holy catholic church by the word of God written; the ten commandments, to know what works thou shouldest do, and what to leave undone; the *Paternoster*, Christ's prayer. . . . He that knoweth less than this cannot be saved; and he that knoweth more than this, if he follow his knowledge, cannot be damned', *EW* 429–30. The overwhelming emphasis here is upon doctrine, not trust. Hooper avoids the idea that mere intellectual assent can save by stressing that man must act in accordance with his knowledge, but this simply underlines the ethical nature of his theology. This also helps to explain his attitude over vestments: if wearing vestments is a wrong action arising from ignorance, then it is immediately a moral problem, as ignorance arises from man's own wilful sinfulness.

[105] *LW* 72.

[106] Hooper's statement here also contrasts strongly with the explicit predestinarianism of the *Confession* falsely ascribed to him: see *LW* 25.

damage that was caused by Adam.[107] He is careful to assert that there can be no salvation outside Christ, and that the Pelagian notion that man can save himself by his own efforts is thus to be condemned.[108] He defines Christ's atonement in the following manner:

I believe that the grace of God, deserved by the passion of Christ, doth . . . freely and without all merits of man begin, teach, and provoke man to believe the promises of God, and so to begin to work the will of God. . . .[109]

Several important issues are raised by this statement. First, Hooper makes no mention in this work of the need to propitiate God's wrath, although it is clear from elsewhere that he did hold such a doctrine. However, its omission from a tract intended as a summary of cardinal points of doctrine is indicative that Hooper does not consider it to be central to his soteriology. The emphasis is not on the need to expiate man's moral guilt, but on the need to teach him to trust God and work his will. If Christ's work is to rectify the damage done through the Fall, then Hooper does not see this damage primarily in terms of moral guilt or bondage, but in terms of ignorance: Christ's work is described not as expiating man's guilt but as providing the basis for teaching man. Again, Hooper emphasizes the close link between salvation and knowledge.

Secondly, this passage might be interpreted as demonstrating that Hooper did not hold to a synergistic view of salvation. Certainly, Hooper here emphasizes the priority of God's action in salvation both in sending Christ and in encouraging man to believe. However, the statement is intended as a description of Christ's role in salvation. As such, it stresses only the action of God in saving man and does not deal with man's response. Synergism is not precluded by the fact that God takes the initiative in offering his grace to the lost sinner and encouraging him to believe; rather, synergism refers to the nature of the sinner's response to the grace offered. Hooper's statement here does not contradict his emphasis upon the decisive role of man's will in accepting God's grace.

In discussing the redemptive work of the Holy Spirit, Hooper places his main emphasis on the preservation of the Church

---

[107] *LW* 72.   [108] *LW* 73.   [109] Ibid.

from error.[110] His role in the salvation of individuals is discussed in a single sentence which states that the Spirit applies those benefits objectively achieved by Christ to the individual. This includes the production of faith and works in the believer, and the resurrection of the flesh and eternal life.[111]

This one comment constitutes one of only two significant references throughout all of Hooper's writings to the work of the Holy Spirit in salvation.[112] There are several reasons for this lack of emphasis. First, Hooper refers sanctification to Christ and not to the Spirit. Secondly, his failure to emphasize man's inability means that there is less need to develop a doctrine of the Spirit's work within man. In turn, this lack of emphasis on the Spirit's work further reinforces the synergistic tendency of his thought: salvation is objectively accomplished through Christ, but its subjective appropriation is developed not primarily in terms of God's subjective activity but in terms of the believer's obligation to have faith in Christ and fulfil the conditions of the contract.

Summary

Hooper makes man's ignorance the cause of the Fall. He also characterizes the saved and the lost in terms of knowledge and ignorance respectively, and thus reflects the emphasis of earlier works. He defines this knowledge in terms of its doctrinal content, and so points towards an understanding of faith which places less emphasis upon trust and more upon assent to doctrine.

He regards the decision to redeem man as the response of the whole Trinity to man's predicament. This decision is not described as a limited decree of election which refers to particular individuals. Redemption is accomplished by Christ. Hooper makes no reference to propitiation in this context. Instead, he emphasizes Christ's teaching role, again reflecting his earlier emphasis. He gives only a brief summary of the Spirit's work in the application, and does not significantly develop this area elsewhere in his writings. This is consistent with his emphasis upon man's role in the appropriation of salvation.

---

[110] *LW* 73–4.

[111] 'I believe that this Holy Spirit worketh the remission of sin, resurrection of the flesh, and everlasting life, according to holy scripture', *LW* 74.

[112] For the other reference, see *EW* 50.

CONCLUSION

Hooper's soteriology is strongly Christological and places very little emphasis upon the role of the Father or the Holy Spirit. He places great emphasis upon the role of ignorance in man's predicament, and sees knowledge as a major factor in man's salvation. Thus, he develops his Christology not so much in terms of propitiation but in terms of Christ the teacher and the imparter of knowledge. Underlying this emphasis on knowledge is a definition of faith which places more emphasis upon doctrinal content than upon trust. This also reflects the strongly ethical concern of Hooper's theology, which he articulates through the concept of a contract between God and man.

Hooper is implacably opposed to any doctrine which might undermine the ethical imperatives embodied in his contract concept. Thus, he attacks the Calvinist doctrine of the eternal decree because of its deterministic implications. Indeed, during his polemic against Traheron, he expresses ideas which point clearly towards a synergistic understanding of salvation. This synergism is expressed only in the context of a controversy in which Hooper might be expected to stress man's responsibility against the Calvinist notion of the decree. As such, it is arguable that Hooper is simply overstating his case to make his point. However, his use of key passages from the *Loci* in this context point to a position akin to that of the synergism of Melanchthon.

It is evident that the interpretation of Hooper's theology as essentially a pale echo of that of Bullinger is no longer tenable. Despite his hard-line stance on the vestment issue, it is clear that Hooper was considerably influenced by the moderate Melanchthon in matters pertaining to salvation. Hooper is clearly in agreement with Bullinger in his contract concept and his division of the work of Christ, but his dependence upon Luther's gentle successor in other doctrinal aspects of salvation cannot be denied. His discussions of election, reprobation, justification, and the use of the law are all indebted to Melanchthon. Moreover, Hooper has imbibed the latter's synergism. Until the precise relationship between the thought of Melanchthon and that of Bullinger is clarified, Hooper must be regarded as owing at least as much, if not considerably more, to Melanchthon in the area of soteriology as he does to Bullinger.[113]

[113] In assessing the influence of Melanchthon on Hooper we are faced with a problem: if Bullinger pointed Hooper to Melanchthon's writings because they supported his own views, then it would really be him, and not Melanchthon, who influenced Hooper. We know that Bullinger read the *Loci* and used it as a textbook for his pupils (see Baker, *Heinrich Bullinger and the Covenant* xiv–xv) but he was also highly critical of Melanchthon's constantly changing views: see the letter in *OC* 14. 481. The relationship between the two men is therefore complex and, until scholarship reaches firm conclusions on this issue, it seems safest to assume that when Hooper borrows from Melanchthon, it is Melanchthon, and not Bullinger who is the influence.

8

John Bradford

BRADFORD'S WRITINGS

BRADFORD'S extant works consist of a large number of devotional prayers and doxologies, a collection of letters, and polemical treatises on election, the mass, and the errors of Rome. He wrote most of these while he was in prison. With the exception of the letters, these writings are not dated and so it is impossible to place them in any meaningful chronological sequence. As a result of this, and of the fragmentary nature of the works themselves, a work-by-work analysis of his writings is pointless. Instead, in order to reconstruct his theology, we must work from the known to the unknown. Thus, we must first deal with those tracts which have specific relevance to his doctrine of salvation, and then, in the light of what we discover there, proceed to gather from his other writings those other fragments of pertinent theological reflection. This eclectic process is, in many ways, a frustrating exercise which demands that many of the conclusions drawn must be tentative. However, the nature of the sources means that it is the best we can do.

ELECTION AND PREDESTINATION

The Polemical Context

Bradford's major writings on salvation were composed in the heat of theological controversy over the nature of election and predestination. During his imprisonment, Bradford came into contact with a group of Protestant separatists who were also being held in the King's Bench prison. This group had acquired the name 'free will men' during the reign of Edward VI, although the primary reason for their persecution appears to have been their separation from the Anglican Church rather than their views on salvation.[1] Information on individual gatherings is scarce, but Joseph Martin has identified over forty free willers from contemporary records. As a movement, it appears to have drawn its support from the lower classes, and to have lacked intellectual sophistication.[2] According to the contemporary records, the leading figure of the movement appears to have been one Henry Hart, who 'exemplified what could result from the sudden impact of the English Bible on a sensitive and articulate layman'.[3] This man Hart was one of Bradford's fellow prisoners, and it was during this period of imprisonment that the two men clashed over the nature of election and predestination.

The doctrinal differences over free will were not the initial source of the controversy. Apparently the free willers objected to the life-style of the Reformers, who were not averse to gambling and passing some of their time in playing games.[4] In contrast to this, the free willers were very strict about their life style. This is evident from Bradford's comment to Cranmer, Ridley, and Latimer that the free willers' heresy is more deadly than that of the papists because their conduct demonstrates the conviction with which they held their beliefs.[5]

However, while differences in life-style provided the initial cause of the dispute, it was the issues of free will and election that came to form the focal point of the controversy.[6] It is not difficult to understand the reason for this. In a letter to Cranmer, Ridley, and Latimer, Bradford summed up the basic error of the free willers as confounding the effects of salvation with the cause.[7] Thus, Bradford saw the dispute as concerned fundamentally with the cause of salvation. For this reason, he focused

---

[1] J. W. Martin, 'English Protestant Separatism at its Beginnings: Henry Hart and the Free-Will Men', *SCJ* 7 (1976), 56; O. T. Hargrave, 'The Freewillers in the English Reformation', *CH* 37 (1968), 271–2.

[2] Martin, *Religious Radicals in Tudor England* (London, 1989), 42; Hargrave, 'The Freewillers in the English Reformation', 280. This lack of intellectual sophistication did not prevent the leader of the movement, Henry Hart, from making some powerful points against Bradford's predestinarianism. For example, he objects to election on the grounds that this makes God's justice general and his mercy only limited. This same objection has been made in modern times against the federal theology of John Owen and Jonathan Edwards by J. B. Torrance: see *Writings* 1. 319; J. B. Torrance, 'The Incarnation and "Limited Atonement"', *EQ* 55 (1983), 92.

[3] Martin, 'English Protestant Separatism', 56.   [4] *Id. Religious Radicals*, 53.

[5] *Writings* 2. 170–1.   [6] Martin, 'English Protestant Separatism', 69.

[7] Writings 2. 170.

his attention not on the superficial differences regarding life-
styles, but on the real theological issues that were involved.

Although the controversy was heated and conducted with a
generous amount of personal abuse, Bradford seems ultimately
to have had some affection for his opponents, referring to them
as 'dearly beloved in the Lord',[8] and even sending them money
and food to help alleviate their suffering in prison.[9] However,
while Bradford was martyred, Hart was eventually released
from prison, and nothing is known of his fate.

During his controversy with Hart, Bradford wrote three
major works on the subject of election: *A Treatise on Election and
Free Will*; *A Brief Sum of Election*; and *A Defence of Election*. The
first two are general statements of the doctrinal issues involved,
while the latter consists of three parts: an essay on the importance
of election as a doctrine; an exposition of the biblical teaching,
based upon Eph. 1; and a point-by-point refutation of a work
by an unnamed free willer. This latter is almost certainly
Henry Hart as Bradford makes several references in his letters
to a refutation of Hart which he has written.[10] Bradford claims
that, in this work, he quotes verbatim passages from a tract by
Hart in order to refute his doctrine. Therefore, if we regard
Bradford as here referring to the third section of *A Defence*,
then this work becomes an important source of information
concerning Hart's position.[11]

In addition to these doctrinal works, Bradford also wrote a
number of letters associated with the controversy which shed
light on the dogmatic aspects of his views. However, purely
doctrinal considerations are only half the story: Bradford's
claim is that election is pre-eminently a practical, pastoral doctrine; thus no study of his views on this matter would be complete
without an examination of the manner in which he applied the
doctrine in his pastoral writings. In this context we are fortunate that so many of his letters from prison have survived, as

---

[8] Ibid. 194.

[9] Ibid. 180. Judging by a subsequent letter, the free willers were very sceptical
about the motivation behind Bradford's generosity: see ibid. 181.

[10] Ibid. 131, 135, 170, 195.

[11] Ibid. 1. 319–20. As there is no extant copy of Hart's original work, it is
impossible to establish the veracity of Bradford's claim. However, the points ostensibly
made by Hart are all plausible and do not appear to have been made over-simplistic. It
therefore appears reasonable to accept that Bradford is telling the truth.

they repeatedly deal with the issue of assurance in the face of persecution and provide first-class material for examining how Bradford applied the doctrine of election in a pastoral context. Thus, after the doctrinal aspects of the controversy have been examined, Bradford's use of election as a basis for assurance will be examined in order to establish whether his pastoral application is consistent with his dogmatic position.

The Importance of Election

The first problem that the controversy raises concerns the crucial importance which Bradford ascribes to the doctrine of election. This is summed up in the opening paragraph of *A Defence:*

Faith of God's election (I mean, to believe that we be in very deed 'the children of God' through Christ, and shall be for ever inheritors of everlasting life through the only grace of God our Father in the same Christ) is of all things which God requireth of us, not only most principal, but also the whole sum: so that 'without this faith' there is nothing we do that can 'please God'.[12]

This passage shows that election is a doctrine of overwhelming importance to Bradford. There are strong theological reasons for this. First, he regards election as the doctrine which most exalts Christ and humbles man. By stressing that God's grace alone, and not any effort on man's part, is the cause of salvation, the doctrine points the believer to the essential mercy of God.[13] Therefore, any doctrine which allows man any credit for his salvation is effectively undermining and undervaluing God's mercy.

Secondly, the doctrine provides an objective basis for assurance. This is a constant theme in Bradford's writings. In *A Defence*, he makes the following statement:

It overthroweth the most pestilent papistical poison of doubting of God's favour, which is the very dungeon of despair and contempt of God.[14]

Election therefore refutes the Catholic idea that only the exceptional believer can know that he is definitely saved. In opposition to this, Bradford constantly emphasizes that this doctrine assures the Christian of God's favour, and that this

---

[12] *Writings* 1. 307.   [13] Ibid. 307–8.   [14] Ibid. 308.

assurance has practical implications for the believer's life. A major criticism he makes in a letter to a free willer is that allowing works a decisive role in salvation precludes the possibility of assurance.[15] Thus, election, by excluding works at the outset, has vital pastoral implications because it provides an objective basis for the certainty of salvation.

However, while these two aspects of the doctrine explain its theological importance, they do not answer the more fundamental question of why it was so important to Bradford in particular. The problem is that election and predestination were not central issues in the early English Reformation. There was the controversy between Hooper and Traheron and the latter's claim that Calvinist predestinarians were in a majority amongst English theologians,[16] but the fact remains that there is no evidence to suggest that election was a major source of tension among the other Edwardian Reformers. Latimer, whose preaching had such a profound effect on Bradford, scarcely mentions the idea. Indeed, it appears that Bradford found it difficult to generate enthusiasm amongst the Reformers for his controversy with the free willers. While those in prison with him were prepared to offer their support, those elsewhere were less than enthusiastic. Bradford sent a copy of *A Defence* to Nicholas Ridley, and at the same time asked him if he would write against the free willers.[17] Ridley's reply indicates his basic caution in these matters:

I have in Latin drawn out the places of the scriptures, and upon the same have noted what I can for the time. Sir, in those matters I am so fearful, that I dare not speak further, yea, almost none otherwise than the very text doth, as it were, lead me by the hand.[18]

It is clear from this that Ridley does not regard election as a particularly proper subject for speculation and is not happy to involve himself in the controversy. Indeed, his reply, while admirable in its caution, amounts in the context to a thinly veiled criticism of Bradford's preoccupation with the doctrine.

---

[15] Ibid. 2. 130.   [16] See Ch. 7.   [17] *Writings* 2. 170.

[18] Ibid. 214. Sadly, this work has not survived. Had it done so, it would undoubtedly have shed much light on Ridley's attitude to both the doctrine and the controversy with Hart. It is significant that he chose to write in Latin, not English, suggesting that he was perhaps concerned about possible pastoral problems which would be raised if the doctrine was taught indiscriminately.

The simple fact is that Eucharistic controversies provided the focal point for English Reformation theology at this time, and that the zeal for the controversy with the free willers originated in only one of the Reformers: John Bradford.

If Bradford's emphasis upon election cannot be explained satisfactorily in terms of the general English context, perhaps the specific situation in prison provides the answer: Bradford is imprisoned in close proximity to Hart whom he considers as leading men astray; thus, he takes up his pen and writes against his erroneous views. This certainly explains why this particular controversy occurred, but it serves only to highlight, and not to explain, Bradford's personal emphasis upon election. The issues he faced were not new to the English Reformation. Tyndale, Frith, and Barnes, to name but three, had all opposed the idea that salvation was not all of grace but involved man's free will as well. They too had touched upon predestination, but all three had tended to focus on anthropological considerations in order to refute their opponents. They stressed the impotence of fallen man, and, when they did emphasize theological aspects of soteriology, such as grace, these were always seen as a response to man's predicament.[19]

Bradford's approach is distinctively different. He does not argue for election primarily as a corollary of man's impotence and justification by faith. Instead, he approaches the subject directly by stressing the reality of an eternal decree of election. This reality he sees as clearly taught in the scriptures and in need of no defence. He simply declares it as a truth.[20] Such an emphasis on an eternal decree of election is not necessarily demanded by a doctrine of man's impotence,[21] and so the confidence with which Bradford states the doctrine is clear proof that he was convinced of both the Bible's teaching on this issue and its importance to the Christian faith before he engaged in controversy with Hart.

If the importance of election to Bradford predates the controversy with Hart, and cannot be explained in terms of the general English situation at the time, then the answer to this problem must lie within his own personal background. A clue

---

[19] See Part Two.
[20] This will be discussed in more detail below: see *The Divine Decree*.
[21] See, for example, the position of G. C. Berkouwer in his *Divine Election*.

to a possible solution is given in the letters which he wrote early on in his Christian life. Bradford was tormented concerning the fraud against the king in which he had been unwittingly involved, and wrote several letters to Traves lamenting the situation. The major problem appears to have been a basic lack of assurance that God would forgive him unless he could make restitution of the stolen money. Although we do not possess the first letter to Traves, we have the latter's reply. This contains the following comment:

Despair not, though all in haste it be not repaid, as though ye were a man forlorn for that the payment is not made. . . . 'But how shall I do, if I die,' say you, 'this being unpaid?'—I say, God hath given you a desire to pay it, but not a power. . . . I believe the sin to be forgiven for Christ's sake.[22]

The clear implication of this passage is that Bradford had written to Traves asking for help because he lacked assurance of his own standing before God. The reason for this lack of assurance was a faulty view of salvation: he felt that he was in jeopardy because he was unable to repay this money. In other words, he was placing his confidence in works. This lack of assurance appears again in other letters written to Traves in 1548, and was a problem with which Bradford appears to have wrestled for some time.[23]

The significance of this personal struggle for election can be seen in Bradford's primary pastoral application of the doctrine: the provision of a secure basis for assurance. In later works Bradford shows no signs of any lack of confidence in God's favour, and it is quite conceivable that this came about as the result of a firm grasp of the doctrine of election. This theory receives some support from a comment Bradford makes in a letter to a free willer:

Only by the doctrine of it [i.e. predestination] I have sought, as to myself, so to others, a certainty of salvation, a setting up of Christ only, an exaltation of God's grace, mercy, righteousness, truth, wisdom, power and glory, and a casting down of man and all his power.[24]

The opening comment of this passage points to the signifi-cance of election for Bradford as a secure base for assurance,

[22] *Writings* 2. 3.   [23] Ibid. 5, 21.   [24] Ibid. 195.

and lends support to the theory that it is this that makes the doctrine so important to him. As he argues elsewhere, only if the believer is sure of God's love, will he do good works in the manner he should. Thus, Bradford would regard any attack on election as potentially lethal to Christian conduct because of the role which the doctrine played in his own experience.

While it cannot be proved that Bradford's own Christian experience caused his zeal for election, such an interpretation does make sense of the facts. However, one final question remains: how was Bradford introduced to the doctrine? Again, any theory that it may have been an English theologian can be dismissed as highly unlikely: Latimer scarcely touches on the doctrine, and Traves does not mention the doctrine as a cure for Bradford's doubts. It is possible that he was in contact with Calvinists, such as Traheron, although there is no evidence for this.

A more likely source of influence is Martin Bucer. Predestination was an important aspect of his theology,[25] and there are similarities between his doctrine and that of Bradford. His Romans commentary was certainly known to Bradford, as the latter translated part of it into English.[26] Indeed, Bradford's reference to him as 'father in the Lord' indicates that Bucer's influence went beyond that of mere teacher.[27] The two became close friends at Cambridge and Bradford must have sat regularly under the preaching and teaching of the great Reformer, and was no doubt impressed by what he heard. Indeed, in *A Farewell to the University and Town of Cambridge*, while listing a number of Reformers whom the town should not forget, it is only Bucer whom he mentions in the context of teaching and doctrine.[28]

Perhaps it was Bucer who first pointed Bradford to the security of his salvation in election. Bucer certainly regarded the doctrine as fundamental to Christian assurance and was critical of those who considered that the doctrine should not be

[25] Stephens, *The Holy Spirit in the Theology of Martin Bucer*, 23; McGrath, 'Humanist Elements', 13–14.
[26] This translation is printed as *The Restoration of All Things*, in *Writings* 1. 351–64.
[27] Ibid. 355.
[28] Ibid. 445. The list includes Cranmer, Ridley, and Latimer, who are to be remembered for their imprisonment because of the truth, and Rogers, Saunders, and Taylor, who have been martyred.

taught.[29] While his influence upon Bradford in this matter
cannot be proved, the similarities between his doctrine and
that of Bradford make such influence extremely probable,
especially in light of the general caution of English ecclesiastical establishment over the issue.[30]

The Foundation of Election

The first important aspect of Bradford's writings on election
is his insistence that all discussion should be based upon the
correct epistemological foundation. In *A Defence*, he is careful
to stress at the very beginning that the will of God is the only
standard by which all things should be evaluated:

> There is neither virtue nor vice to be considered according to any
> outward action, nor according to the will and wisdom of man; but
> according to the will of God. Whatsoever is conformable thereto,
> the same is virtue, and the action that springeth thereof is laudable
> and good. . . .[31]

This statement points to the need to know God's will and to
the difference between the will of God and the wisdom of man.
Man's wisdom is not sufficient for discerning the will of God,
and thus not a proper basis upon which to formulate or evaluate doctrine. Therefore, it is necessary to define an objective
source of knowledge of God's will before any meaningful
statement about doctrine can be made.[32] In *A Defence*, Bradford

[29] See his *Enarratio in Epistolam ad Ephesios* (Basel, 1562), 20.

[30] Bucer's *Enarratio . . . Ephesios*, which inevitably contains much discussion of
election and related doctrines, was originally delivered as a series of lectures in
Cambridge during the years 1550–1. Bradford was himself resident in the town at
this time, and it is therefore highly probable that he would have heard Bucer lecturing
on Ephesians.

[31] *Writings* 1. 310. The notion that God's revelation, and not man's reason, is to be
the only basis for any discussion of election is an idea found in both Bucer and
Melanchthon. Melanchthon's *Loci* appears to have been a favourite with Bradford: he
both translated from the work and lent it to friends, along with the *Loci* of Urbanus
Rhegius. Thus, Bradford could have been influenced either by Bucer or Melanchthon
or both on this issue: see *Enarratio . . . Ephesios*, 25; *OM* 21. 913–14. For Bradford's
references to Melanchthon, see *Writings* 1. 20; ibid. 2. 7.

Rupp ('Patterns of Salvation in the First Age of the Reformation', 64) suggested
that further research on Bradford would reveal Melanchthon as a major influence, but
my own findings suggest that it is Bucer who is the truly decisive influence.

[32] Bradford does not deal extensively with the problem of revelation, but he does
make a number of references to the idea. In *A Fragment on St John's Gospel*, he speaks
of man's inability to grasp the uncreated God. Because of this, God has made himself
known to man through the creation: see *Writings* 2. 266.

immediately proceeds from emphasizing the importance of knowledge of God's will to pointing to the source of such knowledge: the word of God.[33] In the very next paragraph Bradford defines this word as written in the canonical books of the Bible.[34] Elsewhere, in *The Restoration of All Things*, Bradford again emphasizes the scriptures as the revelation of God's will. This time he also stresses that the scriptures define the boundaries of theological speculation and that the human mind must simply confess ignorance concerning those things which the scriptures do not reveal.[35]

From these examples, it is clear that Bradford believes theology must be controlled by God's revelation in his word. This concept, coupled with the mistrust of man's innate wisdom, means that theology is essentially non-speculative. This scriptural principle is important to Bradford's discussion of predestination because he regards election simply as a 'given' of revelation: he considers that the scriptures self-evidently teach that God elected a portion of mankind from eternity. This is sufficient authority, indeed, the greatest authority, for simply asserting the doctrine as a truth above debate. Indeed, he makes the biblical passages which refer to this eternal election the starting point of both his major treatments of predestination, and uses the concept of a decree as a theological axiom. Bradford regards the denial of his interpretation of these passages as a sign of ungodliness. For him, rejection of election does not amount simply to a difference over scriptural interpretation but to a rejection of God's own revelation of himself.[36]

Bradford's doctrine of election is related to his conception of God's sovereignty in providence. In *A Treatise on Election*, he is careful to stress that all things which occur must be foreknown by God. This foreknowledge of God is not simply an objective understanding of events, but is linked to his will. As such, it is a knowledge of what he has predestined, according to which events are not only known but also predetermined:

---

[33] *Writings*. 1. 310.

[34] Ibid. 311.

[35] Ibid. 360. This same idea is expressed by Bucer: 'Nam theologiae principium est, Deus dixit; ex quo omnia sunt nobis demonstranda, quae volumus esse certa; si non possunt inde demonstrari, incerta sunt', *Enarratio . . . Ephesios*, 33.

[36] *Writings* 1. 211–12.

We must grant it [i.e. predestination] therefore, because the word of God doth teach it, but also because it standeth with the very nature of God, that to him not only men, but all things also that have been or shall be forever in all creatures, are not only certain, but so certain that they cannot but be accordingly, and serve his providence; for else God were not God, if any thing were, hath been, or could be without his knowledge, yea, certain knowledge. Which knowledge in God may not be separated of any man from his wisdom, and not so from his will; except we would make two Gods, as did the Manichees. . . . We should certainly know that it is God which is the ruler and arbiter of all things, which of his wisdom hath foreseen and determined all things that he will do, and now of his power doth in time put the same in execution.[37]

By linking God's foreknowledge so closely to his will, and by emphasizing the unity of that will, Bradford is inferring a doctrine of absolute predestination from the being of God.[38] However, by also emphasizing the role of God's wisdom in providence, he avoids expounding a doctrine of impersonal determinism. Providence is intimately related to God's merciful purposes which he is actively working out in history.[39]

Such a formulation of the doctrine of providence has clear determinist implications. However, Bradford is concerned to refute any view which interprets God as working out his purposes in a mechanical manner and which reduces man to the level of a puppet. To do this, he employs the distinction between necessity and constraint or compulsion:

A thing that is done willingly is not to be said to be done by constraint. God is good willingly, but not by compulsion. . . . good men do good willingly, but not constrainedly. . . . So that it is plain, though all things be done of necessity, yet are they not of compulsion and enforcement.[40]

Here, Bradford refers to the idea that all things occur of necessity, and thus points again to a doctrine of absolute predestination.

[37] Ibid. 212; also *A Godly Meditation and Instruction of the Providence of God Towards Mankind*: 'This ought to be unto us most certain, that nothing is done without thy providence, O Lord; that is, that nothing is done, be it good or bad, sweet or sour, but by thy knowledge, that is, by thy will, wisdom, and ordinance . . .', *Writings* 1. 191.

[38] In doing so, it could be said that he is going beyond his own scriptural principle by logically inferring a doctrine from the being of God. However, he would no doubt reply that his position is simply a legitimate application of the biblical teaching concerning God's being.

[39] *Writings* 1. 129, 192, 194–5.

[40] Ibid. 213.

However, by stressing that this is worked out dynamically and in a manner that does not do violence to the orientation of man's will, he is attempting to lessen any mechanistic implications that absolute predestination might imply. This distinction between necessity and compulsion is used by various Reformers in discussions of providence.[41] However, it is quite likely that Bradford borrowed the idea from Bucer who referred to it in his Romans commentary.[42]

The distinction also enables Bradford to assert that God is author of all things, but not of evil or sin.[43] Of course, there is a problem in attempting to use the distinction in this way, because, if God wills all things, then there must be a positive connection between his will and sinful acts. Bradford attempts to resolve this difficulty in his reply to Hart:

God is not the author and cause of sin. To be the author of any act is not to be the author of the evil will that doth the act; as the magistrate may be the author that an executor putteth to death one justly condemned, and yet the executor may put the condemned person to death of a desire of vengeance, wherein he sinneth; and the magistrate which causeth the fact is not to be blamed of the sin committed of the executor.[44]

This explanation is unsatisfactory because it separates sin from action. The analogy of the executioner works only if the act itself can be classified as good but the motivation or will behind the act is evil. This leaves unresolved the problem of those acts which are essentially evil, such as murder. If God has ordained such essentially evil acts, then surely he must be in some sense the author of sin. However, Bradford does not develop any means of explaining this. Instead he simply allows the two truths, that God is author of all things and that God is not the author of sin, to stand side by side.

There is one further problematic area in Bradford's doctrine of predestination. In a letter to a free willer, he makes the

---

[41] e.g. Luther, *Studienausgabe* 3. 206–7; Calvin, *Institutes* 2. 3. 5.

[42] *Enarratio in Epistolam ad Romanos*, 413.

[43] *Writings* 1. 216.

[44] Ibid. 321. Zwingli too uses the illustration of the execution of a criminal in *De Providentia*: see Z VI. iii, 153. 14–22. While there is no evidence to suggest that Bradford borrowed the idea from Zwingli, the two men are similar in approach, emphasizing that God does cause sinful acts but does not cause sin, and that the essence of sin lies in the motivation behind the act: see Z VI. iii, 152. 13–155. 21.

following statement with reference to declarations in scripture concerning God's will:

Sentences determined with God are immutable. . . . Sentences simply spoken are undetermined and mutable, as that of the destruction of Nineveh, of Hezekias' death, of Abimeleh. . . . Some things depend partly on us, and some upon God wholly and altogether. Those that depend partly on us are mutable to us, because we ourselves of ourselves be so; but that depend wholly upon God are immutable, because he is so.[45]

While Bradford immediately proceeds to emphasize salvation as one area which depends entirely upon God and therefore immutably predetermined,[46] the overriding thrust of this passage is that there are matters which are not included in this predetermination. While he is careful to ascribe mutability only to man and not to God, it is still difficult to see how this view can be regarded as consistent with statements elsewhere that God, by his very nature, is the author of all things. This is the only example of this strand of thought in Bradford's writings, and it is thus probably too slender a foundation upon which to build any major conclusions. However, along with the tension concerning sin and predestination, this suggests that Bradford is not entirely happy with the implications of absolute predestination. Later, in the exegesis of certain scriptural passages, he provides contradictory resolutions of problems of interpretation, apparently unsure of which is correct. The impression given is of a man who wishes to maintain predestinarian doctrine, but who is striving to avoid some of the more radical implications of such a position.

It is important to realize the theological function which providence performs in Bradford's thought. He never employs this doctrine as the primary source for his formulation of election, nor does he use the idea as the starting point for his discussion of the doctrine. Instead, in both major treatises on the subject of predestination, he takes the scriptural revelation concerning God's eternal decree of election as the ultimate foundation for the doctrine.[47] Thus, he anchors election primarily in God's

[45] *Writings* 2. 130.
[46] In contrast, Hooper argued God's will to save particular individuals was mutable. This is clear from his exposition of Rom. 9: see Ch. 7.
[47] *Writings* 1. 211, 311.

scriptural revelation and not in his being. However, Bradford does use the idea of providence as a secondary argument against the claims of his opponents that election is dependent upon God's foreknowledge of who will repent.[48] The doctrine of providence is therefore important in so far as it supports his interpretation of the decree.

The Divine Decree

Bradford regards the eternal decree of election as a 'given' of revelation about which there can be no dispute.[49] He uses Eph. 1: 3–14 as his basic text for this assertion,[50] although he sees the doctrine taught 'almost everywhere in the new Testament'.[51]

The fact that the decree of God was made in eternity is of little actual importance to Bradford's doctrine of election. While this aspect of the decree accords with his doctrine of the immutability of God's will, Bradford is not so concerned to emphasize its position in time as he is to stress its cause. This cause is God's will which is not influenced by intrinsic considerations within man.[52] While Bradford does develop an anthropology that stresses man's total inability to turn to God, he introduces this in order to counter the allegation that God's commands imply that fallen man has the ability to fulfil them.[53] He does not use man's impotence as a basis for affirming that God needed to take the initiative in man's salvation. Instead, he simply refers to the concept of an eternal decree which he finds in Eph. 1. Such an approach reveals a clear difference with the English Reformers during the reign of Henry VIII. They did not use the decree as an axiom in their discussions of soteriology, preferring to focus upon grace and justification by faith. It also separates him from the position of Hooper, who specifically formulated his doctrine in opposition to the idea of an eternal decree. For Bradford, eternal predestination is the starting point for the discussion of soteriology.[54]

---

[48] *Writings* 1. 212, 320–1, 322.

[49] Ibid. 211.

[50] Ibid. 311. This choice of text is perhaps the result of having heard Bucer's lectures on Ephesians in Cambridge during 1550 and 1551. However, Eph. 1 is a central passage for any understanding of election, and Bradford's choice does not in itself necessarily indicate Bucer's influence.

[51] *Writings* 1. 211.

[52] Ibid. 312.   [53] Ibid. 216–17.

[54] In a letter to Cole and Sheterden, two free willers, Bradford does approach

As well as being made in eternity and determined solely in accordance with God's own will, the decree is also limited in its extent. When Bradford asserts that God determined in eternity to save men according to his own will, he also stresses the fact that this election encompasses only a portion of mankind.[55] Throughout his writings on election he is careful to avoid any expression of the doctrine which might leave the way open for universalism. Thus, he even places a limitation upon the extent of the atonement, and allows that Christ is a general saviour only in a qualified sense.[56]

Bradford sees this limitation of the decree taught by scripture, pre-eminently in Eph. 1, although he lists other scriptures as evidence and finds further confirmation of this in the fact that not all men have faith (a sure sign of God's election) and not all are justified.[57] However, he regards these proofs from experience as far inferior to the testimony of scripture:

But what go I about to light a candle in the clear sunlight, when our Saviour plainly saith that all be not chosen, but 'few'? 'Many be called,' saith he, 'but few be chosen.'[58]

Once again, Bradford expresses his conviction that election is a truth self-evident in the scriptures and therefore requiring no significant support from elsewhere. However, it is here that a major tension in Bradford's theology emerges. Bradford regards God's revelation in his word as the basis for a correct understanding of election. The problem is that God's word apparently teaches contradictory principles concerning the will of God in salvation. On the one hand, the scriptures teach an eternal decree whereby only a portion of mankind has been chosen for eternal life; on the other hand, they also teach that God would have all men saved and wills not the death of a sinner.

election historically, through the doctrines of creation, the Fall, and redemption, the only example of such an approach in Bradford's writings. As it is a reply to a letter which is now lost, the order may have been determined by questions or issues raised by his opponents: see ibid. 2. 133–5.

[55] Ibid. 1. 211, 311.
[56] Ibid. 320. This issue will be discussed in detail below, in the section 'Election and Atonement'.
[57] Ibid. 313–14.
[58] Ibid. 313.

This problem is very real for Bradford's theology.[59] While he allows for a distinction between what God has revealed and what he has kept hidden, he does not allow that there can be any essential contradiction between these two.[60] To do so, according to Bradford, would be to make two Gods, as did the Manichees.[61] It is therefore extremely problematic when God's revelation itself appears to contain contradictions.

The fact that Bradford himself raises it in the controversy with Hart suggests that he was himself acutely aware of the problem.[62] Here he offers two solutions. The first is to interpret the problem as noetic:

Again, how it is that God 'would have all men saved,' and yet 'whom he will he maketh hard-hearted,' and also 'sheweth mercy on whom he will,' I will be content to leave it till I shall see it in another life; where no contradiction shall be seen to be in God's will. . . . As no man can 'resist his will,' so let no man search it further than he revealeth it. . . .[63]

There is much to be admired in this resolution of the difficulty. Bradford is being entirely consistent with his basic scriptural principle and is not speculating beyond the bounds of scripture. Furthermore, he is attempting to do justice to both statements in scripture, refusing either to deny the sincerity of God's desire that all be saved or the reality of particular election. In doing this, he is also resisting the temptation of solving the problem by means of a dialectical opposition between God's hiddenness and his revelation which could lead to doubts concerning the reliability of the latter. Who could trust the scriptures if God says he desires one thing and wills the opposite?

However, Bradford's solution is not totally satisfactory. Throughout his writings on election, he continually emphasizes the particularity of God's election rather than the universality

---

[59] The problem is indeed very real for all Augustinian doctrines of predestination up to the present day. For an interesting insight into the issues involved, see *CD* 2. 2, pp. 188–94, where Karl Barth outlines the debate which followed Peter Barth's paper at the Congrès international de théologie calviniste at Geneva in 1934.

[60] *Writings* 1. 214, 220, 319.   [61] Ibid. 212.

[62] This occurs in Part Two of *A Defence*, where Bradford is answering Hart's treatise. The point to which he is replying when he raises the issue concerns the nature of God's covenant. Hart makes no mention of the exegetical problems which Bradford attempts to solve: see ibid. 322–3.

[63] Ibid. 324.

of God's desire to save. Therefore his treatment of the subject as a whole does not reflect the balance which he here strikes between the two ideas. In the context of his total theology, the real problem for Bradford is not so much how God can elect only some to life while at the same time wishing all men to be saved; rather, it is how God can will all men to be saved in view of the fact that he has already elected only some to eternal life. The decree effectively casts a shadow over any notion that God actually wills all to be saved. One might object to this that, by making the problem noetic, Bradford does hold the two ideas in tension and does not make the decree determinative in interpreting God's will to save all. This is true. Indeed, if this was all Bradford said on the subject then the above criticism would be nothing more than a suggestion that his statement here does not reflect his overall emphases. However, he does have more to say on the subject. In the very next paragraph, he proposes a second solution to the problem:

If therefore we cannot tie these two together, that God 'would have all men saved,' and yet 'his will is done,' and cannot be withstood, but unto reason there must be some contradiction; yet let faith honour God, that his will is 'just' and not mutable (though his works are now and then altered), how far soever otherwise it seem to 'the flesh': albeit to him that is not curious and contentious, the place how 'God would have all men saved', and how God 'will not the death of a sinner', is and may be well understand of penitent men and sinners; for else they that be impenitent God will damn.[64]

The first half of this statement repeats the same idea as before: that the relationship between the two doctrines is beyond man's understanding and is therefore to be accepted by faith. However, Bradford then proceeds to reinterpret the statement that God wills all men to be saved in the light of the limited nature of the decree of election. Indeed, in the marginal notes to this passage (which are taken from the original manuscript) Bradford declares that when scripture says that God wills all to be saved, the word 'all' does not mean 'everyone in general' but refers either to all of the elect or to all kinds of people.[65] This is not accepting the apparent contradiction in faith;

[64] Ibid. 325.
[65] 'Yea, when the scripture saith that God will have all men saved, it speaketh either of all the elects [*sic*], or of men of all sorts states and conditions', ibid. 325.

rather, it is reinterpreting the plain meaning of the words in order to be consistent with the idea of the decree. The tension is thereby resolved, but the plain meaning of passages of scripture is taken away by allowing the decree to exert a determinative influence upon Bradford's scriptural exegesis.[66]

In Bradford's defence it must be pointed out that he only proposes this solution after he has argued that the paradox should be accepted in faith. The proposition therefore appears almost as an after-thought. This could be interpreted as a simple overstatement of his case in the heat of controversy. However, it must be remembered that it was Bradford, not Hart, who raised the issue, and he does not appear to have been under any particularly intense pressure from his opponents on this point. Alternatively, the problem can be interpreted as the result of tensions within Bradford's own theology. In his attempt to maintain both particular redemption and God's desire that all be saved, Bradford strives to balance apparently contradictory passages in scripture. However, his use of the decree as a basic axiom for his argument exerts tremendous pressure on his theology which leaves him unconvinced that allowing for paradox is an adequate solution and pushes him into modifying his interpretation of universal passages.

This latter solution cannot be proved, but it does explain how Bradford contradicts himself within two paragraphs concerning God's will to save. Like the tensions between his expressions of absolute predestination and his doctrines of sin and the mutability of certain events, the contradictions here suggest once again that Bradford is wavering between the plain meaning of scriptural passages and the logical demands of the doctrine of predestination. His attempt to emphasize God's desire for all to be saved demonstrates a concern similar to that of Hooper, for whom this was fundamental to soteriology. However, the doctrine of the decree is pushing Bradford's thinking far beyond that of Hooper and towards a more rigorously predestinarian position.

---

[66] There are occasions in scripture where the word 'all' cannot be interpreted as meaning 'everyone' in an absolute sense because the context indicates clearly that this is not the intended sense, e.g. Mark 1: 5. However, the context of verses such as 1 Tim. 2: 4 does not necessarily demand that the word 'all' be understood in a limited sense; rather, such an interpretation is based upon prior soteriological presuppositions.

Election and Atonement

One of the accusations Hart levels against Bradford is that his doctrine of election denies that the virtue of Christ's blood extends to all men. To this, Bradford makes the following reply:

Now I ween he will be ashamed (however he thinketh) to extend the virtue of Christ's death to the devil, except he will admit the school-men's distinction of 'sufficiently' and 'effectually'; that is, that Christ's death is sufficient for all, but effectual to none but the elect only: which distinction I desire him to admit. For I take 'the whole world' there, as St. John the Baptist doth in calling Christ 'the Lamb of God which taketh away the sins of the world'; and as Paul doth in saying that 'God hath reconciled the world in Christ': which is to be dis-cerned from that 'world' for which Christ 'prayed not'; for look, for whom he 'prayed not', for them he died not.[67]

There are three basic elements to Bradford's argument here: Christ's death cannot benefit all, for then the devil would be saved; therefore, the scholastic distinction between the suffi-ciency and efficiency of Christ's death must be allowed; and finally, those scripture passages which refer to Christ's death being for all must be reinterpreted in the light of the limited extent of salvation (indicated by Christ's limited intercession) as referring only to the elect. Thus, in effectively denying that Christ died for all, Bradford is again adopting a position anti-thetical to that of Hooper, for whom Christ's death for all without distinction was basic to his doctrine of salvation. This is a further example of the tendency in Bradford's thinking towards a stronger predestinarianism.

A possible source for Bradford's argument at this point is suggested by the passage's close resemblance to the comments of John Calvin on 1 John 2: 2, which happens to be one of the verses used by Hart in this objection to Bradford's doctrine. Calvin makes the following comment:

But here the question may be asked as to how the sins of the whole world have been expiated. I pass over the dreams of the fanatics, who make this a reason to extend salvation to all the reprobate and even to Satan himself. . . . Those who want to avoid this absurdity have said that Christ suffered sufficiently for the whole world but effectively only for the elect. This solution has commonly prevailed in the

[67] *Writings* 1. 320.

schools. Although I allow the truth of this, I deny that it fits this passage. For John's purpose was only to make this blessing common to the whole Church. Therefore, under the word 'all' he does not include the reprobate, but refers to all who would believe and those who were scattered through various regions of the earth.[68]

The basic content of Calvin's argument parallels that of Bradford: universal expiation implies that even the devil is saved; Christ's death can be seen in terms of the sufficient/ efficient distinction; and the word 'all' in relevant passages is to be referred to the elect, not the world in general. The textual differences between the two passages make it impossible to assert that Bradford was definitely relying on Calvin at this point in his controversy with Hart, but the similarities point towards this conclusion.

There are two possible objections to this theory. The first is that while Calvin accepts the scholastic distinction concerning the death of Christ, he rejects its relevance to 1 John 2: 2; Bradford, on the other hand, apparently accepts the distinction without qualification. Therefore, it is possible that he derived the distinction from a scholastic source and that similarities with the passage in Calvin are purely coincidental. While such a theory cannot be disproved, a close reading of the passage in Bradford clearly shows that he does not apply the distinction to those verses which appear to teach universal atonement, whatever his initial comment might suggest. Like Calvin, he refers such universal statements to the elect, not to the hypothetical sufficiency of Christ's death. Both men accept the distinction, but neither actually applies it in this specific context.

Secondly, it might be objected that Bradford's concluding statement, that Christ did not die for those for whom he does not pray, has no equivalent in the passage from Calvin. This is true, and may very well indicate that Bradford was not directly dependent upon this passage of Calvin in this instance. However, it does not point to a fundamental difference between the thought of the two men. Elsewhere, Calvin too makes Christ's intercession decisive for the extent of his atoning work.[69] Both men set their understanding of Christ's death within the context

---

[68] *Commentary on the First Epistle of John*, trans. T. H. L. Parker (Edinburgh, 1961), 244.

[69] See *OC* 52. 29.

of his work as a whole, and thus his work of atonement on the cross cannot be separated from his work of intercession. Therefore, the sufficiency of Christ's atonement is an abstract and irrelevant question.[70]

This passage also reveals the Christological focus of Bradford's doctrine of salvation. He could have deduced the limitation in the efficacy of the atonement from the extent of God's decree of election. Instead, he bases his argument on the extent of Christ's role as intercessor. While there is obviously a close relationship between God's decree and Christ's work, Bradford does not point to this but is content to rest his case entirely on Christ's intercession. It is therefore clear that Bradford does not regard the limited nature of election as demonstrated solely in the decree, but also as an integral part of the work of Christ.

If Bradford's doctrine of the extent of Christ's work is not based directly upon that of Calvin, then it is nevertheless entirely consistent with the latter's statements on this matter. In Bradford's statement that Christ's death must be linked to his intercession, and his work as a whole limited to the elect, he is echoing the position of Calvin. Bradford is allowing the limitation of election to penetrate his Christology, and this further indicates the differences between himself and his friend, John Hooper.

Election and Reprobation

The first important feature of Bradford's doctrine of reprobation is that he does not discuss it in terms of the decree. He regards the decree as God's decision in eternity to elect some to eternal life. This inevitably means that some are not elected, and that reprobation is related to the decree, but Bradford does not make this relationship explicit. Instead, he argues that election and reprobation are not to be seen as analogous to each other:

As for the argument which might be gathered of the contraries, 'If there be not reprobation, *ergo* there is no election', a man of God may see it is not firm. For, though we may well say, and most justly say, that damnation is for our sins, yet can we not say that for our virtue

---

[70] For this aspect of Calvin's thought, see Muller, *Christ and the Decree*, 33–5. Muller's comment (p. 35) with reference to Calvin's theology, that it 'is superfluous to speak of a hypothetical extent of the efficacy of Christ's work beyond its actual application' might just as easily apply to Bradford.

we are saved; even so, because God hath elected some whom it pleaseth him . . . it doth not well follow that therefore he hath repro- bated others, but to our reasons, except the scriptures do teach it.[71]

Once again Bradford is stressing the basic principle that theology is to be derived from God's revelation and not from man's reason. Thus, election cannot be deduced from reproba- tion or vice versa by simply applying logic; instead, the scriptural witness must form the basis for each doctrine.

Bradford sums up what he considers to be the scriptural teaching on election and reprobation at the start of *A Brief Sum*:

God's foresight is not the cause of sin or excusable necessity to him that sinneth: the damned therefore have not nor shall have any excuse, because God, foreseeing their condemnation through their own sin, did not draw them, as he doth his elect, unto Christ. But, as the elect have cause to thank God for ever for his great mercies in Christ, so the other have cause to lament their own wilfulness, sin, and contemning of Christ, which is the cause of their reprobation, and wherein we should look upon reprobation; as the only goodness of God in Christ is the cause of our election and salvation, wherein we should look upon God's election.[72]

While God's will is the cause of election, it is clear from this passage that Bradford regards God's foreknowledge of sin as the basis for reprobation. As God is not the cause of sin, then God cannot be the cause of reprobation. Bradford's formulation of reprobation points to a doctrine of single predestination. While logic demands that the non-election of an individual amounts to reprobation, Bradford is careful to make sin, and not God's decretive will, the cause of damnation. His scriptural principle means that he does not have to succumb to the logical demands of the decree. Indeed, his desire to avoid this is represented by his emphasis upon Christ and sin as the causes of election and reprobation respectively. However, Bradford has formulated a doctrine of the decree, and both Christ and sin stand against the background of God's decision in eternity to elect some and not others. The reality of this is conceded by Bradford in the following extended passage from *A Brief Sum*:

He that will look upon God or anything in God, simply and barely as it is in God, the same shall be stark blind. Who can see God's

[71] *Writings* 1. 325.   [72] Ibid. 219.

goodness, as it is in God? Who can see his justice, as it is in him? If therefore thou wilt look upon his goodness, not only look upon his works, but also his word. . . . Then shalt thou see that election is not to be looked on but in Christ, nor reprobation but in sin. When the second cause is sufficient, should not we think that they are too curious that will run to search out the first cause, further than God doth give them leave by his word? . . . Because God, for the comfort of his children and certainty of their salvation, doth open unto them something of the first cause of their salvation, that is, his goodness before the beginning of the world, to be looked upon in Christ; a man may not therefore be so bold as to wade so in condemnation further than God revealeth it. And forasmuch as he hath not revealed it but in sin, therefore let us not look on it otherwise.[73]

This passage is highly important for an accurate assessment of Bradford's doctrine of election and reprobation. It contains characteristic emphasis upon the unknowability of God outside his revelation and thus the need to base doctrine solely upon his word. However, Bradford here introduces the terms 'second cause' and 'first cause'. While he actually applies these terms only to the idea of election, the implication is that they also apply to reprobation. God has only revealed reprobation in sin, but this does not rule out some ultimate cause which lies behind this revelation. This suggests that Bradford's thought is moving towards a position which regards sin only as the revealed cause of reprobation and allows that the decree may be the ultimate cause.

It would be wrong to regard Bradford's statement here as an affirmation of double predestination. His only positive statements on reprobation demonstrate that he was a single predestinarian. However, this passage does suggest that he was aware of the implications of his doctrine of the decree. As in his discussion of God's saving will, Bradford is attempting to avoid the radical implications of his position, but his thinking unmistakably points towards them.

Summary

Bradford regards election as central to Christian theology because it assures the believer of God's favour. His emphasis upon the doctrine is not explicable simply in terms of the wider

---

[73] Ibid. 220.

English context, as other leading English Reformers were reluctant to engage in controversy over the matter. It is probable that Bradford's love of the doctrine derives from his own early struggles with lack of assurance and his friendship with Martin Bucer. Indeed, the general similarity between aspects of Bradford's doctrine and that of Bucer support such an interpretation.

Bradford is careful to stress that the word of God contained in the scriptures is the only epistemological basis for formulating a doctrine of election. The scriptures teach that God elected a portion of mankind to eternal life before time. This decree is axiomatic to Bradford's predestinarian theology, even limiting the effectual extent of the atonement, an idea possibly borrowed from Calvin. Election is revealed in Christ, while rejection is revealed only in sin.

There are various tensions within Bradford's predestinarianism. His doctrine of providence links God's foreknowledge to his wisdom and his will. This implies a doctrine of absolute determinism, and Bradford does assert that God wills all things. However, he is careful to absolve God of any responsibility for sin, and to support this idea he introduces the distinction between necessity and compulsion. He probably borrowed this distinction from Bucer. A more significant problem is his assertion that God's will in some matters is mutable. While salvation is not one such matter, the problem which this creates with his statements of absolute predestination is clear.

Further tensions are evident in Bradford's contradictory explanations of passages in scripture which speak of God's desire to save all. Here, he attempts to maintain the universal scope of the word 'all' but also allows its meaning to be limited by his doctrine of election. Finally, Bradford implies that sin might only be a secondary cause of reprobation, and thus points towards a doctrine of double predestination.

These tensions suggest that Bradford is attempting to avoid the more radical implications of the position which he is emphasizing in his opposition to the free willers. However, the doctrine of the decree is exerting such pressure on his soteriology that he is reluctantly tending towards a more rigid predestinarianism.

THE PRACTICAL NATURE OF PREDESTINATION

Election and the Christian Life

Bradford does not regard election as an abstract doctrine, but as one which is intensely practical and lies at the very centre of the Christian life. This is clear not only from his polemical writings but also from the letters of pastoral counsel which he wrote from the Tower. There are two major areas in which Bradford applied the doctrine of election: as the basis for the Christian life and as the foundation of assurance. The two ideas are closely connected, and the relationship between them contains certain problems which cannot be avoided in any balanced study of Bradford's thought.

In objective terms, Bradford regards election as the theological basis of the individual's salvation. He joins election in eternity with calling, justification, regeneration, and ultimate salvation, and thus makes it the start of a causal sequence which encompasses the whole of the Christian's life. As such, election can be regarded as the cause of the believer's life in the Spirit.[74]

The purpose of God's decree was not simply to ensure that certain individuals would reach heaven. It also determined that the elect should be conformed to the image of Christ. This conformation is only completed in heaven, but the process of sanctification is started in this life by the presence of the Spirit within the believer.[75] Thus, election determines that the Christian life is one characterised by actual, though very imperfect, holiness.

The decree can therefore be described as the objective basis of holiness, as it is the ultimate cause of regeneration and determines that the believer is to be conformed to Christ. In both cases the direct cause is the subjective activity of the Spirit in the believer's life. However, Bradford regards the reality of election as having a direct existential impact upon the believer as well. The first of these is that election teaches man his true position before God. As Bradford declares at the start of *A Defence*, election is the doctrine that portrays God as most merciful and casts down any pride he may have in his own works.[76] It reveals to man that he is totally dependent upon the sovereign God for his salvation and must look only to the Lord for help.

---

[74] *Writings* 1. 314.   [75] Ibid. 2. 166; cf. Bucer, *Enarratio . . . Ephesios*, 28.
[76] *Writings* 1. 307–8; cf. Bucer, *Enarratio . . . Ephesios*, 23.

Bradford uses this relationship between creature and Creator as a powerful pastoral tool in his letters from the Tower. Throughout these, he makes constant reference to God's control over all events, and thereby encourages those facing persecution to endure suffering with joy.[77] For example, he tells one friend, a Lady Vane, that she will experience suffering only if this serves the Lord's providence, and therefore it shall be for her eternal joy and comfort.[78] Elsewhere he writes to a friend, who is about to be examined before the magistrates, that he should not fear because God controls the interrogators and will make them serve his own purposes.[79] In both cases, the believer is not to become disheartened because the present circumstances are helping to further God's higher providential purposes which ultimately control all events.

Bradford also argues that this idea of the creature's total dependence on the Creator has important existential results arising from its specifically soteriological implications. One of Hart's objections to predestination is that such a doctrine prevents the effective exercise of Church discipline in the form of excommunication. He argues that if no-one but God knows who is elect and who is not, then no-one can know who is truly within the Church, and discipline is therefore irrelevant.[80] In his reply, Bradford does not address the ecclesiological aspect of discipline raised by Hart, but examines the motivation which should underpin excommunication: the desire to restore the fallen brother. As the excommunication must be done in a spirit of love, it is imperative that the excommunicated individual must not be regarded with contempt by other Christians. Only a correct understanding of election can instil such a spirit in believers because only election teaches men the true extent of their own sin and presses upon them the knowledge that they are saved only because of God's mercy. Therefore, the elect understand that others who fall are not to be looked down upon but are to be restored with love. Consequently, the elect will act with more mercy towards them. On the other hand, those who regard their own efforts as decisive in salvation will

---

[77] The theme of providence is to be found in almost all of the letters from the period in the Tower, reflecting the solace which the doctrine gave to those facing imminent death: see *Writings* 2. 34–253 *passim*.

[78] Ibid. 96–7.   [79] Ibid. 156.   [80] *Writings* 1. 327.

see those who fall as somehow intrinsically inferior to themselves and will treat them with contempt.[81] Bradford thus regards election as establishing, not undermining, Church discipline.

It is clear from this that Bradford sees a correct knowledge of God as lying at the centre of man's own practical Christian life. This is further demonstrated by his emphasis on assurance. The need for a secure basis for assurance is one of the primary reasons for Bradford's stress upon election. He does not regard this as important simply for the believer's peace of mind, but also because of the results it produces in the believer's life. This is made clear in a letter of 1554:

According to the revelation and your sense of faith herein, so will you contend to all piety and godliness, as St John saith: 'He that hath this hope will purify himself as Christ is pure'. . . . If we did certainly believe we were members of Christ and God's temples, how should we but flee from all impurity and corruption of the world, which cometh by concupiscence? If we did certainly believe, that God indeed of his mercy in Christ is become our Father, in that his good-will is infinite, and his power according thereto, how could we be afraid of man or devil; how could we doubt of salvation, or any good thing which might make to God's glory and our own weal?[82]

In this passage, Bradford makes assurance of salvation the basic motivation for godliness. It is interesting that Bradford does not here see this motivation primarily in terms of gratitude for salvation but rather as the result of realizing the obligations of the new relationship to Christ. Now that the believer has been engrafted into Christ, he is obliged to be pure because this is what a member of Christ should be. Thus, the purpose of election, i.e. conformity to Christ, is perceived by the believer as the goal towards which he is to strive.

Election is therefore the foundation of the Christian life. In objective terms, it determines that the believer is to be conformed to Christ. In subjective terms, it teaches man his true place before God, assures the believer of God's favour, and indicates the obligations under which salvation places him.

---

[81] Ibid. 328.
[82] Ibid. 2. 122. See also ibid. 154–5. Bucer also makes the same link between assurance and the believer's realization that he must consequently strive to perform good works: see *Enarratio . . . Ephesios*, 20.

The Problem of Assurance

Bradford's formulation of election is intended to provide an objective foundation for assurance. However, his treatment of the doctrine in both polemical and pastoral contexts raises acute problems concerning his achievement of this objective.

In one particularly graphic and memorable passage in a letter of 1554, Bradford directs Joyce Hales to the basis for Christian assurance:

Whom look you on? on yourself, on your worthiness, on your thankfulness, on that which God requireth of you, as faith, hope, love, fear, joy, etc.? Then can you not but waver indeed: for what have you as God requireth? Believe you, hope you, love you, etc., as much as you should do? No, no, nor never can in this life. Ah, my dearly beloved, have you so soon forgotten that which ever should be in memory? namely that, when you would and should be certain and quiet in conscience, then should your faith burst throughout all things . . . until it come to 'Christ crucified', and the eternal sweet mercies and goodness of God in Christ? Here, here is the resting place, here is your spouse's bed: creep into it, and in your arms of faith embrace him.[83]

This passage is a straightforward application of the principle that election is to be looked on only in Christ. This is the idea that Bradford expresses throughout his polemical writings on election. He realizes that introspection can give no sure knowledge of salvation, and thus points the troubled conscience away from itself and towards Christ. Christ is apprehended by faith, and it is the implication of this position that faith must therefore comprehend assurance of election.[84]

There are several problems with Bradford's approach here. The first is the tension it creates within Bradford's own dogmatic formulation of election. The idea that the apprehension of Christ by faith forms the only sound basis for assurance is consistent with Bradford's teaching on Christ as the exclusive revelation of election. However, it is difficult to maintain this position in such a straightforward form because of the reality of the hiddenness of election. The problem is that Bradford himself has asserted the existence of an eternal decree of election which exists behind the revelation in Christ. This decree is ultimately

---

[83] *Writings* 2. 114–15.

[84] This is reflected in Bradford's opening remarks concerning election in *A Defence*: see *Writings* 1. 307–8.

determinative of who will be saved, but the identity of these elect is hidden. This secret decree might therefore be seen as casting a shadow across the revelation in Christ and undermining the idea that the believer can indeed look only on Christ for assurance.

While this problem has been raised as an objection to Reformation formulations of election in modern times, Bradford himself does not appear to have been conscious of it.[85] Throughout his writings on election he is careful to avoid any construction which would imply a dualism within the will of God. While it is arguable that he is not altogether successful in this endeavour, he does make some attempt to maintain a position which regards apparent contradictions in God's will as noetic and not ontic. However, even when the problem of contradictions within God's will is defined as being only apparent, the difficulty with assurance remains, as God's revelation and his hiddenness still appear to the believer to be in tension with each other.

Nevertheless, Bradford lessens this tension in his pastoral letters by making no reference to the eternal dimension of election. He does refer to the immutability of God's will as regards the elect, but this is in order to assure those fearful of the future that God's love towards them will not change. Instead of discussing the decree, he is much more concerned to encourage his friends to trust in Christ and to avoid sin than to speculate concerning their objective election in eternity. In this way, his pastoral emphasis reflects the desire to focus on God's revelation of election and reprobation in terms only of Christ and sin which he referred to in his controversy with Hart. He does not use as pastoral tools such concepts as the decree and the limitation of the atonement, which might be regarded as introducing determinist elements into his theology. Instead he places his emphasis upon the need to trust in Christ and avoid sin.

However, there is another problem in Bradford's doctrine of election: the possibility of apostasy. In both polemical and pastoral writings, Bradford makes reference to the impossibility of the true believer falling away. Faith is dependent upon

---

[85] See Barth's historical analysis of the relationship between the absolute decree and Christ's role as the mirror of election in *CD* 2. 2, pp. 60–78; also his claim that the tension in this relationship leads to the development of an independent works-based assurance, *CD* 2. 2, pp. 333–40, esp. pp. 338–9; also Berkouwer, *Divine Election*, 102–31.

election, and is therefore a true sign of final salvation.[86] The problem is that Bradford's pastoral letters contain continual references to falling away and the very real possibility of apostasy. This is clearly stated in his letter to Humphrey Hales, son of Sir James Hales. Sir James was a leading Protestant under Edward VI, but had then recanted under Mary. Such was his remorse for this that he drowned himself upon release from prison. Bradford writes concerning Hales:

I need not tell you the cause of this [God's judgement] that hath happened unto your father. . . . For you know well enough, that till he forsook God, gave ear to the serpent's counsel, began to mammer of the truth, and to frame himself outwardly to do that which his conscience reproved inwardly—for that which he mingled with the love of God, I mean the love of the world, cannot be in any man without the expulsion of God's love—till then, I say, God did not depart and leave him to himself, to the example of you and me, and all others; that we should fear even ourselves and our own hands, more than man and all the powers of the world, if we therefore should do anything which should wound our conscience.[87]

The example of Hales is therefore directed as an example of God's judgement not primarily to unbelievers, but to believers. The underlying thought in this passage is that Hales was a believer who allowed love of the world to displace love of God and who was consequently rejected by God. Thus Bradford here allows that the believer may indeed fall away. This thought is in simple contradiction with statements elsewhere,[88] but it is by no means the only reference to the idea.[89] Indeed, the reality of apostasy as a possibility undergirds many of his pastoral exhortations. This raises two basic questions: why does Bradford develop such an idea which apparently contradicts his teaching on the certainty of election? and what implications does this have for his doctrine of assurance?

Bradford's development of the idea of apostasy can be explained by reference to the pastoral context within which he was working. One of the major problems he faced during Mary's reign was that of persuading fellow believers not to conform even outwardly to the prevailing Catholic reaction.

[86] *Writings* 1. 313.
[88] Ibid. 1. 298; Ibid. 2. 71, 166.
[87] Ibid. 2. 106.
[89] e.g. see ibid. 49, 52, 125, 230.

Central to this reaction was the re-establishment of the mass, and Bradford was keen to dissuade any believers even from attending a service where the rite was performed. However, Bradford's construction of the Christian life developed in his controversy with Hart was not adequate to deal with this situation. In opposition to the free willers' stress upon works as the cause of election, Bradford had been careful to emphasize the objective decree in eternity. Thus, his polemical writings scarcely touch upon the moral imperatives of the Christian life. Indeed, the idea of election in eternity might even be misconstrued as an excuse for lax behaviour in those who consider themselves elect. This is obviously the fear which lies behind much of Bradford's pastoral advice.

In response to this situation, Bradford emphasizes the judgement of God, as well as his grace. If a believer outwardly conformed to Catholicism, he could expect to be rejected by God. The problem of course is that God's judgement can have no urgent reality for the elect believer if his election has been objectively decreed in eternity. However, if Bradford's exhortations are simply false, warning of something that cannot come to pass, then they lose their basic imperative power and fail to meet the demands of the pastoral situation. Therefore, Bradford does not allow the logic of his doctrine of election to force him into conceding that the possibility of apostasy is not real. While this is in contradiction with both the logic of his doctrine of election and with statements he himself makes, it is not therefore legitimate to conclude that Bradford is less than serious when he issues such warnings. The tension is insoluble, but Bradford regards both election and apostasy as realities.

The second problem raised by this doctrine is that of assurance. By emphasizing man's responsibility to do good works, and by allowing that apostasy will be the result of his failing so to do, it might be argued that Bradford is making perseverance dependent upon works and thereby opening the door to works-based assurance.

Bradford rejects the idea that perseverance is decisively dependent upon good works in a letter to certain free willers:

You say, it [salvation] hangeth partly upon our perseverance to the end; and I say, it hangeth only and altogether upon God's grace in Christ, and not upon our perseverance in any point; 'for then were grace no grace'. You will and do in words deny our perseverance to be any cause, but yet in deed you do otherwise: for, if perseverance be not a cause, but only God's grace in Christ, the whole and only cause of salvation, then the cause, that is to say, grace, remaining, the thing, that is to say, salvation, cannot but remain also. Of which thing if, with the scriptures, you would make perseverance an effect or fruit, then could you not be offended at the truth, but say as it saith, that the salvation of God's children is so certain, that they shall never finally perish, the Lord putting his hand under them that, if they fall, yet they shall not lie still.[90]

In this passage, Bradford asserts that perseverance is the effect of God's grace and thus a fruit, not a cause, of salvation. It is tempting to object that Bradford's own emphasis on the danger of apostasy effectively contradicts what is said here. However, the context of the above quotation is polemical, and Bradford is making a doctrinal statement. In the letters where he refers to apostasy, he is writing in a pastoral context where it is necessary for him to impress upon fellow-believers the imperatives of the Christian life. He therefore emphasizes these at the expense of objective truths such as the immutability of God's sovereign election. Of course, this does not enable us to harmonize these two strands of thought, but it does help to explain their co-existence in Bradford's writings.

Nevertheless, this emphasis upon the believer's obligations still raises the problem of whether Bradford is tending towards a works-based assurance, which is one of the concepts against which his doctrine of election is framed. However, if the believer has to be avoiding sin and doing good works in order to avoid falling away in the manner of Hales, then there will be a tendency for him to look within himself rather than simply to Christ for assurance of his salvation.

In fact, this does not appear to have been a great problem to Bradford. In situations where he is dealing with a troubled conscience, he almost always points towards Christ as the sole means of assurance. It is only when faced with complacency that he goads individuals into action by stressing the moral imperatives of Christianity. His application of theological principles in the pastoral context is determined by the particular demands of each individual case.

[90] *Writings* 2. 165.

One last point concerns a passage which hints that Bradford does allow for introspection as a means of assuring the weak conscience. In a letter to two free willers, Bradford makes the following statement:

Search your hearts whether you have this faith. . . . If you feel not this faith, then know that predestination is too high a matter for you to be disputers of it, until you have been better scholars in the school-house of repentance and justification, which is the grammar-school wherein we must be conversant and learned, before we go to the university of God's most holy predestination and providence.[91]

This passage has been cited as proof that Bradford's theology contains elements that later blossomed in the 'experimental predestinarianism' of the Puritans.[92] This was allegedly characterized by an introspective search for signs of election. However, there are several aspects of this quotation from Bradford which prevent such an interpretation. First, the statement itself is not typical of Bradford's approach: elsewhere, he points the troubled conscience exclusively to Christ for assurance. Secondly, Bradford is not writing to assure a weak conscience, but to attack free willers. In the early part of the letter, Bradford has argued for predestination on the basis of anthropology, i.e. that man's impotence demands God's saving initiative.[93] In the light of this, it is possible that Bradford's plea here is asking his opponents to make sure that they fully understand repentance and justification before they aspire to make pronouncements concerning predestination. This interpretation is supported by Bradford's reference to 'disputers', which indicates that he is thinking of predestination in doctrinal, not pastoral, terms. Furthermore, it is hardly likely that Bradford would point those who reject the doctrine to election in Christ as the basis of assurance. As a result of these considerations, it is impossible to argue that this passage foreshadows later Puritan attempts to construct a works-based assurance.

Summary

Bradford regards election as a highly practical doctrine. It determines that the elect will be conformed to Christ, and the

---

[91] Ibid. 133–4.
[92] Kendall, *Calvin and English Calvinism*, 43–4.
[93] *Writings* 2. 133.

believer perceives this as the goal towards which he is obliged to strive. Election also teaches him dependence upon God and humility. These ideas again point to the influence of Martin Bucer.

Bradford stresses that assurance is to be found in Christ alone, and he does not use the concept of the decree in his pastoral writings. Thus, the problem which the hiddenness of the decree might have caused for assurance does not actually arise. A problem does occur when Bradford allows that those believers who persist in sin will fall away. This is in tension with his insistence on the causal relationship between election and faith, and with his statements that perseverance is a gift of God, not the result of man's obedience. However, Bradford introduces the idea in order to underline the moral imperatives of the Christian life, and he does not allow the possibility of apostasy to lead him to formulate an introspective doctrine of assurance based upon good works.

THE BROADER THEMES OF SALVATION

Any study of Bradford's doctrine of salvation will inevitably devote more attention to election than to other doctrines for the simple reason that this reflects the relative emphases within his extant writings. It is true that Bradford argues that election is central to correct theology, and that his decision to engage in controversy over this issue in particular indicates the importance which the matter had for him; nevertheless, it is also true that the controversy was the result of his contact with the free willers. If he had never had such contact, it is quite possible that Bradford would have written no extensive work on the subject of election. The student would then have had no way of discerning the importance of the doctrine to Bradford and any study of his soteriology would have been significantly different. Therefore, the fact that Bradford devotes comparatively little space to other soteriological doctrines does not necessarily mean that he regarded them as of minor importance; instead, this may indicate only that he had no need to write at length on these subjects. Bradford was not a writer of systematic theology, and when he addressed himself specifically to dogmatic problems, it was exclusively in the context of a contemporary controversy:

the two major topics upon which Bradford wrote dogmatic treatises were the Eucharist and election, the former against the Catholics, the latter against the free willers.

Because Bradford left no extensive work on any other aspect of soteriology, reconstruction of these areas is dependent upon occasional references scattered throughout his writings. These can be gathered conveniently under the following headings: the person and work of Christ; salvation; sanctification; and salvation and the sacraments. The eclectic nature of the task means that the result is somewhat uneven; nevertheless, it does provide a broader picture of Bradford's soteriological concerns.

The Person and Work of Christ

Bradford bases his doctrine of Christ's person on the historic creeds of the Church. However, he is always careful to set these within a soteriological context. This is because he regards the salvation of men as the decisive factor in the incarnation: Christ assumed man's flesh because this was demanded by the nature of the task he was to fulfil. Thus, in his meditation on the second article of the Apostles' Creed, he affirms the Nicene doctrine that Christ is God, co-equal and consubstantial with the Father, and then emphasizes that he became man through the working of the Holy Spirit in order to accomplish salvation for men.[94]

The necessity for God to become man derives from the nature of man's predicament. Bradford expresses this in terms of the Pauline idea of a second Adam Christology:

Jesus Christ, the Son of God and second Adam, by whom we receive righteousness unto life, as by the first Adam we received sin unto death . . . this Christ in our flesh, which he took of the substance of the virgin Mary, but pure and without sin, for the satisfying of God's just displeasure deserved by and in our flesh, did in the same suffer unjustly all kinds of misery and affliction, offering up himself unto his eternal Father with a most willing, obedient heart and ready mind, when he was crucified upon the cross. And, thereby as he satisfied God's justice, so he merited and procured his mercy. . . .[95]

Several important aspects of Bradford's Christology emerge from this quotation. The first is his continuing emphasis upon the soteriological purpose behind the incarnation. Bradford's

[94] *Writings* 1. 142.   [95] Ibid. 2. 277.

doctrine of Christ's person is discussed solely in terms of the salvation which Christ is to accomplish. Secondly, there is a relationship between Christ's task as saviour and the sin of the first Adam. Bradford refers to Adam as the source of mankind's sin and damnation and also to the punishment that has been earned 'by and in our flesh'. The underlying idea in both of these statements is the solidarity of humanity in Adam and in sin. However, both of these ideas find parallels in the work of Christ: Christ gives man righteousness unto life as Adam gave sin unto death; and he assumed our flesh in order to receive the punishment which we had deserved in the same. The use of the term 'our flesh' with reference to Christ not only emphasizes his true humanity, but also his solidarity with mankind, a fact underlined by the title of 'second Adam'. What emerges from this passage is that the need for Christ to assume human flesh is determined by the nature of man's fall in Adam. There can therefore be no separation between Christ's person as the God-man and his work as saviour.

At times, Bradford can emphasize the connection between the union of Christ with humanity in the incarnation and his work of salvation to the extent that he makes this the cause of salvation.[96] Elsewhere, he stresses that it was the whole of Christ's incarnate life that earned redemption for man and thus points to the basic unity between Christ's person and work in his theology.[97] However, a key theme in Bradford's doctrine of redemption is the wrath of God against sin. This wrath exerts a decisive impact upon the nature of Christ's work and focuses attention on Cavalry as the culmination of the propitiation of God's anger.[98] Nevertheless, there is still a close connection between Christ's union with humanity and his sacrificial death. In the last quotation, Bradford draws careful link between the punishment which man's sin deserved in the flesh, and the suffering and sacrifice of Christ, in that same flesh, which purchased redemption. Thus, the incarnation is the presupposition of the atonement on Calvary.

Salvation

Bradford's writings contain few references to how the individual is reconciled to God. The Reformation concept of justification

---

[96] *Writings*. 1. 142–3.   [97] Ibid. 63.   [98] Ibid. 64.

is scarcely mentioned. He does refer to it as part of the order of salvation based upon election.[99] However, he defines the concept only once, in *A Treatise on Election and Free Will*:

Justification in scripture is taken for the forgiveness of our sins, and consisteth in the forgiveness of our sins. This is only God's work, and we nothing else but patients and not agents.[100]

In this passage, Bradford's emphasis is upon the passive role played by man rather than the content of justification. A joint statement of faith issued in May 1554 by eleven prisoners, including both Bradford and Hooper, draws a careful distinction between justifying righteousness and the righteousness which the believer actually possesses as a result of justification.[101] This is the only reference to the imputation of righteousness in Bradford' works and possesses limited value because of the composite authorship of the document.

However, while Bradford may only make the briefest of references to justification, he does provide more detailed discussion of salvation in terms of union with Christ. In *A Defence*, Bradford emphasizes that election is 'in Christ', which he defines as meaning that the elect are 'gathered together in him'.[102] While he does not significantly elaborate the idea with reference to election, he nevertheless applies the concept with more detail to the appropriation of salvation. Bradford's most extensive statement on the subject occurs in the brief work *The Old Man and the New*:

This our Inheritor and 'Husband' Christ Jesus, God with God, 'Light of Light', co-eternal and consubstantial with the Father and with the Holy Ghost, to the end that he might become our 'Husband' (because the husband and the wife must become 'one body and flesh'), hath taken our nature upon him, communicating with it and by it in his own person, to us all his children, his 'divine majesty', as Peter saith; and so is become 'flesh of our flesh and bone of our bones' substantially, as we are become 'flesh of his flesh and bone of his bones' spiritually; all that ever we have pertaining to him, yea, even our sins, as all that he hath pertaineth unto us, even his whole glory. So that if Satan shall summon us to answer for our debts or sins, in that the wife is no suitable person, but the husband, we may well bid him

---

[99] Ibid. 314.   [100] Ibid. 217.
[101] Ibid. 371–2.   [102] Ibid. 312–13.

enter his action against our 'Husband' Christ, and he will make him a sufficient answer.[103]

There is a clear parallel in this passage between Christ's incarnation and the means whereby man is saved: as Christ was physically united with humanity, thus the believer is united spiritually with Christ. The precise soteriological relationship between the incarnational union and the spiritual union is not clear. The reference to the communication of the divine majesty to mankind through the incarnation might seem to imply that this was all that was necessary for individual salvation. Certainly it reveals once again that Bradford constructs his Christology in terms of soteriological requirements. However, it is also evident from the passage that spiritual union is necessary too. Therefore, it is legitimate to interpret Bradford's statement concerning the incarnation as referring to the objective accomplishment of salvation, and that concerning the spiritual union as referring to the subjective appropriation of salvation by the believer.

The legal reference at the end of the passage could be interpreted as a sign of the influence of Melanchthon's doctrine of forensic justification, but the overall tone of the statement emphasizes salvation in terms of the marital union. Indeed, the whole notion of such a union with Christ presents the believer's salvation in decidedly non-forensic terms and Bradford's doctrine is closer to that of Luther's 'joyful exchange' than that of Melanchthon's notion of imputation. Luther expresses the idea that the believer exchanges his sins for Christ's righteousness using the same metaphor of husband and wife as that employed by Bradford.[104] While he died two years before Bradford was converted, his influence on the latter cannot be ruled out: Bradford read Melanchthon, he may well have read Luther.

This spiritual union of the believer to Christ is effected through faith. The fact that faith does save was not an issue over which Bradford engaged in controversy, and he devotes no work to the exposition of this theme. However, he does make one comment which reveals that his doctrine of faith coordinates neatly with his overall concept of salvation:

---

[103] *Writings* 1. 298–9. The idea of the believer's participation in the divine nature through Christ is also present in Bucer: see *Enarratio . . . Ephesios*, 31.

[104] *WA* 7. 54, 31–55, 36. Union with Christ is also an important element in Bucer's soteriology: see *Enarratio . . . Ephesios*, 19, 21, 30, 33, 35, 39, 41, 45; Stephens, *The Holy Spirit in the Theology of Martin Bucer*, 64–5.

O, I beseech thee, good Holy Spirit. . . . Bring me into thy church which thou guidest; that is, guide me, make me holy, and by faith couple me to Christ. . . .[105]

This prayer to the Holy Spirit provides important insights into the role of the third person of the Trinity in Bradford's theology. The Spirit guides and sanctifies the believer. However, more fundamental than either of these two is the fact that the Spirit is the immediate cause of the believer's salvation because he stirs up faith. This faith is the instrument whereby the believer is united to Christ. This spiritual union effects the reconciliation of the individual to God.

In his writings on election, Bradford was concerned to emphasize that the doctrine provided the believer with assurance of salvation. In *The Old Man and the New*, he expresses this same concern with reference to union with Christ:

For this end (I mean that we might be coupled and married thus to Christ, and so be certain of our salvation) God hath given his holy word. . . .[106]

According to this passage that certainty of salvation is dependent upon the believer's union with Christ.[107] This position coordinates with the Christological emphasis in Bradford's doctrine of election. While his doctrine of the decree provides the basic premise of the dogmatic structure of election, he consistently points to Christ as the basis for assurance. Thus certainty of salvation arises from the dynamic relationship between the individual and Christ which is effected through faith. Bradford adopts essentially the same position in the above passage: it is the uniting of the believer to Christ by faith that gives a solid basis for assurance. While he does not mention election as such in this particular context, the emphases upon faith and upon Christ are the same as those in his discussions of election.

Bradford's presentation of the individual's apprehension of salvation in terms of union with Christ reflects the Christocentric manner in which his soteriology as a whole is formulated. It presents the believer's redemption in terms of the dynamic relationship with Christ that is effected through faith, and also reveals the same concern to present a Christological basis for assurance that is found in the writings on election.

---

[105] *Writings* 1. 147.   [106] Ibid. 299.
[107] This same idea is present in Bucer: see *Enarratio . . . Ephesios*, 22.

Sanctification

Bradford does not deal extensively with the theology of sanctification, but he does regard it as essential to the believer. This is clear from *A Sermon of Repentance*, where he links the idea of sanctification to repentance. Bradford defines repentance as comprising two basic elements: sorrow for sins; and trust in God. To these, he adds a third: renewal of life. He declares that the last is not truly a part of repentance, but rather a consequence of the same; however, he allows renewal to be included in order to avoid alienating any who may disagree with its exclusion.[108] His definition of repentance therefore embraces the whole of the Christian's earthly life, as it draws an inseparable link between sorrow for sin, faith, and renewal of life or sanctification.

Repentance remains relevant for the believer because his old sinful nature remains within him. Bradford expresses this using Lutheran terminology:

a man, I say, that is regenerate, consisteth of two men . . . namely of 'the old man', and of the 'new man'. 'The old man' is like to a mighty giant, such a one as was Goliath; for his birth is now perfect. But the 'new man' is like unto a little child, such a one as was David; for his birth is not perfect until the day of his general resurrection. . . . One man therefore which is regenerate well may be called always just and always sinful: just in respect of God's seed and his regeneration; sinful in respect of Satan's seed and his first birth.[109]

Underlying this passage is the idea that the believer's regeneration, though imperfect, will eventually triumph over the sinful nature. This is clear from the analogy with David and Goliath, and the reference to perfection on the day of the general resurrection. The idea also strengthens the proleptic dimension of Bradford's doctrine of justification which emerges in the last sentence. Here, he makes regeneration the basis upon which man is declared to be just. Such a statement does not imply that Bradford allows man's own works any merit in justification. Indeed, this conclusion is precluded by the objective basis of sanctification for which he argues in *A Sermon of Repentance*:

---

[108] *Writings* 1. 45. Melanchthon too adopts a twofold division of repentance into sorrow for sins and faith, but also allows for a third part, renewal of life, to be included for exactly the same reason as Bradford. This suggests that Bradford is following Melanchthon in this matter: see OM 21. 877.   [109] *Writings* 1. 297–8.

Forsooth that, as sin hath reigned to death, as thou seest, to the killing of God's Son, so now grace must reign to life to the honouring of God's Son, who is now alive and 'cannot die anymore': so that they which by faith feel this cannot anymore die to God, but to sin, whereto they are dead and buried with Christ. As Christ therefore liveth, so do they, and that to God, to righteousness and holiness.[110]

Once again, the theme of union with Christ is placed at the centre of Bradford's thought.[111] In discussing election, he described this union as placing ethical obligations upon believers.[112] Here, Bradford echoes Paul's teaching that believers have been united with Christ both in his death and in his resurrection. This ensures that their subsequent life is one lived to God and to holiness.

In formulating sanctification in terms of union with Christ, Bradford is setting the doctrine upon the same conceptual foundation as his doctrine of justification. This indicates a significant theological advance upon the position of the Henrician Reformers, who used the idea of 'double justification' in order to define the relationship between faith and works. Bradford's approach is different in that it focuses upon the Christocentric nature of redemption and relates the whole of the believer's salvation to the dynamic relationship with Christ. Indeed, union with Christ is the focus of election, justification, and sanctification. As such, it forms the point of contact between the three doctrines, and this suggests that the doctrine is very important to Bradford's soteriology.

Although he emphasizes the objective certainty of sanctification in Christ, Bradford does not allow this to lessen the believer's responsibility in the process. On the contrary, the believer is under an obligation to mortify the old man and strengthen the new. This is done through applying the scriptures. The sinful nature is to be put to death by studying the law of God, with its demands of perfect obedience and its threats of judgements.[113] The new nature, however, is to be encouraged

---

[110] Ibid. 76. Bucer also makes union with Christ the basis for the believer's sanctification: see *Enarratio . . . Ephesios*, 19.

[111] Bradford does not emphasize the work of the Holy Spirit in sanctification. He does state that the Spirit begins the process of sanctification here on earth which is only completed in heaven, but he also points to the Spirit as the one who effects the union of the believer to Christ: see *Writings* 1. 147–8.

[112] Ibid. 2. 166.   [113] Ibid. 1. 54–63.

by looking at the unconditional promises which God has made to man. These must be apprehended by faith.[114]

Nevertheless, the law's role in Bradford's theology is not exclusively negative. Indeed, the decalogue forms the basis for the Christian's ethical conduct.[115] Bradford does not make the believer's inability to fulfil its demands an excuse for apathy. Instead, he regards this as forcing the believer to ask God for the strength to perform it more perfectly. This is a constant theme throughout his written prayers, revealing that it was something for which he himself longed.[116]

Sanctification is thus certain because of the union of the believer with Christ. However, the individual is still required to strive actively for holiness, and this holiness is defined by, the decalogue.

Salvation and the Sacraments

Bradford regards the sacraments as confirming that which God's word offers and which faith receives: salvation in Christ.[117] He speaks of only two sacraments: baptism and the Eucharist. The former is a sacrament of initiation into the Church, and the latter is the means whereby the believer is spiritually nourished during his earthly pilgrimage.[118]

Bradford regards baptism as expressing an objective reality and as making subjective demands. Objectively, baptism is a witness of the eternal covenant which God has made with his people. Therefore, baptism fulfils the same role as circumcision did in the Old Testament.[119] Bradford frequently elaborates the role of baptism in terms of Christology. Here again, the theme of union with Christ is dominant: baptism is an engrafting of the believer into Christ's body;[120] baptism unites the believer with Christ through incorporation into the Church,[121] baptism baptises the believer into the death of Christ.[122] Thus, Bradford's baptismal theology continues his emphasis upon the incorporation of the believer into Christ as the central element of salvation.[123]

---

[114] *Writings* 1. 66.
[115] See Bradford's detailed discussion of the decalogue: *Writings* 1. 148–73.
[116] e.g. see ibid. 135, 176, 183.   [117] Ibid. 2. 289.   [118] Ibid. 1. 82.
[119] Ibid. 149.   [120] Ibid. 89; ibid. 2. 271.   [121] Ibid. 1. 347.
[122] The same concern is evident in Bucer's own baptismal theology: see *Enarratio . . . Ephesios*, 48.
[123] *Writings* 1. 384.

Bradford frequently speaks as if baptism actually accomplished this union. He also states that baptism is the means of entry into the Church, of adoption by God, and of regeneration.[124] He never uses terminology which would imply that the sacrament is a 'mere sign'. Indeed, in the one instance where he does refer to baptism as *signifying* a cleansing from sin, he also states that it actually *is* such a cleansing.[125]

However, such statements are balanced by Bradford's stress upon the demands which baptism makes in order for it to be efficacious. For example, infants must first have been elected by God in order for them to benefit from receiving the sacrament. Those who are older, however, must have faith in Christ if they are to experience the reality indicated by baptism.[126] This leads Bradford to emphasize the demands which baptism imposes upon the individual. While emphasizing that faith, regeneration, and holiness are all God's work,[127] he constantly reminds his readers that their baptism constituted a commitment on their part to renounce the world and to struggle against sin.[128] This is a particular theme in his pastoral letters from the Tower, when he is reminding his friends that they must not compromise with sin.[129] Therefore, baptism does not simply articulate Bradford's soteriological concern with the believer's union with Christ, but also indicates the importance which he places upon the need for the believer to have faith and to strive for holiness.

In formulating his doctrine of the Eucharist, Bradford is concerned to avoid two errors: a doctrine which regards Christ as physically present in the elements; and a doctrine which regards the elements as mere signs.[130] The majority of his Eucharistic writings are not concerned with defining the positive relationship between the Eucharist and salvation but with refuting the positions of his opponents.

However, Bradford does relate the Eucharist to his soteriology. For example, he rejects the Catholic notion of sacrifice on the grounds that this undermines the all-sufficiency of Christ's death

---

[124] Ibid. 121, 218, 260.   [125] Ibid. 94.
[126] Ibid. 2. 290. Bradford argues that the children of believers are to be presumed elect and therefore to be baptised, as the children of the Jews were circumcised in the Old Testament: see ibid. 1. 82.
[127] Ibid. 121.   [128] Ibid. 297, 396, 417–18.
[129] See, for example, ibid. 2. 166–7, 203, 235.
[130] Ibid. 1. 95–6.

upon Calvary. Instead he argues that the Eucharist must be regarded as a memorial of Christ's one sacrifice.[131] He also sees it as signifying the salvific union of the believer to Christ. In the Eucharist, the whole Christ, God and man, is present to the believer through faith.[132] The bread and wine are analogous to Christ: as they nourish the body, so Christ nourishes the soul; and as the signs become one substance with the body and sustain physical life, so Christ becomes one substance with believers and sustains their spiritual life.[133]

Even in the brief references Bradford makes to the subject, it is clear that the Eucharist is a reflection of the spiritual union of Christ with the believer. He is again formulating his theology in a way that points to this dynamic relationship and which focuses attention upon the Christocentric nature of salvation.

Summary

Bradford regards the person of Christ as central to salvation. He discusses the incarnation only in terms of the task of redemption which Christ was to fulfil, and regards his union with humanity as the basis for accomplishing the reconciliation of God and man.

In discussing the application of salvation, Bradford does not deal extensively with justification. Instead, he focuses upon the spiritual union of the believer with Christ through faith. This union is analogous to, and dependent upon, the union of Christ with humanity in the incarnation. Bradford regards it as allowing for the exchange of sins and righteousness between the believer and Christ, an idea similar to that of Luther, and as providing the basis for the individual's assurance.

The Christian must grow in actual holiness, and repentance is necessary throughout life. It is possible that Bradford was influenced by Melanchthon on this issue. The believer is to be guided by the decalogue as his ethical code. However, union with Christ provides the objective basis of sanctification. Thus, this union occupies a central place in Bradford's soteriology: it is central to election, Christology, salvation, and sanctification.

Bradford regards the sacraments as reflecting the believer's union with Christ, although he also emphasizes that baptism

---

[131] *Writings* 1. 393; ibid. 2. 315.   [132] Ibid. 1. 435, 450, 456.
[133] Ibid. 2. 82, 88, 105.

places its recipients under the obligation to have faith and to behave as Christians.

Bradford's constant references to union with Christ in his discussions of broader soteriological themes is very similar to Bucer's own approach. This is once again suggestive of his influence upon Bradford's theology.

CONCLUSION

Election is a very important doctrine to Bradford, and this importance probably derives from his own early need to find assurance of God's favour and his contact with Martin Bucer. Certainly, general similarities with the position of Bucer suggest his influence. He stresses that God's revelation is to be the only source of knowledge concerning predestination, and that this revelation teaches that God decreed in eternity to save particular individuals. In using this decree as an axiom, he reveals his clear difference from Hooper, to whom such an idea was anathema. Bradford also develops a concept of God's foreknowledge which implies absolute predestination. However, he hesitates to draw some of the more radical conclusions of such a position. For example, he is unsure how to interpret the biblical statements that God wills all to be saved, and he also declares that God's will is mutable in some matters which do not refer to salvation. These tensions imply that he does not wish to argue for absolute predestination but feels that the deterministic structure of his thought, implied in his doctrine of the decree, is drawing him in such a direction. This ambivalence in his position is further suggested by his hint of a doctrine of double predestination in *A Brief Sum of Election*. In the light of his caution in these matters, it is perhaps surprising that Bradford does commit himself to a doctrine of limited atonement, a concept that indicates the possible influence of John Calvin.

In the context of his pastoral writings, Bradford does not find the idea of a hidden decree a hindrance to assurance, and has no hesitation in pointing believers to Christ for certainty of their salvation. However, he does introduce apostasy as a possibility for believers, even though such a concept contradicts statements elsewhere. This is done for the pastoral purpose of underlining the ethical imperatives of the Christian life.

Bradford wrote no full-scale work on salvation as a whole, and so generalizations about the relative importance of any single doctrine must be tentative. However, the few references in his writings to broader aspects of soteriology all have a common theme: union with Christ. The accomplishment and appropriation of salvation are all described in terms of this union. Indeed, election itself is 'in Christ' and its purpose is to draw men into union with him. It is true that there are only a small number of references to union with Christ in his writings, but they occur almost every time that a soteriological theme is elaborated. This suggests that it is this doctrine, and not election, which lies at the centre of Bradford's theology. Bradford only wrote extensively on election because he wished to refute the ideas of Henry Hart and, if these polemical treatises did not exist, then the soteriological emphases in his other works would appear to point to union with Christ as the central theme. Bradford's development of soteriology in these terms reflects the Christocentric nature of his thought. Furthermore, such a position indicates the probable influence of Bucer on his theology and shows that he has clear affinities with the increasingly Christological structuring of soteriology within Reformed thinking during the middle of the sixteenth century.[134] It is therefore a pity that Bradford did not live long enough to contribute further to the theology of the English Reformation.

[134] See J. C. McLelland, 'The Reformed Doctrine of Predestination According to Peter Martyr', *SJT* 8 (1955), 255; McGrath, 'Humanist Elements', 14–17.

CONCLUSION TO PART THREE

THE CRUMBLING OF CONSENSUS

It is clear from the writings of Hooper and Bradford that the central issues of soteriological debate changed significantly in the years following the death of Henry VIII. During Henry's reign, the controversy over the nature of salvation had taken place along a strict Protestant–Catholic divide. The fundamental points at issue were justification by faith alone, and the relationship of this justification to good works. In dealing with these issues, Tyndale, Frith, and Barnes each demonstrated individual emphases and concerns, but they were in basic agreement on the essentials.

However, under Edward and Mary, soteriology was no longer a central point of conflict between Protestants and Catholics. This role was fulfilled by the Eucharistic controversy which eclipsed disagreements over other doctrines. Instead, soteriology became a point of tension within English Protestantism itself: attention shifted from the enemy without to the enemy within. Furthermore, the basic concerns of the soteriological debate changed. As justification by faith alone became accepted as the official teaching of the Anglican Church, interest moved away from this and focused instead upon the conceptual framework and objective origins of justification, particularly the nature of election. Therefore, the questions being asked were no longer concerned primarily with the relationship of justification to good works; instead, they concerned matters such as the cause of God's election, and the relationship of God's sovereign will to sin.

These questions were not new to the English Reformation. Tyndale, Frith, and Barnes had each treated the subject of predestination. Barnes had even attempted to resolve the problem of the cause of sin which his doctrine of double predestination had raised. However, these issues were not of primary importance. All three dealt with predestination as the corollary of their anthropology and their doctrine of grace. The doctrine was therefore subordinate to the arguments for justification by faith alone, and differences in these areas had not undermined the doctrinal unity of the three men.

During the reigns of Edward and Mary the questions raised by the doctrine of election took on primary importance for particular Protestants and caused considerable tension within the Protestant community. Initially, it is probable that this was the result of the variety of different Reformed opinion that existed in England as exiles returned from various continental cities. Leading foreign theologians, such as Bucer, came to teach in England, and men such as Hooper and Traheron returned from exile with views imbibed at the feet of Reformers in Zurich and Geneva. Certainly, the subsequent debate between Traheron and Hooper can be explained in terms of their chosen cities of exile, and Bradford's love for election was almost certainly the fruit of his friendship with Bucer.

However, the controversy in which Bradford engaged cannot be explained solely in terms of the impact of continental theology on English Reformers. The other protagonists in the debate were members of a semi-Pelagian sect who owed their origins to popular lay piety rather than sophisticated theological reflection. Indeed, the debate in which they engaged Bradford started as a dispute about Christian freedom, not about God's eternal decree, although the latter was ultimately to become the point at issue.

When examining the thought of Hooper and of Bradford, there are significant similarities between their discussions of salvation. In their writings, both are concerned with the same basic problem: the nature of God's election. They also agree about the need to absolve God from any responsibility for sin. However, they disagree about how these problems are to be resolved. Both men have a high regard for the *Loci* of Melanchthon. Both men also stress that Christ is the only cause of election, that sin is the only cause of reprobation, and that God is not to be regarded as the cause of sin. However, these similarities are only superficial. When Hooper speaks of Christ and sin as the causes of election and reprobation, he does this in the context of a decisive rejection of the idea of an eternal decree. Indeed, his entire soteriology is formulated in conscious opposition to the determinist framework of the

Calvinists, a framework which Hooper regards as destructive of the biblical imperatives of repentance and good works. Indeed, Hooper reacts so strongly against predestinarianism that he adopts a synergistic view of election which is further emphasized by his failure to develop clearly the role of the Holy Spirit in salvation.

When Bradford speaks of Christ and sin as the causes of election and reprobation respectively, this is against the background of God's decree in eternity to save particular individuals. Thus, God's will is the ultimate cause of election, and Christ is in reality only the revealed cause. While unwilling to make God's will the cause of reprobation, his use of the ideas of first and second causes, and of the distinction between necessity and compulsion clearly point in such a direction.

To some extent, the differences in emphasis between Hooper and Bradford on the matter of election are the result of the different positions against which they are arguing. In opposition to the Calvinist doctrine which made God the ultimate cause of sin, Hooper inevitably stresses the responsibility of man. In opposition to Pelagian views of man's role in salvation, Bradford inevitably stresses the sovereignty of God. In a strange way, the motivation of both men is the same: a concern to establish a theological foundation for good works. Hooper regards the Calvinist decree as undermining the moral imperatives of the Christian life; Bradford regards the decree of election as essential for assurance and thus as providing the correct motivation for good works. However, the doctrinal differences between the two men are fundamental: their differing attitudes to the eternal decree make their positions irreconcilable.

There are further important areas of difference. Hooper's soteriology is built upon a doctrine of universal atonement, while Bradford is prepared to use the scholastic distinction between sufficiency and efficiency in order to present a consistent doctrine of particular redemption. Hooper sees the idea of a contract between God and man as articulating the soteriological relationship that exists between them, and this is determinative for his view of the law, the Christian life, and the sacraments. However, the evidence suggests that Bradford focuses instead upon the dynamic union of the believer with Christ, a union which is the focal point of his soteriology, his

Christology, the Christian life, and the sacraments. These differences reflect fundamentally different theologies.

It is important to understand the limitations of a study based upon the writings of only two Reformers from the reigns of Edward and Mary. For example, it would not be legitimate to conclude that English Protestantism was so divided over the doctrine of election at this period that the fundamental unity of the Anglican Church was threatened. Questions about election were of secondary importance to leading churchmen such as Cranmer and Ridley when compared with Eucharistic doctrine. Indeed, Cranmer does not appear to have been involved in either controversy, and Ridley's support for Bradford was of the slightest kind, consisting only of a reluctantly composed and studiedly cautious treatise. Even in the particular cases of Hooper and Bradford the issue of election did not rupture their allegiance to the Church: Hooper and Traheron continued to work within the Anglican Church, despite their disagreements; and Bradford's opponents, the free willers, were not part of the Anglican communion anyway. Furthermore, there is no evidence to suggest that there was any personal tension between Hooper and Bradford themselves, despite their differences. Therefore, it is important to avoid using the writings of Hooper and Bradford in order to draw over-generalized conclusions about the state of the Anglican Church as a whole. Instead, it is better to regard their differing views as examples of the variety of soteriological opinion that existed within the Church at that time. As such, they signify early cracks in the Anglican doctrinal consensus. In years to come, these same issues which were raised by Hooper and Bradford were to take a higher profile and haunt English Protestantism again and again with increasingly damaging results. The irony is that it is the views of John Hooper, generally regarded as a proto-puritan, which foreshadow those of later broadchurch Arminianism.

As this study draws to a close, it is perhaps worth asking one final question: is there any thread of doctrine, argument, or emphasis, which gives unity and continuity to the soteriology of the early English Reformation between 1525 and 1556? The answer, I think, lies in the practical concern which we have seen displayed by each of the five Reformers: every one was concerned to construct his theology in a manner which brought honour to God and emphasized the need for the believer to live out his Christian life in a practical, meaningful manner. Tyndale and Hooper spoke of the mutual covenant between God and man; Frith, Barnes, and Bradford wrote about the joyful, loving response of a conscience assured of God's favour. Of course, they had different emphases and, in some cases, different doctrine, but all held that the Christian brings glory to God by the practical outworking of his salvation in works of love towards those around him. On this, there was no disagreement.

BIBLIOGRAPHY

PRIMARY SOURCES

BARNES, R., *Sentenciae ex doctoribus collectae, quas papistae valde impudenter hodie damnant* (Wittenberg, 1530).
—— *A supplicatyon made by Robert Barnes doctoure in divinite unto the most excellent and redoubted prince kinge henrye the eyght* (Antwerp, 1531).
—— *A supplicacion unto the most gracyous prynce H. the .viii* (London, 1534).
BEZA, T., *Tractationes Theologicae* (3 vols.; Geneva, 1570–82).
BRADFORD, J., *The Writings of John Bradford, M.A.*, ed. A. Townsend (2 vols.; Cambridge, 1848–53).
BUCER, M., *Enarratio in Epistolam ad Romanos* (Strasburg, 1536).
—— *Enarratio in Epistolam ad Ephesios* (Basel, 1562).
—— *Common Places of Martin Bucer*, trans. D. F. Wright (Appleford, 1972).
BULLINGER, H., *In . . . Pauli ad Romanos Epistolam . . . Commentarius* (Zurich, 1533).
—— *De Testamento seu Foedere . . . Expositio* (Zurich, 1534).
—— *In omnes Apostolicas Epistolas Divi videlicet Paul XIIII. et VII. Canonicas Commentarii* (Zurich, 1537).
—— *Orthodoxa Tigurinae Ecclesiae ministrorum Confessio* (Zurich, 1545).
CALVIN, J., *Opera quae supersunt omnia* (59 vols.; Brunswick, 1863–1900).
—— *Institutes of the Christian Religion*, trans. F. L. Battles (2 vols.; Philadelphia, 1960).
—— *The Gospel according to St. John 11–21 and The First Epistle of John*, trans. T. H. L. Parker (Edinburgh, 1961).
—— *Calvin's Ecclesiastical Advice*, trans. M. Beaty and B. W. Farley (Edinburgh, 1991).
CRANMER, T., *The Work of Thomas Cranmer*, ed. G. E. Duffield (Appleford, 1964).
Documents Illustrative of the Continental Reformation, ed. B. J. Kidd (Oxford, 1911).
ERASMUS, D., *Enchiridion Militis Christiani* (Cambridge 1685).
—— *Collected Works of Erasmus*, trans. R. A. B. Mynors (66 vols.; Toronto, 1974 ff.).

FOXE, J., *Acts and Monuments*, ed. J. Pratt (8 vols.; London, 1877).

FRITH, J., *The Works of the English Reformers: William Tyndale and John Frith* 3, ed. T. Russell (London, 1831).

—— *The Work of John Frith*, ed. N. T. Wright (Appleford, 1978).

HAMILTON, P., *Patrick's Places*, trans. by J. Frith in J. Knox, *History of the Reformation of Religion within the Realm of Scotland* 2, ed. W. C. Dickinson (London 1949).

HOOPER, J., *Early Writings of John Hooper, D.D.*, ed. S. Carr (Cambridge 1843).

—— *Later Writings of John Hooper D.D.*, ed. C. Nevinson (Cambridge, 1852).

LUTHER, M., *D. Martin Luthers Werke: Kritische Gesamtausgabe* (63 vols.; Weimar, 1883–1987).

—— *D. Martin Luthers Werke: Kritische Gesamtausgabe: Die Deutsche Bibel* (12 vols.; Weimar, 1906–61).

—— *Lectures on Romans*, trans. W. Pauck (Philadelphia, 1961).

—— *Studienausgabe* 3, ed. H. Delius (Berlin, 1983).

MELANCHTHON, P., *Opera quae supersunt omnia* (28 vols.; Brunswick, 1834–60).

MORE, T., *The Complete Works of St. Thomas More*, 8, eds. L. A. Schuster *et al.* (Yale, 1973).

Original Letters relative to the English Reformation, ed. H. Robinson (2 vols.; Cambridge, 1846–47).

Patrologia Graeca, ed. J. P. Migne (162 vols.; Paris, 1857–66).

Patrologia Latina, ed. J. P. Migne (221 vols.; Paris, 1844–64).

THOMAS AQUINAS., *Scriptum super 'Sententiis' Magistri Petri Lombardi* (4 vols.; Paris, 1947–56).

—— *Summa Theologiae*. Translated by T. Gilby *et al.* (61 vols.; London, 1964–81).

—— *Opera Omnia Sancti Thomae de Aquino* 23 (Rome, 1982).

TYNDALE, W., *Doctrinal Treatises and Introductions to Different Portions of the Holy Scriptures*, ed. H. Walter (Cambridge, 1848).

—— *Expositions and Notes on Sundry Portions of the Holy Scriptures, together with The Practice of Prelates*, ed. H. Walter (Cambridge, 1849).

—— *An Answer to Sir Thomas More's Dialogue*, ed. H. Walter (Cambridge, 1850).

—— *The First Printed English New Testament*, ed. T. Arber (London, 1871).

ZWINGLI, H., *Sämtliche Werke* (14 vols.; Berlin, 1905 ff.).

SECONDARY SOURCES

ALTHAUS, P., *The Theology of Martin Luther*, trans. R. C. Schultz (Philadelphia, 1966).

—— *The Ethics of Martin Luther*, trans. R. C. Schultz (Philadelphia, 1972).

ANDERSON, C. S., 'The Person and Position of Dr. Robert Barnes, 1495–1540: a Study in the Relationship between the English and German Reformations', unpubl. Th.D. diss. (Union Theological Seminary, 1962).

—— 'Robert Barnes on Luther', in *Interpreters of Luther*, ed. J. Pelikan (Philadelphia, 1968), pp. 35–66.

BAINTON, R., *Here I Stand* (Tring, 1978).

BAKER J. P., 'Offices of Christ', in *New Dictionary of Theology*, ed. S. B. Ferguson and D. F. Wright (Leicester, 1988), 476–7.

BAKER, J. W., *Heinrich Bullinger and the Covenant: The Other Reformed Tradition* (Ohio, 1980).

BARTH, K., *Church Dogmatics 2. 2*, trans. G. W. Bromiley (Edinburgh, 1957).

BEEKE, J. R., *Assurance of Faith: Calvin, English Puritanism and the Dutch Second Reformation* (Bern, 1991).

Berkouwer, G. C., *The Triumph of Grace in the Theology of Karl Barth*, trans. H. R. Boer (Grand Rapids, 1956).

—— *Divine Election*, trans. H. Bekker (Grand Rapids, 1960).

BORNKAMM, H., *Luther and the Old Testament*, trans. E. W. and R. C. Gritsch (Philadelphia, 1969).

BROOKS, P. N., *Thomas Cranmer's Doctrine of the Eucharist* (London, 1965).

—— Review of D. D. Smeeton, *Lollard Themes in the Reformation Theology of William Tyndale*, *Journal of Ecclesiastical History*, 39 (1988), 638.

BURNABY, J., *Amor Dei: a Study of the Religion of St. Augustine* (London, 1938).

CAMERON, A. (ed.), *Patrick Hamilton: First Scottish Martyr of the Reformation* (Edinburgh, 1929).

CLARKE, F., *Eucharistic Sacrifice and the Reformation* (Oxford, 1967).

CLEBSCH, W. A., *England's Earliest Protestants 1520–35* (Yale, 1964).

DAVIS, J. F., 'Lollardy and the Reformation in England' *Archiv für Reformationsgeschichte*, 73 (1982), 217–37.

DICK, J. A. R., 'A Critical Edition of William Tyndale's "The Parable of the Wicked Mammon', unpubl. Ph.D. diss. (Yale, 1974).

DICKENS, A. G., *The English Reformation* (London, 1967).

—— 'The Early Expansion of Protestantism in England 1520–58', *Archiv für Reformationsgeschichte*,78 (1987), 187–221.

DOERNBERG, E., *Henry VIII and Luther: An Account of Their Personal Relations* (Stanford, 1961).

DOWLING, M., 'The Gospel and the Court: Reformation under Henry VIII', in *Protestantism and the National Church in Sixteenth Century England*, eds. P. Lake and M. Dowling (London, 1967), 36–77.

—— *Humanism in the Age of Henry VIII* (London, 1986).

DUGMORE, C. W., *The Mass and the English Reformers* (London, 1958).

ELTON, G. R., *Reformation Europe 1517–59* (London, 1963).

FELDMETH, N. P., 'Humanism', in *New Dictionary of Theology*, 322.

FENLON, D., *Heresy and Obedience in Tridentine Italy: Cardinal Pole and the Counter Reformation* (Cambridge, 1972).

FISHER, N. H., 'Robert Barnes and the English Reformation', unpubl. MA diss. (Birmingham University, 1950).

FLESSEMAN-VAN LEER, E., 'The Controversy about Scripture and Tradition Between Thomas More and William Tyndale', *Nederlands Archief voor Kerkgeschiedenis*, 43 (1959), 143–65.

—— 'The Controversy about Ecclesiology Between Thomas More and William Tyndale', *Nederlands Archief voor Kerkgeschiedenis*, 44 (1960), 65–86.

FULOP, R. E., 'John Frith (1503–1533) and His Relation to the Origins of the Reformation in England', unpubl. Ph.D. diss. (Edinburgh University, 1956).

GERRISH, B. A., '"To the Unknown God": Luther and Calvin on the Hiddenness of God', *Journal of Religion*, 53 (1973) 263–92.

GREAVES, R. L., 'The Origins and Early Development of English Covenant Thought', *The Historian*, 31 (1968), 21–35.

—— 'John Knox and the Covenant Tradition', *Journal of Ecclesiastical History*, 24 (1973), 23–32.

GREENHOUGH, G. H., 'The Reformer's Attitude to the Law of God', *Westminster Theological Journal*, 39 (1976), 81–99.

GREENSLADE, S. L., *The English Reformers and the Fathers of the Church* (Oxford, 1960).

—— 'The Faculty of Theology', in *The History of the University of Oxford*, ed. J. McConica (Oxford, 1986), 295–334

HAGEN, K., 'From Testament to Covenant in the Early Sixteenth Century', *Sixteenth Century Journal*, 3 (1972), 1–24.

HAIGH, C., Review of M. Bowker, *The Henrician Reformation: The Diocese of Lincoln under John Longland 1521–1547* (Cambridge, 1981), *English Historical Review*, 98 (1983), 370–73.

HARGRAVE, O. T., 'The Doctrine of Predestination in the English Reformation', unpubl. Ph.D. diss. (Vanderbilt University, 1966).

—— 'The Freewillers in the English Reformation', *Church History*, 37 (1968), 271–80.

HEADLEY, J. M. 'Thomas More and Luther's Revolt', *Archiv für Reformationsgeschichte*, 60 (1969), 145–59.

HOEKEMA, A. A., 'The Covenant of Grace in Calvin's Teaching', *Calvin Theological Journal*, 2 (1967), 133–61.

HUDSON, A., *The Premature Reformation* (Oxford, 1988).

KAUFMAN, P. I., *Augustinian Piety and Catholic Reform: Augustine, Colet, and Erasmus* (Macon, 1982).

KENDALL, R. T., *Calvin and English Calvinism to 1649* (Oxford, 1979).

KENNY, A., *Wyclif* (Oxford, 1985).

KNAPPEN, M. M., *Tudor Puritanism* (Chicago, 1939).

KNOX, D. B., *The Doctrine of Faith in the Reign of Henry VIII* (London, 1961).

KOHLS, E.-W., 'The Principal Theological Thoughts in the *Enchiridion Militis Christiani*', in *Essays on the Works of Erasmus*, ed. R. L. DeMolen (Yale, 1978), 61–82.

KÜNG, H., *Justification: The Doctrine of Karl Barth and a Catholic Reflection*, trans. T. Collins *et al.* (London 1981).

LAUGHLIN, P. A., 'The Brightness of Moses's Face: Law and Gospel, Covenant, and Hermeneutics in the Theology of William Tyndale', unpubl. Ph.D. diss. (Emory University, 1975).

LEADER, D. R., *A History of the University of Cambridge 1: The University to 1546* (Cambridge, 1988).

LETHAM, R. W. A., 'Saving Faith and Assurance in Reformed Theology from Zwingli to the Synod of Dordt', unpubl. Ph.D. diss. (Aberdeen University, 1979).

LIENHARD, M., *Luther: Witness to Jesus Christ*, trans. E. H. Robertson (Minneapolis, 1982).

LOCHER, G. W., *Zwingli's Thought: New Perspectives* (Leiden, 1981).

LOEWENICH, W. VON, *Luther's Theology of the Cross*, trans. H. J. A. Bouman (Belfast, 1976).

LOHSE, B., *Martin Luther: an Introduction to His Life and Work*, trans. R. C. Schultz (Edinburgh, 1986).

LUSARDI, J. P., 'The Career of Robert Barnes', in *The Complete Works of St. Thomas More*, 8, 1365–415.

LYALL, F., 'Of Metaphors and Analogies: Legal Language and Covenant Theology', *Scottish Journal of Theology*, 32 (1979), 1–17.

—— Metaphors, Legal and Theological', *Scottish Bulletin of Evangelical Theology*, 10 (1992), 94–112.

McGIFFERT, M., 'William Tyndale's Conception of Covenant', *Journal of Ecclesiastical History*, 32 (1981), 167–84.

McGOLDRICK, J. E., *Luther's English Connection* (Milwaukee 1979).

MCGRATH, A. E., ' "Augustinianism?" A Critical Assessment of the so-called "Medieval Augustinian Tradition" on Justification', *Augustiniana*, 31 (1981), 247–67.

—— 'Humanist Elements in the Early Reformed Doctrine of Justification', in *Archiv für Reformationsgeschichte*, 73 (1982), 5–30

—— *Iustitia Dei. A History of the Christian Doctrine of Justification* (2 vols.; Cambridge, 1986).

—— *The Intellectual Origins of the European Reformation*, (Oxford, 1987).

MCLELLAND, J. C., 'The Reformed Doctrine of Predestination According to Peter Martyr', *Scottish Journal of Theology*, 8 (1955), 255–71.

MCSORLEY, H. J., *Luther: Right or Wrong? An Ecumenical–Theological Study of Luther's Major Work, 'The Bondage of the Will'* (Minneapolis, 1969).

MARTIN, J. W., 'English Protestant Separatism at its Beginnings: Henry Hart and the Free-Will Men', *Sixteenth Century Journal*, 7 (1976), 55–74.

—— *Religious Radicals in Tudor England* (London, 1989).

MAYOTTE, J. M., 'William Tyndale's Contribution to the Reformation in England', unpubl. Ph.D. diss. (Marquette University, 1976).

MØLLER, J. G., 'The Beginnings of Puritan Covenant Theology', *Journal of Ecclesiastical History*, 14 (1963), 46–67.

MOZLEY, J. B., *A Treatise on the Augustinian Doctrine of Predestination* (London, 1855).

MOZLEY, J. F., *William Tyndale* (London, 1937).

MULLER, R. A., *A Dictionary of Latin and Greek Theological Terms* (Grand Rapids, 1985).

—— *Christ and the Decree: Christology and Predestination in Reformed Theology from Calvin to Perkins* (Grand Rapids, 1988).

MURRAY, I. H., *The Forgotten Spurgeon* (Edinburgh, 1973).

MURRAY, J., *The Covenant of Grace: a Biblico-Theological Study* (London, 1954).

NIESEL, W., *The Theology of John Calvin*, trans. H. Knight (Philadelphia, 1956).

OBERMAN, H. A., *The Harvest of Medieval Theology: Gabriel Biel and Late Medieval Nominalism* (Grand Rapids, 1967).

—— *Masters of the Reformation* (Cambridge, 1981).

—— *The Dawn of the Reformation* (Edinburgh, 1986).

—— *Luther: Man between God and the Devil*, trans. E. Walliser-Schwarzbart (Yale, 1989).

OPIE, J., 'The Anglicizing of John Hooper', *Archiv für Reformationsgeschichte*, 59 (1968), 150–76.

PARKER, T. H. L., Introduction to *A Declaration of Christ and his Office* by J. Hooper, in *English Reformers*, (London, 1966), 185–8.

POTTER, G. R., *Zwingli* (Cambridge, 1976).

PREUS, R. D., *The Theology of Post-Reformation Lutheranism: Prolegomena to Theology* (St Louis, 1970).

RIDLEY, J., *John Knox* (Oxford, 1968).

RIST, J. M., 'Augustine on Free Will and Predestination', *Journal of Theological Studies*, NS, 20 (1969), 420–47.

RIVIÈRE, J., 'Mérite', in *Dictionnaire de théologie catholique* 10, ed. A. Vacant *et al.* (Paris, 1928), 574–785.

ROBERTS, L. D., 'Indeterminism in Duns Scotus' Doctrine of Human Freedom', *The Modern Schoolman*, 51 (1973), 1–16.

ROSS, D. S., 'Hooper's Alleged Authorship of *A Brief and Clear Confession of the Christian Faith*', *Church History*, 39 (1970), 18–29.

RUPP, E. G., *Studies in the Making of the English Protestant Tradition* (Cambridge, 1949).

—— *The Righteousness of God* (London, 1953).

—— *Six Makers of English Religion 1500–1700* (London, 1957).

—— 'Patterns of Salvation in the First Age of the Reformation', *Archiv für Reformationsgeschichte*, 57 (1966), 52–67.

SHARP, L. D., 'The Doctrines of Grace in Calvin and Augustine', *Evangelical Quarterly*, 52 (1980), 84–96.

SHOFNER, R. D., 'Luther on "The Bondage of the Will": an Analytical-Critical Essay', *Scottish Journal of Theology*, 26 (1973), 24–39.

SIGGINS, I. D. K., *Martin Luther's Doctrine of Christ* (Yale, 1970).

SMEETON, D. D., 'The Pneumatology of William Tyndale', *Pneuma: Journal of the Society for Pentecostal Studies*, 3 (1981), 22–30.

—— *Lollard Themes in the Reformation Theology of William Tyndale* (Missouri, 1987).

SMITH, P., 'Luther and Henry VIII', *English Historical Review*, 25 (1910), 656–69

—— 'Englishmen at Wittenberg in the Sixteenth Century', *English Historical Review*, 36 (1921), 422–33.

—— *Erasmus: a Study of his Life, Ideals, and Place in History* (New York, 1962).

SMITHEN, F. J., *Continental Protestantism and the English Reformation* (London, 1927).

SPLITZ, L. W., *The Religious Renaissance of the German Humanists* (Harvard, 1963).

STEPHENS, W. P., *The Holy Spirit in the Theology of Martin Bucer* (Cambridge, 1970).

—— *The Theology of Huldrych Zwingli* (Oxford, 1986).

STREHLE, S., *Calvinism, Federalism, and Scholasticism: A Study of the Reformed Doctrine of Covenant* (Bern, 1988).

STRYPE, J., *Ecclesiastical Memorials* (Oxford, 1822).

STUPPERICH, R., *Melanchthon*, trans. R. H. Fischer (London, 1966).

THOMPSON, W. D. J. C., 'The Sixteenth Century Editions of *A Supplication unto King Henry the Eighth* by Robert Barnes, D.D.: a Footnote to the Royal Supremacy', *Transactions of the Cambridge Bibliographic Society*, 3 (1960), 133–42.

—— 'The Two Regiments: the continental setting of William Tyndale's political thought', in *Reform and Reformation: England and the Continent c.1500–c.1750*, ed. D. Baker (Oxford, 1979), 17–33.

THOMSON, J. A. F., *The Later Lollards 1414–1520* (Oxford, 1965).

THOMSON, S. H., 'The Philosophical Basis of Wyclif's Theology', *Journal of Religion*, 11 (1931), 86–116.

TJERNAGEL, N. S., *Henry VIII and the Lutherans: a Study in Anglo-Lutheran Relations from 1521 to 1547* (St Louis, 1965).

TORRANCE, J. B., 'The Incarnation and "Limited Atonement"', *Evangelical Quarterly*, 55 (1983), 83–94.

TRINTERUD, L. J., 'The Origins of Puritanism', *Church History* 20 (1951), 37–57.

—— 'A Reappraisal of William Tyndale's Debt to Martin Luther', *Church History*, 31 (1962), 24–45.

URBAN, L., 'Was Luther a Thoroughgoing Determinist?' *Journal of Theological Studies*, NS, 22 (1971), 113–39.

VOS, A., *Aquinas, Calvin, and Contemporary Protestant Thought: a Critique of Protestant Views on the Thought of Thomas Aquinas* (Washington, 1985).

WALLACE, D. D., *Puritans and Predestination: Grace in English Protestant Theology, 1525–1695* (North Carolina, 1982)

WALLACE, R. S., *Calvin, Geneva and the Reformation* (Edinburgh, 1988).

WATSON, P. S., 'The Lutheran Riposte', in *Luther and Erasmus: Free Will and Salvation*, eds. E. G. Rupp *et al.* (London, 1969), 12–28.

WATT, H., 'Hamilton's Interpretation of Luther, with Special Reference to "Patrick's Places"' in A. Cameron (ed.), *Patrick Hamilton: First Scottish Martyr of the Reformation*, 28–36,

WENDEL, F., *Calvin: the Origins and Development of his Religious Thought*, trans. P. Mairet (London, 1965).

WEST, W. M. S., 'A Study of John Hooper with Special Reference to his Contact with Henry Bullinger', unpubl. doctoral diss. (Zurich University, 1953).

—— 'John Hooper and the Origins of Puritanism', *Baptist Quarterly*, 15 (1954), 346–68.

—— 'John Hooper and the Origins of Puritanism', *Baptist Quarterly*, 16 (1955), 22–46, 67–88.

WILLIAMS, C. H., *William Tyndale* (London, 1969).

WILLIAMS, G. H., *The Radical Reformation* (London, 1962).

WRIGHT, D. F., 'Martin Bucer 1491–1551: Ecumenical Theologian', in *Common Places of Martin Bucer*, 15–71.

—— 'The Ethical Use of the Old Testament in Luther and Calvin: a Comparison', *Scottish Journal of Theology*, 36 (1983), 463–85.

WRIGHT, N. T., 'Introduction' in *The Work of John Frith*, 1–80.

YOST, J. K., 'The Christian Humanism of the English Reformers, 1525–1555: A Study in English Renaissance Humanism', unpubl. Ph.D. diss. (Duke University, 1965).

—— 'Tyndale's Use of the Fathers: a Note on His Connection to Northern Humanism', *Moreana*, 6 (1969), 5–13.

INDEX